PHILOSOPHY, FEMINISM,
AND FAITH

Indiana Series in the Philosophy of Religion
Merold Westphal, general editor

Philosophy, Feminism, and Faith

EDITED BY

RUTH E. GROENHOUT

AND

MARYA BOWER

INDIANA University Press

Bloomington & Indianapolis

This book is a publication of

Indiana University Press
601 North Morton Street
Bloomington, IN 47404-3797 USA

http://iupress.indiana.edu

Telephone orders   800-842-6796
Fax orders   812-855-7931
Orders by e-mail   iuporder@indiana.edu

© 2003 by Indiana University Press

MANUFACTURED IN THE UNITED STATES OF AMERICA

Library of Congress Cataloging-in-Publication Data

Philosophy, feminism, and faith / edited by Ruth E. Groenhout and
Marya Bower.

p. cm. — (Indiana series in the philosophy of religion)

Includes bibliographical references and index.

ISBN 0-253-34177-9 (cloth : alk. paper) — ISBN 0-253-21561-7
(pbk. : alk. paper)

1. Women and religion. 2. Feminism—Religious aspects. 3. Feminist
theory. I. Groenhout, Ruth E., date II. Bower, Marya, date III. Series.

BL458 .P48 2003

200'.82—dc21

2002011674

1 2 3 4 5 08 07 06 05 04 03

CONTENTS

ACKNOWLEDGMENTS / vii

INTRODUCTION / 1

Part I. Setting the Context

1. Judaism and the Love of Reason
MARTHA C. NUSSBAUM   9

2. Feminism, Socialism, and Christianity Revisited
MARY B. MAHOWALD   40

3. "Philosophizing on Saturday": Faith and the Philosophical Life
WINIFRED WING HAN LAMB   60

4. Three Aspects of Identity
SR. MARY CHRISTINE MORKOVSKY   76

5. Reflections on Identity
JEAN BETHKE ELSHTAIN   88

Part II. Tensions and Integrations

6. Yes
MARIANNE SAWICKI   105

7. Into the Crucible: My Art of Living
JACQUELINE SCOTT   120

8. Learning to Question
PATRICIA ALTENBERND JOHNSON   140

9. I Can't Say No: Self-Sacrifice and an Ethics of Care
RUTH E. GROENHOUT   152

10. Seduction: Does How You Get to "Yes" Still Matter?
CAROLINE J. SIMON   175

11. Living within Tradition
LAURA DUHAN KAPLAN   190

12. Hagar on My Mind
AZIZAH Y. AL-HIBRI   198

Part III. Challenging Traditions

13. A Skeptical Spirituality
NEL NODDINGS   213

14. Faith, Philosophy, Passions, and Feminism: Dangerous Attractions
IRMGARD SCHERER   227

15. On Being a Christian Philosopher and Not a Feminist
M. ELAINE BOTHA   243

16. Toward a Visionary Politics:
Phenomenology, Psychoanalytic Feminism, and Transcendence
MARILYN NISSIM-SABAT   260

17. My Life Speaks
SARA EBENRECK   282

CONTRIBUTORS / 297

INDEX / 299

ACKNOWLEDGMENTS

The editors would like to acknowledge the assistance, support, and encouragement provided during the process of developing this manuscript. All the contributors are due special thanks for their patience and willingness to see the project through to completion. Special thanks to Merold Westphal for encouraging us to pursue the project, to Martha Nussbaum for supporting our efforts from the beginning of the project, and to the editors at Indiana University Press, Dee Mortensen and Jane Lyle, who provided guidance, encouragement, and assistance along the way.

PHILOSOPHY, FEMINISM, AND FAITH

Introduction

Commitment to any one of the terms listed in the title of this volume seems to preclude commitment to either of the other two. Philosophical skepticism seems inimical to religious faith. Traditional religious faith is often understood as standing over against feminism. And feminist theories have frequently placed themselves in opposition to male-stream philosophy. So how can one live with the seemingly immiscible combination of being a philosopher, belonging to a traditional religion, and being a feminist? How can we make sense of being, as Diana Tietjens Meyers phrases it, "intersectional selves"[1] when those selves are at the intersection of opposing systems of belief?

This is the question that began this anthology, a question that the anthology cannot fully answer. There is no one answer about how these three strands of existence may come together in people's lives, any more than there is a single answer to Freud's plaintive question about what women want. Searching for a single answer in this context is as misguided as looking for the necessary and sufficient conditions of something's being a game. But there are many answers, and in the answers gathered here there is both philosophical and practical wisdom, both theoria and praxis.

The essays that comprise this anthology offer a range of approaches to creating the complex texture of a mature human life, a life that recognizes the potential for conflict in multiple allegiances, but also recognizes the creative potential the tension between these allegiances may generate, as well as the potential for creating mutually supportive coherence out of those same allegiances. Thus the aim of this anthology is to begin to open up a space for thinking through the variety of ways one could organize, synthesize, or simply live three complex commitments that may shape one's life. It focuses on three life-formative commitments, philosophy, feminism, and religion. Philosophers were asked to reflect on how these commitments play out in their own understanding of their scholarly lives. In several cases this reflection takes an autobiographical tone, as the thinker reflects on the experiences of living these tensions. In other cases the reflection begins from the perspective of the intersection of these three commitments, turns toward a particular philosophical puzzle that can be seen from that vantage point, and so speaks from the intersection rather than reflecting on it. These latter essays offer a less autobiographical reflection on the three commitments; they offer instead a sense of how working from within tensions can generate fruitful philosophical reflections. Before turning to the essays themselves, however, it is worth thinking about the three commitments that form the framework for this volume.

Becoming a philosopher seems to commit one to several things. Academic philosophy usually requires a commitment to reason, though there are philosophical traditions that challenge this commitment. Jürgen Habermas, in fact, begins the *Theory of Communicative Action* with the claim that

> One could even say that philosophical thought originates in reflection on the reason embodied in cognition, speech and action; and reason remains its basic theme. . . . If there is anything common to philosophical theories, it is the intention of thinking being or the unity of the world by way of explicating reason's experience of itself.[2]

Philosophy requires a dedication to the life of the mind in some sense, and places a high value on theoretical work. Though the issue could be debated, it also seems that philosophy commits one to following reason where it leads, regardless of the practical consequences, political ramifications, or religious conclusions of the journey. To the extent that these conceptions of philosophy are accurate, both religious commitments and feminist commitments are thrown into question by an identification with philosophy.

Feminism commits one to a political agenda that seeks to end oppression. It requires that one adopt techniques of analysis that incorporate an awareness of the intersection of power and gender. This means that one's theoretical commitments require scrutiny, and it requires a willingness to reject those commitments if they impede or prevent the full development of human abilities and gifts in oneself or others. Feminist philosophical work has frequently developed critiques of reason and the purity of the conclusions particular reasonings have purported to achieve. In addition, feminism acknowledges the importance of our lived experiences as embodied beings and generally requires that one's work be grounded in the practical and the everyday. These feminist commitments seem to prohibit an unqualified commitment to reason. They also seem to require a scrutiny of religious traditions, particularly when those faith traditions have impeded women's development, and this scrutiny appears at odds with a wholehearted faith commitment.

Religious faiths require other commitments from their practitioners. Reason may need to be subordinated to the demands of a metaphysics or a revealed truth that is said to be more fundamental or more transcendent than mere human reason. In addition, religious traditions may ask one to subordinate practical experience or wisdom to authorities or institutional structures far removed from the challenges and joys one experiences in life. This has been an especially problematic aspect of traditional religion for many feminists, including several who write for this volume, and is one of the reasons many give for rejecting religious faith. While traditional religions have sometimes provided opportunities for women to exercise political, religious, or social power, they have sometimes been potent forces for denying such opportunities. The subordination of practical experience to doctrine, and the denial of opportunities to women have often gone hand in hand. When women do not have the authority to speak in public, their experience cannot challenge religious doctrine. And when religious doctrine denigrates women and their experience, that doctrine carries enormous political weight in many cultures. So traditional religions are rarely comfortable environments for cultural critics such as feminists, or for critics committed to the primacy of reason such as philosophers.

That there are tensions between philosophy, feminism, and faith is not hard to see. The existence of the tension is not the interesting question, however; the interesting question is how to respond to that tension. And this is the issue to which the authors in this volume address themselves. Some do so in a way that reflects a feminist commitment to the personal. These essays offer autobiographical reflections on constructing a life in the midst of tangled commitments. Other essays use the tension as one might use the tension of a springboard—they pose a philosophical question from the perspective afforded by these three commitments and use the tension inherent in those commitments to generate philosophical scrutiny of a particular philosophical issue. And some essays straddle the autobiographical-philosophical divide, using issues generated by autobiographical reflections to illuminate a particular philosophical question.

The first essays provide multiple perspectives on the historical context of the questions this volume poses. The authors trace their participation in the feminist movement as they experience it within the context of religious traditions that sometimes support and sometimes discourage activism. They also present alternative ways that philosophy can be conceptualized, from an Enlightenment account of pure reason to a more postmodern notion of multiple traditions of socially constituted knowledge. Finally, they offer an array of responses to the challenges that this integration poses.

Some authors discuss decisions to change from one faith tradition to another, while others describe their decision to work for change from within a faith or intellectual tradition.

The second group of essays includes some writers who believe that these three commitments fit together seamlessly, or with little effort. All three commitments are important parts of these individual's lives, and all three are understood to be mutually compatible and reinforcing. These authors have achieved a certain peacefulness; they have constructed a unified account of their lives. This section also includes some authors who have not been able to achieve this type of unity. Instead, these authors attempt to live with paradox, to accept and work with tensions that cannot easily be resolved or reorganized. Although they feel themselves pulled in contrary directions, they can also see the serious implications of giving up any of their commitments, and they refuse to settle for a truncated set of primary commitments. These authors illustrate, among other things, the nature of eschatological writing and living. They embody the experience of living in present circumstances that must be changed while fighting for a vision of the future one may never see fully realized.

The final group of essays includes authors who argue for a more radical vision of life, one that moves beyond one or another of the three primary commitments that frame this book. Some suggest that what is needed is a new conception of religion or spirituality, or a secularization of religious tradition. These authors want to move toward a resolution that accommodates their other commitments more clearly, or causes less conflict within their lives. They seek new sources of strength and hope, leaving behind old disciplines and traditions that seem outmoded and ill-suited for the task of creating the future. Others challenge us to reconceptualize philosophy or feminism, to make our commitments more inclusive, our critiques less rationalistic.

All of the essays are interesting for their own sake, but they also are important because of their relationship to difficult questions about what it means to live as a full member of the human community. Full and responsible membership in a community requires rejecting both hyper-individualist accounts of the self and naïve accounts of the social construction of human nature. The authors respect the extent to which identities are created by communities, while simultaneously recognizing their responsibility to critique and change those communities. The tensions they experience as they engage in these activities are a central part of what makes human life human. The accounts of their struggles and triumphs offer alternatives for carrying out the project of constructing human life within community.

These accounts also offer reflections on what it means to live as a self with multiple identities, as opposed to the unified Cartesian ego so often assumed in a philosophical context. Few of us find ourselves to be completely single-minded. One of life's challenges is to decide whether we strive to achieve unity or learn to live with inner diversity. Either way there are difficulties and benefits, and both are explored in the essays in this volume.

In addition, this volume highlights religion in the identities of feminist philosophers. Many feminists, both academic philosophers and others, have reacted against religion in becoming feminist, and there are many good reasons for such a reaction. Some of these issues were mentioned above, but among those good reasons are the hostility in many religious traditions to women's authority and autonomy. Viewed as a whole, religious traditions have barred women from roles of leadership within particular religions, and they have actively subordinated women's civil rights in the broader society. For several of the authors in this book these provide reasons for moving away from particular religions, or even all religions. For other feminists, however, religion is something that cannot be given up; in a number of cases their religious beliefs have been and continue to be instrumental in their development of a feminist consciousness. This volume offers more evidence of the diversity that flourishes in a feminist context.

Finally, it is our hope that these essays will offer younger philosophers a resource for thinking through the complexities of their lives. Accordingly, we have included writers who are at different points in their life journeys. Some of them are distinguished professors, reflecting on the course of illustrious and productive careers. Other authors are at an early stage in their professional development or have chosen less traditional paths in their lives. All of the authors share their stories of challenge and tension, of integration and wholeness, from their own perspective and with a vision of their own and our possible futures.

NOTES

1. Diana Tietjens Meyers, "Intersectional Identity and the Authentic Self? Opposites Attract!" in *Relational Autonomy: Feminist Perspectives on Autonomy, Agency, and the Social Self,* ed. Catriona Mackenzie and Natalie Stoljar (New York: Oxford University Press, 2000), pp. 151–80.

2. Jürgen Habermas, *The Theory of Communicative Action,* vol. 1: *Reason and the Rationalization of Society,* trans. Thomas McCarthy (Boston: Beacon Press, 1984), p. 1.

Part I

SETTING
THE CONTEXT

ONE

Judaism and the Love of Reason

MARTHA C. NUSSBAUM

The barbaric days are gone when . . . it was regarded as sinful to
place the woman on the same level as the man.
—*Aaron Chorin (leader of Reform Judaism in Hungary), 1820*

9. In the public worship of the congregation,
there shall be no discrimination made in favor of the male
and against female worshippers.
—*Resolution, Congregation KAM (Kehilath Anshe Ma'rav,
"Congregation of the People of the West"), Chicago, 1859[1]*

The highest stage of wisdom is incontrovertibly doing
that which is good.
—*Moses Mendelssohn, Letter, September 1777*

Love truth! Love peace!
—*Moses Mendelssohn,* Jerusalem, *1783*

I

I am an Enlightenment Jew. My Judaism is marked by a commitment to
the primacy of the moral, to the authority of truth and reason, and to the
equal worth of all human beings. That this Judaism is both feminist and
cosmopolitan follows from its commitment to these three great organizing
values. Like the intellectual leaders who gave rise to Reform Judaism in Germany, I conceive of God's kingdom as the kingdom of ends, a virtual poli-
ty, containing both true autonomy and true community, that organizes our
moral hopes and efforts in this world of confusion, herdlike obedience, and
unenlightened self-interest. As Moses Mendelssohn expressed it,

In God's wise and harmonious government the goal for which human politics strives is achieved to the fullest extent, namely, that every individual fur-
thers the common good in pursuing his own well-being; then no reasonable
being can pursue his own true well-being without being a benefactor of all
creation, since the particular and general interests are so exactly, so indivisi-
bly connected.[2]

In this essay I shall draw on the history of Judaism in the Enlightenment
and of Reform Judaism in Germany and the United States to paint the picture of the type of Judaism that inspires me; I shall discuss both feminism
and cosmopolitanism, issues that have been at the heart of the Reform
movement since its inception and to which Reform Judaism gives, in my
view, more satisfactory answers than do other varieties of Judaism.

   But because I am a convert to Judaism, and have thus, already a rationalist, *chosen* Judaism, I shall also have to face the question: if your religion
is this rationalist, why do you call yourself religious at all? Moses Mendelssohn and the other Jewish Enlightenment thinkers were stuck with a problem: how to reconcile their Enlightenment beliefs with a Judaism that birth
and prejudice made an inevitable part of their lives. In producing the Haskalah (Jewish Enlightenment), they sought to reconcile these two organizing elements of their histories. Similarly, the great founders of European
Reform Judaism[3] in the nineteenth century, and of the American Reform
movement in the nineteenth and early twentieth, sought to reconcile a Judaism they loved with the world of modernity to which they were also committed[4]—and, in the case of the Americans, to make Judaism fully at home
in the liberal democracy of the United States, which seemed to offer all immigrants so much in the way of liberty and equality.[5] Why have I, stuck
with no such problem, moved from a Christian childhood into both the
Enlightenment and Judaism, more or less at the same time? And what does
being a Jew mean to me, given my rather Kantian views about religion and
the supremacy of the moral? In keeping with the nature of the present volume, I begin, then, with an account of how I came to Judaism.

II

I was raised as an Episcopalian, in Bryn Mawr, Pennsylvania, on Philadelphia's fashionable "Main Line." It was fashionable to be an Episcopalian;
the Presbyterians down the street were regarded as slightly less fashionable,
although they did everything in their power to emulate the Episcopalians.[6]
Methodists and Baptists were thought to be very low-class; one would not
ordinarily wish one's child to visit such a church. Catholics were not permitted to buy houses in this community. My father's explanation for this

policy was that their large family size would drive up property taxes because of the stress on the school system, and thus property values would be lowered. Like so many economic explanations, this one was both irrational (ignoring parochial schools) and a screen for darker motives.

Jews, of course, were nowhere to be seen. The year I graduated from high school, a house on my street was sold to a Jewish doctor by the widow who had owned it. The received interpretation of this act of betrayal was that the owner had had a nervous breakdown after the death of her husband and had become insane. Two years after that, when my parents sold our house, Bill Cosby made an offer for it. My father rejected the offer, saying to me that he had never liked our neighbors, but he did not want to take revenge on them to that extent. (I thought that Cosby, who already seemed an admirable person, had had a lucky escape.)

But in my early childhood, the harmony of Bryn Mawr was undisturbed. Episcopalians and Republicans ruled the land, and they were one and the same. (When I worked for local candidates, I noted that the only registered Democrats in Bryn Mawr were the teachers at my school.) The Church of the Redeemer was a fine church, with three very dedicated ministers and one of the best organs in Pennsylvania. Nonetheless, it increasingly struck me, as I moved from childhood into adolescence, as a smug bastion of hypocrisy and unearned privilege, to which people came in order to be seen and to avoid seeing those whom they would rather not see.

It was possible for a child to ignore, for a time and up to a point, these social features of the Church. I believe I was only dimly aware of them until I was in my teens. I was very serious about Christianity between the ages of ten and sixteen. My deepest connection to the Church was through music: I sang in both the child and the adult choirs, thus going to two services every Sunday, and I took organ lessons from the choir director, a gifted musician. The emotions of joy and pain and longing that were embodied in the music we performed were my route to an understanding of religious ideas, and I had a very deep longing for the salvation that I heard represented there. Because my mother was an alcoholic, my home was an unhappy one, and I believe my search for salvation was motivated, above all, by a fear of my own anger at her and a desire to be forgiven for the terrible cauldron of emotions that I felt in myself every time I came home from school and smelled bourbon in the kitchen air.

I therefore went not only to the two services, but also to the Sunday school classes for high school students. I conceived the plan of becoming an Episcopalian minister. Our assistant minister, a timorous character, told me that women would never be ordained; I doubted this because I had little confidence in this man's judgment. Around this time, two new young ministers joined the Church: a deacon named Mr. Bartholemew, a real intellectual who taught us Tillich and William James in Sunday school, and our new assistant minister, the newly ordained priest Frank Tracy Griswold III —elected in 1997 as Presiding Bishop of the Protestant Episcopal Church of the United States of America.

Mr. Griswold, as we then called him, was no radical. Although he has since been a strong defender of the ordination of women, I recall no daring pronouncements on that topic, and since that time he has owed his great success to diplomacy and moderation. Nonetheless, I felt that he took my intellectual aspirations and my dedication to the Church very seriously, and I felt encouraged. And because he was, in addition to his many other fine qualities, the most magnetic man I had ever set eyes on, it became a habit with me to volunteer to carry poinsettias to the sick—because this was Mr. Griswold's department, and I could get to talk to him about the itinerary. One time he actually showed up at our house to thank me and bring me a poinsettia, a moment of sharp joy that remains etched in my memory. When cast as an angel in the Christmas pageant, I dutifully drilled, holding my arms horizontal for twenty minutes, strapped in heavy wings.

But at this time the civil rights movement was in full swing, and the political environment of Bryn Mawr began to seem stifling. I argued with my father ceaselessly about race. And although prominent Episcopalians—in particular our bishop, Bishop De Witt—were strong advocates of civil rights laws,[7] the Church of the Redeemer increasingly began to seem to me elitist and exclusive. I had been a volunteer campaign worker for Barry Goldwater, because I had thought that individual choice could solve the problem of race. I believed, and still believe, that Goldwater was a deeply moral man who held this view also and was personally committed to racial integration. But the people I met in Goldwater headquarters were elitists and racists, and they were working for Goldwater out of racism, as their best hope for stopping change. I saw the same resistance to change in most of my fellow parishioners. It occurred to me that one might connect this resistance with the other-worldly message of Christianity itself. (I simply report my views at that time; I do not now hold the same view about the potential inherent in Christianity.)

It seemed to me that there was a synergy between Republican libertarianism and Christianity: it was morally permissible to believe in either only if there were no extremely urgent issues of earthly justice that took priority over the next world (or, what came to the same thing, the utopian fantasy of voluntary individual compliance with norms of racial justice). During a summer on a student exchange program in Wales, I lived with a family of factory workers and saw how real poverty grinds down the human spirit. I therefore finally rejected the libertarian idea that we could allow justice to depend upon individual choice. Nor was I prepared to leave justice for the life after death. It seemed to me that Jesus encouraged complacency about poverty and indignity in this world, telling people that they could wait for the next to receive their due reward. I preferred the idea of the Jews, that the Messiah should do his work for the downtrodden here and now. I went off to college with many doubts in my heart, and I went to church less often. I preferred outsiders and underdogs. I looked for anyone who would not be invited to the Junior Dance Assembly.

After two years at Wellesley College, one year as an actress, and two years at NYU (during which I sang in one of the best Episcopal church choirs in New York, but with religious skepticism), I found myself in love with a Jewish man whose family was reluctant to accept a non-Jewish spouse. At this point, all the doubts about Christianity that had for a long time pushed me from the Church crystallized in a preference for Judaism. Here I found a this-worldly religion, a religion in which the primacy of the moral, and of this-worldly justice, informed not only judgments but also, or so it seemed to me, the entirety of a tradition. I felt a passionate sympathy for my future husband's family, refugees from the Holocaust and dedicated social democrats of the sort who read I. F. Stone and *The Nation*. I had an intense desire to join the underdogs and to fight for justice in solidarity with them. I read Martin Buber and understood that virtually every relationship I had observed in Bryn Mawr had been an I-it relationship, involving no genuine acknowledgment of humanity. And I saw, I think, that the best solution to the problem of personal anger and guilt at anger lay in some form of "reparation," a dedication to good deeds that seemed well embodied in Jewish ethical norms.

At this time in the U.S., the strong and traditional affiliation between Judaism and socialism made it easy to think of Judaism as centrally about the search for social justice, the resistance to oppression. Writer Grace Paley put it this way:

> *What was your sense of what it meant to be Jewish when you were growing up?*
>
> Well, it meant to be a socialist. Well, not really. But it meant to have social consciousness. . . . It was a normal sense of outrage when others were treated badly, and along with that the idea that injustice not be allowed to continue. Blacks, for example. When I was a little kid, I said the word "nigger," my big sister hauled off and socked me. When I tell her this, she's absolutely amazed. She really doesn't remember it. But those are the feelings that seemed to me very important, that seemed to me for some peculiar reason connected to being Jewish.[8]

As I shall later argue, this connection is not at all accidental or peculiar, but a central part of the history of Judaism in general, and Reform Judaism above all. This sense of outrage, and the combination of joy and relief I found in entering a community in which outrage at injustice was normal, propelled me strongly toward conversion.

I therefore embarked on the conversion process. A rabbi in Passaic, New Jersey, a friend of my future husband's family, agreed to instruct me. He was Orthodox, but he understood that the family was not, and he never expected me to keep a kosher home. Nor, however, did he introduce me directly to the ideas of the great Reform leaders—that I had to discover much later, on my own, finding a confirmation of ideas to which I had already come in my own thinking. Rabbi Weinberger was himself, however, in some crucial respects a Mendelssohnian:[9] he believed firmly in the priority of the practical, and he understood the Biblical revelation as (essentially moral) legislation that demanded performance, rather than as metaphysical dogma demanding belief, or as mystical experience demanding faith. He taught me in the spirit of Mendelssohn's interpretation of Mosaic law:

> Among all the prescriptions and ordinances of the Mosaic law, there is not a single one which says: *You shall believe or not believe.* They all say: *You shall do or not do.* Faith is not commanded, for it accepts no other commands than those that come to it by way of conviction. All the commandments of the divine law are addressed to man's will, to his power to act.[10]

Weinberger believed this, I think, for Mendelssohn's reasons: he saw belief as something that could not be commanded, whereas conduct could be commanded. For Rabbi Weinberger himself, as for Mendelssohn, the commandments to do were both ritual and moral. But knowing from the start that my practice was highly unlikely to be Orthodox, he presented ritual practice to me not in Mendelssohn's way—as legislation binding on a specific historical group—but, rather, in a manner consistent with the practice of nineteenth century German Reformers such as Abraham Geiger—as options I should consider, pondering the wisdom that might be encompassed in tradition, but recognizing that the choice to adopt or reject resided with my own conscience.

In consequence of this commitment to the primacy of the moral, our discussions focused almost entirely on the tradition of Jewish ethics. Because Rabbi Weinberger, long accustomed to a rather non-intellectual congregation in Passaic, New Jersey, was pleased to have a philosophical discussion partner, we increasingly focused on *Pirke Avoth* and other great writings on moral matters. In the process, I learned too little Hebrew (studying on my own from a wretched phonetic text from which my husband had learned at age ten), something that still inhibits my participation in services. I came to see Judaism as a religion of argument, with a profound faith in the worth of reason. In great contrast to my Christian education, focused on catechism and professions of faith, I discovered that in a Jewish conversion process it was possible to dispute about everything. Always I was asked what I had learned and what I was resolved to do, never what I believed.

My gender was never a problem in this process. I knew that everyone involved respected me as an equal, and indeed admired my intelligence and dedication. I thought it somewhat ridiculous to go to the *mikvah* during the conversion ceremony. I found it embarrassing and extremely uncomfortable to go to that dark, run-down, cold building in Paterson and immerse myself, while three rabbis sat on the other side of a screen. I had already told Rabbi Weinberger in no uncertain terms that I found the idea of ritual sexual abstinence during menstruation and ritual female cleansing after a menstrual period degrading. He had responded by simply saying, softly and tentatively, that sometimes in a marriage it is good for the two parties to get away from one another. Rabbi Weinberger's wife was unstable and had repeatedly been hospitalized for mental illness. Sometimes she interrupted our tutorials to express intense anger about some matter, in a violent and scary way. So I sympathized with his statement, but saw it as having no bearing on my actions. He understood my views, and made no objection to my flat rejection of menstrual custom. Thus my arrival at the conversion *mikvah* was surrounded by an agreement that the aspect of the *mikvah* I found degrading was already repudiated by me on the basis of good reasons.[11] I quickly got out of the slimy cold water and emerged to be shown off in discussion with the rabbis as Rabbi Weinberger's prize pupil. Nobody involved suggested that my intelligence and ambition were other than great assets in this process.

Shortly after the *mikvah* came the marriage ceremony, performed by Rabbi Weinberger in a Reform temple near my mother's home in suburban Philadelphia. My sister, a professional organist and choir director (in Christian churches), played the organ, and we marched out to the Coronation March from Meyerbeer's *Le Prophète*.[12]

We moved to Cambridge, where, for the next twenty-five years (attending more and less regularly, most regularly during the three years before my daughter's *bat mitzvah*) I belonged to a Conservative minyan at Harvard, the Worship-Study congregation, among the first Conservative congregations to be fully egalitarian in sex roles. Reform Judaism was not strong at Harvard; this Conservative group, led by the remarkable and deeply inspiring Ben-Zion Gold, a survivor of Auschwitz and a profound scholar, had all the points that I value in Reform now: sex equality, a passion for argument, a deep concern for social justice. It also had traditional ritual observance and traditional melodies, which I found and find deeply satisfying. On Saturday mornings we would argue about Israel and Palestine; about Hellenism and Judaism; about racial justice; about sex equality.

Also, importantly, about whether God acted rightly in asking Abraham to kill his son. I firmly believe that he did not. That is, I believe that this is a morally heinous myth that does not accurately represent the actions of any being whom I could call God, that either the Bible is wrong in portraying God this way, or else the myth is to be interpreted as that of a test that Abraham fails when he chooses obedience over morality. The fact that I can say this and not be tossed out of the group is one of the crucial factors that keeps me within Judaism today. I note that even our most fundamentalist citizens, both Christian and Jewish, do not hold that laws against homicide impose a substantial burden on any individual's free exercise of religion. I infer from this silence that they agree with me about the real world, judging that no human being can claim exemption from these laws on account of a belief in a divine command. I see no reason to think that things were different several thousand years ago. I am not enamored of Kierkegaardian leaps, nor yet of obedience, where the death of a child is at issue. The moral law is the moral law, and any mystery that is incompatible with it is a snare and a delusion.[13] I do believe that serious moral dilemmas exist; once given God's command, Abraham, a man of deep faith, had just such a dilemma. The myth in that way invites us to meditate on the plurality of moral values that are not always harmoniously situated in our lives. But that, to me, does not morally justify the command itself, nor would I concede that it is inappropriate to raise questions of moral justification about it. My view is by no means isolated: it is one of the interpretations that my congregation is asked to ponder, and it has been defended by Jewish thinkers in both remote and modern times.[14]

Many Jews find these views objectionable; there are many views of many Jews that I find objectionable. I knew from the beginning of my conversion, however, that I was entering a religion in which disagreement about fundamental matters was invited and was seen as a part of religion itself. (This I believe to be true of Conservative Judaism, and indeed of many strands in Orthodox Judaism, as well as of Reform.) My awareness of the prominence of contestation and argument in the recent history of Judaism made it easier for me to conclude that I could pursue my own political and moral concerns within Judaism.

I have officially been a Reform Jew only since moving to Chicago, where I found that temple more passionate about social justice and more committed to debate than the local Conservative temple. I was also delighted by the even more thoroughgoing sex equality, which extends to the language of the ritual itself: we speak of the (four) mothers as well as the (three) fathers, and address God as "you" rather than "he." And it is consequently only recently that I have become fascinated by the ideas of the founders of Reform and have read their eloquent articulations of beliefs that I held in a more inchoate form.

III

It would, of course, be beyond the scope of this chapter to provide either an extended historical discussion of the genesis of the central ideas of Reform Judaism or an extended critical discussion of alternative views. I shall, instead, simply describe some of the ideas that form the core of my own understanding of Judaism. Nonetheless, since the history may be quite unfamiliar to many readers of this book, I shall attempt to insert historical references into the text, in a way that may lead the reader to the sources I shall only briefly describe.

I shall be referring to several distinct strands of Jewish Enlightenment thinking: the Haskalah, or Jewish Enlightenment, of which Moses Mendelssohn (1729–86) was the most famous and influential exemplar; the early German Jewish Reformers, especially Abraham Geiger (1810–74) and Samuel Holdheim (1806–60); the early leaders of Reform in the United States, most influential among whom were Isaac Mayer Wise (1819–1900) and David Einhorn (1809–79); and "Classical" Reform Judaism, among whose many leaders two Chicago rabbis Kaufmann Kohler (1843–1926) and Emil Hirsch (1851–1923) are particularly important for my discussion. In addition, I shall refer to several official documents of American Reform Judaism: the Pittsburgh Platform (1885), the Columbus Platform (1937), and the San Francisco Platform, "Reform Judaism—a Centenary Perspective" (1976). Obviously many of the ideas I derive from these sources are controversial; many Reform Jews do not accept all of them, and some may deny them all—especially at present, when, in the aftermath of the Holocaust, many Reform Jews have lost the rational optimism that once characterized the religion as a whole. (As will become evident, I have a number of problems with some current trends in Reform Judaism, particularly the ascendancy of Zionism and a certain pulling back from the cause of social justice.)

One prefatory qualification is unavoidable. The early Reformers were Enlightenment Jews. They were also Germans. They believed their views were right; but they also knew that such views would promote assimilation. Sincere rethinking of the tradition is difficult to separate from many Jews' desire to have a religion whose observances German Christians would accept and respect. As my mother-in-law, who left Vienna in 1938, said to me about her confirmation (a sex-equal ritual introduced by the Reformers as an alternative to the then all-male bar mitzvah), "You could never com pletely remove the German from it." This ambiguous aspect of Reform was less prominent in the U.S., but social discrimination by German Jews against newer immigrants from Eastern Europe was certainly played out in the preference for the "orderly" rituals of Reform over the allegedly chaotic praying of non-Reform synagogues. My own relation to the ideas of Reform, as a convert who simply liked the ideas and connected them from the start with Judaism, is thus easier and simpler than that of non-converts, who have to grapple with the fact that by embracing Reform they are in a way embracing Germany, or Judaism's tragic embrace of Germany. Many younger Jews have my own relation to the tradition. But I understand why many contemporary Jews, especially older Jews, find it much more difficult than I do to say: These are good ideas, let's keep them.

A. *The Primacy of the Moral: Kant and the Prophets*

It would not be an exaggeration to see the thought of the early Reformers as an extended conversation with Immanuel Kant. In *Religion Within the Limits of Reason Alone,* Kant had defended a view of religion focused on the moral law and the worth of humanity. He urged readers to find this moral core in all the great religions, beneath the sometimes deceptive trappings of custom and text. At the same time, however, Kant discussed Judaism in a highly critical manner, portraying it as an authoritarian and legalistic religion centered around non-moral laws, rather than around the regard for humanity that should properly be central to religion. He also saw Judaism as particularistic rather than universalistic. Mendelssohn and other distinguished thinkers of the Haskalah sympathized with Kant's view about what religion properly is; but they believed that he was dead wrong about Judaism. They set out to prove that, in essence, Judaism was the most Kantian religion of all. Far more than most other religions, as they saw it, it put regard for humanity and imperatives of moral conduct at its very core. For a Jew the primary obligation is to act for the sake of justice and right in this world. The this-worldly character of the religion, combined with the priority it attaches to practice in contrast to belief and metaphysics, makes it ideally suited to be the vehicle of a Kantian program of rational religious reform.[15]

In so writing, the Reformers did not see themselves as innovators. Instead, they saw themselves as returning the religion to its original Biblical core, from a period of rabbinical dominance that had, in their view, corrupted its essence. Thus "Reform" means not "modernizing transformation" but "return to authenticity." For Mendelssohn, who was not himself a Reformer, the moral core of religion was fully universal, but Jews were bound in addition by the entire Biblical tradition, which he understood as enjoining conduct and not belief. But Mendelssohn thought that the tradition of rabbinic law was part of the Biblical legislation, which Jews might question and debate, but which they were bound (with a few exceptions) to observe.[16] Thus his concept of practice included the dietary laws, and he never explicitly took the view that morality was more important than other aspects of the life Jews had been commanded to lead. He did, however, move in that direction with his endorsement of a famous story about Hillel:

> . . . all of God's commandments and prohibitions are fundamental. Should you, nevertheless, want to obtain their quintessence, listen to how that great teacher of the nation, Hillel the Elder, . . . conducted himself in this matter. A heathen said: "Rabbi, teach me the entire law while I am standing on one foot!" Shammai, whom he had previously approached with the same unreasonable request, had dismissed him contemptuously; but Hillel, renowned for his imperturbable composure and gentleness, said: "Son, *love thy neighbor as thyself.* This is the text of the law; all the rest is commentary. Now go and study![17]

Mendelssohn thus stresses the antiquity of the view that the core "text" of Judaism is a (rather Kantian) idea of universal regard for humanity, and that the core of "study" is moral practice. Kant congratulated Mendelssohn on *Jerusalem,* finding it a development of his own ideas. There was some wishful thinking in that reading, but there was also truth.

It was left to the nineteenth century Reformers, however, to make Judaism thoroughly Kantian. Holdheim in particular stressed the idea that the moral core takes precedence over any other idea of law, and that proper religious practice *is* moral action.[18] But all the early Reformers took a related line. It was for this reason that one of their most salient religious innovations was the introduction of the vernacular sermon, which they saw as a key to moral education and deliberation. The Jewish education of (Reform) children, from the early nineteenth century on, stressed that the most important value of Judaism is morality, and that rituals are means to the instilling of moral values.[19] The American Reform movement went in some ways even further: the Pittsburgh Platform states that among the Mosaic laws *only* the moral laws are to be regarded as binding. Kaufmann Kohler defined Judaism as an "eternal moral idea."[20]

One common strategy in developing this line of argument was to give a central place to the prophets, claiming that Reform was returning Judaism to a prophetic urgency about social justice that had been lost in an era of rabbinic legalism. Geiger explicitly called his version of Judaism "Prophetic Judaism," continually drawing attention to the prophets' concern for the poor and oppressed, their disdain for any ritual act not animated by a passion for justice.[21] An extreme but not uncharacteristic statement of this view was given by British Reformer Claude Montefiore (1858–1938), who wrote that if a Jew were to build a synagogue today, without reference to past custom, he "would not put scrolls of the Law into an ark and make that ark the most sacred part of the building. If he had such an ark, he would put in it the prophecies of Amos, Hosea and Isaiah, rather than the Pentateuch, for the Prophets are more primary and more essential than the Law."[22]

B. The Priority of Conscience over Text and External Revelation

In keeping with their regard for reason, all Enlightenment Jews, from the Haskalah on, insisted on the priority of the internal authority of conscience over external revelations, including both miracles and texts. Mendelssohn already expressed the central idea: a wise and beneficent God would surely not create human beings stunted in their faculties, and leave them to wait for miracles to figure out what they should do. Such a view would surely "detract from the omnipotence or the goodness of God."[23] A far more fitting expression of God's power would be to "grant them the powers to discover these truths themselves."[24] Reformers Geiger and Holdheim, no longer committed, as was Mendelssohn, to Orthodox practice, made this claim in an even stronger way: human beings are both rational and autonomous, and moral reason is the test for both belief and practice. Holdheim went so far as to say that conscience *is* the revelation; Geiger, similarly, held that obedience to God is obedience to the voice of moral reason within us.[25] Kaufmann Kohler, similarly, insisted that all revelation is internal, and concluded, "The Bible is holy *not because it is inspired, but because and insofar as it does still inspire.*"[26] Reformers insisted that this line was not foreign to the Jewish tradition: rationalist readings of the core of Judaism have been common throughout the tradition. Maimonides, very important to the thought of Mendelssohn, is frequently mentioned as a precedent.[27] (Spinoza is important too, but most Reformers refrained from citing this more radical name.)

One motivation for taking this line was a concern for making the Jew autonomous in a Kantian sense. Another related motivation was a concern for universality. All revelations, as Mendelssohn observed, are particularistic; they are given to one people and not to another, to one individual and not to another. Morality, by contrast, is universal; thus it must have a source in us that is itself universal. Mendelssohn, like Kant, believed that the Biblical text, appropriately studied, would yield, over time, the universal moral truths. But as time went on the Reformers preferred to place less weight on the vicissitudes of textual interpretation and more on the autonomy of the individual Jew. Thus the first article of the Pittsburgh Platform speaks of "the consciousness of the indwelling of God in man" as the core of Judaism's idea of divinity, and "the central religious truth for the human race."

C. The Core of the Moral: Love of Humanity, Social Justice, Peace, Mercy

Jewish morality has meant many things to many people. The Reformers were well aware that for many of their gentile contemporaries Judaism meant wrath, revenge, and all-powerful authority. When it did not mean these things, it meant base dedication to money-making. To counter such popular stereotypes, it was therefore not enough to stress that Judaism has a moral core; it was necessary to say what lay within that core. Mendelssohn (following Hillel) understood the core of the core to be love of the neighbor; in this he was followed by all the great Reformers, who stressed the urgency of the fight for social justice in the here and now. Mendelssohn turned to Pausanias's speech in Plato's *Symposium* for the image of a "heavenly" politics that will ennoble people whose vision has been corrupted by bad social trends: just as Plato's Heavenly Aphrodite is more noble than her "Everyday" cousin, so too the true politics of Judaism is a reproof to the false politics of "power, the circulation of money, commerce"—all of which gives Jews a "false point of view, from which we are in the habit of regarding the true interest of human society."[28] Geiger, similarly, stressed that Judaism is a religion of compassion, not of might, of mercy, not of wrath.

The idea of peace has been very central to Reform Judaism, as indeed it is to all Jews. Many Jews have been pacifists. Reform Judaism has never taken that line as a body, because it has in general held to the prophetic view that peace is to be sought only in conjunction with justice and righteousness. Nonetheless, it is not surprising that Reform Jews have been among the leading advocates of international disarmament, of international peacekeeping agencies, and, more recently, of peace in Palestine.[29] As with commerce, so with war: Reform set out to establish that stereotypes of Jewish morality as hawkish and aggressive, reveling in vengeance for its own sake, are pernicious and false. The God of Judaism is a god of mercy and love, who seeks a peace built on a foundation of social justice for all.

The leaders of Reform, both in Germany and in the United States, insisted, indeed, that insofar as the Jewish people have a particular mission in the world, it is to take the lead in the struggle for social equality, world peace, and the elimination of poverty. Samson Raphael Hirsch, an Orthodox Jew whose ideas are in some ways closely linked to those of early nineteenth century Reform (although he in fact opposed Reform), imagined a future in which every Jew would be a "respected, widely influential priestly exemplar of justice and love, disseminating not Judaism—which is prohibited[30]—but pure humanity among the nations!"[31] This idea keeps returning: Einhorn held that Jewish particularism was a type of priestly garb that the Jew could take off only when justice had been achieved.

But it was in America that the moral mission of Judaism was most thoroughly mapped out and pursued—because American Jews had full civil rights, were not preoccupied with struggling for their own political liberty, and were in a position to influence the development of society, a privilege they eagerly took up. David Einhorn, the intellectual architect of early American Reform, called slavery "the cancer of the Union," and attacked rabbis who defended it. In 1861 he had to flee Baltimore for his life as a result of his crusade. Coining the term "Radical Reform," he insisted on an uncompromising stance against evil: "truth, which means peace with God, must stand higher than peace with humans and a stormy turbulent sea must be more precious than the calm of a stagnant swamp that exudes only polluting vapors."[32]

In the late nineteenth and the twentieth centuries, the moral mission of Reform Judaism has been understood, above all, as a commitment to economic justice. The last article of the Pittsburgh Platform reads: "In full accordance with the spirit of Mosaic legislation, which strives to regulate the relation between the rich and poor, we deem it our duty to participate in the great task of modern times, to solve, on the basis of justice and righteousness, the problems presented by the contrasts and evils of the present organization of society." The Columbus Platform states that Judaism calls for the "elimination of man-made misery and suffering, of poverty and degradation, of tyranny and slavery, of social inequality and prejudice, of ill-will and strife"; that Judaism takes a stand against child labor and in favor of workplace safety regulations; that Judaism makes the right of all workers to an adequate living standard prior to "the rights of property"; that Judaism seeks a society in which the sick, the elderly, and the unemployed will be protected against "material disabilities." Finally, it states that "Judaism, from the days of the prophets, has proclaimed to mankind the ideal of universal peace," and calls for international action to seek universal disarmament on a foundation of justice and collective security.

The San Francisco Platform regrettably soft-pedals these commitments in favor of a commitment to the State of Israel and a far vaguer support for "universal justice and peace." I feel more comfortable with Columbus. The fact that Reform Jews are no longer immigrants, but prosperous leaders of society, seems to have made it impossible to gain a consensus on the moral imperatives that were at the core of the religion in earlier years. We should ask whether material comfort has not corrupted our moral vision, leading us to embrace Mendelssohn's "false politics" of power, money, and commerce.

Despite this retreat, the call for social justice remains central to many Reform congregations and their leaders. My own Rabbi Arnold Wolf put things this way in a 1987 sermon:

I believe that Judaism mandates a quite specific political ethic which is binding upon all Jews. I include among our political obligations the amelioration of inequality, offering sanctuary to those fleeing oppression and tyranny, and a perpetual struggle for peace, even at some risk to our own security and safety . . .

There are specific entailments of this view that I do not propose to ignore. We are not permitted to make war against the government and people of Nicaragua. Jews must support the rights of the victims in South Africa, in the Soviet Union—*and* in the United States. . . . Jews must endorse a freeze on nuclear weapons, a rapprochement between the nuclear powers, and an ultimate disarmament that will make war far less lethal, if not actually impossible. I believe that Jews must support the legitimate right of Palestinian self-determination, with no illusions about the meaning of that right: a Palestinian state beside Israel—though not, of course, instead of Israel. I believe that these "left-liberal" political goals are precisely mandated by Judaism as I understand it, and that no Jew is free to abstain from them. . . .

God will complete our imperfections. She will not forgive our self-defensive cowardice or our fear of failure.[33]

As Arnold Wolf knows, these are fighting words; many Jews will strongly disagree with the specifics. But his hope, and my own, is that the underlying commitment to justice for the oppressed will remain so deeply at the heart of all Jews that disagreement will be only about specifics, not about the more general goal of a just society in this world.

D. A Cosmopolitan Religion: Universalism and Israel's Moral Mission

Any Jew who holds that moral laws are universal must find some way of explaining the particular role of the Jewish people in history, and must give some account of her Jewish particularism. Some contemporary Jews have decided that this cannot be done: the Jews who founded the Ethical Culture society and those who joined the Unitarian-Universalist Church consciously left aside their separate identity as Jews in order to join humanity. Similarly, in the eighteenth and nineteenth centuries, many assimilated German Jews had concluded that Judaism had to be left behind in order to join universal rational humanity. Reform Judaism was thus confronted at its inception with the problem of articulating the relationship between Judaism and cosmopolitanism: only in this way could it attract again to Judaism many who had left it behind; and only in this way could the Reformers show that a Kantian ideal of universal morality could be realized within Judaism. This is an issue that has always confronted Judaism, but it arises with special force within a Judaism dedicated to Enlightenment values.

Mendelssohn, as I have mentioned, understood the moral law to be universal, and criticized revelation on the grounds of its particularity. But he also held that Jews are bound by a particularistic legislation that extends to many non-moral matters. He insisted that it was good that society should contain a diversity of religions, each with its own religious laws. Such a pluralism, he argued, is good for social justice, since each group will protect itself from oppression by adopting universally some political policies, such as the liberty of conscience and the liberty of speech and press, that are everywhere valuable.[34] (Mendelssohn was thus on the track of a central idea of Rawlsian political liberalism, although he ran the justification in the opposite direction, justifying pluralism by appeal to its role in promoting liberty, rather than justifying liberty as an appropriate response to the fact of pluralism.) In this way Mendelssohn avoided a conflict between Jewish particularism and cosmopolitan values: Jewish particularism itself serves the cosmopolitan value of liberty.

The leading Reformers, both in Germany and in the United States, departed from Mendelssohn's view, attempting to produce a Judaism that was internally cosmopolitan. Holding strictly to the idea that only the moral law is binding, they refused to allow that anything that could not be universalized belonged to the core of Judaism. On the other hand, they emphasized that universal obligations to humanity may reasonably be performed from within a community with a distinctive historical character; as I have mentioned, they frequently expressed this character as that of a special messianic dedication to social justice and equality.

Thus Samson Hirsch coined a term that well expressed the conception of the Reformers: the Jew should understand himself as a "Mensch-Jissroeïl,"[35] a human being pursuing the universal within a particular tradition. As the Columbus Platform put it, "Judaism is the historical religious experience of the Jewish people. Though growing out of Jewish life, its message is universal, aiming at the union and perfection of mankind. . . . We regard it as our historic task to cooperate with all men in the establishment of the kingdom of God, of universal brotherhood, justice, truth and peace on earth. This is our Messianic goal." The San Francisco Platform keeps that part of the tradition intact, stating "that the ethics of universalism implicit in traditional Judaism must be an explicit part of our Jewish duty." (Once again, however, notice the pulling back from earlier claims that this was the *whole* of our Jewish duty.)

In keeping with this cosmopolitan commitment, Reform was anti-Zionist since its inception. The first striking change introduced into traditional liturgy by the early German Reformers (in the Hamburg prayerbook of 1810) was the removal of references to a return to the land of Israel and the reestablishment of the Temple. As Zionism grew, leading Reformers explicitly and routinely attacked it. Especially in America, Jews were concerned lest the identification of Judaism with Zionism persuade Americans to judge that Jews are not fully loyal to America. The Pittsburgh Platform states: "We consider ourselves no longer a nation, but a religious community, and, therefore, expect neither a return to Palestine, nor a sacrificial worship under the sons of Aaron, nor the restoration of any of the laws concerning the Jewish state."

The events of the twentieth century changed all this. Already in 1937, the Columbus Platform attempts a compromise between strong American loyalty and a moderate Zionism:

> In all lands where our people live, they assume and seek to share loyally the full duties and responsibilities of citizenship and to create seats of Jewish knowledge and religion. In the rehabilitation of Palestine, the land hallowed by memories and hopes, we behold the promise of renewed life for many of our brethren. We affirm the obligation of all Jewry to aid in its upbuilding as a Jewish homeland by endeavoring to make it not only a haven of refuge for the oppressed but also a center of Jewish culture and spiritual life.

The San Francisco Platform affirms these two propositions—the loyal citizenship of all Jews in their respective nations and the importance of Israel—urging that the attitude of non-Israeli Jews toward Israel can "show how a people transcends nationalism even as it affirms it, thereby setting an example for humanity which remains largely concerned with dangerous parochial goals." (This is to me a dubious proposition: too often the attitude of American Jews to Israel shows nothing like a transcendence of nationalism, but a kind of double nationalism, and an indifference to the suffering of the oppressed that is difficult to square with the Jewish tradition.) At the same time, the Platform demands the full recognition of Reform Judaism in the state of Israel—a problem that today, twenty-two years later, is placing increasing strain on the relationship.[36]

My own view is that the early Reformers are in principle correct: cosmopolitan Jews should cease to focus on a Jewish homeland as a goal worthwhile in itself. However, history—and especially the world community's culpable unwillingness to accept Jewish refugees from genocide or to act on their behalf—has made clear the *instrumental* importance of such a homeland for the protection of Jewish life, speech, and culture. A cosmopolitan Jew may therefore cautiously support the existence of the state of Israel, while deploring its unjust conduct to the Palestinians and its refusal to extend fully equal rights to Reform and Conservative Jews (and therefore to female Jews of all sorts). I believe that a cosmopolitan Jew should also oppose the establishment of Judaism as the state religion of Israel, in the light of the way in which this fact has been used to turn non-Jews into second-class citizens. Israel may continue to be a Jewish state by extending preferential immigration policies to Jews; but once citizens are present they should be fully equal no matter what their ethnic or religious origins. In general, I have difficulty seeing contemporary Israel as a place in which any worthy Jewish ideal is realized. Given the ideas that led me to Judaism, it comes as a rude shock to me to observe Jews who take delight in dominating others, getting revenge on others, and expressing loathsome prejudices concerning others. Such attitudes are a "false politics" in the Mendelssohnian sense, and should be repudiated by all Jews. Obviously one also encounters many admirable attitudes, and many Jewish politicians (for example in the judiciary) who do attempt to carry out the highest moral ideals of Judaism. One can only hope that such attitudes will prevail.

E. A Historical Understanding of the Tradition

Enlightenment Jews must give some account of those parts of the tradition that seem not to express universal moral law. Mendelssohn's way was the least historicist: he saw the non-moral parts of the tradition as binding legislation. Even he, however, understood ceremonial law to be "a kind of living script" that was differently realized in different periods;[37] and he challenged much of the rabbinic tradition in the name of the Biblical core of the religion.

Most of the Reformers went much further, understanding a great part of the tradition to be a historical record. For some, the Mosaic core is distinguished from Halacha (rabbinic law), the latter being historical and nonbinding. Both Holdheim and Geiger went further, holding that no text has binding authority, given that human beings are autonomous moral agents. Geiger was particularly concerned with overturning the authority of the rabbinic tradition; he argued that the rabbis had systematically distorted the Biblical text to gain authority for themselves, although he insisted that their works were still important spiritual sources. Holdheim, more radical, said modernity was totally discontinuous with earlier times, and texts written in earlier times therefore offer little guidance for modern moral reasoning: for example, Jewish proponents of women's equality should not even try to gain authority for their view by reading it back into the Talmud, they should just say that it was right.

As time went on, most Reform Jews understood the Biblical text through the lens of modern historical scholarship, and they came to believe that the truths revealed by scholarship made Reform the only defensible version of Judaism. As Emil Hirsch put it in 1886, "Modern scholarship has spoken and its voice cannot be hushed. It has shown that Moses is not the author of the Pentateuch; that Sinai is not the cradle of what is highest and best in Biblical Judaism . . . that the whole apparatus of priestly institutionalism is of non-Hebraic origin. . . . "[38] Judaism, Reformers held, is "a progressive religion, ever striving to be in accord with the postulates of reason" (Pittsburgh Platform). This meant acknowledging the truths revealed by scholarship and revising one's conception of text and tradition accordingly. As the Pittsburgh Platform puts it: "We hold that the modern discoveries of scientific researches in the domains of nature and history are not antagonistic to the doctrines of Judaism, the Bible reflecting the primitive ideas of its own age, and at times clothing its conception of Divine Providence and justice dealing with man in miraculous narratives."

F. Ritual as Moral Instrument and Moral Expression

This being the case, Reform Judaism has struggled to work out an adequately modern conception of the role of ritual in Jewish life. Already in the early nineteenth century, progressive congregations in Germany insisted on the use of the vernacular in the service, on sermons in the vernacular, and on "decorum" during the service—holding that the customary chaos of individual praying was not conducive to moral reflection. (Often this emphasis was used as a device of ethnic prejudice: both in Europe and in America the Jews of Eastern Europe were found wanting from the point of view of "decorum" by contrast to German Jews.) Nonetheless, ritual was not altogether disdained: Geiger, for example, saw rituals as bearers of moral truth, to be maintained so long as they "stimulate our moral and religious sensibility."[39] In America, David Einhorn insisted that symbols were important vehicles of moral ideas.

That has been the view of most Reform Jews: the test for ritual practice is its relation to the inner moral life of the participating Jew. Thus the Pittsburgh Platform condemns the dietary laws by saying that "[t]hey fail to impress the modern Jew with a spirit of priestly holiness; their observance in our days is apt rather to obstruct than to further modern spiritual elevation." Some were harsher still: Emil Hirsch called the dietary laws "a survival of a species of totemism," and Kaufmann Kohler called the wearing of the *talit* "fetishism."[40]

Two broad currents can be discerned within this general critique of ritual. On the one side are Reformers like Geiger, David Einhorn, and Kaufmann Kohler, all of whom emphasized the positive value of ritual observance in expressing human need and aspiration, in sharpening reflection, and in motivating the individual to seek justice; on the other are sterner rationalists, such as Emil Hirsch, who had little room for liturgy and viewed symbolism as a distraction from the important task of pursuing justice out in the world.

My own sympathies are definitely with the former group. I believe that ritual observance is extremely important for many people who seek to live a moral life, and especially important for children, in connecting abstract moral truths to particular musical and emotional memories. Nor do I believe that ritual is only instrumental. I think that the acts of imagination and emotion that one performs when one participates in a ritual well are intrinsically valuable human acts, acts expressive of moral dedication, of fellowship, of longing for justice. Music and poetic language can frequently inspire us to express ourselves morally in a more adequate and focused way; and those expressions themselves have worth, in addition to their worth in motivating us to act. In general the inner moral life itself has moral worth; it is not just a preparation for action, but part of moral virtue itself. I think it was definitely a mistake on the part of the early Reformers to prune the liturgy, stripping away much of the traditional poetry and translating everything into the vernacular. They made, often, a worthy and bland soup, rather than anything interesting enough to be called a meal. (For example, early Reform Haggadahs took out all the Talmudic disputation that provides much of the historical richness and the humor of the Passover seder.)

Indeed, one of the great barriers I have found in moving from Conservative Judaism into Reform is the strangeness of the Reform attitude to liturgical music and language. In their eagerness to be Enlightenment Germans or Americans, the early Reformers stripped away a great deal of poetic and musical beauty, substituting, often, language and music of appalling banality. Instead of the thrilling sound of the *shofar,* in most Reform temples (until recently) one would find a decorous trumpet. Instead of traditional Jewish melodies, with their haunting wild beauty, one encounters organ music that is so decorous that it expresses no authentic sentiment or idea. Instead of the traditional poetic texts, one often finds modern prose and poetry, often hacked to bits and inserted oddly into the middle of a service that is about something else. (I remember my dismay at running across a stanza of Stephen Spender, unattributed, plunked down in the middle of the Kol Nidre service.) At one time, Reformers eliminated the Kol Nidre prayer, the most beautiful and stirring prayer of the entire Jewish year, on the grounds that they did not want the Germans to believe that they would not keep their promises.[41]

And as for music, always one of my central connections to religion, my husband's view of Reform temples was that that was where they play the guitar and sing folk songs. This is not altogether wrong—except that they don't sing anything as interesting as folk music. A recent concert of new Jewish music in my temple showed me that Jewish liturgical composition is in a dismal state. It is neither good music of its own time nor traditional music. We don't commission new works from demanding and excellent Jewish composers such as Shulamith Ran (whose opera based on Agnon's *The Dybbuk* contains some of the best Jewish music I know). Instead, the music seeks to be what will alienate nobody. It is the Hallmark greeting card of music. In this one respect alone, I miss Christianity: while my sister plays works by composers from Bach to Verdi to Poulenc to Britten to Messiaen, we are stuck with mediocrities who could not command respect for five minutes in Symphony Hall. Nor do we play the great Jewish composers of the past: the many Baroque masters; the portions of Mahler's music that are evidently Jewish in character; the Kol Nidre of Schoenberg; Bernstein's Kaddish symphony. If I can even imagine Ran or Schoenberg performed at KAM, I know the misery and outrage with which much of the congregation would greet it. Christians are more used to having liturgical music challenge and educate, rather than just soothing, their musical sensibilities. Fortunately my temple, ritually at the Conservative end of Reform, uses many of the traditional melodies and thus manages to create real musical beauty, despite the goyish organ playing (which is not even highly skilled for the most part, as if it had to apologize for being in the synagogue by being unobtrusive and bland).

G. Sex Equality in the Context of Cosmopolitan Morality

Judaism as traditionally practiced is, obviously, a patriarchal religion. Thus, as leading Jewish feminist thinker Judith Plaskow rightly notes, "For many people—from secular feminists to observant Jews—the notion of a feminist Judaism is an oxymoron."[42] But the patriarchal character of Judaism came under attack from the very beginning of the Reform movement. Indeed, the religious needs of Jewish women were among the forces that gave birth to Reform in Germany; the fact that women were not educated in Hebrew was among the primary reasons for holding the service in German, as the 1818 Hamburg congregation explicitly stated. All the early German Reform congregations urged women to attend services—including young unmarried women, who had traditionally not been encouraged. Although women were still seated apart from men until around the 1850s, they were given more seats, often seated on the same floor rather than in a gallery, and were not put behind a screen. Mixed seating became general by the 1870s, but came in earlier in America (1851 in Albany), where the custom of families attending church together led Jews to favor a "family pew."

Confirmation services symmetrical for women and men displaced the traditional bar mitzvah as early as 1810.[43] In 1855, the female congregants in Baden protested against the restoration to the liturgy (notice that it had already been eliminated once) of the prayer in which men thank God for not making them women. The women note that *they* are thanking God for modernity, which makes it unnecessary to put up with things like this! In Breslau in 1846, women began to be counted in the minyan, the quota of participants necessary to pray (which in Orthodox Judaism means male participants). Increasingly, too, the marriage ceremony was rewritten to create symmetry between male and female: in the U.S. in 1830, such a reformed wedding service was used in the first Reform prayer book to be published. In 1869, David Einhorn's prayerbook emphasized equal participation of men and women in the marriage ceremony. During this period, Reform Jews also abandoned the religious divorce and the *get* (religious document of divorce that cannot be obtained by the woman without the man's consent), and opened civil divorce to both male and female Jews.

Women continued, nonetheless, to play a subordinate role in their congregations. They were leaders, often, in religious education and charitable functions, but they played no role in leading the service. Despite a certain degree of feminism, most leading Reform Jews shared the view that a woman's primary role was as wife and mother. Reform rabbis were not radicals when it came to women's suffrage: the Conference endorsed it only three years before the passage of the constitutional amendment. Even radical Emil Hirsch held that women and men were unequal by nature, although he allowed Jane Addams to preach a sermon in Sinai temple. As is frequently the case in progressive cultural movements generally, the subordination of women to men was not questioned as profoundly and as thoroughly as were other forms of subordination (such as class- or race-based inequality). In this respect Reform Jews were people of their time and place. They went beyond their time in some respects, but they could not envisage a reorganization of the family or of the rabbinate.

Women did not accept this situation passively. By 1893 the American Jewish Women had organized nationally to demand a larger role in temple life; they had the support of Kaufmann Kohler, who said that Reform needed female leaders. The iconoclastic Reform woman Ray Frank preached in temples in the 1890s, and even officiated at High Holy Day services. In Britain, meanwhile, Lily Montagu (1873–1963) played a leading role in the development of Liberal Judaism (the British analogue of Reform).

But the really large changes had to wait for a time of more general social change. The 1976 San Francisco Platform affirms the full equality of women as participants in Judaism; and indeed the first Reform female rabbi was ordained in 1972.[44] Laura Geller, among the first to be ordained, notes that female rabbis have encountered the "glass ceiling" that greets so many working women: she is the first to have been hired by a very large influential congregation, and that only recently. But she thinks that female rabbis have brought about a widespread transformation, particularly in worshippers' attitudes to the gender of God. Before, even if Reform Jews rejected the idea that God is male, they tended to imagine a male being. "As long as their rabbi is male, they are not even aware that they associate him in some way with a male divinity." Now, the combination of liturgical reform with the presence of a female officiating at the service has made Jews "begin to confront directly their images of God" and to ask how those unexamined images have been linked to other thoughts and responses.[45] Even when the rabbi is not female, the congregation's awareness of this possibility—together with the frequent presence of a female cantor[46]—makes a significant difference. Changes in liturgical language and in the practice of even male rabbis when referring to the deity (note Arnold Wolf's "she" in the 1987 passage cited above) carry the transformation further.[47]

In short, I see no reason to believe that Judaism is inherently patriarchal, or that it has been a retrograde force in the struggle for women's full equality. Some Jews have been retrograde, and I believe that Orthodox Judaism still has many problems on that score. But Judaism has also been in advance of its surrounding culture in some respects, and just of a piece with its surrounding culture in most others. The messianic fervor with which Jews have championed the rights of the poor has not been matched by a comparable zeal for sex equality—until very recently. But secular leftist movements in America have often been far more patriarchal than left-wing Judaism was, so I see no reason to blame religion itself for our slow progress in this regard. (Marxism, for example, is rarely blamed for sexism; and yet Marxist movements have been at least as sexist as Reform Judaism, and probably far more so.)

Some critics of Judaism say that Judaism is inherently or originally patriarchal, and that modern reforms are changes and reconstructions. Orthodox and Conservative feminists frequently engage in strenuous denials of such charges, pointing to the evident fact that early Biblical texts show women playing strong roles (Deborah, for example), and that God ought properly to be conceived as beyond gender. But let us consider what both the charge of patriarchy and its refutation take for granted. They assume without argument that the original core of Judaism is a set of authoritative Biblical texts, and perhaps also the tradition of Halacha.[48] If one takes seriously the idea that the core of Judaism is, instead, a set of universal moral ideas that are partially expressed in the texts, and to some extent also in the legal tradition, then one should not conclude anything of the kind. One should conclude that Judaism never was misogynistic or patriarchal at its core: erring human beings, blinded by habit and culture, put that construction upon it. We recall it, in this way, to its purity.

IV

It will hardly escape the notice of readers of this volume that up until now I have said little about God or prayer. And this is deliberate. The moral core of Reform Judaism has coexisted with many different ideas of God, running the gamut from traditional belief in a personal anthropomorphic God to Deism and even agnosticism. The Haskalah was strongly influenced by Deism, and the early German and American Reformers pondered many possibilities, some taking Spinoza as their lead. At the 1871 Reform convention in Cincinnati, a famous debate on this issue took place. Rabbi Jacob Mayer of Cleveland stated: "I believe not in a personal God, neither do I address my prayer to a personal God." The enormously influential Isaac Mayer Wise, founder of Hebrew Union College, agreed with him, urging the convention to adopt a Spinozistic conception of God as "the substance, unlimited, eternal and infinite." He told the assembled rabbis that the personal God was a Christian, not a Jewish, idea, "a philosophical fiction to explain the incarnation."[49] Wise was attacked by many people, including David Einhorn and Kaufmann Kohler, who immediately wrote impassioned statements of their own belief in a personal God; nonetheless, views of this sort continued to be solidly represented within Reform. Emil Hirsch defined prayer in purely human terms as "the attempt to bring home to man from the emotional side of his nature, and to sharpen within him, the sense of duty and responsibility." He defined God by citing Matthew Arnold: "that Power, not ourselves, which makes for righteousness." And he frequently spoke of his view as "moral theism," meaning by this that the Jew lives not by faith but by works.

The creation of the Ethical Culture Society, a break-off sect originating from Reform Judaism, led to a lot of questioning, as Reform Jews who chose to remain within Judaism tried to respond to the challenge posed by the morally high-minded agnosticism of Felix Adler and his group. Emil Hirsch preached that Judaism was itself an ethical culture movement, but one based upon history and tradition.[50] Others, like Kohler, attacked Ethical Culture more sharply, reasserting their theistic beliefs. On balance, the existence of Ethical Culture as an alternative reinforced the theistic commitments of Reform Judaism. Nonetheless, the spectrum of belief about the deity represented within Reform remains wide. In the 1940s, for example, the "religious humanists" within Reform argued that God is not transcendent and omnipotent but finite, struggling for humanity from within the natural world. Prayer was therefore not petition to the transcendent, but "meditation on the best we know." This has remained a minority view; and in the 1980s one entire congregation that officially denied the existence of God was denied admission to the Reform Union. Nonetheless, all Reform platforms have stressed the respect for argument and for diversity of belief that has always been the movement's hallmark. The San Francisco Platform, for example, while committing itself to belief in one God, states:

Reform Jews respond to change in various ways according to the Reform principle of the autonomy of the individual. However, Reform Judaism does more than tolerate diversity; it engenders it . . . We stand open to any position thoughtfully and conscientiously advocated in the spirit of Reform Jewish beliefs. . . . [W]e accept such differences as precious and see in them Judaism's best hope for confronting whatever the future holds for us.

In that spirit, therefore, I shall attempt to state my own views, which are at the Kantian/Deist end of the traditional spectrum.

First, what I do not believe: I do not believe that morality needs the existence of an eternal or transcendent divinity to back it up. Nor do I think that it is appropriate for us to focus on transcendence of our own mortality in a life after death. Our moral task is in this world, and if it should happen that there is a life after death, that would make no difference to what we have to do here and now. I don't think we have any reason to believe that there is such a life, unfortunately, but I also think that this does not diminish us or make our efforts less worthy. Focusing on the other world has, in fact, done great harm to this-worldly morality; I came to Judaism precisely in search of a moral view of religion, and that is what I continue to find there. From the Greeks I have learned that it is the conditions of this-worldly life that give virtues such as justice and benevolence their point; morality thus seems to me a peculiarly this-worldly phenomenon.

I don't believe in a personal God, and the idea of an eternal infinite substance means nothing to me. Nor do I think that humanity is precious only if there is something more than human about it. My beliefs are thus closest to those of the religious humanists, who think that what is worthy of respect and awe is humanity itself, struggling with its problems within history. I also find attractive the conceptions of prayer articulated by Hirsch and the humanists: prayer is (for me) essentially emotional and moral, a sharpening and focusing of one's moral energies, which are usually blunted by the distractions of daily life. But I am not taken with Hirsch's Matthew Arnold view of divinity: I think that if we are ever to do right, the power to do it has to come from us. Otherwise our actions would be by rote, and would not be virtuous actions.

Beyond this, I have great uncertainty. I do think that there is mystery and sublimity in our lives; but I think it would be a cop-out to say that we need to derive that sublimity from an external source. Nor do I agree with Kant about the need for a specific hope for life after death to sustain our moral efforts. But I do think that humanity is not just a machine pushed around by the natural world: that, as both Seneca and Kant said in their different ways, there is something in humanity that is deeply awe-inspiring, that goes beyond mechanical causality. If that makes enough room for a conception of God—as whatever it is that makes us not mere machines and objects, but ends, capable of loving and worthy of being loved—then I have a conception of God. As I have said, the thought of God's kingdom plays for me something of the role played by the kingdom of ends in Kantian morality: an ideal of social justice that can focus thought and motivate conduct.

Given these views, why do I not join the Ethical Culture Society? Many Reform Jews have asked themselves this question, and there is almost certainly considerable overlap between the beliefs of Reform Jews and the beliefs of members of Ethical Culture—especially today, when Ethical Culture is in steep decline. There are some easy answers: I don't go to Ethical Culture because everyone there is over eighty; because the music is even more ridiculous than the music in a Reform temple; because the movement scorned ritual to such an extent that (like the Humanist Society) it never developed an emotionally satisfying form of worship; because it has no history and no tradition, things that are important to people for fixing their thoughts on ethical ideals; because I want to find a community of like-minded people, and Ethical Culture now no longer contains that. Certainly Ethical Culture is a barren place to raise a child, for all of these reasons. And it was very important to me to raise my daughter within a religion, because I think that traditional forms of worship are very helpful in the transmission of ethical values.

But I suppose I also have deeper reasons, having to do with the idea of awe. I think Ethical Culture was a rather reductionist movement, which read science as implying that we are simply objects within the natural world. Maybe I'm wrong about that, since I have only once been to an Ethical Culture service. But I think that a sense of openness to the mysterious and (morally) transcendent is lacking there, and, of course, wonderfully present in the traditional Jewish liturgy. I also think that the question of God's existence is not a closed but an open question, and I like to be in the company of people who have views more traditionally theistic than my own, so that I can learn from those beliefs and keep asking myself what I believe. Especially, I would like to think that there is some source of forgiveness for our aggressive and selfish actions and thoughts that goes beyond the individual forgiveness of individual people, and I focus on that portion of the liturgy with great attention, considering different ways of conceiving of this idea.

I think that something like this has been the position of many Enlightenment Jews, so I am comforted in my unease and ambivalence by finding myself in a long tradition of speculation and struggle.

Most of all, I find all these things very difficult and very mysterious. Many Enlightenment people reject religion out of hand because they think they know what's what, or at least how we would go about finding out

what's what. I don't have such confidence in the adequacy of our understanding of ourselves; so while I do believe that in the end we have to make
up our minds what we are going to do, I think it is valuable to focus on the
mysteriousness of life and death in a way that makes us keenly aware of the
shortcoming of our own explanations. In that sense, the humanist idea of
prayer seems to me narcissistic and smug; prayer is meditation on what we
do not know, as well as on the best we know.

But I remain with Mendelssohn in this: "The highest wisdom is incontrovertibly doing that which is good."

NOTES

For comments on an earlier draft of this essay, I am extremely grateful to Jacob Adler,
Lisa Bernstein, Rob Katz, Abner Mikva, Richard Posner, Stephen Schulhofer, David Strauss,
Josef Stern, Cass Sunstein, Paul Weithman, and Laurie Wohl. I know that I am far from
having answered all their questions. Rachel Nussbaum (my daughter) helped me learn
about the history of German Jews in the eighteenth and nineteenth centuries. At a time of
severe illness, Sara Nussbaum (my mother-in-law) generously talked with me about her religious education in Vienna in the 1920s. She died in March 1999; this paper is dedicated to
her with love. I am especially grateful to my Rabbi Arnold Wolf for fighting with me about
this paper, as about many other topics, and getting me to make it better. Also for the blunt-
ness of his initial reaction when he phoned after reading it through: "You know what the
trouble is with you? You're a goddamn Reform Jew."

1. KAM is one of the three ancestors of my own congregation, KAM Isaiah Israel.
Founded in 1847, it was the first Jewish congregation in the Midwest. Although initially
Orthodox, it quickly moved into the Reform camp and has remained there ever since,
defining a type of moderate, ritual-friendly Reform Judaism that contrasts with types of
radical Reform that question the role of ritual in Jewish life.

2. Moses Mendelssohn, "Rhapsodie Über die Empfindungen" in Moritz Brasch, ed.
Schriften zur Psychologie und Aesthetik (Leipzig: Verlag Leopold Voss, 1880), p. 123.

3. It is difficult to know at what point we should use the term "Reform Judaism,"
rather than speaking of various reformers. I use the term somewhat anachronistically of the
German reformers, since the movement became an organized entity primarily in America,
and only in the 1850s and later.

4. For an excellent overall history of the Reform Movement, to which I am much in-
debted, see Michael A. Meyer, *Response to Modernity: A History of the Reform Movement in
Judaism* (Detroit: Wayne State University Press, 1988), hereafter Meyer, *Response*. See also
Michael A. Meyer, ed., *German-Jewish History in Modern Times*, vol. 2: *Emancipation and
Acculturation, 1780–1871* (New York: Columbia University Press, 1997), hereafter Meyer,
History. (Although this is an edited collection, the chapters to which I shall refer are all authored by Meyer, except where noted.) The strong anti-Zionism of the American Reform
movement in the nineteenth century and the first half of the twentieth is closely connected
with the Reformers' admiration for America: they did not wish to seem to long for any
other land in which to realize their aspirations. See Meyer, *Response*, Ch. 8. Nor was this attitude without precedent. From the beginning of German Reform, the idea of the return to
the land of Israel came under criticism: the Hamburg Temple prayerbook of 1818, for example, already excluded all mention of the return (see Meyer, *History*, p. 124).

5. On the love of the Reformers for America, see Meyer, *Response,* Ch. 6. Isaac Mayer Wise, the most influential nineteenth century American Reformer and founder of the Hebrew Union College, where Reform rabbis have been trained ever since, went so far as to state that George Washington and his revolutionary compatriots were "chosen instruments in the hands of Providence," and that the insights of Judaism would help America "work out a new and peculiar destiny," fulfilling prophetic ideals in the modern world. Wise even believed that Reform Judaism, as a universalist, progressive, and non-authoritarian religion focused on the supremacy of the moral, would become the common faith of all Americans (Meyer, *Response,* p. 227). Such sentiments were common. In 1882, Rabbi Adolf Moses of Mobile, Alabama, preached (in German!) that "[f]rom America salvation will go forth; in this land will the religion of Israel celebrate its greatest triumphs" (Meyer, *Response,* p. 253). Things haven't changed all that much: my High Holy Day prayer book includes both "America the Beautiful" and "The Star Spangled Banner"—and, just for good measure, "O Canada" as well.

6. I refer here only to a single congregation, not to the Presbyterian Church as a whole; even in that case, I report memories that may well be colored by my own evolving social attitudes.

7. In particular, De Witt took a strong public stand on the integration of Girard College, a preparatory school founded by Stephen Girard for "poor white male orphans." The forced integration of Girard (racial, not, of course, sexual) was the first instance of the setting aside of a will on grounds of racial discrimination, and was thus much disputed. My father, a lawyer specializing in trusts and estates, conducted a heated correspondence with the Bishop, objecting both to the content of his position and to the fact that a religious leader would speak publicly on a divisive issue.

8. Melanie Kay/Kantrowitz and Irena Klepfisz, "An Interview with Grace Paley," in *The Tribe of Dina: A Jewish Women's Anthology* (Montpelier, Vt.: Sinister Wisdom Books, 1986). In a similar vein, Abner Mikva tells me that Rabbi Harold Kushner quoted a female friend as saying: "When I was young, I was taught that being Jewish meant: You don't cross picket lines, you work for peace, you fight for social justice, you never forget the suffering of your people as a link to the suffering of others."

9. Mendelssohn himself was orthodox in practice, as were most of the Enlightenment Jews of this period. For the best overall account of Mendelssohn's views, see David Sorkin, *Moses Mendelssohn and the Religious Enlightenment* (Berkeley: University of California Press, 1996); the best biography is Alexander Altmann, *Moses Mendelssohn: A Biographical Study* (New York: Oxford University Press, 1988).

10. Moses Mendelssohn, *Jerusalem,* trans. Allan Arkush, Introduction and Commentary by Alexander Altmann (Hanover, N.H.: University Press of New England, 1983), p. 100. Mendelssohn points out that the Hebrew term that is standardly translated "faith" is better rendered as "trust" or "confidence."

11. See, in this connection, the discussion of feminist reinterpretations of the *mikvah* in Sylvia Barack Fishman, *A Breath of Life: Feminism in the American Jewish Community* (New York: The Free Press, 1993; reprint, Waltham, Mass.: Brandeis University Press, 1995), p. 116; understandings include a general idea of purification from daily inattention and from corroding resentment; also an idea of oneness with a source of physical and spiritual energy.

12. Orthodox Jews do not permit instrumental music in the synagogue, believing that it is forbidden to play a musical instrument on the Sabbath, on Yom Tov, and during certain prescribed mourning periods. (On other occasions, however, music could be played; during the Renaissance, for example, Jewish instrumental music was written to be performed just before Shabbat.) Some less strict Orthodox Jews and Conservative Jews permit a non-Jew (e.g., my sister) to play an instrument; but organ music in the temple was among the earliest and is still among the most characteristic marks of Reform. Meyerbeer is the Jewish operatic composer who was hated by Wagner and who is the primary target of his *Judaism in Music.*

13. Among the Meditations in the front of my High Holy Day prayerbook is a paragraph by one John D. Rayner stating that the Akedah proves that Judaism "teaches reverence for life as its highest principle." The author derives this conclusion from the fact that Abraham (having agreed to sacrifice his son) is ultimately told that he need not do so. I find this hardly satisfactory.

14. My colleague Josef Stern believes that this may have been Maimonides' view; I shall not digress to consider his complex and subtle argument. Jacob Adler suggests to me that there is a similar *reductio* in Ps. 82, "God takes his stand in the divine assembly . . . " This psalm seems to assert the existence of other gods, who are then described as dying. Such a statement would be incompatible with the monotheism of the Psalms. So we might interpret the Psalm as follows: "Suppose there were other gods. They would be mortal and fallible, therefore not gods. Therefore, there are no other gods." Similarly, Adler suggests, the Akedah might be interpreted to say, "Suppose God commanded a pious person to sacrifice his/her child. . . . "

15. See Meyer, *Response*, p. 65.

16. For example, he was willing to modify burial customs, in light of evidence that there was a danger of premature burial of living persons. Here the overriding principle of preserving life superseded, for him, the customary practice of rapid burial. See Meyer, *Response*, p. 15. He admitted having "detected human additions and abuses in my religion which, sadly, all too much dim its luster."

17. Mendelssohn, *Jerusalem*, p. 102.

18. See Meyer, *History*, pp. 143, 150.

19. Meyer, *History*, p. 117.

20. Meyer, *Response*, p. 271.

21. Meyer, *Response*, pp. 95–96.

22. Meyer, *Response*, p. 215.

23. Mendelssohn, *Jerusalem*, p. 94.

24. Mendelssohn, *Jerusalem*, p. 94. This argument is found already in some medieval texts.

25. Meyer, *History*, p. 147.

26. Kohler, *Hebrew Union College and Other Addresses*, quoted in Meyer, *Response*, p. 273.

27. Maimonides argues that what makes the Torah divine is not the identity of its author but its content or "final cause," which is to make us intellectually perfect. So, we can infer that the Torah was authored by God because it is divine; it is not divine because it was authored by God. (I am grateful to Josef Stern for these observations.)

28. Mendelssohn, *Jerusalem*, p. 131.

29. This essay was written in 1999. Now (June 2002), I believe that these remarks about Israel are lacking in nuance. For a more complex discussion of my views about Israel and the current situation, please see my article "The Other Israel," *The Nation*, July 17, 2002.

30. Jews have frequently held that it is wrong to try to convert non-Jews. Prospective converts must repeatedly ask to be instructed, and even then it is the rabbi's duty to dissuade them. Hirsch may be referring to these traditions; or he may be referring to rabbinic strictures against teaching Oral Torah (rabbinic interpretation) to non-Jews.

31. Hirsch, *Igrot tsafun*, quoted (and translated) in Meyer, *History*, p. 146.

32. Quoted in Meyer, *Response*, p. 249. Wise was less radical than Einhorn in all respects; by character a consensus-seeker, he defended states' rights.

33. Arnold Jacob Wolf, "A Theology of Activism," in *Unfinished Rabbi: Selected Writings of Arnold Jacob Wolf* (Chicago: Ivan R. Dee, 1998), pp. 76–79.

34. Mendelssohn, *Jerusalem*, pp. 137–38: "At bottom, a union of faiths, should it ever come about, could have but the most unfortunate consequences for reason and liberty of conscience. . . . I fear it would be . . . a first step again to confine within narrow bounds the

now liberated spirit of man. Begin only by binding the faith to symbols, the opinion to words, as modestly and pliantly as you please; only establish, for once and for all, the articles: then woe to the unfortunate, who comes a day later, and who finds something to criticize even in these *modest, purified* words! He is a disturber of the peace. To the stake with him!

Brothers if you care for true piety, let us not feign agreement where diversity is evidently the plan and purpose of Providence . . . Our noblest treasure, the liberty to think, will be forfeited . . . Pay heed to the *conduct* of men; upon this bring to bear the tribunal of wise laws, and leave us *thought and speech* which the Father of us all assigned to us as an inalienable heritage and granted to us as an immutable right."

35. Meyer, *History*, p. 139, with his interpretation of the phrase. Another possible interpretation is that the modern Orthodox Jew combines modernity (secular education, a professional education, participation in Western culture) with Judaism and Torah.

36. See the good discussion of this history in Arnold Jacob Wolf, "Israel as the False Messiah," in *Unfinished Rabbi*, pp. 155–58 (written 1988).

37. Mendelssohn, *Jerusalem*, p. 102.

38. Cited in Meyer, *Response*, p. 273.

39. Meyer, *Response*, p. 151.

40. Circumcision has provoked some of the most intense controversies within Reform. On the one hand, it seems hard to deny that everything said about the dietary laws applies to circumcision as well. Historicizing Jews quickly understood it as a type of initiation ceremony familiar in many tribal peoples, and many also pointed to its connection with the patriarchal aspects of Jewish culture that they were united in rejecting. On the other hand, the connection of circumcision with persecution and its absence with cowardly assimilationism has caused most Reform Jews to cling to it. (In Israel today, even the staunchest secular Jews still have their male children circumcised.)

The dispute is a long-standing one. Reformers in Baden demanded the abolition of circumcision already in 1831. In 1843, a major controversy broke out in Frankfurt over whether an uncircumcised male could be admitted to the community. The Friends of Reform favored an initiation ceremony, similar for male and female infants, in place of circumcision.

But these radicals did not prevail; Reform as well as Orthodox rabbis affirmed its centrality in Judaism. This has been so ever since. Although leading Reformers have expressed private skepticism, the ritual has been maintained for infants, although it is frequently set aside for adult male converts. Indeed, today Reform Jews have begun to train their own *mohalim* (ritual circumcisors), rather than relying on Orthodox or Conservative ones.

41. The Kol Nidre prayer, recited on the evening before Yom Kippur, the Day of Atonement, states that the Jew is released from all vows made to God should they have proven honestly unable to fulfill them. The release does not apply to promises made to other human beings.

42. Judith Plaskow, *Standing Again at Sinai: Judaism from a Feminist Perspective* (San Francisco: Harper and Row, 1990), p. vii.

43. See the fascinating period drawing of such a confirmation in Meyer, *History*, p. 124. The *bar* and *bat mitzvah* were reintroduced—in addition to the confirmation—in this century.

44. For a chronology of related events, see Alice Shalvi, "Geopolitics of Jewish Feminism," in T. M. Rudavsky, ed., *Gender and Judaism: The Transformation of Tradition* (New York: NYU Press, 1995), pp. 231–42. For other recent discussions of sex equality in Judaism, see *Judaism since Gender*, ed. Miriam Perkowitz and Laura Levitt (New York: Routledge, 1997), and Fishman, *A Breath of Life*.

45. Laura Geller, "From Equality to Transformation," in *Gender and Judaism*, pp. 243–53.

46. KAM has had a female cantor for the past two years, and I think she has played an extremely important role in shaping the congregation's ideas of gender, both through her cantorial role and through her leading role in religious education.

47. See also Plaskow, *Standing Again,* chapter 4, "God: Reimaging the Unimaginable." Plaskow documents the way in which—although most Jews would agree that God is incorporeal and not literally male—the dominant male imagery through which God is traditionally seen creates a deeply gendered understanding of God that has had harmful political consequences.

48. See also Plaskow, *Standing Again,* p. xvi: "Often the question of boundaries identifies Judaism with its elite, mainstream rabbinic expression; and further, with certain aspects of rabbinic Judaism that are assumed to be unchanging and essential." Plaskow draws on dissident popular and rabbinic traditions as well as on moral ideals to construct her own feminist account of Judaism. She therefore places greater emphasis than I do on the task of struggling with a history that contains unpleasant elements and yet is unavoidably a part of one's own Jewish identity.

49. Meyer, *Response,* p. 259.

50. Meyer, *Response,* p. 266.

TWO

Feminism, Socialism, and Christianity Revisited

MARY B. MAHOWALD

Nearly three decades ago, I wrote an article in which I identified myself as ideologically committed to feminism, socialism, and Christianity.[1] The invitation to contribute to this book provides me with an opportunity to review those commitments and what they mean to me now. As then, I acknowledge the gap between my theory and my practice.

In that early essay, the crucial distinction I used to sketch the understandings of feminism, socialism, and Christianity to which I was committed was between individualistic and communalistic interpretations of the three terms. I defined an individualistic interpretation as one that emphasizes self-interest, whether the self be construed separately or through identification with a particular group, and I defined a communalistic interpretation as one that emphasizes concern for an ever-widening community, an orientation that is essentially outward and open-ended. In what follows, I employ the same distinction.

FEMINISM THEN AND NOW

In the early 1970s, I had but recently been awakened to the fact that sexism prevails in society. Having lived and thrived in a community of women for more than a decade, I had come to know and admire strong women and counted myself among their number. Reading Simone de Beauvoir's *The Second Sex* and experiencing gender-based biases in others' expectations of me, particularly after I married and mothered, evoked my consciousness of the sexism that I had hardly noticed in my youth. Joining the Society for Women in Philosophy brought me into contact with women who felt similarly. Like them, my commitment to feminism was born of the desire to challenge sexist stereotypes both theoretically and practically. Through the years, feminists I met then and subsequently have nurtured this commitment.

My commitment to feminism was also nourished by my teaching and research, through which I increasingly noticed the sexism of some of my favorite philosophers. As a remedial effort in behalf of my students, my profession, and myself, I compiled a collection of texts that philosophers had written about "woman."[2] In the majority of cases, their views were inconsistent with what they had written about "man" or "human nature." In other words, their concepts of generic "man" applied to male human beings only; women were typically defined as lacking or deficient in the superior traits of men, such as rationality and physical strength. Women were also described as destined by nature to be subject to men, fulfilling their principal function as "helpers" to men and bearers of their children.[3]

For pedagogical purposes, I included popular sources in the introductory section of the first edition of my collection of philosophers' writings on woman; these illustrated different feminist orientations as well as perspectives antithetical to feminism.[4] In the former category, I distinguished between the "moderate" feminism of Betty Friedan and the National Organization for Women (NOW), which she founded, and the "radical" feminism of Ti-Grace Atkinson and Shulamith Firestone. The moderate feminists argued for reformation of current social structures so that women would have equal opportunities with men. Friedan, for example, declared that her primary goal was "to get women into positions of power," i.e., positions predominantly held by men.[5] She challenged "the idea that women are primarily responsible for raising children," and called for men and society "to be educated to accept their responsibility for that role as well."[6]

In contrast, radical feminists argued for the transformation of social structures through elimination of the "institutions" of marriage and heterosexuality. Atkinson, who had resigned her presidency of the New York Chapter of NOW because of "irreconcilable ideological conflicts" within the organization, proposed "to destroy the positions of power."[7] She and other radical feminist groups supported class action on behalf of women against the class enemy of women, viz., men. One group not only excluded men from membership but also stipulated that no more than one-third of its members be married.[8] While NOW aligned itself with the individualism of American culture, the exclusionary practices of some radical feminists thus exhibited a class- or gender-based form of individualism.

Moderate and radical feminists alike belonged to the Society for Women in Philosophy. At times there were disagreements between these groups, just as there were (and are) among other feminists. In general, however, both groups were united in three basic claims: that women in general have been oppressed throughout history, that this is morally unjust, and that the oppressive situation should be rectified. The main difference between the two groups was the meaning and means of "rectification" (e.g., reform or revolution). Another claim was less often expressed than it is now, but it underlay the others: the empirical and moral validity of women's experience in fashioning a society that embodies gender justice.

All of these claims have been central to feminism throughout its history. In 1993, however, when I revised my anthology for a new edition, a number of feminist writings had joined the list of those I wanted to incorporate to illustrate theoretical orientations such as psychoanalysis,[9] socialism,[10] pragmatism,[11] and analytic philosophy.[12] I inserted these into sections previously dominated by nonfeminist authors. In addition, I deleted the popular material (both feminist and anti-feminist) because I thought it was no longer needed for pedagogical purposes. The distinction between moderate and radical feminism had become woefully inadequate to describe the variety of feminisms that had emerged since the first edition. Accordingly, I added a new section of selections by current feminist authors, most of whom are philosophers; these pieces represented liberal feminism,[13] socialist feminism,[14] pragmatist feminism,[15] maternal or cultural feminism,[16] lesbian feminism,[17] postmodern feminism,[18] multicultural feminism,[19] and environmental feminism.[20]

The distinction between individualism and communalism cuts across the different versions of feminism mentioned in the preceding paragraph. Some liberal feminists, for example, are more inclined toward individualism; I call these libertarian liberals. Other liberal feminists are more inclined toward communalism; I call these egalitarian liberals. Pragmatist feminists may be more inclined to follow the individualistic spirit of William James or the emphasis on community found in Charles Sanders Peirce or John Dewey. Postmodern feminists, I believe, tend to be individualistic; environmental feminists and socialist feminists are communalistic. Maternal feminists, lesbian feminists, and multicultural feminists may be individualistic with regard to the group for whom they advocate, or communalistic if their advocacy extends to other groups as well. Many of the different versions overlap, and within each of the versions mentioned, there may be further differentiation. Some lesbian feminists, for example, support lesbian separatism; others do not.

Different versions of feminism represent different ideologies in their own right, and these are sometimes at odds with one another. Consider, for example, the opposition between libertarian liberal feminism and socialist or Marxist feminism. The former is primarily committed to women's liberation; the latter to women's equality with men. Feminist philosophers cannot consistently embrace all versions of feminism. Those with which I continue to identify are open to the commitments I have to particular understandings of socialism and Christianity. Similarly, the understandings of socialism and Christianity with which I identify are open to my understanding of feminism. These understandings give priority to social equality or justice rather than individual liberty. The notion of gender justice that I support includes concerns about respect for the autonomy of all individuals. It incorporates those concerns into an overall emphasis on equitable distribution of material goods and capabilities as essential to fulfillment of the autonomous goals of individuals.[21] In other words, to use the jargon of contemporary bioethics, respect for autonomy does not trump beneficence or nonmaleficence; rather, to use traditional philosophical jargon, all three of these are *prima facie* principles, to be ordered in specific instances according to the priority of gender justice and justice in general.

This communalistic interpretation of feminism is more coherent, I believe, than versions that are individualistic.[22] To the extent that feminism focuses exclusively on women either as individuals or as a class, it can only inadequately promote gender justice across the spectrum of cultural, racial, economic, and other groups in which women find themselves. A libertarian liberal feminism, for example, ignores the obstacles that economically impoverished women face in achieving their autonomous goals. By opposing government-based redistribution of goods and services that would promote equality, a libertarian orientation advantages affluent women and exacerbates the disparity between them and those who are already economically disadvantaged. In addition, it fails to address the burdensome impact on many women of the inequities experienced by their children and the men to whom they are related.

SOCIALISM THEN AND NOW

During graduate school, my study of the writings of the young Marx precipitated my ideological commitment to socialism. The contrast between the views I read then and the views I had heard imputed to Marx by the U.S. government and religious leaders in the 1950s and 60s was remarkable. In particular, Marx's notions of *Gattungswesen* and *Gemeinschaft* appealed to me.[23] Unlike the philosophers whose concept of "man" was male, Marx's concept of *Gattungswesen* (awkwardly translated as "species being") was applicable to both sexes. Human beings, for Marx, are free, conscious, social beings, and part of nature, which is essentially material. In Marx's dialectical materialism, however, human beings are producers as well as products of their environment: they are not only shaped by nature, but they shape nature through their conscious agency.

For Marx, the level of human progress, i.e., the progress of human beings as such, may be measured by the degree to which the man/woman relationship reflects and respects this capacity. As Marx put it,

> the relationship of man to woman is the *most natural* relationship of human being to human being. It thus indicates the extent to which man's *natural* behavior has become *human* or the extent to which his *human* essence has become a *natural* essence for him, . . . the extent to which he in his most individual existence is at the same time a social being.[24]

In our own day, David Landes makes a similar point: "the best clue to a nation's growth and development potential is the status and role of women."[25] This gauge of human development can of course measure regress as well as progress. A recent example of the former is the cruel repression of women under the Taliban government in Afghanistan. Not only was human progress thereby thwarted for the entire country; what progress had already been achieved was markedly reduced.

To indicate the dehumanizing impact of capitalism, Marx used the analogy of prostitution: just as women are used as objects of pleasure for men, wage labor makes prostitutes of the proletariat. The bourgeoisie are the "Johns" who pay workers fixed wages while setting no limits to the capital they themselves acquire. The captains of industry thus expand their own options by constraining those of the people who do the work on which their profits depend.

The young Marx apparently construes the egalitarian ideal of *Gemeinschaft* ("community") as a realizable goal. Through the transformation of consciousness, an educative process by which the bourgeoisie gradually recognize their solidarity with the proletariat, the first stage of communism (sometimes called socialism) would be transcended and true communism (Marx's ideal) attained.[26] The first stage is the necessary reversal of the capitalist status quo, where workers are dehumanized by being treated as tools of production by the producer/elite; this is what Marx called the temporary dictatorship of the proletariat. This stage is more egalitarian and democratic than a capitalist system in which the interests of a minority of wealthy individuals predominate over those of the majority; however, it is not as egalitarian or democratic as the classless society of the second phase of communism. Only in the second phase can both individual liberty and social equality be maximized for everyone.

In the years since I first studied Marx, socialism has been repudiated in many quarters. To some extent, my idealism regarding the possibility of achieving, or at least approximating, a truly egalitarian society has been tempered by my experience of the individualism of many human beings, including myself, and by the failure of so many attempts to establish Marxist states. I have nonetheless been drawn to a socialist version of feminism, as distinct from a Marxist version, because it represents a better approximation to my egalitarian ideal than other versions of feminism.[27] Marxist feminism has been distinguished from socialist feminism based on the centrality each attributes to the oppression of women in comparison with economic oppression in general. In Marxist feminism, the primary oppression is economic and other forms of oppression flow from that. In socialist feminism, the primary oppression is that of women; other forms of oppression, including economic, flow from that.

The socialist version makes more sense to me because the man-woman relationship is more fundamental in human history and human experience. As Marx and Friederich Engels put it, "[t]he first division of labor is between men and women for the propagation of children."[28] And as Engels added: "The first class opposition that appears in history coincides with the development of the antagonism between man and woman in monogamous marriage, and the first class oppression coincides with that of the female sex by the male."[29] As has been evident in so-called Marxist states, the overall achievement of economic equality has not eliminated sexism either in the domestic sphere or in the workplace. Until and unless the man-woman relationship is truly egalitarian, other forms of oppression are likely to remain. Despite the preceding definition of Marxist feminism, then, Marx's suggestion of a criterion for evaluating human progress seems to support the priority that socialist feminists assign to the elimination of sexism for a just society.

Although most socialist and communist systems have been overthrown during the past decades, some societies, such as secular communes, Hebrew kibbutzim, and other religious communities, preserve the egalitarian orientation of those systems. Indeed, these communities flourished long before Marx proposed his political theory. But socialist and egalitarian concerns and commitments are also present in people who live in individualistic forms of society and government. As might be said of communism in its second phase, i.e., communism as a completely classless society: it has never been tried. The same may be said of capitalism: a thoroughgoing form of it has never been tried.[30] Rather, from the first days of our democratic republic, our free enterprise system has been accompanied by government regulations restricting the lives of individuals in various ways, limiting the development of monopolies, and requiring income taxes that curb the wealth of the affluent to some extent. In other words, a completely *laissez-faire* system has never been implemented in American society. Fortunately.

In *The Origin of the Family*, Engels developed Marx's views about gender equality more fully. Drawing on the work of Lewis Morgan, he described the defeat of "mother-right," i.e., "exclusive recognition of descent through the mother and the relations of inheritance which in time resulted from it" and its replacement by a patriarchal system and "monogamous" marriage.[31] Within the family, according to Engels, the husband "is the bourgeois and the wife represents the proletariat."[32] Monogamy, he says, "is based on the supremacy of the man, the express purpose being to produce children of undisputed paternity" so as to insure that they "come into their father's property as his natural heirs."[33] The practice of private property, so inimical to Marxism, thus precipitated the sexual double standard by which women were bound by the requirement of monogamy because of their economic dependence on their husbands. In contrast, men were free to obtain sexual pleasure with unmarried women, either concubines or prostitutes.

The analogy between capitalism and prostitution is one that Vladimir Lenin developed as well. "[C]ommerce in women's bodies," he wrote, occurs in the marketplace as well as the bedroom, as capitalists exploit millions of female workers through the wage labor by which they attempt "to 'earn' an extra crust of bread for themselves and their families."[34] The prostitution commonly practiced in bourgeois society doubly victimizes women—first through "its accursed system of property," and second through "its accursed moral hypocrisy."[35] Rather than support the legalization of prostitution, he argued for an end to the conditions that precipitate it: "Return the prostitute to productive work, find her a place in the social economy."[36]

Both Engels and Lenin acknowledged the discrepancy between communist ideology about gender equality and the practices of the majority of communist men. "Scratch the Communist," Lenin observes,

> and a philistine appears. . . . To be sure, you have to scratch the sensitive spots, such as their mentality regarding women. Could there be any more palpable proof than the common sight of a man calmly watching a woman wear herself out with trivial, monotonous, strength- and time-consuming work. . . .Very few husbands, not even the proletarians, think of how much they could lighten the burdens and worries of their wives, or relieve them entirely, if they lent a hand. . . . But no, that would go against the 'privilege and dignity of the husband.'"[37]

His call for practical efforts to provide women with equal opportunities to men (public catering establishments, universal child care, etc.) and for an end to men's sexist attitudes and practices extends to all women:

> We demonstrate thereby that we are aware of these needs and of the oppression of women, that we are conscious of the privileged position of the men, and that we hate—yes, hate—and want to remove whatever oppresses and harasses the working woman, the wife of the worker, the peasant woman,

the wife of the little man, and even in many respects the woman of the propertied classes.[38]

Although the preceding set of views is consistent with a communalistic interpretation of socialism, some features of socialist theory and practice illustrate an extended form of individualism or class-based individualism. Marx's dictatorship of the proletariat, for example, while intended as a means rather than an end, is an inversion of the inequality suffered under capitalism. Lenin's theory of the "revolutionary elite," i.e., a group of like-minded people who would provoke and lead the proletariat to overturn the bourgeois power structure, may also be interpreted as an extended form of individualism. Only in the second phase of communism, when classes or revolutionary elites no longer exist, can the communalistic orientation of communism or socialism be achieved or best approximated.

CHRISTIANITY THEN AND NOW

In the late 1960s, I was particularly interested in tracking the theme of community in various philosophers. My involvement in community activism and religious community no doubt contributed to this interest. Because of their explicit emphasis on community, the writings of Josiah Royce both surprised and appealed to me.[39] In his mature writings, for example, Royce claimed that community was his main metaphysical principle. Although his philosophy of religion eschewed sectarian dogma, he chose to illustrate his view of the universality of religious experience through an examination of Christianity. The key religious ideas to which he imputed universality were threefold: the experience of finitude, i.e., human need or limitation; an ideal that represents the overcoming of this need or limitation; and an account of how the gap between the need and the ideal can be bridged. For Royce, Christianity expresses the universal experience of need in its doctrine of original sin; the life of Christ is the ideal, which human beings are called to pursue through efforts to overcome their flaws or limitations; and the story of redemption and doctrine of grace are the means by which human beings can bridge the gap between the need and the ideal. The community of believers who make up what Royce calls the "invisible Church" provides indispensable support in utilizing the means by which to achieve the ideal.[40]

Christianity is subject to a more individualistic interpretation than Royce's account provides. In fact, that interpretation is supported by the defining datum of Christian faith, redemption or salvation through Christ. Christians, for example, have persistently been counseled that each one's primary concern ought to be the salvation of her or his own soul. For "[w]hat will a man gain if he wins the whole world and ruins his life?"[41]

Protestant Christianity has particularly stressed the interests of the individual in obtaining salvation. In the colonizing of America, such religious individualism reinforced the ideal of rugged individualism to meet the demands of frontier life. Ironically, this individualistic interpretation of Christianity offered a religious rationale for assessing ethical worth through material success. It is an interpretation that continues to strengthen the underlying theory of capitalism.

Beyond their emphasis on individual salvation, Christianity and other religions have exhibited a gender-based individualism through their concurrence in, and replication of, the patriarchal structure of society. With few exceptions, men have dominated the leadership positions of various institutional religions, and women have often been explicitly excluded from those positions even though they predominate as congregants.

A term that may best describe the communalistic nature of Christianity is "church," defined as "people of God" rather than as an institution or hierarchical structure that exists apart from, or regardless of, lay Christian believers. This distinction is comparable to Royce's distinction between the visible and invisible church. As people of God, the church is necessarily composed of individuals whose primary interest extends beyond themselves and their own lives. Because the human Christ was one whose life was lived for others, Christians are called to emulate this spirit by living similarly. The primary interest of the Christian church is thus the entire community of humankind.

That entire community, for Christians and many of those who align themselves with other religious traditions, is the work of a Creator God. But to believe in the existence of a Creator is to accept the Creator's effective definition of human nature. Jean-Paul Sartre put the relevant counter-argument plainly: if God exists, then human beings are not free because their nature is determined by God, who made them to be as they are.[42] But human beings are manifestly and essentially free; therefore, God cannot exist.

Belief in a Creator of humankind is thus incompatible with a Sartrean conception of human freedom, which rejects any and all limitations. But belief in God *is* compatible with a conception of freedom as partial or limited; this conception is crucial to the Christian doctrine of sin and punishment for sin. As Augustine (among others) has pointed out, human beings are free to sin but not to avoid the consequences of sin. Further, since to be human is to be an *imago Dei*, one is only "free" to be human by sustaining that resemblance through avoidance of sin. "By abusing free choice," Augustine claims, "man loses both it and himself."[43] On a more philosophical level, Aquinas distinguishes between free choice and the necessitated will. "[S]ince choice is not of the end, but of the means," he writes, " . . . it is not of the perfect good. . . . Therefore, man chooses, not of necessity, but freely." On the other hand, "if the will be offered an object which is good universally and from every point of view [i.e., God], the will tends to it of necessity. . . ."[44] Ultimately, a Christian interpretation of freedom is thus limited through beliefs in creation, a final end, and the inevitable consequences of moral decisions.

To assert that Christian freedom is limited, however, does not imply that Christianity is communalistic. For a communalistic concept of freedom, Paul's letter to the Galatians provides a helpful source. For Paul, the liberty to which Christians are called by Christ is essentially a freedom for service to others. "Be careful," he warns, "or this liberty will provide an opening for self-indulgence. Serve one another, rather, in works of love, since the whole of the Law is summarized in a single command: Love your neighbor as yourself."[45] In other words, love is the core of the gospel and of Christian life, but freedom is the precondition for love even as it is for sin. To use freedom to serve others lovingly is necessarily to build community, since love involves a dynamic and open-ended relationship between or among persons. Even as Plato described it in the *Symposium,* love is essentially life giving and nonexclusive. Love is thus communalistic rather than individualistic; it is essentially a caring relationship to others.[46]

By believing in the doctrine of original sin, Christians acknowledge that human beings are naturally inclined toward selfishness. Nonetheless, their doctrine of grace provides a basis for faith that egoism can be overcome and replaced by a truly communalistic spirit. Since grace is a sharing in God's life, graced Christians become one in a life which is essentially communalistic. Their initial and continuing participation in that life always occurs in a communal setting. The priesthood in which all Christians share is a call to build community in order to mediate the presence of God to people. "Where two or three meet in my name," Christ said, "I shall be there with them."[47] The most effective sign of Christ's presence is Eucharist, where the being-for-others of Christ is recalled and relived as Christians are strengthened to be-for-others also.

By virtue of their belief in creation, original sin, and grace, Christians affirm a communalistic concept of equality. A question of Paul evokes realization of creaturely equality: "What do you have that was not given to you?"[48] Since each one's needs and talents are God's gift, there is no justification for regarding or treating one person as better than, or superior to, another. Further supporting the imperative that people be regarded as equal is the example of Christ, who loved the sinner even while despising the sin. Recognition of equality is reinforced by the eschatological dimension of Christianity—because the same finality applies to all, regardless of their natural differences. Only moral differences, based on each one's freedom, affect differences in eternal destinies.

A FEMINIST STANDPOINT
TOWARD RELIGION AND PHILOSOPHY

The desire for continuity in one's life and consistency in one's values is probably widespread; a tendency to rationalize with regard to these themes is probably widespread as well. Like many people, then, I desire continuity and consistency, and I doubt that I am an exception to the tendency to rationalize. Whether rightly or wrongly, however, I remain committed to communalistic interpretations of feminism, socialism, and Christianity. Two themes that have been prominent in my thinking and acting during the past decade support the continuity and consistency of my interpretations: one is a specific concept of equality, the other a theoretical framework that entails a strategy for promoting my ideal of social equality. The latter is identifiable as a perspectival or standpoint theory of knowledge. Because this approach has been well elaborated recently by feminists, it may also be characterized as "feminist standpoint theory."[49]

The concept of equality that underlies my feminist standpoint is not one of "sameness," which is often the meaning attached to the term in popular parlance.[50] Rather, it is a concept that acknowledges differences between and among everything and everyone, but posits that, despite those differences, every human being is of equal value.[51] This concept of equality is surely defensible as a starting point or assumption for moral philosophy, but, like Aristotle's first premises (and perhaps like other philosophers' "intuitions"), it is unproved and unprovable. A religious belief in creation and sustenance by God supports my concept, but these beliefs are neither based on, nor refutable by, philosophical argument. My belief in, or affirmation of, this concept of equality matches Peirce's definition of belief as the resolution of doubt: a decision or plan of action.[52] It means, in other words, that I intend (whether I succeed or not) to act toward people as if they are all of equal value.

My philosophical assumption and religious belief about human equality grounds my notion of an obligation to respect all other human beings equally. However, my observation of differences in people, coupled with my own experience of finitude, impels me to acknowledge that others have abilities, insights, and talents that I lack. The perspectival view of knowledge developed by Peirce and James supports this acknowledgment.[53] Feminist standpoint theory also supports it.[54]

A feminist standpoint differs from the impersonal standpoint that Thomas Nagel describes as crucial to ethics. "Ethics and political theory," he observed, "begin when from the impersonal standpoint we focus on the raw data provided by the individual desires, interests, projects, attachments, allegiances and plans of life that define the personal points of view of the multitude of distinct individuals, ourselves included."[55]

Yet if ethics focuses on the moral responsibility of persons as persons, it is ironic as well as illogical to insist that personal considerations be excluded from ethical judgments. If Nagel is right, we are morally required to separate our personal religious beliefs from our moral judgments. To some extent, I have attempted to do that in much of my academic life. When religious subjects, such as the existence of God, are broached with students or colleagues, I have deliberately addressed them without disclosing my own belief. Moreover, in the clinical setting in which I have worked for many years, I think my credibility in communicating with individuals from various ethnic, disciplinary, and religious backgrounds has been enhanced by their recognition that I do not speak for, or claim expertise in, a specific religious tradition. As I review my own behavior, however, I doubt that I have consistently or wholly succeeded in separating my unproved and unprovable assumptions from our discussions; neither am I sure that I should have done so even if I could.

For Nagel, an impersonal standpoint is achieved through a process of abstraction that critics such as Donna Haraway consider neither feasible nor desirable. Haraway affirms the "embodied nature of all vision" against the pretense of objectivity that denies the situatedness of human experience.[56] Although the term "standpoint" generally refers to a particular position from which something is viewed, the concept of an impersonal standpoint suggests the "god trick of seeing everything from nowhere."[57] From an empirical perspective, this is impossible; from a psychological perspective, it is pretentious; from a religious perspective, it is blasphemous.

Haraway's proposed alternative is "a doctrine of embodied objectivity," involving "partial, locatable, critical knowledges sustaining the possibilities of webs of connections called solidarity in politics and shared conversations in epistemology."[58] Only through the accumulation of partial perspectives, she claims, can we approach objectivity. Haraway defends her proposal against the anticipated charge of relativism by pointing out that, like the concept of an impersonal standpoint, "relativism is a way of being nowhere while claiming to be everywhere equally."[59] Clearly, her concept of "situated knowledges" does not conform to this definition of relativism. The difference between partial knowledge and relativism supports the epistemological validity of standpoint theory. Sandra Harding's notion of "strong objectivity" offers further support for this critique.[60]

Unlike Peirce, Haraway uses the term "knowledge" so broadly that it may encompass beliefs, including religious beliefs. Her concept of "situated knowledges" supports the notion of complementarity between religious belief and philosophical knowledge. Recognition of the situatedness or perspectival nature of knowledge is essential to the development of less inadequate knowledge on the part of dominant individuals. Many women are not only nondominant by gender but in other ways as well. Accordingly, a feminist standpoint calls for the attribution of a privileged standpoint to all nondominant groups, e.g., those who are not white, male, heterosexual, able-bodied, or socio-economically advantaged. The purpose of this "privilege" is to reduce the inevitable limitations of the dominant perspective that generally defines the world for everyone. Feminists who, like me, are white, middle-class academics obviously belong to dominant groups. To treat the myopia associated with these forms of dominance, we need to privilege the input of those on whom our dominance depends, i.e., men and women of color, and those who are socio-economically disadvantaged.

STANDPOINT THEORY AND FEMINIST WOMEN

Being explicitly feminist, whether in the context of religion, philosophy, or society in general, adds another dimension of nondominance to the experience of many women and some men. Rarely if ever is feminism accorded privileged status; in fact, it is often a liability. If incorporated at all into mainstream philosophy or mainstream religion, feminism is typically regarded as tangential. This makes it difficult to embrace or persist in a commitment to feminism, and understandable (while regrettable) that some do not. I was not surprised, therefore, when I once asked an audience of bioethicists to raise their hands if they considered themselves feminists, and few did so. I then argued that if justice is a cardinal principle of contemporary bioethics and gender justice is a subset of justice, a commitment to bioethics demands a commitment to feminism. While I probably converted no one, I consider this argument compelling not only for bioethicists but also for anyone to whom justice represents a basic moral obligation, whether on philosophical or religious grounds.

Like many who read this essay or have contributed to this volume, I have been tangentialized both as a woman and as a feminist. In the university setting, I have been a token from time to time—serving on committees as the necessary (only) woman, teaching feminist courses that the department wants taught but hardly respects, participating in conferences so that the program planners look like they care about diversity. Even so, my token presence in various situations has afforded me the opportunity to raise issues unlikely to be identified by others, and I feel morally and happily compelled to take advantage of such opportunities. From my privileged position within the dominant power structure of academia, I believe I reach a fair number of dominant types whose nearsightedness may thereby be reduced.

In philosophical and feminist circles, I have mainly been a closet Christian, and within that context, a closet Catholic.[61] This article is, in a sense, my coming-out piece. I have been closeted in part to avoid the antagonism toward religion that I have observed in those settings. While I cannot document the point, I suspect many philosophers, especially but not exclusively those who work in secular surroundings, are closet believers in some religious tradition. It is difficult, however, to identify connections between religious *belief* or *practice* (as distinct from the academic enterprise of theology) and philosophy, including feminist philosophy. For several years in the 1970s I reviewed books in feminist theology, but saw little convergence between them and feminist philosophy.[62] In my teaching and writing, however, I use authors on whom some theologians place great reliance, such as Thomas Aquinas, finding their original texts much more open to my views than the accounts of their interpreters.[63]

In Christian circles and in my Catholic parish, I seldom articulate my philosophical and feminist interests. My reticence is due in part to an assumption that the views of most people are more conservative than mine, and to a desire not to separate myself from them solely on the basis of that difference. Women and men who share my disagreement with official church teachings on various moral and social issues have challenged this assumption; they comprise a community of support and hope for me. Despite my disagreement with certain practices and pronouncements, I am proud of the strong critiques of social and economic injustice, including capitalism, that have been articulated by church leaders. I am also proud of specific members of the church with whose views I do not totally agree, such as Cardinal Joseph Bernardin and Mother Teresa, whose lives exemplified a moral ideal I fall far short of.

Of course I am angry about the sexism that remains within Christianity in general and Catholicism in particular, as in other religions. Over twenty years ago, I was so angry about a papal pronouncement about mothers working outside the home that I wrote a letter to Pope John Paul II, indicating my disagreement with the pronouncement. In my letter I alluded to commonalities between the Pope and me, viz., our training in philosophy and our religious commitment, but I also mentioned several relevant differences between us: that I was a woman, married, and a mother, and he was not. The Pope had claimed that the primary responsibility of mothers is to raise their children, and work outside the home compromised that. I countered that, from a faith perspective, the primary responsibility of both parents is to raise their children to live not just for themselves but also for the wider community. That lesson, I suggested, is conveyed much more effectively by example than by words. Parents may thus fulfill rather than compromise their primary responsibility to their children by working outside the home in behalf of others.

I realized that the Pope would probably never see my letter, but writing it was a way of re-examining, affirming, and articulating my egalitarian feminist standpoint to whoever might read it. As an "idealistic pragmatist,"[64] I was hopeful that the nearsightedness of anyone who read the letter might thereby be reduced. Despite little likelihood of systemic change within the church, challenging opinions or practices I consider unjust, at least from time to time, has long been a means by which I attempt to avoid complicity in them and remind myself of my own core values.

My commitment to an egalitarian version of feminism has been reinforced by simultaneous commitments to certain understandings of philosophy (socialism and pragmatism) and religion (Christianity). The epistemological tradition of classical pragmatism has given me grounds by which to affirm the legitimacy of belief and of partial knowledge, the inseparability of thought and action, and a communal process of inquiry. Socialist thought has elaborated a persuasive critique of individualism and an egalitarian social ideal. Christianity has provided me with a model of the kind of person I want to be and want to help others to be. As already suggested, these sources coalesce around the central theme of feminism, gender justice, which necessarily involves justice for all marginalized or nondominant groups.

Because women and some of the men to whom we are related belong to diverse nondominant groups, an egalitarian feminist standpoint calls for the inclusion of all nondominant groups in the development of philosophical views or religious beliefs. A democratic understanding of socialism calls for that inclusion as well. But genuine openness to inclusion of others requires humility, a virtue notably lacking in philosophers who purport to have ascertained "the truth" through their rational analyses. Apparently, humility is also lacking in Christian leaders—despite the priority that Christian teachings assign to this virtue—who purport to have ascertained "the truth" through their religious beliefs while denying women and other minorities any role in the ascertainment or interpretation of those "truths." The virtue of humility may itself be defined as "truth" because it entails truthful acknowledgment of one's human limitations as well as one's abilities or talents, and those of others. The unearned advantages (intellectual, physical, social, etc.) of the dominant group lead to their dominance despite the inevitable limitedness of their vision. Reduction of their myopia is the rationale for granting privileged status to the vision of those who are nondominant.

Genuine humility involves a tension between acknowledgment of limitation and assertion of privilege. Many women are prone to resolve this tension by not asserting their privileged standpoint; many men are prone to do the opposite. The same proneness applies to other nondominant and dominant groups. Either excess is a "sin" against humility.[65] To be socially constructive and conducive to an egalitarian goal, the tension needs to be sustained.

Sustaining the tension is probably impossible for lone individuals. Community is thus practically as well as theoretically crucial to nondominant groups and individuals if egalitarian advances are to be made. As feminist, socialist, and Christian, I have at times succumbed to the temptation to ignore or deny the privilege of these standpoints as I understand them. In doing so, I have sustained another kind of tension: between the I that I am and the I that I would be. In my graduate school days, I attempted to practice the Cartesian doubt by eschewing all that I had believed without rational proof. I found that I couldn't; I just did believe in God and most of what I had learned and embraced of Christianity and Catholicism, especially the meaning of Jesus as one who lived his life for others. In other words, my own religious faith, including its criticisms of sexism within the church, was part of me. Like my skin, I couldn't shed it. Something similar may be said for my philosophical "faith" and my feminist "faith." I remain a philosopher despite my criticisms of traditional philosophy, and a feminist despite my criticisms of some versions of feminism.

NOTES

1. Mary B. Mahowald, "Feminism, Socialism, and Christianity," *Cross Currents* XXV (1975): 33–50; reprinted in *An Anthology of the Best of Cross Currents, 1950–1990,* ed. W. Birmingham (New York: Cross Road, 1989), pp. 138–62. Personal circumstances associated with this article may be pertinent here. My main objective was to clarify some of my own complicated views and values. I wrote the piece just after teaching a course entitled "The Concept of Woman," in which my students and I compared and contrasted various philosophers' concepts of "human nature" or "man" with their views about women. When the course began, I was in the early stages of pregnancy, but neither my students nor I knew that, while examining the *concept* of woman, I was also developing the *reality* of one. By the end of the course, it was obvious that someone else had been attending; after delivery, I quipped to friends that the reality of her sex attested to the veracity of the concept we had been studying. My daughter's manner of arrival also suggested an important theme of feminism. Rather than be induced on July 4th (Independence Day), as planned by my doctor, she came on her own on July 3rd. This apparent declaration of independence has been symptomatic of her disposition ever since.

2. I used the term "woman" rather than "women" as a clearer correlate of "man" as a generic term.

3. Consider, for example, Aristotle: " A woman is as it were an infertile male, . . . a deformed male"; Aquinas: "Woman is naturally subject to man, because in man the discernment of reason predominates"; and Nietzsche: "All in woman hath one answer:—that is

childbearing. . . . Man shall be trained for war, and woman for the recreation of the war-rior." All of these quotations are from selections by their authors in Mary Briody Ma-howald, ed., *Philosophy of Woman: An Anthology of Classical to Current Concepts,* 3rd ed. (Indianapolis: Hackett Publishing Company, 1994), pp. 24–25, 55–56, 193.

4. Mary Briody Mahowald, ed., *Philosophy of Woman: Classical to Current Concepts* (Indianapolis: Hackett Publishing Company, 1978). Popular sources were used to demon-strate the need for clarity in conceptions of woman. Midge Decter and Esther Vilar were the anti-feminist sources.

5. Quoted by Ti-Grace Atkinson in *Amazon Odyssey* (New York: Links Books, 1974), p. 10.

6. Betty Friedan, "Our Revolution Is Unique," in *Voices of the New Feminism,* ed. M. S. Thompson (Boston: Beacon Press, 1970), p. 40.

7. Atkinson, p. 9.

8. Manifesto of "The Feminists: A Political Organization to Annihilate Sex Roles," in *Notes from the Second Year: Women's Liberation,* ed. Shulamith Firestone (New York: P.O. Box AA, Old Chelsea Station), p. 116.

9. Karen Horney, "Feminine Psychology," and Juliet Mitchell, "Femininity," in Ma-howald, ed., *Philosophy of Woman,* 1994, pp. 246–69. References 10 through 20 below are also taken from this anthology.

10. Charlotte Perkins Gilman, "Women and Economics," pp. 300–308.

11. Jesse Taft, "The Woman Movement from the Point of View of Social Conscious-ness," pp. 325–30, and Jane Addams, "Democracy and Social Ethics" and "Peace and Bread in Time of War," pp. 331–37.

12. Joyce Trebilcot, "Sex Roles: The Argument from Nature," pp. 349–56, Christine Pierce, "Natural Law Language and Women," pp. 356–68, and Elizabeth V. Spelman, "Woman: The One and the Many," pp. 369–97.

13. Zillah R. Eisenstein, "The Radical Future of Liberal Feminism," pp. 400–11.

14. Heidi I. Hartmann, "The Unhappy Marriage of Marxism and Feminism: Towards a More Progressive Union," pp. 411–25.

15. Charlene Haddock Seigfried, "Where Are All the Pragmatist Feminists," pp. 425–42. Drawing less on John Dewey and more on Charles Sanders Peirce, I have developed a different account on the topic in "A Majority Perspective: Feminine and Feminist Elements in American Philosophy," *Cross Currents* XXXVI (1987): 410–17.

16. Sara Ruddick, "Maternal Thinking," pp. 442–51. I use the term "maternal femi-nism" to characterize a range of views that emphasize an ethic of care based on women's ma-ternal role. Rosemarie Tong refers to these as "cultural feminism."

17. Sarah Hoagland, "Lesbian Ethics," pp. 451–64.

18. Jane Flax, "Postmodernism and Gender Relations in Feminist Theory," pp. 465–86.

19. bell hooks, "Black Women: Shaping Feminist Theory," pp. 486–95.

20. Karen Warren, "Feminism and the Environment: An Overview of the Issues," pp. 495–510.

21. Cf. Amartya Sen's account of equality as capability, as elaborated in *Inequality Re-examined* (Cambridge, Mass.: Harvard University Press, 1992), pp. 73–87. Sen's view goes beyond the equality of opportunity elaborated by John Rawls and those who embrace Rawls's theory as developed in *A Theory of Justice* (Cambridge, Mass.: Harvard University Press, 1971) and *Political Liberalism* (New York: Columbia University Press, 1993). The lat-ter work is even more resistant to my and Sen's account of equality.

22. This interpretation should not be equated with "communitarianism," a more re-cent coinage, which I find problematic because it risks complicity in exploitative practices by communities and fails to deal with dilemmas arising from the fact that most individuals belong to multiple communities with potentially conflicting priorities.

23. Cf. Mary B. Mahowald, "Marx's *'Gemeinschaft':* Another Interpretation," *Philoso-phy and Phenomenological Research* XXXIII (1973): 472–88.

24. Karl Marx, "Economic and Philosophical Manuscripts," in *Writings of the Young Marx on Philosophy and Society,* trans. Lloyd D. Easton and Kurt H. Guddat (Garden City, N.Y.: Doubleday Anchor Books, 1967), p. 303. Italics are in the text.

25. David S. Landes, *The Wealth and Poverty of Nations,* cited in Nicholas D. Kristof, "The Veiled Resource," *New York Times,* Dec. 11, 2001, p. A27.

26. Although socialism is sometimes viewed as a theory quite distinct from communism, Marx, while critiquing utopian socialist systems, describes communism as socialist also.

27. In recent years, I have used the term "egalitarian" rather than "socialist" to describe the version of feminism that I support. "Egalitarian" can have different meanings also, but it is less likely than "socialist" to be demonized by its interpreters.

28. Engels quotes this statement by Marx and himself in *The Origin of the Family, Private Property and the State,* in Mahowald, ed., *Philosophy of Woman,* 1994, p. 278.

29. Engels, p. 278.

30. The same has been said of Christianity: it has never been thoroughly tried, i.e., in a manner that represents the entirety of its teachings applied consistently.

31. Engels, pp. 274, 278. Although the accuracy of Morgan's account has been challenged, it apparently provided Lenin with a credible explanation of the origin of sexism in society.

32. Engels, p. 282.

33. Engels, p. 277.

34. Vladimir I. Lenin, *The Emancipation of the State,* in Mahowald, ed., 1994, p. 289.

35. Lenin, p. 291.

36. Lenin, p. 291.

37. Lenin, p. 298.

38. Lenin, p. 296.

39. Cf. Mary L. Briody, "Community in Royce: An Interpretation," *Transactions of the Charles S. Peirce Society: A Journal in American Philosophy* 4 (1969): 224–42.

40. Josiah Royce, *Sources of Religious Insight* (New York: Charles Scribner's Sons, 1914), p. 277.

41. Matthew 16:26.

42. E.g., Jean-Paul Sartre, *Existentialism and Human Emotions* (New York: Philosophical Library, 1957), p. 15.

43. Augustine, *Enchiridion* XXX (PL 40,246), cited by Aquinas in Anton Pegis, ed., *Basic Writings of Saint Thomas Aquinas,* vol. 1 (New York: Random House, 1945), p. 788.

44. Thomas Aquinas, *Summa Theologica* I–II, in Pegis, ed., pp. 262, 285.

45. Galatians 5:13–15. Although Paul stresses the connection between redemption and liberation in this epistle, in other places he clearly illustrates the sexism of his (and our) time; e.g., Ephesians 5:21.

46. I am aware of the problematic meaning of love and its relationship to "care." The latter concept, as developed in the literature of social psychology, is problematic for feminists despite its association with women's experience. Those who view "love" as hazardous for women include Mary Wollstonecraft, who describes friendship as the preferable relationship between married partners, and Ti-Grace Atkinson, who calls it a "euphoric state of fantasy in which the victim transforms her oppressor into her redeemer" (Mahowald, ed., *Philosophy of Woman: Classical to Current Concepts,* 1978, pp. 136, 28, respectively). Nel Noddings and Sara Ruddick advocate an ethic of care based on mother love; I have developed a notion of "just caring" to address the potential for exploitation that maternal love or care involves. Cf. Noddings, *Caring: A Feminine Approach to Ethics and Moral Education* (Berkeley: University of California Press, 1984); Ruddick, *Maternal Thinking: Toward a Politic of Peace* (New York: Ballantine Books, 1989); Mary Briody Mahowald, *Women and Children in Health Care: An Unequal Majority* (New York: Oxford University Press, 1993), pp. 255–69; and Mary B. Mahowald, "Care and Its Pitfalls," in *Ethical Dimensions of Phar-*

maceutical Care, ed. Amy M. Haddad and Robert A. Buerki (New York: The Haworth Press, 1996), pp. 85–102.

47. Matthew 18:20.

48. 1 Corinthians 4:7.

49. To avoid monolithic interpretations of feminism, I prefer to speak of "feminist standpoints" or "a feminist standpoint" rather than "the feminist standpoint." As shall be clear in what follows, nonfeminist philosophers, especially pragmatists, developed the major arguments of feminist standpoint theorists prior to their being called "feminist," without applying their rationale to women. My understanding of feminist standpoint theory has been enriched by these earlier sources but is largely based on more recent writings: e.g., Nancy C. M. Hartsock, *The Feminist Standpoint Revisited and Other Essays* (Boulder, Colo.: Westview Press, 1998), pp. 107–26, 228–30; Terry Winant, "The Feminist Standpoint: A Matter of Language," *Hypatia* 2 (Winter 1987): 123–48; Nel Noddings, "Ethics from the Standpoint of Women," in *Theoretical Perspectives on Sexual Difference,* ed. Deborah L. Rhode (New Haven, Conn.: Yale University Press, 1990), pp. 160–73; Alison M. Jaggar, *Feminist Politics and Human Nature* (Totowa, N.J.: Rowman and Allanheld, 1983), pp. 369–71, 377–89; Ruddick, pp. 127–39; Catharine A. MacKinnon, "Feminism, Marxism, Method, and the State," in *Feminism and Methodology: Social Science Issues,* ed. Sandra Harding (Bloomington: Indiana University Press, 1987), pp. 85–96; and the following in *Signs: Journal of Women in Culture and Society* 22, no. 21 (1997); Susan Heckman, "Truth and Method: Feminist Standpoint Theory Revisited," with commentaries by Nancy C. M. Hartsock, Patricia Hill Collins, Sandra Harding, and Dorothy E. Smith, and Heckman's reply to the commentaries, pp. 341–402.

50. With regard to philosophical interpretations, Sen suggests that all theories of justice are egalitarian in some sense. The key difference among them is their different answers to the question: equality of what? Even Robert Nozick, for Sen, is egalitarian in that he demands "equality of libertarian rights." Cf. *Inequality Reexamined,* p. 13. Needless to say, my concept of equality is incompatible with Nozick's.

51. Note that equal value is attributed to human beings rather than to specific differences within them, which are not of equal value. Some philosophers seem to identify the differences with the individuals themselves. E.g., Allen Buchanan writes that "any two (or more) persons, simply because they are different individuals, will be unequal in *some* respects." Unequal "respects" do not make the persons unequal. Cf. Buchanan, "Equal Opportunity and Genetic Intervention," *Social Philosophy and Policy* 12, no. 2 (1995): 112.

52. *Charles Sanders Peirce: The Essential Writings,* ed. Edward C. Moore (New York: Harper and Row Publishers, 1972), pp. 125–26.

53. Peirce's doctrine of fallibilism, for example, by which he acknowledged the inevitable limitations of individual perspectives, impelled him to advocate a collaborative method of inquiry that gives rise to beliefs, rather than knowledge, as modifiable plans of action. And James defines philosophy itself as "our *individual way of just seeing* and feeling the total push and pressure of the cosmos" (my italics). Cf. John McDermott, ed., *The Writings of William James* (New York: Random House, 1967), p. 362.

54. The term "theory" refers to the rationale that supports the standpoint and strategies for implementing it.

55. Thomas Nagel, *Equality and Partiality* (New York: Oxford University Press, 1991), p. 11.

56. Donna Haraway, "Situated Knowledges: The Science Question in Feminism and the Privilege of Partial Perspective," *Feminist Studies* 14 (1988): 581.

57. Haraway, p. 581.

58. Haraway, p. 584.

59. Haraway, p. 584.

60. Sandra Harding, "Rethinking Standpoint Epistemology: What Is 'Strong Objectivity'?" in *Feminism and Science,* ed. Evelyn Fox Keller and Helen E. Longino (New York: Ox-

ford University Press, 1996), pp. 235–48. Harding quotes a relevant passage from Haraway at the beginning of her article: "Feminist objectivity means quite simply situated knowledges" (p. 235).

61. I guess the closet door was open enough to prompt the editors to invite me to contribute to this book.

62. E.g., the following review articles: "For Men and Women," *Cross Currents* XXII (1973): 231–35; "On Experiencing 'the Feminine,'" *Cross Currents* XXIV (1975): 514–16; "Feminism, Religion and Socialism," *Cross Currents* XXV (1975): 206–11; "On Liberating God and Other People," *Cross Currents* XXVIII (1979): 491–94; "Is Non-Sexist Religion Possible?" *Cross Currents* XXXIII (1980): 222–24.

63. For example, Aquinas's Treatise on Law offers a broader and more persuasive understanding of natural law than I have read elsewhere. Although philosophers in bioethics tend to ignore or discredit the contributions of Catholic moral theologians, those contributions, many of which draw heavily on the writings of Aquinas, are often more meaningful and helpful to clinicians and the public in their analyses of issues than the esoteric arguments of some philosophers.

64. I have long characterized myself as such, having published my first book on the pragmatic element of the philosophy of the idealist, Josiah Royce. Cf. Mary Briody Mahowald, *An Idealistic Pragmatism* (The Hague: Nijhoff, 1972).

65. I use the term "sin" because of its religious connotation, but without theological or doctrinal underpinnings.

THREE

"Philosophizing on Saturday": Faith and the Philosophical Life

WINIFRED WING HAN LAMB

SITUATING THE PHILOSOPHER

G ood philosophies have typically been constructed by authors "with at least one eye out for the human condition," and part of the human condition is a sense of alienation and tension between "that intuition of ourselves as one with the whole . . . and that [of ourselves] as separate beings. . . ."[1] According to the philosopher David Cooper, it is out of this latent tension that good philosophy arises and the failure to resolve it is not only an intellectual debacle, it is also a human tragedy.

As a Eurasian Christian woman from Hong Kong doing philosophy in Australia, I would agree with Cooper but would also have to say that the tension that he expresses is not the end of the matter! Just as Cooper introduces us to the worlds that philosophy has to traverse—the world of clear thinking and rigorous deliverance of ideas, and the world in which there is often more ambiguity than clarity, more letting be than rigorous application, so being a middle-aged Christian, immigrant woman also adds to the sense of possible and actual worlds. Philosophers, and feminist philosophers in particular, have presented us with the challenge of "the everyday,"[2] and the importance of "common understanding."[3] While this resonates with the Christian desire to honor the "common things" and godly non-academic wisdom, there is more that could be said. For Christians, there is also the not-yet, in the truth that is not-yet-delivered. In addition is the deep awareness that knowledge is not neutral, in a way that is now philosophically acknowledged, but also in the sense that there is no innocence in knowing because of sin. This essay addresses these challenges of the "not-yet" for philosophy, symbolized by the reference to Saturday in the title, for Holy Saturday comes in between the despair of Good Friday and the hope of Easter Sunday as I will elaborate below.

Having recently returned to philosophy after some years at home with children, I also feel the tension between what is regarded as the proper "career chase" and the awareness that life is short and nothing must be allowed to become all-consuming. That tension arises not only from the embrace of the Christian sense of values, but also from the perspective of middle age with its constant demand for the re-evaluation of what is important, so that success cannot be so easily measured by cleverness, productivity, and image but must also be reflected in a way of being and of the life that is lived. Current, ruthless education cutbacks in Australia under a Liberal (i.e., conservative) government have created a climate of scarcity and competitiveness that further exacerbates the danger of idolizing academic success and recognition. Within such a climate, peer evaluation and the judgment of one's academic betters dominate, to the extent that it seems, at times, that one's whole life becomes an exercise of public self-justification. This is, for me, a genuine source of unease. Should the worthwhileness of my person and of my life not be judged more appropriately by my family, my friends, and my God?

The question of how one is to be assumes an everyday urgency. Colleagues with whom one shares and talks with some honesty sense that their autonomy and integrity are often at stake in the game of surviving in this world. As a result, the challenges experienced by academic philosophers in Australia in the late 1990s are not confined to questions of knowledge, or the modes of pursuing knowledge, i.e., the question of academic integrity in the theoretical sense, but more. There is also the question of personal integrity—the question of how one is oriented in the world of academic philosophy, with all the political and economic realities of the day, and with all the non-philosophical choices that surround it.

Professional insecurity, which many Australian academics have experienced in recent times, has occurred against a general background of important national issues, especially surrounding policies governing the relationships between indigenous and non-indigenous Australians. 1997 was an important year for such issues to be brought out into the open, and in such an emotionally challenging way that, as one indigenous leader put it, it was as if the nation was facing its demons. Many, if not most, academics have been bitterly disappointed with the way in which the government in power has dealt in a mean-spirited fashion with what most Australians acknowledge as past wrongs and acts of gross injustices against indigenous Australians.

The year 1997 saw the presentation to Parliament of the report of the "stolen" children from indigenous peoples, which included a compilation of stories of many who were removed from their parents.[4] For a brief period, national attention was given to these harrowing stories, narratives that many could not read or hear without feeling totally wrenched. In that year, such stories from the margins challenged the traditional version of Australian history. The powerful potential of such narratives has been appreciated by people from both sides of the reconciliation process, and the profound disagreements expressed have occurred over different ways of reading Australian history. Most people have also appreciated the fact that one question at stake in all this is whether we will allow such stories to rupture national consciousness. It is perhaps not surprising that such events have occurred against the background of a bolder voice of racism in the country.

As an Australian from Hong Kong, I faced another event of some "ontological" import, since 1997 was the year of the handover of Hong Kong to China, an event that has the potential, in spite of assurances from China, of drastically changing the nature of Hong Kong society and the direction of its history. When one's place of origin undergoes a major change of this nature, what happens to one's sense of stability and identity, and how does that affect the way one engages in philosophical activity?

These are demoralizing times for academics in Australia. Drastic cutbacks and corporatizing tendencies do not augur well for intellectual life since they create an environment that is hardly affirming, either for the life of the mind or for the task of teaching. Professional insecurity, added work pressures, and threats to collegiality create the kind of demoralization that can easily lead to a profound sense of victimhood. In the midst of all this, philosophy is hardly the pure activity of disinterested spirits!

As philosophers, we are concerned with truth. What notion of truth is adequate to the tensions and variety of concerns I have outlined? All too often, in philosophical circles, especially of the Anglo-American analytic tradition, "truth" is a somewhat etiolated concept that is confined to theories and arguments. But such a concept is insufficient to address the disparate concerns of truth as well as issues of philosophical and personal orientation that I have so far mentioned. For the palpable concerns that I have expressed, I need to mine another, fuller notion of truth to orient me in the world of the academy and of my own unstable place within it.

Whereas statements can be called true and it is proper that philosophy should consider in what their truth consists, this linguistic conception drastically narrows the scope of truth and leaves out other dimensions and nuances that are meaningful.[5] In particular, it does so by perpetuating the idea of disengaged, ratiocinating individuals, agreeing or disagreeing over views.

But what about their struggle to maintain temporal continuity and stability amidst the tensions and contradictions of life where an individual's truthfulness requires her integrity and authenticity?

The Hebrew notion is serviceable for us here, since *emeth* is conceptually connected with faithfulness and means "the reliability, the unshakeable dependability, of a thing or word, and accordingly also, the faithfulness of persons."[6] Accordingly, to be "in the truth" is to be faithful, and to be faithful is "to act with integrity and insight towards others and the reality in which we are situated."[7] At first glance, the notion may suggest a posture of obedience and submissiveness, but that is far from the case for the life of faithfulness. In the light of what I have described as my situation and context for philosophical enquiry, an obedient, passive stance will hardly do. Working out what it means to be faithful is demanding of practical judgment, self-understanding, and integrity. "Faithfulness" expresses my existential predicament and struggle to maintain a sense of personal continuity in the midst of change and of disparate concerns. It calls attention to my historicity, my finitude as well as my freedom. There is adventurousness and there is also risk. The philosopher Søren Kierkegaard comes to mind here since he was supremely interested in the question of how the individual could live the truth by refusing to conform to relative values, but rather be personally responsible to the experience of the transcendent.

What then, does faithfulness mean for me in my work as a philosopher in the light of concerns, both ultimate and everyday? *Emeth* spans both dimensions of my life in philosophy, faithfulness with regard to the reality in which I am situated, and faithfulness toward others. What does it mean for me to show reliability and unshakeable dependability as a philosopher, and to philosophize with integrity and insight with respect to the reality in which I am situated? Such challenging questions. It is not surprising then that there is a common way of avoiding them in philosophy. This way of avoidance is found in the view of truth which has prevailed in the twentieth century, truth as the exclusive feature of statements and the accompanying assumption that such truth is found in the attainment of a kind of atemporal objectivity, a "view from nowhere" which "dissociates" from the realities which face us in our philosophizing. The theologian H. Richard Niebuhr said that both atemporal objectivity, and its opposite extreme, subjectivism, are ways of avoiding the "egocentric predicament," and both are impossible attempts to transcend the dialectical situation of subject and object.[8] In contrast, the notion of faithfulness addresses concerns that are existentially palpable in the challenges of the everyday, as well as the extraordinary, events in our lives. In addition, faithfulness for me involves transcendent truth and the binding address of a transcendent God to whom I am also ultimately answerable.

FAITHFULNESS AND PHILOSOPHICAL INQUIRY

"How shall we sing the Lord's song in a strange land?"

Philosophers who belong to a faith community can find the philosophical terrain a strange one. George Schlesinger refers to the transition that needs to be made, in his case, from the intensely religious Talmudic community of which he is part and the "radically differently motivated community" consisting mainly of secular philosophers and of free-thinking academics.[9] He speaks of the "almost impassable gulch" that separates these areas of study, in terms of their prevailing methodologies, intellectual attitudes, and emotional climates.[10] Given that we "sing the Lord's song in a strange land," what does faithfulness mean when we are philosophizing from a faith community? In what follows, I will explore some of the connections that arise between existential and philosophical truthfulness and their importance for philosophy.

Humility and the "Big Picture"

In discussing the stance that the religious person takes to philosophical activity, Schlesinger refers to the importance of humility, which he characterizes as "the supreme form of moral rectitude."[11] Whereas philosophers have always been concerned with the question of truth, Schlesinger reasons that this concern should issue in true humility since it springs from a genuine objectivity, and a kind of faithfulness to the reality in which they are situated. This is because true objectivity gives a wide perspective against which one's work is found to be "only a fraction of a percentage of the entire harvest of human genius." From that "objective" point of view, even the most remarkable individual achievement is "but a single element in the vast mosaic produced by creative people throughout the generations. . . ." A truly humble person will therefore dwell "only briefly and infrequently on what is notable specifically about himself."[12]

Attention to the big picture of human achievement and concern creates the virtues of other-directedness, self-forgetfulness, and evenhandedness, for humility requires that one set one's ambitions among the many wants, ambitions, and longings to be found in the world. The acknowledgement that one's philosophical activity is only a small part of human concern, activity, and achievement immediately orients one more realistically and faithfully toward the reality in which she is situated. That same objectivity will also shape the questions that are raised and the areas of philosophical concerns that engage one. However, faithfulness to reality in another sense is also required in philosophy.

Standing Tall and Feeling Fragile

Many philosophers, especially feminist ones, have pointed out that much of Western philosophy has operated on the assumption of a neutral space. This has posited a picture of knowers as abstract, generalized individuals, disengaged from circumstance and situation and disengaged also from complexity and chaos.[13] Accordingly, the human knower is often assumed to be a rational and autonomous agent. Faithfulness, however, compels us to acknowledge other aspects of human experience within which the person is not an autonomous agent. Analytic philosophy especially has not been good at acknowledging aspects of human experience for which reason seems inadequate and in which there is more ambiguity than rationality and more passivity than human agency. Is this because the attention to reason that is at the heart of such philosophy is ultimately incompatible with the admission of human frailty? For frailty is associated with passivity and confusion rather than agency and clarity. The question of the limits of clarity and the nature of rationality is too large for this essay, but a story can illuminate aspects of their relation.

A friend and colleague died while I was putting in a proposal for this anthology. She was struggling with cancer while trying to complete a thesis on the philosophy of love. Even though her cancer was well advanced, she hung on to life, finding it very hard indeed to leave her children behind (for what mother would not fight to stay with her children?). However, on Good Friday 1997, she died peacefully. On Maundy Thursday evening, she had asked to be wheeled into a quiet service at the Anglican palliative care place where she had been staying. By the end of that week, she had faced the inevitable. It seemed, from a report I heard at the funeral, that she finally embraced faith, and she had asked her children to join her at the little service, saying that she did not want to see them "left in a spiritual vacuum."

For Christians, Good Friday is associated with deep suffering, coming before the hope and vindication of Easter Sunday. According to George Steiner, however, the non-Christian and atheist both know analogously of the significance of these days. For they both know "of the injustice . . . the interminable suffering . . . the waste, the brute enigma of ending which so largely make up not only the historical dimension of the human condition but the very fabric of our personal lives. [They] know, ineluctably, of the pain . . . the failure of love . . . the solitude which are our history and private fate."[14] And while, for Christians, Sunday signifies an "intimation, both assured and precarious, both evident and beyond comprehension, of resurrection, of a justice and a love that have conquered death," for the non-Christian and the non-believer, the "lineaments of that Sunday carry the name of hope and signify the day of resolution."[15] For, as Steiner adds, hope is "undeconstructably" human.[16]

But for us all there is "the long day's journey of the Saturday . . . ." For us all is "an immensity of waiting . . . [b]etween suffering, aloneness, unutterable waste on the one hand and the dream of liberation, of rebirth on the other."[17] "Saturday is waiting day, limbo day, the day of unsureness, indifference, numbness. . . ."[18]

The meaning of these days holds a lesson for philosophy. If it is to be faithful, philosophy should address, not only the dark reality of Friday, or the resolution of Sunday, but also the ambiguity and irresolution and the "immensity of waiting" which is our human life. Faithful philosophy must embrace the "not-yet" and the tensions that are part of the human condition, the tensions between doubt and conviction, self-transcendence and self-regard, self-centering and aloneness. If philosophy is to keep an eye out on the human condition, part of that condition is the experience of events that try our capacity to hope, to maintain integrity, and to be faithful to what we hold dear. Indeed, as Kierkegaard saw it, to exercise faith is to change one's life into a trial, a daily test, in which one is taken outside the comfort zone of the conventional and the expected, even to be uncomfortably "suspended more than 70,000 fathoms," in realms where philosophical reasoning is no longer a sure guide.[19] Accordingly, philosophy that is faithful must not depend on sewn-up, victorious arguments. On the other hand, one must hasten to add, philosophy, especially if it is passed on to the young, must not leave people in despair through processes of relentless skepticism. It cannot advocate heterogeneity for its own sake and endless choice without direction, without also providing a place for the young to stand.

How then does philosophical enquiry reconcile the tension between Friday and Sunday, between fragility and triumph, weakness and victory? How can it be faithful, on the one hand, to the weakness of my friend on Holy Thursday, and, on the other hand, to the rigorous and powerful displays of argument in the typical seminar? How do we reconcile the truth and reality of human loss and mortality with intellectual triumph? Must we demand such a continuity? If good philosophy is to be true to the human condition, can it afford to forget the fact of mortality and of ultimate weakness? Should not the experience of powerlessness and loss interrogate autonomy and agency and the confident thrashings of energy in philosophical sparring? Those "too, too solid" displays of intellectual power to establish what is the case must somehow be challenged by the experience of emptiness and the fact of human frailty. On Holy Thursday, my friend finally let go of the prowess that we celebrate in philosophy, to embrace her ultimate powerlessness.

"A More Kind Knowing"

Faithfulness to the human condition in these respects should, without sacrificing rigor, lead to "a more kind knowing," that is, a knowing that is more concerned with wisdom than with mere enquiry or mere intellectual victory.[20] The philosopher R. K. Elliott says that enquiry presents us with the choice between "hunting" and "shepherding." Hunting is inherently aggressive and celebrates prowess and skill for its own sake. It is an acquisitive form of enquiry which is characterized by a "restless hurrying on" of the process.

In contrast, shepherding is a more kind knowing which cares for the objects of enquiry, and in which understanding is sought through friendship and contemplation with the known. Contemplation has the character of resting in the subject in such a way that there is no "restless hurrying on" in order that nothing "comes between the mind and its original object."[21] Friendship describes the spirit of unconditionality toward the object of knowledge since it carries "a patient unaggressive insistence that the object show itself as it is . . . rather as a friend is willing for one to 'be oneself' in her company."[22] The opposite of friendship is a conditioned acceptance which is extended only when "the objects of knowledge exhibit, or can be made to exhibit aspects which conform to a certain pre-given system of concepts and other conventions."[23] This way of knowing is like catching prey in a net, for the sake of what one can go on to do with it when it is caught, or for the sake of the hunting. It is an acquisitive and masterful approach to the objects of knowledge.

In contrast, I have often been struck by the mystery of enquiry, how it is carried by the expectation of reward and how it points to a richness and plenty which we hope to find. Indeed, contemplative experience often has the character of a gift that reaches to the depth of our being and harmonizes its many aspects.[24]

"The Invincible Love of Yahweh"

Christian creation theology speaks of the plenitude of Being on which we instinctively depend. It speaks of a creation that is eloquent and rich because it springs from the "invincible love" of Yahweh.[25] If love is indeed the fundamental character of reality, then understanding will evoke desire and thankfulness and be attended by intimations of grace. If creation is rich and eloquent, it will reward the enquirer with surprise and joy and feed the spontaneity and vitality of her quest. Intellectual eros will then be a human response to the love that is at the heart of creation.

But the conventional wisdom in the West regarding people of faith is that they are far from being open-minded and far from being lovers of truth. The perception is that faith presents a psychological impediment to the openness of friendship. This, unfortunately, is true of some people of faith, especially of fundamentalist faith, but the opposite can also be true. Faith in the Transcendent can lead us to a respect for difference rather than epistemic closure, since transcendent truth itself resists domestication and conditionality. With its themes of eloquence and the "sociality of harmonic difference," Christian creation theology encourages the respect for otherness and the expectation of the unexpected in all our enquiry.[26] Indeed, theologically framed in this way, intellectual eros is a worship and celebration of the rich gifts of God.

The "Open Heaven"

A large view of transcendence is conveyed by the idea of an "open heaven" which can be found in the work of the Dutch philosopher Hermann Dooyeweerd.[27] The concept expresses the transcendental structure of creation that allows for the possibility of radical community in the midst of genuine difference. According to Dooyeweerd, temporal societal relationships should ideally express this "supra-temporal community" of humankind within which is openness because of the largeness of God's nature.[28] Under an "open heaven," the believer finds that she is addressed, warned, and taught in ways she does not expect, and often she will be surprised by a God more generous than she had imagined. Under an "open heaven," she finds that reality and truth are not "sewn up," indeed, that all are at risk of being enlarged by many intimations of a loving God who gifts us with a rich and eloquent world. The phenomenology of intellectual eros aptly reflects faith in such an "open heaven."[29]

This affects the way I see philosophy. For several years I have been involved with teaching and developing a philosophy course for senior secondary students, aged between sixteen to eighteen years.[30] There is a good deal of evidence in pedagogical research that even very young children take naturally to philosophy. What then is the place of philosophy in human life?

If, as noted earlier, good philosophy addresses the sense of alienation that we all experience, the tension between "that intuition of ourselves as one with the whole . . . and that [of ourselves] as separate beings . . . ,"[31] such a view of philosophy has implications for how we teach it, especially to those who are being introduced to it for the first time. It seems to me that teachers of philosophy will not be able to endorse any narrow idea of their task, as being merely the "piecemeal clarification of puzzling terms";[32] instead they will view philosophy in terms of the whole person, and in the context of care.[33] Care that students will learn to love truth and value integrity, and care too that they will not be overwhelmed by critical skepticism.

Whereas liberal skepticism is wary, sometimes with good reason, of "thick" notions of the good that go unjustified in our teaching activities, there is a very real sense in which teachers of philosophy should be concerned about where philosophy leaves those in their charge. I like the phrase "epistemological homebuilding" for the reminder that philosophy could serve the task of centering people in the world.[34] "Homebuilding" in philosophy seeks the continuity between common and academic understandings, and between students' experiences and questions and the questions of philosophy. It seeks to provide a rich, profound, and synoptic understanding,[35] rather than one taken over by academic concerns dissociated from life. I have found that as teachers of philosophy we are ideally placed to provide a "background map" for our students to the range of their knowledge.[36]

While the notion of epistemological homebuilding may strike some as a dangerously value-laden notion of education, it also flies in the face of the radical postmodern belief in the incommensurability of disciplines and discourses. This raises a large question that touches the core of the academic enterprise today, but it is beyond the scope of this paper. However, the problem of fragmentation in learning and the curriculum is also exacerbated by the political climate in Australian education today.

In the Face of "Managerial Newspeak"

Speaking about philosophy as epistemological homebuilding is rather out of kilter with the current Australian political climate of "economic rationalism"[37] and "managerial newspeak."[38] "Economic rationalism" in education refers to its commercialization and to a market-oriented view of education as career training. Accordingly, discussions on education have become dominated by the language of the market. For example, senior bureaucrats are often heard referring to knowledge as a "product," and these days they are also urging (or threatening) universities to become more service oriented or risk irrelevance and loss of market share.[39]

Is it possible in such a climate to articulate the value of something like philosophy without appealing to its many external benefits? The difficulty arises because of a conceptual loss promoted by this climate so that we are now unable to articulate the treasure that philosophy is. The "form of speaking" that we need to advance the worth of philosophy "has gone dead on us."[40]

But it is important that we not justify philosophy (indeed, the humanities in general) solely in terms of external benefits, since the value of an enquiry like philosophy is at least partly its capacity to nourish the life of the mind. Indeed, it could be said that the lucidity and reflection that are valued in and intrinsic to philosophy are goods without which our whole lives will suffer. In other words, the relationship between philosophical reflectiveness and personal authenticity is not an extrinsic one since notions such as authenticity and integrity characterize the very nature of a rich inner life. For this reason, Raimond Gaita argues, rightly in my view, that truth is a necessity of the soul because an indifference to truth in one's life, including one's emotional life, results in superficiality and loss of self-knowledge.[41] Gaita cites the avoidance of sentimentality as an illustration of how those committed to what is true are also committed to truthfulness, for sentimentality is both a form of falsehood and a form of untruthfulness.[42] If truthfulness is thus intrinsic to truth, then virtues like authenticity and integrity are also prerequisites to thinking well. However, this continuity between truth and truthfulness is missed by instrumental approaches in education today when the emphasis is on the extrinsic value of knowledge as a "product."

Care and concern for one's own inner life and that of the others in one's care should therefore extend to the care for and protection of one's subject. Faithfulness to one's subject involves the art of shepherding, an "art of tendance," which seeks to protect one's subject from the spirit of hunting in acquisitive, instrumental enquiry. The "art of tendance" in philosophy is nurtured by the love of wisdom as well as the appreciation that the lucidity and reflectiveness cultivated through philosophy are of vital personal importance in philosophical education. This is because the concern for truth, the striving to see things as they are, rather than as one would wish them to be, is all-important for self-making, a process of individuation that is constitutive of a "critically realized individuality."[43]

Indeed, we come to understand the kind of value that truth is in the lives of people we meet which have been deepened by it. We learn about truth by being moved, through the example of those who mediate it to us, as we see their lives of truthfulness and faithfulness. A subject like philosophy cannot finally be justified by words, rather its worth becomes apparent through its inspired teaching.[44] For teachers of philosophy, this is both a privilege and a responsibility. I feel this keenly, especially when I am teaching philosophy to those who meet it for the first time.

"Absolutely toward Absolute Ends"

Contrary to the value of "managerial newspeak," therefore, my life in philosophy cannot be viewed as simply a career, or even as a profession. For that life must extend beyond the world of philosophers and beyond particular fashions and values that may prevail. Just as a proper notion of transcendence calls me beyond my parochialism to embrace difference, so my life is called to be judged prophetically against what is of ultimate value. In Kierkegaardian terms, being faithful to the absolute involves "making the relationship to the absolute *telos* absolute, and the relationship to the relative ends relative."[45] As Kierkegaard understood it, such a calling can take one outside the scope of what is considered rational and acceptable and beyond what are considered to be natural responses to one's fate in the world. Whereas Kierkegaard spoke of a freely chosen individuality that brings with it vulnerability and loneliness, there is a kind of vulnerability that one would not have freely chosen. I referred earlier to the demoralization of the Australian university and the pressures that it has created. Funding cutbacks and loss of positions threaten collegiality and professional security. Pain is all around, so too is resentment, and suspicion of institutions at large. Amidst the postmodern culture of distrust, it is easy to slip into a cynical reading of the situation, and it is tempting to fall prey to a sense of victimhood that is prevalent. But faithfulness challenges us to move beyond the comfort zone of these responses. Under an "open heaven" I am transcendentally addressed in my vulnerability, confusion, and complacency to be, at times, reassured, occasionally surprised, and sometimes warned, but also constantly challenged to think more largely, beyond the lure of victimhood.

Victimhood is indeed a lure. Nietzsche has shown splendidly how it lives in unlovely collusion with resentment and how it then becomes the heartspring of dissembling thoughts and manipulative actions.[46] But victimhood, and the enjoyment of that state, is also unhealthy because it is based on a theologically unstable dichotomy between tyranny and impotence. Victimhood is also ultimately based on the brute view of power as mastery, since it does not allow for the possibility of *mutual* empowerment. Neither does it allow for the many occasions in which pain and humiliation can be redeemed, when inwardness can be deepened through being made aware of one's own dissemblings and manipulation of power. The stance of victimhood is like being stuck in "Good Friday time," without moving on in hope. It cannot lead us to wholeness.

Such reflections and agonizings in the midst of the accomplishments of the academic life may seem unnecessary and overwrought to those not so disposed. Philosophers are always concerned about truth and objectivity, but the concern for objectivity in philosophy, as we have seen, need not touch us at any deep or personal level. When we struggle in this way with the degree to which our work is infected with dissemblings and manipulativeness, we are concerned with a level of inwardness and private objectivity that only makes sense if we view philosophy in a certain way, i.e., as a calling and a vocation, a life's work in which one's integrity and self-making are bound.[47]

"The Candle of the Lord"

In the light of self-making, philosophy, truth, and reason embrace wide dimensions of meaning, and ultimately are not opposed to spirituality, beauty, and the complexity of human life. This conception of reason is not narrow and instrumental. Nor will it be advanced through agency and clarity alone. Indeed, reason can nurture my soul with a "holy resonance,"[48] and lead me to joy. Under an "open heaven," reason is part of the cosmic drama, leading us, as a seventeenth century divine described it, as "the candle of the Lord."[49]

The Christian feminist theologian Sara Maitland said that, as believers in a profligately loving God, Christians should revive an amazement, an "Oh Wow!" in the course of each day. Indeed, she says that this is an ethical imperative in response to God's creative power and love, in the midst of contingency and risk, in the long day's journey of the Saturday. What Maitland says about joy reminds us of faithfulness, for joy is a way of being that is deeply caring of the great virtues of hope, faith, and love. Joy is produced when these virtues are steadfastly held in the face of not old or fundamentalist certainties, but of old and new insights, both about the nature of the universe and our human situation. Maitland says that the deep awareness today of our historicity and even of our contingency must be embraced along with *koinonia,* the sense of fellowship provided by our faith tradition. With its store of wisdom and struggle, faith provides a sense of solidarity and a safety net for the journey of faithfulness. In a parallel way in philosophy, we can say that the "deep problem of truth" in our time is not addressed by returning to Platonic timelessness or detached objectivity, but by recognizing our historicity and drawing upon the resources provided by others, across space and time, others who have struggled with those deep questions of truth. The history of philosophy also provides *koinonia,* for in it we find "an enduring intellectual homeland with ancestors who are able to play the role of liberators."[50]

We now recognize as never before that knowledge of the human situation cannot be achieved by some transcendent, spectatorial stance, since knowledge of ourselves and of the human situation does not occur because of the transparency of our own being. Rather, truth is achieved by standing firm, by establishing, by supporting, and by bearing. It is not a timeless state of affairs, achieved once and for all, but its reliability "must be shown again and again."[51] If indeed we are not spectators, but part of the show, and by nature embedded in life, we must vindicate truth with our character and life by displaying that "binding directedness to cleave to how things are."[52] The essentially temporal nature of truth and faithfulness, as we have seen, is well captured by Kierkegaard. His account of faithfulness to the Absolute emphasizes the loneliness of the path of truth. Somehow, I prefer Maitland's picture of the tightrope walker because of the beauty in that image, beauty in the risk taken and the hope exercised. She writes:

I often dream I am a tightrope walker. I climb the rope ladder slowly, carefully, adjusting to its wrigglings. The wooden slats mutter to me all the way up. The rungs my right foot stands on say, "If you are afraid of falling, you will fall," and the rungs my left foot presses say, "If you believe you cannot fall, you will fall."

Eventually I arrive on the little platform at the top. I strip off my track suit and am revealed in all my sequinned glory. I look out and down at the upturned eyes, sparkling brighter than my costume. Then the spotlight pins me, and I hear its mocking tones.

It says, "And probably in the end you will fall anyway."

And in my dream, I always listen politely and know it is true, and then I go out sparkling, flashing and dance on the void. That is the challenge, the moment of hope: to dance as near to the edge of destruction as is possible, to be willing to fall and still not fall. And the audience cheers, because it is beautiful and because they know that this time, I may indeed fall and because they know that this is precisely why it is beautiful, and I have made it beautiful.

That is a good dream.[53]

It is a good dream too for me because in God's invincible love, reality is eloquent and rich. It is good for me too, that from the dizzying heights, a safety net of *koinonia* and truth is provided. We do not dance into the future alone. Because of this, faithfulness is worth the effort.

NOTES

The title of this chapter is inspired by Graeme Garrett's "Preaching on Saturday," *St. Mark's Review* 171 (Spring 1997) (Journal of St. Mark's National Theological Centre, Canberra, Australia). This essay is a testimony to the *koinonia* and collegiality to which I refer. I am grateful to colleagues, friends, and "fellow travelers," for the many conversations (electronic and otherwise) and many instances of support that have helped me to write this. I thank Sarah Bachelard and Heather Thomson for comments on an earlier draft of this paper. In addition, I acknowledge my indebtedness to Prof. R. K. Elliott whose work has continually inspired me. Finally, I am grateful to Raina Verrills, for what she has taught me.

1. David Cooper, *World Philosophies: An Historical Introduction* (Oxford: Blackwell, 1996), p. 61.

2. See, for example, Lorraine Code, *Rhetorical Spaces: Essays on Gendered Locations* (New York: Routledge, 1995).

3. R. K. Elliott, "Education and the Human Being," in *Philosophers Discuss Education,* ed. S. C. Brown (London: Macmillan, 1974).

4. *Bringing Them Home,* Report of the H. R. E. O. C., Australia, 1997.

5. Richard Campbell, *Truth and Historicity* (Oxford: Clarendon Press, 1991), p. 395.

6. *Truth and Historicity,* p. 437.

7. *Truth and Historicity,* p. 438.

8. H. Richard Niebuhr, ed., *Faith on Earth: An Enquiry into the Structure of Human Faith* (New Haven, Conn.: Yale University Press, 1989), p. 27.

9. George Schlesinger, "Truth, Humility, and Philosophers," in *God and the Philosophers: The Reconciliation of Faith and Reason,* ed. T. V. Morris (New York: Oxford University Press, 1994).

10. "Truth, Humility, and Philosophers," p. 249.

11. "Truth, Humility, and Philosophers," p. 251.

12. "Truth, Humility, and Philosophers," p. 253.

13. *Rhetorical Spaces,* pp. x–xiv.

14. George Steiner, *Real Presences: Is There Anything in What We say?* (London: Faber and Faber, 1989), pp. 231–32.

15. *Real Presences,* p. 232.

16. *Real Presences,* p. 232.

17. "Preaching on Saturday," p. 6.

18. "Preaching on Saturday," p. 6.

19. Søren Kierkegaard, *Journals and Papers,* trans. H. V. Hong and E. H. Hong (Bloomington: Indiana University Press, 1967), entry 1142, X4A 114.

20. The phrase is from William Langland, author of the religious allegory *The Vision of Piers Plowman,* cited in R. K. Elliott, "Education, Love of One's Subject, and Love of Truth," *Proceedings of the Philosophy of Education Society of Great Britain* 8, no. 1 (January 1974): 141.

21. "Education, Love of One's Subject, and Love of Truth," p. 142.

22. "Education, Love of One's Subject, and Love of Truth," p. 142.

23. "Education, Love of One's Subject, and Love of Truth," p. 143

24. "Education, Love of One's Subject, and Love of Truth," p. 146

25. Pedro Trigo, quoted in J. Richard Middleton and Brian J. Walsh, *Truth Is Stranger Than It Used to Be* (Downer's Grove, Ill.: InterVarsity Press, 1995), p. 153.

26. John Milbank, quoted in *Truth Is Stranger Than It Used to Be,* p. 157.

27. Herman Dooyeweerd, *A New Critique of Theoretical Thought,* vol. 3 (Philadelphia: Presbyterian and Reformed Press, 1957), pp. 582–83. See also R. Mouw and S. Griffioen, *Pluralisms and Horizons* (Grand Rapids, Mich.: Eerdmans, 1993), pp. 158–77.

28. *Pluralisms and Horizons,* p. 170.

29. For more extensive development of this topic, see my discussion in "The 'Open Heaven': Understanding Other Faiths in God's World," in *The Task of Theology Today: Doctrines and Dogmas,* ed. Victor Pfitzner and Hilary Regan (Edinburgh: T & T Clark, 1999), pp. 163–89.

30. The course is called "Theory of Knowledge," and it is discussed in Winifred Wing Han Lamb, "'TOK' at Narrabundah College: Content Approach and Rationale," *Critical and Creative Thinking* 7, no. 2 (1999).

31. *Faith on Earth,* p. 27.

32. *World Philosophies,* p. 4.

33. For a fuller discussion of this point, see Winifred Wing Han Lamb, "The 'Whole Child' in Education," *Journal of Philosophy of Education* 35, no. 2 (2001): 203–17.

34. The phrase comes from *Truth Is Stranger Than It Used to Be,* p. 171.

35. See R. K. Elliott, "Education and Human Being," in *Philosophers Discuss Education,* ed. S. C. Brown (London: Macmillan, 1975), p. 69.

36. The phrase is from Mary Midgley, *Wisdom, Information, Wonder* (London: Routledge, 1989), p. 8.

37. "Economic Rationalism" is a political position that advocates less government intervention for growth in a market economy. The term is often used pejoratively by Australian economists like Michael Pusey, who question whether such "rationalizations" are of

benefit to the nation and to its citizens. See Pusey, "Australia: Once the Lighthouse Social Democracy of the World—The Impact of Recent Economic Reforms," *Theses Eleven* 55 (1998): 41–59.

38. The phrase is Raimond Gaita's and refers to what he describes as the "debased" speech patterns of educational administrators, speech that reflects the emphasis on career training and market outcomes over intellectual development. See "Truth and the Idea of the University," *Australian Universities Review* 40, no. 2 (1997): 14.

39. From a speech given by Mike Gallagher, First Assistant Secretary, Higher Education Division, Department of Education, Training and Youth Affairs, at the conference, "The Idea of the University: Enterprise or Academy?" at Australian National University, July 2001. Reported in "Universities Told to Swim or Sink," *Canberra Times,* 28 July 2001.

40. "Truth and the Idea of the University," p. 14.

41. "Truth and the Idea of the University," p. 17.

42. "Truth and the Idea of the University," p. 17.

43. "Truth and the Idea of the University," p. 18.

44. "Education, Love of One's Subject, and Love of Truth," p. 147.

45. Søren Kierkegaard, *Concluding Unscientific Postscript,* trans. David F. Swenson (Princeton, N.J.: Princeton University Press, 1941), p. 365.

46. Friedrich Nietzsche, *On the Genealogy of Morals,* trans. Walter Kaufmann and R. J. Hollingdale, and *Ecce Homo,* trans. Walter Kaufmann (New York; Vintage Books, 1967). See especially the Second Essay in *Genealogy,* sections 16–25, pp. 84–96.

47. R. K. Elliot, "Education and Objectivity," *Journal of Philosophy of Education* 16, no. 1 (1982): 49–62.

48. Sara Maitland, *A Big Enough God: Artful Theology* (London: Mowbray, 1995), p. 153.

49. Dr. Whichcote, quoted in *A Big Enough God,* p. 153.

50. "Education, Love of One's Subject, and Love of Truth," p. 140.

51. *Truth and Historicity,* p. 437.

52. *Truth and Historicity,* p. 437.

53. *A Big Enough God,* pp. 145–46.

FOUR

Three Aspects of Identity

SR. MARY CHRISTINE MORKOVSKY

1. EXPERIENCES

A believer who came to feminism through philosophy—that is how I would characterize myself. Chronologically, I was born into a Roman Catholic family and baptized as an infant; after becoming a religious Sister, I was trained in philosophy; and in the 1980s I became aware of and content with the fact that I am a feminist. Some autobiographical details will explain how this unfolded. Then I will discuss the tensions and rewards that ensued.

My family of origin is from Moravia in the Czech Republic. Mother was born there and emigrated to Texas at the age of five. Raised in rural Lavaca County, Texas, where being Catholic and being Czech were practically synonymous, my parents met when they worked in San Antonio, Texas, during the Depression. They chose to settle and raise their family in this city. Two of my father's brothers became priests, and all ten of us children were baptized by one of these two uncles shortly after birth. My godfather, who was still a seminarian when I was born, later became the bishop of Galveston-Houston.

My father took us to Mass every Sunday, to Confession on many Saturdays, and to other services such as Benediction and Lenten devotions at St. Cecilia's parish church, about two miles away from our house. If we didn't attend the Stations of the Cross during Lent, he would sometimes conduct them at home. Although our family had been consecrated to the Sacred Heart, with a certificate on the wall to prove it, we did not say prayers together except before meals, when my father said a prayer in Czech. During a thunderstorm, we would light a blessed candle and say a mantra attributed to my paternal grandmother: "God is with us; evil begone." (I am recalling what I experienced as the eldest of ten children; when there were more of us, some of these customs were not so strong.) My introverted father was more "pious" than my mother in that he promoted regular, recited prayers —as they did in his family. Mother's faith was less legalistic. She was an extrovert with great spontaneous interest in people, who once said her favorite devotion was to the Holy Spirit "because he was the most neglected person of the Holy Trinity." Her parents probably had a somewhat Jansenistic upbringing; they thought they should go to Confession just before receiving Communion. But Mother was never afflicted with such scruples. I think we tended to identify religion with going to church and saying prayers. Only looking back do I appreciate the moral uprightness of my parents, their generosity to anyone who was needy, and their great charitableness in speech. These aspects of true religion were just taken for granted, as was the unquestioned belief that God was ultimately in charge of this world and indeed of all that occurred.

Reinforcing the religious views at home was the instruction we received from the Sisters at St. Teresa's Academy, a grade school and high school located across the street from our house. Their Society had been founded in Barcelona early in the twentieth century, and most of the Sisters hailed from Spain or Latin America. Their devotion to their patroness, St. Teresa of Avila, was manifested in their frequent practical efforts to teach us meditative prayer suitable to our age. In grade school we prayed often and memorized the catechism. I remember that even in the first grade Sister Concepcion led us in vivid meditations where we were to imagine our own death and whether we were ready for it. We also had a club called "The Little Flock of Jesus," whose members had a special song, marched in a procession about once a month, and promised to lead a good life. When I received first Holy Communion in the second grade, I was vaguely aware that this was a solemn occasion; but the memory of the pretty rosary and prayer book I received is stronger. In the early grades we were encouraged to check out lives of the saints from the classroom library, and around the sixth grade the whole class began to go to chapel once a day to recite the rosary. Every Friday, our teacher had us memorize the Gospel for the following Sunday. Around the age of twelve, I received the Sacrament of Confirmation in the parish church after a few instruction sessions from the assistant pastor. From seventh grade on, we made an annual three-day retreat in February with priests who gave us conferences. Each year they were sure to discourse on the need to consider what vocation we would follow—single, married, or religious.

In high school religion classes, we followed the "Quest for Happiness" series and a series on the New Testament with our Sister home room teacher. Three times a week all the students in this girls' high school gathered for instruction from Monsignor Patrick Geehan, the Sisters' chaplain who was also the Vicar General of the Archdiocese. His method of asking questions from the catechism and demanding exact answers frightened us. But he also elaborated on the material in the orthodox and precise manner of one trained in Canon Law. He held my interest to the point that one day at home I asked my uncle, Father John, to "explain" the mystery of the Trinity—and was able to make sense of his answer, which involved the "processions." As a junior, I attended a religious meeting at a downtown hotel with adults from the parish. During the small group discussions, to my own surprise I was able to articulate the importance of Jesus' Resurrection to our faith. I consider myself fortunate to have had solid religious instruction and encouragement to take on "mainline" devotions such as the rosary and mental prayer. No one encouraged me—nor was I tempted—to get caught up in apparitions of Mary or fears of evil spirits or other fringe movements. To this day, I have had no extraordinary or mystical prayer experiences.

My only experience of Protestants was neighbors who called us "Bohunks" or "Catlickers." They were hardly prone to dialogue, and anyhow the archbishop said we should never attend their services. After World War II, two of my mother's brothers married women who were not only non-Catholic but non-Czech! Both of them were baptized before their wedding, and we loved them dearly; but we always were aware that they did not have the same background as we did.

During high school I became more connected to the parish through membership in the youth club and playing the organ for the adult choir. Helping to teach religious vacation school for public school students in the summer, I met some seminarians. Our teen-age "gang" members were all from the parish and concentrated mostly on having fun. I would engage in personal meditative prayer a few times a week and recite the rosary to myself in bed before falling asleep. After my junior year, the doctor ordered me to spend the summer in bed because of rheumatic fever. This provided more time for reflection, and I became aware that I would really like to become a religious Sister. I felt I knew quite a bit about that way of life from observing the great variety of teachers I had experienced down the years, but I kept my plans to myself. My health improved so that I spent a fairly normal senior year, climaxed by my solo piano recital and reception of a scholarship to Our Lady of the Lake University. I'm not sure why I favored this college over the other girls' college in town, Incarnate Word College. Perhaps I remembered going with my uncle, Father Alois, to OLL one summer when I was about seven years old to read in Czech to his class of Sister-students. I also had memories of concerts on campus and of the fine nativity scene that appeared in the chapel at Christmastime. (My family used to visit creches in many churches during the Christmas holidays.)

During my freshman year of college, I observed the ways of the Sister-teachers while I studied for my courses, and I reached the decision during the annual retreat in February that I would ask to join them. I told my mother shortly afterwards, but it was only in the summer that I consulted one of the Sisters about how to enter the Congregation of Divine Providence. Our class was fairly large, over twenty. We were postulants for nine months and novices for one year before receiving our first assignments.

How did my faith grow during that period? I think the good foundation from home and previous schooling was strengthened rather than amended. It was taken for granted that we knew and kept the Ten Commandments and laws of the church and were serious about entering on the "way of perfection," which was another name for religious life. This meant vowing to be celibate, to share all material goods with the community, to follow directions from superiors, and to devote ourselves unstintingly to the service of others. This was the minimum requirement for being "a religious" and not very different from the way I had lived heretofore. We were expected to grow in the appreciation of this chaste, poor, and obedient life, sustained by daily public and private prayer, spiritual reading, a monthly Sunday of reflection, an annual retreat, and all the give and take of living and working with a group of like-minded women. Whoever had no outstanding family or psychological problems, enjoyed adequate health, and could willingly follow all the directives adapted easily and even joyfully.

In the house of formation, there were plenty of opportunities and encouragement for self-denial and not much encouragement of initiative. I was willing to major in English or music and was told it would be music because there was greater need in that area. I did not experience any crisis of faith or vocation during this time; so at nineteen I was a professed religious Sister teaching and at the same time taking a few courses to finish a BA degree. "Out on the mission," I found more challenges such as tailoring instruction to different children, learning to live harmoniously with a small group of Sisters, and making more personal and professional decisions (in my case, about pianos, music books, and management of personal study time). Contact with laypeople was minimal, and almost always I would be giving them support in their faith rather than receiving support from them. We very much identified ourselves with and by our work, our "apostolate," rather than our personal gifts and talents. The "common good" definitely took precedence over individual wishes and plans. Probably our life resembled the military more than anything else. Someone else looked after us, and we were ready to be sent wherever we were needed.

Around this time, directives from Rome about modifying our habit and receiving better professional preparation were being communicated to us. We opened a house of formation for high-school-age girls, and I was assigned there to teach. Now the need was for an English teacher, so I changed my major. Soon I was chosen to go on for higher studies in philosophy to be able to work in formation.

My journey into philosophy began with a summer course in metaphysics, where I felt utterly lost but fascinated. To this day, I really love to ask and try to answer ultimate questions. The teacher, a Vincentian priest, apparently saw some potential in me and recommended higher studies in philosophy. I had all the required prerequisite courses but one in Natural Theology when I enrolled for the MA degree at St. Louis University. At twenty-four, I was one of the youngest of a class of about a dozen Sisters also preparing to do formation work for their communities. The Sister Formation movement, spearheaded by Sister Emil Penet, IHM, was gathering steam, and a philosophy major was considered the best preparation for our future work. For my personality, philosophy seemed to be a good field, given my introversion, intellectual curiosity, perseverance at tasks, and ability to objectify. I am predominantly a head person. The required philosophy courses at St. Louis University in the 1960s consisted of history of ancient, medieval, and modern philosophy along with extensive reading lists and oral exams in each of these three areas. Required systematic courses in metaphysics and ethics were taught from the Thomistic perspective, and most elective courses were on individual philosophers from every historical period.

Graduate school exposed me to a variety of companions from different parts of the country whose histories and viewpoints didn't always match my own. Still, all of us in the house of studies for Sisters had in common our belief systems, our daily prayer routine, and a similar outlook on life. I experienced what was probably the first intellectual challenge to my inherited faith, which never really questioned the existence of God but took it for granted along with all church teachings. With permission from officials in the archdiocesan chancery, I was reading books on the Index. I continually felt that I had inadequate background and intelligence and was frightened by the experience of accepting a philosophical position that was new and seemed good to me, only to have the teacher severely critique it in subsequent classes, leaving me with the task of deciding what *I really* thought. My basic belief in God and fidelity to religious practices remained, but I was threading my way through a dense jungle of reasons for numerous new positions. Some very intelligent authors didn't believe what I believed; others did. Both kinds gave reasons. It was a kind of dualism—stability in practice and externals but great flux and uncertainty in my head. My habitual tendency to mistrust my own insights was due in some part to my socialization in a thoroughly patriarchal society, but recognition of this fact came only a decade or more later. I attributed my success in studies to divine Providence and was increasingly grateful for God's care. Being able to cope adequately in graduate school surprised me, but it also gave me a growing confidence in my own reasoning powers.

Although classes, required reading, and research for seminars occupied most of my time, I could not be unaware of current events and issues. John F. Kennedy was elected and assassinated; Martin Luther King came to speak to the students in a gym auditorium full of police and secret service agents; a few graduate students went to march in Selma; people whose neighborhood had been demolished moved into the nearby notorious Pruitt Igoe housing project; Dan Berrigan spoke at an ecumenical prayer service on the topic, "We Are *Not* Sheep." We sang freedom songs at hootenannies, discussed the meaning of Fellini and Ingmar Bergman films, admired Sister Corita's serigraphs, and got used to the Mass in English. We conversed informally on current affairs; but they did not enter into the courses I was taking, nor did I relate them to my topics of research. A new professor was starting to teach phenomenology, and existentialism was an exciting new school to dip into.

Moreover, the revolutionary second Vatican Council was in session. Following instructions from Cardinal Archbishop Ritter, almost everyone on campus formed mixed groups of about ten people to discuss the documents as they came off the press. There was a sense that the old order was giving way. Aggiornamento meant learning more about non-Catholics, stripping the liturgy of centuries of accretions, singing new hymns in English, challenging traditional customs of religious life, and getting back to the animating vision of the founders of our respective Congregations. Theologians had a new freedom that seemed similar to the liberty philosophers customarily enjoyed to explore ideas without threat of being accused of heresy. My dissertation was on Henri Bergson, Jewish proponent of the *élan vital,* who wrote in his last book about Christ as the culmination of life's natural tendency to hoard energy and release it, that is, to spread love to all humankind. Experimentation was not only tolerated but encouraged, and optimism abounded among us graduate students—if not among our older relatives and friends. In our familiar circles, there was no great distinction between men and women as far as freedom to discuss was concerned. I had come a long way from unthinking conformity. Living away from my community, I had worked out my own schedules and personal priorities and had a sense that I was better informed about church matters than the Sisters who had stayed at home. I believed God existed and took care of me, of us, and of the church. I had learned through friendships that other religious orders were not so different from our own and laypeople had some views about life that were worth considering.

I remember one sincere lecturer who convinced me that any conflict between faith and reason was only apparent. Tenets of belief were true, and if they *seemed* to be unreasonable, one just needed to think more or more deeply or wait a while until more facts were available or until better thinkers than I would explain how they harmonized. My superficiality became somewhat apparent to me when a few years later an educated woman on a plane asked me rather elementary questions about the relationship between believing and proving God's existence. I had to write to a smart companion from graduate student days for enlightenment, for the kinds of questions she asked had not been part of the curriculum.

I did not go into religious formation work after all, for now our college was in need of a philosophy teacher. Teaching full-time, living in a student dorm as a prefect, and fulfilling various duties as a sponsor and committee member were completely absorbing. I began each class with a spontaneous personal prayer. The students' questions were increasingly about ethical decisions, war and peace, prejudice and discrimination, and above all "relevance." The customs of traditional on-campus religious societies as well as the notion of premarital chastity seemed naive to many of them. More older students started to enroll, and they posed new questions about business ethics. One of them, a black Baptist woman, paid me a compliment I greatly appreciated when she said, "Sister, you know you're really not a Catholic. You're a Christian." The curriculum was revised, and several liberal arts requirements—including philosophy—were decreased to make room for disciplines like sociology and psychology. Competency-based education was the rage, and we introduced concentrated courses that were offered only on alternating weekends.

Meanwhile, in the Congregation we were renewing big time, and some of us younger Sisters were delegates to the general chapters that made momentous decisions. The religious dress or habit was gone; the daily schedule was almost entirely left to personal choice; we started to view our work as ministry and the quality of our relationships as extremely important. My personal relationship with God, though not very intimate, became a kind of anchor in the midst of continual change. On the one hand, as a group we were trying to be more organized, efficient, and up to date; on the other hand, we were starting to share prayer and views with each other on deeper levels than ever before. Superiors consulted us more and ordered us around less. Large communities broke up into small living groups. A number of Sisters, including my younger sister, decided to leave the Congregation to find greater satisfaction and use their talents better elsewhere. Even in the church, the opportunities for women, married or single, were diversifying and increasing.

When I celebrated twenty-five years of religious profession, the contrasts between the present Congregation and the one I had entered were quite obvious both in externals and in the individual Sisters' viewpoints and attitudes. When I entered the convent, who could have foreseen that I would live in a predominantly Mexican federal housing project, would research shipwrecks for a state agency, would visit a Baptist retreat center, would make friends with the ecumenical Brothers of Taizè, and would spend semesters studying alone abroad? I felt like I had lived through two different churches without ever changing my religious denomination.

I was secure as a tenured professor, teaching and publishing in philosophy even though the college no longer offered a philosophy major; and I was continuing to learn from my students, who were increasingly Mexican-American. They challenged me to teach subjects I had never been taught, such as non-Western philosophies. In the course of exploring Latin American philosophy, I met the philosopher-theologian Enrique Dussel and co-translated his book *Philosophy of Liberation*. My encounter with Dussel convinced me that European philosophy was ultimately at the root of much oppression. He proposed a theoretical framework for a different philosophy and convinced me that philosophers had a responsibility to liberate the oppressed—views quite opposite to all I had been taught. Not only minorities but women were still among those oppressed. I also began to see Christ more as a power that was not completed in the past but continues to be revealed in men and women today.

Some of our younger Sisters were becoming feminists, but at first I didn't take them too seriously. After all, I said to myself, everyone should know the word "man" is still a term in English for the whole human race! In the mid-80s, Elizabeth Schussler-Fiorenza's *In Memory of Her* helped me to see how language can legitimate societal oppression and the cultural marginality of women. Not only philosophy but theology also by definition is engaged for or against the oppressed. The writings of thinkers like Rosemary Radford Ruether, rather than my personal experiences, led me to ponder my images of God and the interrelation of human beings with nature. Feminists to me were people who noted exclusion and oppression, not only of women but of anyone anywhere, and took steps—in my case, speaking and writing—to eliminate such discrimination. I began to speak out for women even though I did not think that I myself experienced oppression.

Craving more challenges, I renounced tenure and accepted a position as head of the philosophy department in a small Roman Catholic seminary in upstate New York. All the students were men who majored in philosophy, so I was delighted to teach a variety of courses each year. In addition, I got a closer look at the "inside" of the church and the life of priests. All the faculty members were deeply involved in daily church services and in the spiritual formation of the seminarians. It was the best experience I have had to date of a discipleship of equals. On Saturdays I volunteered to teach Hispanic prisoners in the local penitentiary the basics of their faith. I reactivated my keyboard skills, learned to cross-country ski, earned an MA in Religious Studies, actively chaired the social justice committee, and imagined I would remain there until retirement.

A high point of this period was delivering a lecture on "A Process View of Divine Providence" to a gathering of Sisters from about twelve different Congregations that were named "Providence." I developed a philosophically consistent worldview which illuminated divine providence as an aspect of God and showed some of its implications for our daily lives. Bergson, and some of Whitehead, helped me view God as both more intimate and more challenging; liberation thought suggested some practical applications. We are co-Creators with a God who constantly lures us to transcend ourselves and to further goodness. God is a liberator and asks us to liberate ourselves, others, and the earth from numerous kinds of oppression.

A low point of this period was a personal experience of discrimination against me as a woman. My happy life in the college seminary was disrupted by a new rector who saw women predominantly as servants and would not honor the contract that for years had given me virtual equality with priests on the faculty. Comfortable within the religious "system," I now found myself outside, excluded from its benefits. Almost sixty years old, I could not find a philosophy position. Even though I was disenchanted with and very critical of the organization of the church which allowed and even promoted the discrimination I was experiencing, I kept in mind the distinction I believe exists between the Reign of God we are all charged to promote and the Roman Catholic Church. To me they are not antithetical, but the church has a long way to go before it is the community of disciples Jesus envisioned and directed us to build. My views on the church were influenced by Leonardo Boff. I was impressed by Jon Sobrino's insistence that the ultimate for Jesus is not simply God or church or the kingdom of heaven but the Kingdom of God, or God's concrete relationship with us in history. The Reign of God is the establishment of justice and right with regard to the poor, whom God favors. It is here but also still coming in its fullness.

Process thinking also strengthened my desire to accept what I believe are invitations from a provident God; so when the employment situation was no longer life-giving, I set out on a new life in the Midwest as a member of the spiritual formation team at a Roman Catholic seminary for older candidates. Here I tried to help seminarians see and take steps to become integrated, holy human beings ready to collaborate with others in furthering the Reign of God in their ministries. Idealistic? Definitely! Unrealistic? I hope not. Challenging? Absolutely.

For the past three years I have been an elected General Councilor in my religious Congregation. Although I do not teach in a classroom, I find almost daily opportunities to share not only faith but feminist and liberationist views.

2. TENSIONS

The tension I see between philosophy and religious faith is stimulating rather than stifling. Philosophy can forestall superstitious idolatry, and faith can situate human beings and human reason in their proper non-supreme place in the scheme of things. Neither sentimentality nor conformism co-exist well with a demand for reasons and principles. But the one God, immanent and transcendent—and ultimately mysterious—is never fully comprehensible to any finite mind.

A certain philosophical insight aided greatly in releasing me from religious formality or conformism. St. Thomas's critique of Aristotle led to his metaphysical insight that existence (*esse*) is an act but not a form. Accepting the primacy of act helped me put into perspective a number of items. What is formed can be conceptualized or defined, but abstract concepts cannot capture the full, vibrant reality of existents. I think Bergson shared this insight when he said intuition, rather than intellect, coincides with enduring being. The positive relation and distinction between act of existence and form is analogous to the distinction between intellectual intuition and intellectual conceptualization; life and law; and Reign of God and church. The first member of each "pair" actualizes the second, not vice versa.

The moral philosophy I was taught stressed careful reasoning and acceptance of personal responsibility, but it tended to separate personal from social ethics. Liberation thought has shown me that "the personal is political." Individuals are in systems, which we as individuals and groups are responsible to change when they are exclusive and oppressive.

My basic faith convictions are expressed in the Apostles' Creed or the Nicene Creed, but I am aware that creeds employ language appropriate for the historical period in which they were articulated. In every generation those with a talent for thinking need to re-express basic truths concerning God, and some expressions seem more adequate than others. My image of God is of a being eminently alive and loving, and Jesus is the best expression of God. In Jesus—whom I know through Scripture, personal prayer, and others' insights—I can best tell who God is and what God wants of us.

Feminism has uncovered for me many faults in my church. I do not find feminism conflicting with the most basic tenets of my faith, which have not always been expressed accurately in particular traditions or customs. I believe we are all equally children of God. Close reading of the Gospels shows me that the Herald of God, Jesus, not only did not exclude women or other marginalized people even though he lived in a very patriarchal culture, but actually was partial to them. I believe that the Spirit within and among us continually calls us to more inclusive care and service of neighbor. I would like to believe (but facts often deny it) that the consciousness of humankind as a whole (through education, communication, and other means) is developing. At our particular historical period, the work of many women (and some men) is sharpening our awareness of how whole groups, and especially women, have been excluded from benefits available to human beings and is suggesting means to make them equal participants. Some have shed blood; others have been persecuted and ostracized for pointing out such discrepancies. I benefit from their sacrifices and am grateful to them all, known and unknown.

When I accepted a philosophical view that was predominantly European, I had a more hierarchical view that was prone to consider women inferior. This outlook was incompatible with the basic metaphysical views of some of these same philosophies—in particular with process and liberation philosophies as I came to know them. But it was quite compatible with views of God as absolutely almighty, immutable, and omniscient. Such theologies of divine supremacy do not seem to harmonize well with the God presented in Scripture, who is affected by relationships with creatures, so I have become increasingly critical of them.

In sum, while I can see ways in which tensions have existed between philosophy, feminism, and faith, it seems to me that contradictions between and among them can be minimized or even eliminated. Thomistic philosophy gave me a metaphysical framework; liberation and process thought provided a basic anthropology and social philosophy; Scripture studies enlarged the vision of God I had from dogmatic theology; and feminism has helped me keep focusing on current conditions in our world. Now in my seventh decade of life, I think faith (not to be equated with a particular religion or church) for me is the most basic yardstick such that I will persistently question new views that I don't (or don't yet) see to be compatible with what I believe about God and creation. I would like to stay in dialogue with any view that is new to me and try to determine whether it fits with everything that I know and believe. As a trained philosopher, my criteria for what I accept as reasonable are, I think, quite strict. But I don't think that my reason, or any human reason, can encompass *all* reality and truth.

3. REWARDS

Although I can imagine more exciting periods of history than our own, I am grateful to be alive at a time and place when a woman can be a believer, philosopher, and feminist—and be asked to write about it! To remove any one of those components from who I am would for me be crippling indeed. Secure in the love of God for me as an individual, I feel more free to explore various philosophical positions and am more daring in speaking out against injustice and struggling for women's liberation. I am committed to ever-greater trust in God, to continual search for reasonable explanations, and to emancipatory efforts for oppressed human beings. In my fifty years as a professed religious, God has been lavish in love and mercy, and I can never be grateful enough for the opportunities to know God better and appreciate divine concern and support. I have something in common with all mono-theists, philosophers, and liberators. Even though I would also differ from them in many respects, if we do indeed agree on a few basic principles, mutual dialogue and enrichment are possible.

The criteria given by Thomistic, liberation, process, and feminist thought, along with the praxis of Jesus, also enable me to see the poverty of what I consider to be extremes in the areas under discussion, such as: believers interested only in converting others to their religious systems; relativistic philosophers unwilling to adhere to any basic principles; or feminists hostile to promoting the welfare of anyone except women. I have not met many such people. I do continue to meet persons whose views correct and complement mine. May we continue to awaken in one another a fuller appreciation of divine and human reality and truth.

FIVE

Reflections on Identity

JEAN BETHKE ELSHTAIN

When I was a graduate student of medieval and reformation history, I picked up and read a work that had a rather dramatic impact on me as an academic-in-training in the human sciences who was soon to find herself stifling within the confines of the then-dominant positivistic and behaviorist models in social science. That book was Erik Erikson's *Young Man Luther*.[1] When *Young Man Luther* was first published, there were a number of excited discussions about "psycho-history" and restoring a rich understanding of human subjects in the social sciences. Although the book was not assigned in any of my graduate seminars—I was doing graduate work in history before the tumult of the times and my own calling bade me turn to political theory and ethics—it did surface in discussions from time to time, almost surreptitiously—rather like a dotty relative people don't invite to parties but who turns up anyway.

For one particular seminar, we had read excerpts from Luther himself—always a treat and occasionally terrifying given Luther's volcanic eruptions—and, if memory serves, portions of Roland Bainton's biography of Luther. During our discussion session, no doubt brandishing my hardcover edition of *Young Man Luther* as I did so, I queried our instructor, a young man fresh out of Harvard. (He went on to become a very famous historian). Had he read this work, I wondered, and if so what had he thought? The professor smiled benignly, then said he had not and he doubted that he would as a number of other distinguished Reformation scholars had already, and in no uncertain terms, expressed disinterest in the "anal" theory of history. To me, this assessment of Erikson's Luther, made off-handedly, was far more reductionistic than anything in Erikson's treatment of Luther. *Young Man Luther* struck me then and strikes me now as powerful (in its own way) and appreciative, written, of course, from a specific and well-spelled-out angle of vision. Was there really nothing of value to be learned from Erikson's *Young Man Luther*? Apparently not, if my professor was right.

But I persisted in my conviction there was much that was compelling to be derived from Erikson's Luther, formulations and nuanced analyses having to do with the self and with the seriousness of what it means to "mean it." For there are among us children who, at a tender age, are overtaken by an unspecified but nonetheless clear seriousness of purpose and intent and who grow up to be adults who are determined, somehow, to "mean it." I knew because I was one such: an earnest graduate student even as I had been an earnest child, an earnest participant in my Lutheran Confirmation Class, where we had worked at memorizing Luther's great pedagogical work, that classic in Christian formation, the Small Catechism. I yearned for the day when I would be able to state boldly what Luther proclaims so often at the conclusion of his wonderfully direct and pithy expositions of each article of the Apostle's Creed. These words are: "This is most certainly true." This is most certainly true.

If only. For by 1963 I had become a doubter. In fact, I think I had taken to calling myself an "agnostic." That sounded so sophisticated and mature. And the faith of my mothers and fathers had fallen under a cloud of suspicion, first, in undergraduate school and, now, the cloud growing ever darker, looming larger, in graduate school. Somewhere along the line I had picked up a higher-education leitmotiv: reason and the higher learning are one thing; faith another.

The twain rarely, if ever, meet . . . or should. In this scheme of things, faith is reduced to simplistic fideism while reason, on its own separate track, zooms ahead, compelling the mind to go in any direction and to think any thought, but only after it has jettisoned any and all barriers to thought, like that albatross of atavistic belief! That, at least, was the dominant story—not couched so brazenly, of course; rather, it was simply there, part of the air one breathed as a graduate student in the late 1960s.

During my undergraduate years I had taken to heart all the rationalistic world-views being presented. I recall thinking myself a deist for about three weeks when we studied the Enlightenment in a history honors course. After all, I didn't want to be one of those left behind at the station when the engine of history lunged forward, true to its teleology of certain progress and spreading Enlightenment. These goals demanded casting away all sources of error and darkness, including faith: all slated to disappear. And I was enjoined, by the prophets of rationalism, to have done with all of this—to shed this debris—without regret; if anything, with a kind of smug self-certainty.

But this wasn't working for me by the early 1960s. The only existentialist I found sympathetic was Albert Camus—and he insisted that he was not an existentialist at all; rather, he was a man torn between belief and unbelief, a man in a lifelong dialogue with Christians. Camus helped me to settle one point—you could be a good person without being Christian. Slowly I realized (very slowly, I should add) that that wasn't, finally, what Christian belief and theology were all about. There were all sorts of ways to acquire the skills of decency, perseverance, even fellow-feeling. Rather, the gravamen of faith lay elsewhere. Reading Erikson's *Luther,* I learned of the great reformer's torment and grief, his doubts, his fit in the choir when he declared, according to legend, that he was nothing; that he no longer existed; that he had lost his *identity*—the word crept into my vocabulary. "Ich bin's nicht." A dark obliteration and then the moment—saved by faith alone. *Sola fides.* I was drawn to Luther's humanness, his gargantuan appetites, capacities, and energies and his struggle, frequently with himself as "his own worst enemy," a saying of which my mother was inordinately fond.

Why the pull of Luther? He was part of my familial past and my by-then unraveling faith. More importantly, his doubts mirrored my own. I no longer knew exactly who I was. The daughter of my parents, granddaughter of my grandparents; a sister; a wife and mother; a niece; an aunt—all the family markers were in place. But once I had been a Lutheran Christian. Now I wasn't sure. Once I had wanted to be a writer full stop. Now university teaching was beckoning and seemed, to boot, more reconcilable with motherhood. I had married my high school sweet-heart, a four-star athlete and champion wrestler. Young and uninformed, we had three daughters in less than four years. One of these girls—the eldest—was born with brain dysfunction and mild mental retardation. My then-husband couldn't handle it—not in a way that served my daughter's well-being. Things did not go well for us. By 1964, when that marriage ended officially, in addition to three daughters, the oldest of whom was four, I had a B.A. in history and an M.A. earned under the auspices of a Woodrow Wilson Fellowship, and I was applying to Ph.D. programs to begin work toward a degree in political science, with a focus on political culture and philosophy. I remarried, bore a fourth child, and by age twenty-six I was en route to the Ph.D. in politics, at Brandeis.

You might think that things were pretty clear for me: that I had a smoothly paved career path (as we say these days) before me. Not so. Something was off, wrong, incomplete, missing. Remember: I had learned the word *identity*—I and just about everyone else in my generation. And therein lies much of the turmoil of our recent past. Identity became a fashion more frequently than it became a serious accomplishment. The texture and depth of Erikson's vision—what had attracted me to his work in the first place—faded as pop versions of identity, identity crises, and identity reversals and transformations soared.

But Erikson was no pop-therapeutic nostrum trafficker. His work was serious in the best sense of the word. He was poignantly aware of the ways in which the firm foundations of identity may shiver and quake. He had in mind the immigrant experience, tied, for so many tens of thousands in the aftermath of World War II, to the refugee experience. All the moorings of life unleashed as individuals and families were compelled to begin all over again in a new land, with a new language, a new culture. I wasn't that far removed from the immigrant experience myself. My maternal grandparents hadn't been fleeing persecution, but they had been folks under tremendous pressure and the signs, for them, weren't good in turn-of-the-century Russia. They were part of a group called Volga Deutsch—ethnic Germans living in Russia. I would muse sometimes about how contingent were our existences when I thought of their story and its overlapping happenstances: if my grandparents, who met and married in America, hadn't been children in émigré families, not only would I not exist, they would have been killed or exiled during World War II. A lucky thing, coming to America. As a result, I had no doubt, none whatsoever, about my national identity: I was an American through and through. I loved school. I loved the English language. I loved to read. I loved stories of our heroes and founding documents. Being an American: that was a source of both pride and responsibility.

I discovered that for many of my fellow students in the late 1960s, being an American seemed a source of shame or chagrin. I was stunned by the level of animus displayed by young people my age with their whole lives before them, many of them privileged. Maybe it's the East Coast, I would muse, for I was now at Brandeis University in a new Ph.D. program in politics. Endless hours of talk about what a horrible, repressive, oppressive, imperialistic, lord-knows-what, country we were forced to live in. As classmates declaimed, I, while not denying various grievances, even horrors, reminded them that America was the place in which they were getting the best education money could buy and they and their dear ones lived in safe and secure homes in a stable civil society. This is what the rest of the world yearned for and lacked much of the time. The civil rights revolution, to be sure, was a revelation to me and led me into deeper questioning of America's failure to live up to her own most cherished premises—something I had already begun to do in any case with American Indians. (I'm from a small town in Colorado so the focus is natural, if you will. It was but a few years on from the Wild West when I was growing up.) So you make things right. You follow Dr. King, who loved America and yearned for a "beloved community" and who tapped all my deepest Christian impulses about love and service to one's neighbor. And he did so from a generous, full-hearted, stance, not an anemic and sour one. So I was shocked to hear King attacked and violence celebrated by privileged college students who wouldn't pay the price for violence in the streets.

I argued that we needed to affirm, not simply negate. Because Erikson agreed with me, I drew Erikson into debates and peppered my papers with Erikson quotes—this by contrast to a rising cult of violence among my peers, as if violence could wash away and destroy the old and leave something new and whole rather than something devastated and torn in its wake. I was told that I was "anti-progressive" or just simply "bourgeois," about the worst thing anybody could be called in those days! But my family, my faith background, and the great people I read and clung to (Camus was especially important) helped me to avoid all-or-nothing fits and starts. For the task and challenge of identity was that it named an ongoing effort to forge the "self" into a coherent "something." This involved striving for wholeness (in Eriksonian terms) through various and complex affirmations and negations. Should negation triumph, all would be bitterness and gall, one's life as ashes in one's mouth.

I was struck by the bitterness manifest in so much of the rhetoric of student "radicals." Everything stank. You couldn't trust anybody over thirty. The "system" controlled everything. The United States government was part of a vast, interlocking conspiracy aimed at crushing proletarians and peasants everywhere. And should one point to hopeful signs and possibilities? Well, these, too, were ground up in the negation machine as so much "artificial negativity"—women protesting toxic waste sites, or African Americans protesting segregation—looks good, sure, but it isn't really "negativity" as the "system," that all-controlling menace, can absorb protest and render it moot.

What happens to the quest for meaning and integrity in these situations? From Erikson, I learned that in order to "experience wholeness," a young person must feel a

> progressive continuity between that which he [sic] has come to be during the long years of childhood and that which he promises to become in the anticipated future; between that which he conceives himself to be and that which he perceives others see in him and expect of him. Individually speaking, identity includes, but is more than the sum of, all the successive identifications of those earlier years when the child wanted to be, and often was forced to become, like the people he depended on.[2]

What I saw at work in many of my classmates was the brittle *totalism* Erikson contrasted to a more fluid and flexible *totality.* The "more primitive" black or white, all-or-nothing demands of totalism drove so much political and cultural thinking in that era. Either America was the greatest country on earth or she was imperialist Amerika, the fascist fraud. Perhaps what shocked me most was the frequently and openly voiced vituperation against one's parents, up to and including demands that the family be smashed as a repressive institution. Parenting was regressive; you were a slave of the system if you had kids. This was news to me. Sure, I felt like a slave to my kids often enough, but so far as I knew we weren't taking orders from some subliminal source that controlled every aspect of our lives.

Words like ingratitude would come into my mind when I heard such fulminations. I wanted to say: Shame on you. How could anyone talk about his or her family like that? Were there that many worthless, distracted, controlling, reactionary, cruel mothers and fathers abroad in the land? Whence the animus? Why should one expect one's parents to "fully understand" everything one was doing? The hostility toward parents seemed the flip side of wildly over-inflated views of unending parental warmth and symbiosis with no friction: not growing up, in other words. I understood this as an intellectual argument but I never felt I got to the heart of the matter. Not really. My relationship with my own parents had been fractious from time to time, especially with my mother, but I loved them and was close to them and knew that my most basic struggles and accomplishments were tied to identifications with both of them.

The youth culture rapidly got pinioned in a whirligig of its own making—with lots of help from various commercial/cultural forces. Because you had to avoid at all cost seeming a sucker or a sell-out or being co-opted —the really awful thing—you could never commit yourself to anything or any person for very long. So you were to drop out. But what, exactly, did that mean anyhow? You were supposed to undermine the machine. Which machine? How does one do that? You had to f— the system. But if the system is everywhere and controls everything, there is no coherent strategy available for attacking it. And all of this rhetoric was couched on such an abstract level it had no critical purchase in dealing with actual social and political arrangements. Nevertheless, people tried to reorder their identities around such negations and totalisms. As all these tumultuous cultural struggles were swirling all around me, I was also, as a student of political science, grappling with a regnant view of the human person that struck me as utterly fantastic. I refer to a view that sees the individual as an atomistic calculator of marginal utility, a view that was on display in political science and the social sciences more generally. Would I—could I—survive this mechanistic approach to politics, with its reductionistic construal of identity? There was a rather delicious irony that suggested itself amidst the confusion and hard work and by-now permanent sense of upheaval and cultural dislocation, and that was that the disconnected, self-serving self of what later became rational choice theory in social science and the disconnected, alienated, mistrustful self of much of the student culture were not opposites at all. They were peas in a single pod. Ultimately everything came down to "me" in these schema.

In the student culture, this me was a "don't tread on me" me, although together we could do lots of treading on other people. This was the era, remember, when "exclusive relationships" were condemned in the name of a wholly abstract vision of total individual freedom, when some of my acquaintances hid their marriages or lied about how intense a relationship was because an "exclusive relationship" meant that you had "sold out." I was on the suspect list from the start, being married with children, hence guilty of perpetuating a—here a new word of opprobrium was now available—patriarchal family. I had been raised in a matriarchy, so the uniform image of oppressive Fathers had no resonance for me and was hard to square with all the reading I was doing about the mild, conforming organization man, featuring father as a hard-working nerd who takes orders all of his life.

One way or the other, whether in "hard" social science or in much—not all—of the student culture, what was being repudiated was one's own origins. Erikson was apropos here as well. He ties identity to a "basic trust in one's origins—and the courage to emerge from them."[3] That, surely, was something very different from smashing one's past or embracing modes of analysis that made unintelligible the care and tending one had received that helped one to grow up, perhaps to become a social scientist who could then negate human sociality and interdependence and embrace a model of a free-standing utility maximizer. One way or the other, folks seemed incapable of holding "change and continuity" in a single frame. The irony here is that if Erikson was right, it was the "well-established identities" that did best with radical change because these identities didn't fly apart and break into brittle little pieces.[4] Those strong enough to perdure were the ones gifted with a fighting chance to transform themselves and the world around then in meaningful ways—not through huge cataclysms but through the patient building up of a more decent world.

Well, it is more than a few years on from those tumultuous times. Many of the people my husband and I knew then dropped out, never to be heard from again. A few killed themselves; a few went mad; others spend their days reliving the good old days, telling war stories about student strikes and sit-ins and communes. Many got things together (in an Eriksonian sense) by animating their capacities for generative activity, for love and for work, and they do what most people do—try to raise families, be decent neighbors, and make a living, The reductionistic model triumphed in much of social science, even though the epistemology that drives it has been so thoroughly critiqued it is a rather hollow shell of a building.

There is another phenomenon that reached the "take-off" point over the past fifteen years or so, and it is not unrelated to the forces I have described that preceded it, namely, so-called *identity politics*. In one dominant mode of expression, identity politics speaks to a collective loss of trust and hope in our capacities to act in common with others. As American culture moved into the era of identity politics, the thinker who had helped to name so many of the discontents of his own time—Erik Erikson—faded from view.

When Erikson died a few years ago, it was as if he had fallen off the face of the earth—at least insofar as the human sciences were concerned, where the regnant rational choice model of the human had triumphed utterly, a model based on a being, in other words, who cannot distinguish qualitatively as between different "utilities." But the rushing tide of econometrism cannot be the entire explanation for Erikson's disappearance from academic scholarship. More critically, I think it is simply that Erikson's theory is complex and puts pressure on any and all who wish to be simplistic by trafficking in One Big Idea as the key to open all secrets, whether that One Big Idea is rational choice or evolutionary strategies derived from macro-biology, or some other perspective that takes hold and spreads well beyond its sphere of reasonableness and competence. If to this one adds our parlous political times, it helps explain why Erikson is, at least temporarily, eclipsed. For Erik Erikson, identity isn't simply given by what we used to call an "ascriptive" characteristic like race or ethnicity or sexual orientation or gender. Rather, identity is a task and an achievement. Much of the stuff of identity is given, or many features are, but identity is also about how we deal with what has been dealt, drawing on our familial, individual, and cultural repertoire.

For hard-core practitioners and theorists of identity politics, however, identity emerges more or less automatically given such predetermined criteria as race, ethnicity, sexual orientation, and so on. You are what you are. If you seem to abandon what you are, then you are a phony or fake version of what you are. An example of such narrow identity definition occurs when advocates of a narrow feminist identity politics describe a female candidate or officeholder who espouses political views other than their own as a male in female drag, as "male-identified," suggesting that all "authentic" women/feminists will think alike, especially on the high-voltage issues like abortion. Such a clumsy (and fundamentally anti-political) notion can only be supported if one believes there is such a thing as the female or the woman's point of view, a claim that was once considered sexist and is now, in all too many circles, the purview of *bien pensant* spokeswomen.

These narrowing imperatives extend, if anything with more vehemence, to race and ethnicity. So we have "white culture" and "black culture" and "queer culture" and so on. Now, of course, we have a rough-and-ready notion about "black culture"—we think of jazz and hip-hop and Motown and other cultural phenomena that have entered into, transformed, and enriched American cultural life beyond measure. They are "black" but they are also ours as Americans. For strict identity politics advocates, however, this sharing is itself bogus and means that non-blacks are trying to appropriate "black culture," even to "steal it." Furthermore, consider what on earth "white culture" might mean. I have absolutely no idea. Race just isn't a coherent category for thinking about culture. We would have to know whether a person's parents were recent immigrants or long residents; hailed from the Scottish Highlands or Naples; were Catholic or Calvinist; on and on. Identities are particular, not generic and not reducible to race—a pernicious idea that has tormented this century.

Let's take a closer look at the presuppositions that undergird identity politics, beginning with the notion that one cannot in principle make common cause with those who do not share one's identity. Just beneath the surface of such adamant claims, mistrust, fear, a hopeless sense that one will be swamped or beguiled by another are at work. What gets lost is the constructive conviction that, through dialogue and trust, we might come to know a good in common we cannot know alone, or, for that matter, with those others who are "just like me." Here is a good place to issue a reminder of what Erikson calls those "human strengths" that are constitutive of strong yet flexible identities. Hope is profoundly important in building strong identities, rather than rigid and brittle ones. To be able to impart this strength from generation to generation builds trust. "Hope," Erikson writes, "is both the earliest and the most indispensable virtue inherent in the state of being alive . . . trust [is] the earliest positive psychosocial attitude, but if life is to be sustained hope must remain, even where confidence is wounded, trust impaired."[5] Erikson ties hope to maternal experience—to warmth and care and tending. We learn in childhood to reach out to others hopefully rather than to retreat from others fearfully. He then moves on to will and determination and other virtues. Surely, and in light of the fact that, however varied our early maternal experiences, we were cared for by somebody or bodies or we wouldn't have lived to tell the tale, it is a counsel of despair to claim that others, in principle, cannot understand one's own experience—the thesis of incommensurability that is so much a part of contemporary identity politics and identity politics scholarship in the academy. We all started out as helpless, dependent beings, and the stirrings of our helplessness stay with us yet. We can deny these and shove them away from us—I won't be bossed! I won't be managed! I won't be smothered!—or we can embrace others as we were once embraced, not as mother to helpless child, but as friend and fellow human being and citizen, each of us fully aware of our shared vulnerabilities, hopes, and fears.

Those of us who have lived through identity politics totalism have many unpleasant memories of the times when, for example, a male professor of my acquaintance, though expert in the subject matter, was not permitted to teach a "woman's studies" course because, *qua* male, he was "unqualified" by definition as he could never enter sympathetically into women's experiences. In art and literature we do enter into the experience of others all the time, or used to. A totalizing race for purity reminds me of the arguments of anthropologist Mary Douglas in her superb book *Purity and Danger.*[6] Douglas assays primitive notions of taint and taboo and the putative dangers of mixing, of permitting some "impure" element into what had been pure. Identity politics of the totalistic sort longs for the pure and for a version of identity that inexorably links culture to race, with culture construed as epiphenomenal, a direct outgrowth of a racial given. If you buy into this sort of thing, all men and women can do is to bleat at one another from across a great distance. All blacks and whites can do is stay at arm's length. But this generates a politics of resentment and victimization. Coalitions and alliances are shunned in favor of going it alone with one's identity group. The worst forms of groupthink are fueled by the harshest forms of identity politics. Identity reductionistically construed, remember: blood, race, sex. The identity absolutists tell us that we cannot work together; we cannot live together; we have nothing in common as Americans. What we have are demands for recognition based on exclusive claims to difference.

Think about how odd this is on the face of it: I demand that you recognize that we have nothing in common with one another. The dialogic aspects of identity are foresworn in such positions. Erik Erikson talked at great length about forms of mutual activation, about the ways in which aspects of who we are are brought to light and even to life by others who challenge, support, beguile, and vex us. But this more capacious possibility is not what so many young people hear—even in some of our institutions of higher learning.

And what young people hear is vital, because ideas bear performative implications: we act in behalf of concepts and categories. If you are convinced that hope is mushy sentimentalism and that only the hard and the tough will inherit the earth; that trust is for suckers; that you've got to look out for #1, then you are likely to behave toward others in ways quite different from those of a person who has embraced a more hopeful, dialogic, social, active, dialectical view of identity in all its depth and complexity.

Let me add to our list of thinkers one of the great complexifiers of identity, St. Augustine, in order to further underscore these points. Now Augustine was no stranger to identity conflict. Here we think invariably of his *Confessions*. But I have, for the moment, several of his great theological and historic works in mind, including *De Trinitate* and *De Civitate Dei*. Augustine shares his struggles with us. He describes years of "living behind his own back," of shutting his "heart away." Slowly light begins to dawn. We must awaken to that dawn in community: we need interlocutors and friends. We need the practices and saving presences of a community. We are too weak—epistemologically speaking—to discover all the truth by individual reason alone, unaided by powerful feeling and experience. Augustine tells us his heart went into labor and gave birth to humility and this, in turn, catalyzed—activated—understanding. His "credo ut intelligam" is not a counsel of irrationalism or simplistic fideism but an insistence that the mind must be open to many sources of illumination that lie outside itself, so to speak, but that enliven it. Augustine's credo? I doubt, therefore I am. One must live with contingency and in recognition of finitude.

The self should be neither scattered—broken into pieces, incapable of pulling itself together coherently (totality and integrity, Erikson's terms, come to mind here)—nor should it operate from a presumption of what Augustine calls the "Selfsame." The Selfsame is "That which exists always in the same way, which is not now one thing and again something else." Such Selfsameness is for God alone, not for mutable creatures caught in temporality. "Man's mind, called rational, is changeable, never the same. Sometimes it wishes, sometimes it does not wish; sometimes it knows, sometimes it does not know; sometimes it remembers and sometimes it forgets. No one has, therefore, Selfsameness from himself."[7] The self-absorbed person cannot get out of himself and acknowledge his own incompleteness. He wishes to be the "origin of himself," like so many of my student peers a quarter of a century ago, weighed down with the knowledge of their mortality and interdependence. Such a self gets caught in a whirlpool of its own devising and it spins further and further away—from self, from neighbor, from engagement with the created world. For Augustine, many of our modern forms of identity triumphalism would constitute a repudiation of the transcendent nature of the Selfsame. Instead, the category is (so to speak) immanentized and applied to Selves presumed to be their own perduring principle of unchanging self-constitution.

Augustine warns that those overtaken by a need to cast off all recognition of interdependency, those who claim Selfsameness for themselves, are those most controlled by the need to dominate others. They have forgotten how to "yearn" and to live in hope, for it is "yearning," he tells us, "that makes the heart deep." I cannot recall what Erikson's term for what Augustine calls "false pride" might be. Certainly Erikson describes the phenomenon symptomatically. Augustine argues that the fruits of false pride, which we see all about us, include the presumption that we are the sole and only ground of our own being; a denial of both birth and death (that is, finitude); denial of dependence on others to nurture and to tend to us; denial of interdependence on friends, family, colleagues to sustain us. Augustine includes, of course, denying our Maker. "Every proud man heeds himself, and he who pleases himself seems great to himself. But he who pleases himself pleases a fool, for he himself is a fool when he is pleasing to himself."

The recognition of interdependence advanced by Augustine is not a form of self-abasement but, rather, awareness that no one simply "goes it alone." Augustine could very well recognize the strength of many of his own arguments; the beauty of some of his own formulations. But when he writes of them it is from a kind of appreciative distance; his prose doesn't call attention to itself. He is inviting us in. And what he warns about incessantly is what many theologians call the ever-present fruits of the "noetic effects of sin." Simply: in a broken, fragmented, contingent world in which we are not "at one" with God or nature or our fellows, we cannot seek to attain on the level of thought that which eludes us in other ways. Such efforts are driven by totalism in Erikson's sense, in contrast to that good totality which remains open to new discoveries and truths. Epistemological self-certainty circles the wagons round on the assumption one can attain a kind of epistemic completeness and then stop. You could mount a very powerful critique of many philosophic systems on the grounds that they require or encourage this sort of epistemological solipsism.

Let me say just a bit more about why I find Augustine such a great interlocutor in the matter of identity. He is vexed over how we come to know and what it is that knows. Can the mind ever really know itself? I was always flabbergasted by the absolute certainty voiced by many of my peers. Let's go back to a horrid example from the radical student politics of the late 60s–early 70s. Some among my class argued along the following lines: It simply would be the case that if Boston elected a racist mayor (one Louise Day Hicks), African-Americans in Roxbury (the predominantly black section of Boston) would ignite an urban revolt and there would be radical change in Boston. So what radicals should do, these students argued, is to work to elect Louise Day Hicks as mayor of Boston in order to force an explosion and revolutionary change. They clung to this as if it were as absolutely true as the gravitational constant. The wily ins and outs of a pseudo-Marxist teleology of pseudo-history assured them of its truth. When I raised questions about the justifiability, ethically speaking, or the feasibility, politically speaking, of such a stance, I was once again chided for displaying my bourgeois faint-heartedness. Then came the clincher. "To make an omelet, you've got to break some eggs." But those eggs are not your own heads and homes, I said. You can skip away to mom's New York apartment or the summer beach cottage on the Cape. You won't pay the price for this advocacy. Never mind. They saw themselves as sparks to get the flames going. Of course, black leaders saw them as naive nuisances, but that's a whole other matter. Augustine understood this human capacity for cruel delusion very well and recognized that there is never a bright, continuous spotlight shining and showing us what is the best thing to do and what decisions will turn out right.

But we are not without hope. Self-knowledge brings both sorrow and delight. We do live in darkness, but there is a light shining in that darkness. We can come to know, not absolutely but resolutely; we know imperfectly but we do know. We form concepts. We imagine. We believe many things exist that are not personally known to us. How? Through trust, through the shared language that makes possible communication between persons. We yearn for the truth and labor to know it. We come to know through the "beauty of minds brought together in fellowship by listening to and answering questions through signs that are known." Augustine builds a powerful argument against philosophical solipsism, based on his argument against constituting the self as its own ground. We must learn to pay attention, real attention, to our selves, to others, to the world. The world both beckons and enchains us. This is not an "either . . . or," it is a "both . . . and." Knowledge of the world is not a form of violent appropriation but an appreciation of the integrity of things.

So despite it all—the troubles, the pain, the frustrations, the dangers of self-pride or excessive self-abnegation—through it all, trust, hope, and, for Christians, the greatest of all: love. Let us add thankfulness to the list—gratitude. One of our grandsons, our dear Bobby, now three, said to me when he was just barely two and I was swinging him in the backyard on a sunny, crisp day as a slight breeze stirred the leaves in the trees, "Everything is everywhere." This was said as he looked at me after having gazed for a time at the sun, the rustling leaves, the expanse of yard, a cat frolicking nearby: everything is everywhere. It is that childlike awe and wonder at what is that Augustine underscores in words that are so often achingly beautiful.

Delight and wonder are part and parcel of hope and trust. Without hope and trust our hearts are locked away, as Augustine would say. I can understand why children brutalized at an early age are too damaged to come to know hope and trust. But I still puzzle about my peers, my somewhat long-in-the-tooth by now "age cohort." Why were so many of us so hostile? So angry? So prickly? Why did so many of us many embrace a feckless, hence false, view of freedom? Why did so much of the life-affirming joy get destroyed by loveless sex and mind-numbing drugs? I do not know. But this I do know: I have come full-circle, returning to the place from whence I began, which is, of course, a vastly different place given the complex journey I took en route: from doubt to disbelief in dialogue with belief, back to belief in dialogue with disbelief. This move over many years has permitted me to reappropriate and to reappreciate much of what was always "mine" but in a simpler, less nuanced (because childish) form. The upshot: many more questions! I doubt, therefore I am.

NOTES

1. Erik Erikson, *Young Man Luther* (New York: W. W. Norton, 1958).

2. Erikson, *Insight and Responsibility: Ethical Implications of Psychoanalytic Insight* (New York: W. W. Norton, 1964), p. 92.

3. *Insight and Responsibility,* p. 95.

4. *Insight and Responsibility,* p. 96.

5. *Insight and Responsibility,* p. 115.

6. Mary Douglas, *Purity and Danger: An Analysis of Concepts of Pollution and Taboo* (New York: Praeger, 1966).

7. Augustine of Hippo, *Selected Writings,* translated by Mary C. Clark (New York: Paulist Press, 1984), from Homilies on the Psalms, Psalm 121, p. 238.

Part II

TENSIONS AND INTEGRATIONS

SIX

Yes

MARIANNE SAWICKI

Yes has a lot of no in it, or so I have found during my five decades on this planet. I must say some no's to the common premises of this anthology, so that I can profoundly and genuinely affirm its spirit of commitment to philosophy, faith, and feminism. Thus, I start with three refusals.

First, I am no daughter of Sophia. The project that would become this volume began as a family affair. Invitations went out to any who might count herself "among Sophia's daughters." I wanted in, but I wanted out too. Sophia is not my mother. We are just *friends*. But that says a lot. To the Greeks, a "philosopher" was a befriender of wisdom—not a "lover of wisdom," as the textbooks say. Friendship, in the elite Athenian milieu that bequeathed us the academic discipline of philosophy, was the foundation of political and economic power. You needed a network of influential friends to do favors for you; and in turn you would be loyal to them. Making friends with wisdom, then, meant to rely upon her for help and guidance in good times and bad, and in turn, to lend wisdom your support whenever she was neglected or abused. My own "philo-sophy"—my affective relationship with wisdom—feels more like this sort of chosen and mutually beneficial alliance than like the organic and necessarily passionate bond between a mother and a daughter. Sophia did not bear me; we have just befriended each other.

Second, I cannot say I am "committed" to my Christian faith or to my feminism in the same way that I have committed myself to the practices of philosophy. Prior to faith I have no memory of myself; prior to feminism I was not who I am. Faith and feminism are constituent components of my intellectual life, rather than optional commitments that I could just as easily have declined to make while remaining this same human being. Like other aspects of my personal identity, feminism and faith are gifts originating in the special circumstances of my birth into a Polish- and German-American working-class Catholic family in the port city (and historic arch-diocese) of Baltimore. That is the context in which the mothering analogy has its place. I am the church's daughter, and feminism runs in our family.

Third, and despite the distinctions just made, it is difficult for me con-ceptually to separate "philosophy, feminism, and faith" into three contrast-ing activities. This difficulty has been a real handicap for me as I have tried to understand the struggles that other women and men experience, and even more, when I have tried to work with people who embraced one or two of these activities while rejecting the other. In my experience, these phenomena essentially implicate one another. This is not to discount or deny the conflict that many intellectual religious women and men report. I believe it, I have seen it, I respect it—but I just do not know what it feels like to experience the separation and opposition of these components.

Why? Let me tell you how I learned to read. In 1955, as a child of five, I took a seat in a classroom in Saint Francis of Assisi School and watched a woman write G-O-D on the wall. I would learn to call that wall "the black-board" (though it was green), I would learn to call the woman Sister Joseph, and I would watch her put the same signs on the board each morning for a year "because, children, God is the beginning and the end of everything."

"Everything" was everything else that went up on that board, that day, that year, and for the first sixteen years of my formal education: number facts, grammar rules, geographical data, historical events, Bible stories, civics, literature, biology, art, physics, poetry, geometry, French, music, po-litical science, theology, and philosophy. A woman's hand began this for me. The blackboard, moreover, was an egalitarian public space for displaying and asking questions about any sort of content. This, I think, was the cru-cial mechanism in establishing the integration of faith and reason for me. Nothing that crossed the board was above questioning; rather, to question was a way of studying and cherishing.

This is not to say that the religious institutions of my girlhood held nought but sweetness and light; nevertheless the basic ethos of the Catholic classrooms that I inhabited was one of confident openness to any honest in-quiry. (My first experiences of being ridiculed for asking questions occurred in graduate school, at the University of Pennsylvania. The Jesuit college that I attended had neglected to instill in me due reverence for the sacred preju-dices of the Ivy League.)

But there is a lot of no in yes. The blackboard, symbolizing and bring-ing about equal scrutiny for sacred and secular subjects alike, also was a venue of cruel exposure for children less quick-witted than myself. I re-member the ritual humiliations of any who stumbled in their spelling or addition exercises at that board. We did laugh at them. I laughed, and I am sorry for it. Today as a teacher I write on the board, "This is a safe place." That is how I write the name of the deity, for I now know that the one who is the beginning and end of everything is not cruel, but compassionate. With compassion, too, I criticize the administrative misogyny that contributed to the famous cruelties of the Catholic school classroom: the presumption that a black veil *on* the head of a nineteen-year-old made her competent to stand in front of sixty little desks, no matter what was *in* that head. Sister deserved, and eventually got, a better professional preparation for her tasks. When I became a teacher of teachers myself, I tried to convey to professionals what Sister in her ignorance already knew at nineteen: there is nothing more important on earth or in heaven than *this* student standing before me right now. Heaven holds its breath as reality offers itself to the learner in the words of the teacher, and as the learner decides to accept or refuse. It is not the content that makes teaching a holy thing; it is the mystery of assisting a human being to take possession of the rationality that the Creator designed for us and to assent to truth as it confronts us.

Our basic assent *to be* the rational-emotional creatures we *are,* with the particular histories we have, is never going to be a perfect and total assent. But I think it can be a creative crescendo of affirmation, both within each life and as lives join together. Being a woman, at this point in history, with the duties of co-creating oneself and nurturing others, is a way of being human. Being human is the way I experience the creative act of the deity. As far as I can tell, the deity favors those actions and conditions that are conducive to women's holy affirmation of the holy reality that is their created and co-creative being. This seems like a very simple and intuitively clear notion to me: that God glories in women's intelligence and wants us to develop it. And conversely, whatever wills the hobbling of women's creative intelligence is not God, nor is it from God. Therefore we are obliged to withhold our worship and obedience from any such idol. Of course, it is easier to state this than to implement it. In our "doing," we often have to proceed by trial and error; but that very fact, too, seems to be part of the human condition and therefore calls for my acceptance and cooperation rather than my denial or regret.

With these introductory paragraphs, then, I have identified myself religiously and philosophically: as a Catholic Christian and as a realist phenomenologist. The sense in which this identity is also *feminist* will become clear in the next section.

BEHAVING FEMINISTLY

I wish we could stop using "feminist" as a noun and an adjective. I wish we could restrict the term to its adverbial sense. Feminism is a *mode* of acting, a distinctive *way* of setting an agenda and going about various intellectual and practical tasks. "Feminisms," understood as contrastable sets of theories, are no more interesting (and no less) than any other corpus of texts that can be manipulated with philosophical tools. To be sure, in academia there exist feminist classics and feminist dogma and various "schools" or branches of feminism. I have written about such orthodoxies myself in other places. But here, it seems more useful to address the *practice* of feminism, or rather, the competencies and habits through which we exist "feministly" in our institutions, communities, families, and partnerships, regardless of the particular theoretical schools to which we may subscribe.

Once again, my starting point is the classroom. In the early 1990s I was twice called upon to teach a course on feminism: a graduate course at Princeton Theological Seminary in "feminist pedagogy," and the undergraduate philosophy seminar in feminist theory at the University of Kentucky. Deliberately, in each course, the learners and I chose not to structure the syllabus around "important books" or "leading figures" or "key issues." Instead, we organized our work according to desirable competencies, available resources, and emerging questions. The freedom of this procedure was enjoyable, but in each case the students—being good academics!—eventually asked me for a summary statement of "what we have learned in this course." Collaboratively, we then found that any such statement would have to include imperative as well as declarative sentences.

The following list of directives is culled from that work. For the participants in those classes, the directives recall our discussions. I share them here because I think they have some enduring value on their own, as an alternative way of specifying what is meant by "feminism." They are standards to which I hold myself as I aspire to live feministly, and to do my philosophical work feministly. (Readers who are familiar with the classic texts of feminism will easily identify the background of some of these directives.)

1. Before describing women's experience, ask women.

2. Where you find distinctions, make connections. Try to link up the widest possible range of factors in any webwork of explanation. Try to provide for the broadest possible participation in any plan of action.

3. Where you find connections, make distinctions. Question the automatic assignment of personal traits to the categories of gender, class, or race. Watch out for hidden agendas. Slice through stereotypes.

4. Ask who profits from a particular social configuration, and who loses.

5. Refuse to define and to be defined.

6. Refuse authority without negotiation. Take good care of those whom you have vested with power.

7. Investigate origins. They are of three kinds: historical, ideological, and systematic. Philosophy has origins. Rationality has origins. Religion has origins. Investigate them all.

8. Love questions more than you love answers. Decide how you will transmit what you love to the rising generations.

9. Walk the fine line between being excluded and being co-opted. Work on your own timetable and your own agenda.

10. Take the friendship of women seriously.

11. Trust your mothers and aunts. Consult your mothers and aunts.

12. Avoid the "attack mode" in philosophy. Look for the balance point between self-reliance and dependence upon others. Study the works of women as a source of encouragement and energy for yourself.

13. Share. Network.

14. If words are not the appropriate response, then do something.

15. Say yes to yourself. Say it profoundly and with all the deliberation and joy that is in you. You are that yes.

16. Receive actively: stitch today's experiences into the pattern of your knowledges and competencies. Take it; but take it on your own terms, and put it into perspective.

17. Refuse unreal loyalties. Decide whose judgment you will take seriously. Decide for whom and for what it is worth spending your life. Work for that.

18. Choose laughter rather than a pedestal.

19. Ask yourself once in a while, "What are you paid for your silence?" Don't sell your mind for money.

20. Know that everything that is has been written. But know that you too can write.

SAWICKI'S REPORT CARD

Since participating in the formulation of these directives in 1990 and 1991, I have followed some of them more successfully than others in the course of my academic work in philosophy and in earliest Christianity. Several of them can be selected now to serve as criteria for reviewing my work. This review will illustrate how I have experienced the interplay of philosophy, feminism, and faith, under the rubric of a brief examen or "report card."

Stitch New Experiences into the Existing Pattern of My Knowledges and Competencies (#16)

The metaphor behind this directive is mending: a traditional women's practice of renewing old garments by reinforcing holes with patches of newer material. This practice resists the consuming ethos of American culture; it favors continuity with the past and a gentle use of earth's resources. In scholarly life, it means that I try to conserve what I already have by selectively using new material to accommodate the demands of ongoing engagement with reality. In religious life, it means I do not discard the garment of my baptism, but I do maintain it and make alterations so that it fits me as I grow.

When I began graduate studies in philosophy, I was forty years old and had already been teaching for a number of years at the university and graduate seminary level. My earlier academic interests had been in hermeneutics and religious education, especially the instructional practices of the earliest churches. I had formulated the principle that gospel texts were more than the *testimony* of Christian teachers: the texts offered *evidence* of the practices and events that had shaped the content of what was taught after Calvary. With that principle, I recognized that I had split the seams of my earlier professional training: a doctorate in religious studies from the Catholic University of America. Clearly there were holes in my scholarly preparation: I needed to know some more Greek philology, and I needed a detailed technical understanding of the differences between witness and evidence. By coincidence, my career suffered an unexpected tear just then as well. I was fired from my teaching job at a Protestant seminary with no warning and no explanation, just after my husband and I had accepted responsibility for helping my sister raise her three young sons. Thus there was no way to mend my career by relocating to another job. I had to stay put where I was. I sought part-time teaching work at a nearby university, and that is how I came to begin studying for my second Ph.D.

The patches that I needed presented themselves in the guise of post-structuralist social theory, both in philosophy classes and in seminars in the anthropology and geography of gender. Feminist discussions in philosophy of science offered me a new dimension of analysis beyond the literary theory funding the feminist theology and exegesis that I had known up until that time. Social science is oriented toward practices and artifacts. It regards gender as a way of organizing a people's labor, use of property, inheritance patterns, and so forth. In applications such as archaeology and economic history, this kind of science provides a way to observe gender practices as real factors in the production of artifacts—including production of texts. Moreover, gender practices cannot be understood in isolation from the practices that constitute race and socio-economic class. By the early 1990s, revolutionary studies were beginning to appear in the archaeology of gender, race, and class. I was able to transpose the implications of that work onto the question of gender in the archaeology of Greco-Roman Galilee. At a more theoretical level, I came to recognize that the doctrine of the bodily resurrection of Jesus depends upon what is meant by "body," and that that question in turn requires philosophical and anthropological investigation. The central chapters of my 1994 resurrection book[1] argue in favor of a bodily resurrection; but in doing so *realistically*, they insist upon a rigorous examination of how the human body was experienced in Antiquity and how it is experienced in our own culture. Christian resurrection belief, I found, first emerged as an elaboration of first-century Judean-Jewish understandings of the human body's fate, patched over with Greek cultural material. The truth of resurrection claims can be accessible for us today *only* through the historical emergence of resurrection belief, as a culturally conditioned event of the past; yet obviously the facts of the belief's historical emergence do not alone warrant its truth. That truth is not confined to the first century, and so it must be warranted by something equally present in the first century and today. In other words, the fact of resurrection must be neither separated from, nor reduced to, the facts about the historically earliest occurrences of resurrection belief.

The seamstress succeeds when her mendings outlast her. It is too early to tell whether my arguments will hold up. In the short run, though, I was disappointed by the failure of my work to persuade colleagues in the Catholic Theological Society of America that the *historical events* of the emergence of resurrection belief are of decisive significance for faith, or, more generally, that historical investigation of the life, times, material circumstances, and gender practices of Jesus is required by Catholic Christian faith. Before theologians can believe that such historical knowledge is required and decisive, they must first be shown that it is possible and reliable. That is precisely a philosophical task, and I am still working on it.

Study the Works of Women;
Avoid the "Attack Mode" in Philosophy (#12)

For the subject of my doctoral dissertation in philosophy, I chose the early work of Edith Stein.[2] Stein was the student of the great phenomenologist Edmund Husserl from 1913 to 1916, and then became his assistant and collaborator. She published four major philosophical treatises; these were written before her baptism and subsequent turn to topics in spirituality and theology. In addition to those treatises, Stein left extensive comments about her everyday work and her colleagues, both in her correspondence and in notes for an autobiography. Thanks to those personal sources, I was unable to (nor did I want to) hold up Stein's philosophical texts at arm's length for dispassionate examination. Yet her phenomenological arguments work independently of the personal insights afforded by the non-technical writings. Those technical arguments were designed to lead the reader step by step through recognitions of the evidence for the theory that Stein was advancing—a theory of evidence itself, the evidence of the presence of other persons within one's own immediate experience. Stein called that "in-feeling" or "feeling-into"—*Einfühlung*—translated as "empathy" for want of a more appropriate term in English. I found that Stein had elaborated a theory of literacy with hermeneutic and poietic dimensions, and I was fascinated to discover that her own practices of reading and writing did not always accord with her theory.

Perhaps most significantly, I was able to follow how Stein assisted other people to write. In fact, she composed certain important passages of the second book of Husserl's *Ideas,* and he went on to use her published treatises as sources for his social writings of the early 1920s—just after he had declared, in a lukewarm letter of recommendation for Stein, that women had no professional contribution to make to academic philosophy! In practice, then, the phenomenological movement in philosophy was much more collaborative and full of borrowings than it is typically portrayed to be. My own conclusion is that we do an immense disservice to students when we teach philosophical "positions" by indexing them to the famous names of those who supposedly originated those positions—like some rogues' gallery, or a deck of face cards. Philosophy, rather, is a practice of reading and writing, and so can be pursued in modes that are more or less adequate, more or less productive. This practice intersects with social practices of gender and race at various points; for example, in the individualization and ownership of "positions" by men and in the systematic suppression and obliteration of women's participation. The gendering of philosophy may be a guilty practice. But more significantly, it is an intelligible, fascinating, and quite reformable practice. It is possible and imperative, I believe, to practice philosophy—the befriending of wisdom—in ways that expose and subvert philosophy's earlier complicity in the stupidities of gender and racial bias. We do not need new face cards in the deck we deal; we need to understand what it means to deal in faces.

The role of racial identification in early twentieth-century German philosophy is among the questions that I bring to my study of Stein, who was born a Jew in the Polish-German city of Breslau. In 1934 Jews were expelled from teaching posts, and a 1943 philosophical dictionary carefully labels the Jews among the great men of German intellectual life. Both the authorship and the substance of Stein's philosophy came under attack by the ideologues of National Socialism. Phenomenological empathy theory holds that the human body itself is the principle of the possibility of understanding between any two persons. This principle was "disproved" by the Nazi dogma that cultural understanding is possible only on the basis of shared blood, soil, and history. Race became the hermeneutical principle for National Socialism. Thus empathy theory, which asserts the indispensable value of each body and every culture, was officially discredited in the late 1930s and 1940s.

Stein seems to have regarded Jesus Christ as a figure who overcomes nationalist and racist divisions, facilitating the availability of human persons to one another and to God. Before studying her theology in depth, however, I am at present trying to understand her theories of human decision at the individual and the community level. Stein's philosophy of science, employing the common phenomenological distinction between motivation and causality, offers a means of escaping the paralysis of cultural relativism that afflicts contemporary social theory. I continue to devote my energy to the study and translation of her work because of these considerations, although I first took notice of her because I felt I had already spent enough of my life reading dead white men.

Apart from my work on Stein, I have not had much success with "avoiding the attack mode" and finding encouragement and energy in the works of women. An initiative to identify common factors in the teaching and interpretive practices of women in the late 1980s failed utterly. Academic feminists, it seems to me, have not yet learned the art of giving and receiving criticism. (This is less true of electronic exchanges than of exchanges in the traditional fora of conferences and journals.) On three or four occasions, book reviews that I wrote with great care and enthusiasm have been met with stony silence or even with tears. This means I have not found an effective way to engage the author in a discourse whose rules are acceptable to us both. On the other hand, when it comes to my own publications, women's reviews of them generally have seemed less acute than men's and they more often miss the point entirely. On one occasion this occurred because the reviewer was using an exceptionally narrow canon or approved list of "feminist" theorists, and simply was unaware of the divergence of empirical social-science feminist theory from literary feminist theory. So I must say that in my intellectual pilgrimage I have not yet reached that promised land where women scholars dwell in mutually stimulating research relationships. Nowadays if I meet someone on the way who claims to be a feminist, I grow wary, and I wait to see how she behaves herself. (I do the same when I meet self-advertised philosophers and Christians and Jews.)

Take the Friendship of Women Seriously (#10)

This is both a historical principle and a principle for prioritizing my own professional relationships. In history, I make the methodological presupposition that transactions among women could be significant factors in shaping events, practices, and institutions. For example, in the archaeology of the Galilee of Jesus, we must ask where and how indigenous women (as brides, caterers, craft workers, midwives, etc.) traveled across the countryside, across villages, and across the doorsteps of village houses—and how those patterns changed when the city of Tiberias was established on the Kinneret lakeshore about 20 C.E., or when the city of Sepphoris near Nazareth was rebuilt during Jesus' childhood. And we must also ask about connections among elite Greek-speaking women in those cities and in Jerusalem. Going on the presupposition that women's friendships existed and could affect events, I have used textual and archaeological data to argue a case that the Passion-Resurrection narratives as we find them in the gospels cannot have come into existence without a certain creative compositional step that—in *that* particular time and place—could have been accomplished *only* by women with a certain kind of elite education and cultural habit. That argument takes several chapters to present in my 1994 book. But its implication can be stated quite briefly. The recognition of the resurrection of Jesus was the accomplishment of intellectual, *philosophical,* women friends after Calvary. It is in no way a product of patriarchy (as the Last Supper/Passion narratives are, I argue). What about before Calvary? Based upon material and textual evidence, in current work I argue the historical likelihood of a friendship between two women in the neighboring seaside towns of Magdala and Tiberias—Mary and Joanna (Luke 8:1–3)—that predated the friendship of either woman with Jesus and that helps to explain how he became influential in Herodian and Roman circles.

As I pursue these arguments, unfortunately, I find that in my professional relationships I cannot continue to "be friends with" all the women I would like to have as friends. The reigning feminist interpretation of Jesus, in Catholic biblical studies, holds that any *historical* investigation of him is to be dismissed as a project of patriarchal positivism. I confess that I have become very discouraged over my inability to convince feminists that the words of women can be detected within the canonical gospel narratives and deserve to be heard. Once again, part of the difficulty is that feminist scholars in biblical studies generally are relying too much upon feminist *literary* theory and are unaware of feminist philosophy of science, much less interpretive techniques for the non-textual evidence, the evidence of material culture.

More generally, friendship negatively impacts the academic fields and practices of philosophy, theology, and biblical studies. When you forget that wisdom is your best friend, you risk setting up exclusive cliques rather than networks to promote inclusion of women in academic life. I would like to see a reconsideration of the ethics of "networking." I would like senior academic women to examine their consciences concerning their desire to "mentor" younger women. The would-be mentor may really want to collect disciples of her own, to clone herself. In such a case the younger person is unfree to reject the "mentoring," upon pain of exclusion from the preferred flock. I have paid dearly for having expressed honest disagreements with powerful women early in my career. The doctor-mother under whom I wrote my first dissertation would not even shake my hand after the defense, and as far as I know has not uttered my name from that day in 1983 to this. To be sure, the generation of women just ahead of my own was horribly abused in the course of their own academic formation; but the generation now in power has got to ensure that those intellectually abusive practices go no further. The seminar room must become "a safe place."

Work on Your Own Agenda, on Your Own Time,
Being Neither Excluded nor Co-opted (#9)

Perhaps the most exhilarating aspect of feminist experience is giving yourself permission to choose your own values and then holding yourself accountable to them. But I can say the same thing in religious and philosophical terms. There is only one God, the God who limits work and frees slaves; that is the only God who deserves to be the focus of human efforts. In biblical Hebrew the same word (*'-bad*) means work and worship. Mary of Nazareth uses this word in her own self-portrait, or so Luke implies with his Greek translation of Mary's words: "Look at me, I am the servant of God only, the only God." (*"Idou hë doulë kyriou,"* Luke 1:38.) This pronouncement depicts a moment of self-recognition, which is at the same time God-recognition, which in turn is the conception of the Savior, the *yes* made flesh for once without any no. In the Torah, carving and inscribing seem to be regarded as identical gestures. The one whom we worship must not be imaged by carving or inscribing: God's image is neither the written word nor the graven idol, but only human beings in our intellectual, emotional, gendered, bodily being (Genesis 1:26–27). This is not to say we worship ourselves. Rather, we worship the one who is shadowed by the least of us, by the least common denominator of us, by that which is prior to and creative of everything that we rightly or wrongly make of ourselves.

Sometimes my undergraduate ethics students ask me what religion I am. I tell them that I worship the God who created their ability to think and feel, and that this is why I work so hard to help students burnish their rational faculties, the mirror in which they can most reliably see their creator. This answer satisfies me but not them, of course, for it presupposes an appreciation of intellectual autonomy that can only be achieved through sustained philosophical study that the students have not yet undertaken. In my own case, it so happens that I learned about this autonomy *as a dogma in the catechism* long before I was ever capable of an intuitive insight into its validity. Children in Baltimore's Catholic grammar schools learned this dogma in four steps:

1. that God created me in the image of God for the purpose of knowing God;
2. that this image still functioned after having been damaged by sin (no matter what the Protestants said);
3. that my own conscience would be my ultimate moral criterion, provided I formed my conscience honestly (no matter what the Pope said); and
4. that I therefore had the responsibility to form my conscience honestly day by day.

This I learned as a girl, before I was ten—in the sense that I could have repeated it back to you correctly. But as an adult I am still learning it from the inside out. It seems to me that this insight is the transcendental root for my feminism, my faith, and my philosophy alike—regardless of the various historical and social influences that have surely shaped them.

So it is this profound and self-defining sense of responsibility for knowing truth and doing right which makes me a feminist, a philosopher, and a religious believer. It is a very personal experience; but I think it can be communicated, even if only indirectly. Before I say how, let me admit that in real life I find I can sustain this insight only for a few moments at a time. Mostly I am dispersed into the various sorts of academic co-optations and preoccupations that I recognize to be such from the vantage point of the insight. But my own inconstancy seems unimportant.

What seems important is that this insight, though self-validating, is also validated secondarily by being communicable and being communicated. It is witnessed to by the behaviors of feminists who find ways to refuse that social disparagement of women that our culture hands us, and find ways of teaching other women to refuse it as well. It is witnessed to by the behaviors of those of us who pursue philosophy in the face of severe economic disincentives. It is witnessed to by the behaviors of religious people who defy the expectations of governments, cultures, or neighbors in order to stay true to their own values. These behaviors indirectly communicate this: that the individuals who do them are free because within themselves they have access to evidence of their own responsible freedom. I do not see a great many of these witnessing, communicative behaviors; but I have seen enough to give me hope.

SAWICKI'S HOPES

Hope is the best we can do when evidence is mixed and testimony is equivocal. Hope became the quintessential Christian intellectual mode when the precanonical Greek-speaking churches, confronting the Platonic fork between the way of knowing and the way of being rhetorically persuaded (*Gorgias* 453a–455a), chose to go with persuasion—*peith, pistis,* "faith." But hope is a philosophical and feminist virtue as well. The grand philosophical systems that we display before students—Platonism, Idealism, Empiricism, Pragmatism, Existentialism, Phenomenology—are all failed attempts at being seamless garments, "one size fits all" universal answer-dispensers for questions that may never be asked. Their ambitions, not their accomplishments, define them. They subsist on hope: not only on the hope that the system will always generate persuasive answers, but also on the hope that people will continue to care enough to ask. And feminism, by definition as the practice and theory of women's liberation, hopes for the happy ending that will put it out of business at last. Like philosophy, feminism exhibits a delayed eschatology as an essential component. As eschatologies, both philosophies and feminisms gradually wear out during use, never quite arriving at the achievement of that to which they aspire. Yet, incongruously, only religious eschatology is commonly regarded as irrational.

Truly, hope is the most rational of all behaviors in the human repertoire. I do not advocate feminist practice because I am a perfect feminist, but because I have managed to be only a C-minus feminist so far. I do not teach philosophy because I am such an excellent thinker, but because I am so poor a thinker that I need the students to do better. There comes a point when a garment has had all the patching it can take; mending is no longer an option. Its fate then is to yield scraps for another kind of stitching: for *quilting.* A quilt is a beautiful and functional new design made from salvaged portions of totally outworn garments. God did not raise Jesus from the dead by merely patching up his tattered body. No, God quilts. (It was my feminist-Calvinist seminarians who figured this out.) What God did with Jesus is meant to be done with us too. We will recognize the pattern in our future, but not until then. And on whose authority do I assert this— Epictetus the pagan, Jesus the Jew, or Edith Stein the Christian? All three thinkers eloquently advocated confidence in divine providence, to be sure, but their testimony alone is not enough to authorize mine. Their testimony, plus my own experience of the essentially teleological and eschatological orientation of human intelligence, authorizes my testimony. And my testimony can do no more than encourage you to look for your own evidence.

This is why I insist so strongly upon a realist stance: a "real feminism" or realist feminism, as I put it in my 1997 book.[3] History is real and is basically knowable through concrete traces persisting in the present; moreover, human choices produce the real future. Therefore it is irresponsible, and thus ultimately irrational, to interpret texts as though their references were inconsequential. On the one hand, texts do eventually cash out in terms of real privilege and, correspondingly, deprivation for various groups of people. On the other hand, information is carried and is readable from artifacts that are not texts. All texts need checking. The Bible is a text. The Bible is an invitation for us to check it; the Bible does not want to be an idol or a last word.

To maintain hope, you have to be willing to acknowledge your fears and then consciously withdraw your assent from the fear. Let me conclude with a litany of things that we—as philosophers, feminists, and women of faith—can decide to fear no longer.

Let's not be afraid of facing historical and personal facts, honestly.

Let's not be afraid of hard intellectual work and discomforting conclusions.

Let's not be afraid of intimidation by powerful people, even powerful feminists, mentors, philosophers, clergy, colleagues, students. Let's not be afraid of losing "friends" or of being betrayed by "friends."

Let's not be afraid of detours and derailments in our academic careers. Let's not be afraid to take time off and time out for the needs of children and teens and seniors and lovers and other friends. Let's not be afraid to keep time for ourselves.

Let's not be afraid of impoverishment and menial labor, when the alternative is dishonesty.

Let's not be afraid of appearing irrational, "strident," impolite, or impious. Let's not be afraid of anyone's judgment but God's.

Let's not be afraid of "going to the board": to public display, discussion, testing, and evaluation of our beliefs before communities of scholars, of women, and of various secular and religious faiths, whether acknowledged or unacknowledged. Let's not be afraid to offer testimony about the evidences that we have experienced. Let's not be afraid to teach.

Let's not be afraid to rely upon Sophia, our best friend and God-given companion.

Let's not be afraid of who we are. We are the women whom God made to know, love, and serve God on earth. This is what it means to be with God, and there is no other way to be happy.

NOTES

1. *Seeing the Lord: Resurrection and Early Christian Practices* (Minneapolis: Fortress Press, 1994). The original title was *Making Jesus: Resurrection and the Practices of Gender, Race, and Class.*

2. Information about Edith Stein (1891–1942) id offered online through links listed on my web page: http://jewel.morgan.edu/~sawicki/steinstuff.html

3. *Body, Text, and Science: The Literacy of Investigative Practices and the Phenomenology of Edith Stein,* Phaenomenologica 144 (Dordrecht: Kluwer Academic Publishers, 1997).

SEVEN

Into the Crucible:
My Art of Living

JACQUELINE SCOTT

I think of philosophy, feminism, and Judaism as communities to which I belong because I have made commitments to them, but also because they have made investments in me. It is less the case that I chose to join them, and more accurate to say that they chose me. The relationship I have with them is often frustrating, and yet generally enlightening. They are the burden I "can neither bear nor throw off."[1] At the same time, they are integral to my identity, and so perhaps, "burden" is entirely too strong a word. As with my race, there are times when I wish that I did not have to contend with some of the baggage that goes along with being a philosopher, feminist, and Jew, but to reject those identities would be to change me fundamentally; to become someone different. And so I struggle with those aspects of my identity and try to make them coexist. In order to bring about this coexistence, a binding agent is required.

Gumbo is a food in which the ingredients vary widely. The distinguishing characteristic of gumbo is the roux—which binds and holds the ingredients together. The "roux" that binds philosophy, feminism, and faith in my life is this notion of "the art of living." Practicing the art means consciously trying to flourish by resisting offered definitions and actively seeking to define oneself. Friedrich Nietzsche referred to these offered (he might also use the verb "imposed") definitions as "nooks."[2] They are sometimes nooks of comfort and security, but they can also be nooks of imprisonment. The first philosophy I read was by the type of writers Alexander Nehamas calls "philosophers of the art of living," and since then it is the type of philosophy I have found the most personally compelling.[3] It is also the type that has had a profound influence on my own formation. As a black Jewish female feminist philosopher, I am continuously on the margins of the various communities in which I have found myself, and so it has been alternatively easy and difficult to resist placing myself in "nooks." On one side, there is no single nook (that I know of) in which I would easily fit, but on the other side people often try to ignore or reduce the importance of one or more facets of my identity in order to "nook" me more easily.

As I result, I have had to make conscious decisions about how I conceive of myself. Philosophy, feminism, and Judaism have all played an important role in helping me to arrive at the person I am now. I see my coming into being regarding these three categories as temporal: first as a feminist, then as a philosopher, and lastly as a Jew. But it has not always been neatly linear, in that with the temporal progression, the three areas have informed one another. I want to explore the ways in which my practice of the art of living has informed my understanding of philosophy, feminism, and spirituality, but also the ways in which those three areas have informed my practice of the art of living. In other words, I want to analyze the symbiotic relationship between the art of living on one hand and philosophy, feminism, and spirituality on the other.

THE ART OF LIVING:
THEORY AND PRACTICE

A few years ago, I was at the Eastern Division meeting of the American Philosophical Association and was waiting in line for the registration desk to open. We had all formed a single line behind the one open window when a second window opened and a group of people at the end of the line hurriedly lined up in front of the second window. Those of us at the front were dismayed that they had jumped the line, and we joked that they all probably specialized in ethics. This joke is humorous only if one knows that philosophy is commonly understood primarily as a theoretical discipline with little practical import, and by extension that philosophers are understood as only studying the discipline and not living it. While such an understanding of philosophy is not new, I am always caught off guard by the number of philosophers who are proud of the fact that their research is not "practical." In short, in contemporary philosophy there is an abyss between the theory and practice of it that very few try to cross.

At the same time, the joke also works only if one assumes that what philosophers study *should* affect their personal conduct. There is a part of us that would hope that ethicists would try to be ethical people. When I first started studying philosophy, I certainly had that expectation, and sixteen years later, while I am no longer so naive about the discipline, I still long to bring theory and practice closer together. As Alexander Nehamas has pointed out in his book *The Art of Living*, philosophy has not always been solely a theoretical discipline, and it is not solely one now.[4] It is this type of philosophy that first drew me to the discipline, and it continues to be the type that I find the most compelling today. By the art of living, I do not mean exclusively what is commonly called "applied philosophy" (e.g., business ethics), which generally entails applying theory to "real life" situations. The art of living denotes a broader category in which the theoretical and the practical are wedded in the *act* of conceiving, structuring, and living one's life. It involves melding the theory and practice of living well so that they become inseparable. It is a form of alchemy in which each is burnished in the crucible of life such that their intrinsic chemical properties are permanently altered.

The art of living involves making conscious decisions as to how one conceives of oneself and practices a meaningful life. The assumption underlying this art is that one's identity and conception of a meaningful life are "up for grabs." With the art of living, then, one does not "discover" one's self, one creates it. This art of living can take on an infinite number of forms, but for our purposes here, I would like to broadly distinguish between two approaches to it: active and passive. These two approaches should be understood as extremes at either end of a continuum, with no one ever truly embodying either extreme. The two approaches are characterized by the extent to which one depends upon others in conceiving and practicing the art of living, with the most active depending on no one else and the most passive being wholly dependent on others.

My own notion of the art of living has been heavily influenced by Nietzsche, and I will use his conception of it in providing an account of the theoretical underpinnings of my practice of it. For Nietzsche, there is no inherent meaning in life to be discovered, and therefore, humans must somehow contend with this meaninglessness of existence.[5] But this meaninglessness presents humans with a paradox: we must create meaning in life, but any meaning we create will eventually decay (meaning that it will no longer be effective in helping us affirm our lives), and we will return to the state of nihilism (a complete lack of meaning in life), which Nietzsche claimed would lead to mass suicide.[6] In order to move away from the danger of nihilism, we have to create meaning in our lives, but the fact that this meaning will decay means that we never permanently escape the threat of nihilism. Nietzsche's conception of the art of living, and its relationship to our human existence, can best be explained by way of an extended metaphor. The void in meaning is like the sea in which we must live, but as human beings we cannot live in a state of nihilism because it will lead to mass suicide. In order to avoid it, he said that traditionally we have created rationales for existence that acted like rafts. One group, whom Nietzsche labeled weak decadents, built rafts that simulated the stability of the earth (*terra firma*). These rafts—think of an oil rig—convinced their inhabitants (passive types) that the raft was the nature of existence: stable and unchanging. In this way, these traditional moralists ignored the existence of the vast fathomless ocean, and in a sense fabricated an alternate existence in which life was static, predictable, and thus intelligible. The problem with such an approach is that eventually either the ocean will overwhelm the raft or the raft will be worn away by the incessant motion of the unpredictable and powerful sea. In either case, its inhabitants will not know how to swim because the life on the rig had denied the existence of the ocean. They will "drown" when they realize that the only truth of existence is that there are no objective, universal truths.

Nietzsche's proposal was not that we should refrain altogether from building rafts (creating meaning in life), but instead that we should refrain from building rafts that give the illusion of permanence. The denizens of an oil rig–like raft either might not survive the shock of the revelation of its insufficiency or, if they do survive, will be too weak to create other rationales. In other words, they might drown immediately or drift aimlessly on the sea. Nietzsche suggested that instead of building oil rig–like rafts that deny the ocean, we create rafts that acknowledge the ocean and its unintelligibility. These rafts would allow their inhabitants to enjoy the ocean, would allow their builders to celebrate their own creativity and to explore the ocean as they saw fit. Most important, this type of raft builder must always acknowledge that any type of raft they could build would eventually fall apart. They must emphasize their ability to create continually new rafts.

To step back from the metaphor, Nietzsche's contention was that we must move away from attempting to discover Truth and instead should try to create values that do not deny their own subjectivity. These values would celebrate and affirm the lives of individuals and others like them. Their purpose is the enhancement of the creator, a celebration of the creator's flourishing, and by extension the enhancement of the species. The type who create such values are a strong type for Nietzsche because they are actively creating values in the face of the meaninglessness of life, and acknowledging this meaninglessness as the opportunity for self-creation. People of this type are not only forming their identity (in Nietzsche's parlance, "becoming what one is"), but also determining the standards of a meaningful life and continually re-creating both as they develop and as the circumstances around them change.[7] Nietzsche acknowledged that most people are not strong enough to carry out this self-creation—and especially throughout their lives—and so they passively depend on others to provide them with both an identity and meaning in their lives. They have someone else build the raft for them.[8]

So that is the art of living in theory. In practice, I have found it to be an arduous yet often satisfying process. At the same time, it is an "art" that I wonder if anyone can truly "master." I did not come to practice this art after having studied it in theory; rather, because of the circumstances of my life, by trial and error, I have undertaken its practice. I grew up in an upper-middle-class suburb of Chicago, and we were one of very few African American families in the area. Because my race, class status, and gender together made me a minority, I had few easily accessible role models to guide me in my identity formation. Moreover, my trusted guides in this formation (family, friends, teachers) warned me that many of the stereotypical role models presented to me by society were a danger. I was then put in the situation of carving out an identity with little guidance and having to resist actively those identities offered to me by the communities around me.

The downside to the art of living is that it is quite easy to second-guess oneself—much easier than if one were depending on a notion of a god, on historical precedent, or on images offered by society. In the latter case, there is an established source of one's identity that is recognized as legitimate. Without this legitimization, one is often left feeling fragmented. Rarely is there one community of people in which one's whole self is fully accepted, and in which the self is mirrored. It is hard to keep from falling apart. I have found myself fighting to remember that those parts of me which others tell me are contradictory, I consider to exist naturally within me. In the end, though, it often only takes a word, a phrase, a glance to dissolve the glue holding me together, for the various aspects of my identity to fall apart, and for me to be plagued with self-doubt as to just who I think I am. "Why study philosophy? Everyone knows that it has nothing to offer black women, and that black women don't have the aptitude to study it. Who do you think you are?" This is the voice of my "doubt spiders," and sometimes they serve as a needed cautionary reminder. Generally though, they are the internalized voices of those who would like me to conform to their expectations of a black person, a woman, a feminist, a philosopher, a Jew. They throw me into a state in which I am plagued by self-doubt and I wonder what I am doing with my life. It is during these times that the art of living seems like a fantasy and I just want the comfort and security of a nook. I want to conform; I am willing to scrap all of the identity formation I have done to that point for the wholehearted acceptance of an established community. This state of cognitive perplexity brought on by seemingly inconsistent ideas is referred to in philosophy as *aporia*. It is this state that, in order to maintain my mental health, has forced me to find, and sometimes to create, various communities that affirm aspects of me, and by extension, affirm my practice of the art of living. Three important aspects of my identity for which I have found supportive communities are as philosopher, feminist, and Jew. In the rest of this essay, I want to examine my commitments to the various communities that have supported me in my attempt to develop that aspect of my identity.

FEMINISM

I cannot remember a time when "feminist" was not part of my vocabulary or when I did not consider myself one. I grew up in a household in which both of my parents considered themselves feminists, and in which, even while she stayed home with her three young children, my mother was an active member of the Panel of American Women. The Panel was one of the few feminist organizations in the mid-sixties to late seventies whose goal was to bring together women of different races, ethnicities, and religions. The Panel was based on the assumption that if women of diverse backgrounds were to band together, share their stories with one another and with others, then they could demonstrate that race, ethnicity, and religion need not be divisive. The members of the Panel avoided preaching theory to the Rotary clubs, school, and religious groups to whom they spoke. Instead, a black, a Jewish, a Catholic, and a White Anglo-Saxon Protestant woman would each present her personal story, and then as a group they would have a discussion with the audience. My mother was the black woman in her chapter of the Panel, and beginning at a very early age, my sister, my brother, and I would be taken to meetings, where we were expected to play, read, or color quietly in the next room or in the corner. I believe it is at these meetings, as well as from the women and men who attended them and acted as my surrogate parents, that I learned about multicultural feminist ideas.

More important in the formation of my feminist sensibilities is the fact that my parents did not just call themselves feminists and talk about it, they also enacted it. Everyone in the family was expected to help at home. Dinner was begun by whoever got home first (often my brother and I would start dinner and then my father would finish it when he got home). My father not only took off from work and went on field trips with our school, but he also stayed home and took care of us when my mom became national president of the Panel and had to travel. I always got the sense that my parents were partners.

My understanding of myself as a feminist is best encapsulated in my adolescent fantasy of my grown-up life. I would imagine that I had my own apartment in which I could eat and read whenever I wanted. I was not a princess, a mother, a successful businesswoman, or someone's soul mate, but a grown woman who had her own space in which she could be quiet and be by herself. Based on this early fantasy, it is probably no surprise that I became an academic—a career in which having a room of one's own in which to work and think is so important.

Another important aspect in my self-formation as a feminist has been my involvement in organized sports. Because of bomb threats leveled against our family, my parents decided to send my siblings and me to a progressive private college-preparatory school starting in kindergarten, and we all stayed through high school graduation. At this school, beginning in seventh grade everyone was required to play at least one competitive sport, and every member of the team was guaranteed to play in the games. It made for less-than-stellar teams, but it also lessened the stigma (particularly for girls) of playing sports. During my time at the school, I played basketball, softball, and field hockey. I do not think I would have tried to play those sports if they had not been part of the school curriculum. The emphasis was on learning skills and playing together as a team, and winning was tertiary. While I proved to be a bad basketball player (I lasted only one season), an average softball player (though I loved it), and an above average field hockey player, I soon came to define myself as an athlete. My older sister was also an athlete, and neither of us ever felt that we surrendered any of our identities as girls by playing sports avidly—and my sister began modeling at the age of thirteen.

By the time I was choosing where to go to college, I was a feminist who assumed that women should assume leadership positions; bond together across religion, ethnicity, and race; be physically strong, smart, independent, and outspoken; and take on the responsibility of ending oppression—in all its forms. After much deliberation, I chose to attend Spelman College, a historically black college for women in Atlanta, Georgia. I decided that I wanted to experience life in the majority—especially in terms of race. It was only in my sophomore year that I realized how profoundly attending a women's college would affect me. I was surrounded by black women who wanted to succeed or who had already succeeded. For the first time, I met other black women who were interested in academic endeavors and who were proud of it. I had black women professors who were ready role models for me, and I had white male and female professors who pushed me to "become what I was."

I strongly doubt that I would have chosen to major in philosophy or to go to graduate school if I had gone to a predominantly white school. It was at Spelman that I first studied feminism, particularly feminisms of women of color, and learned about the intersections of race, class, and gender. I learned the theory that underlay some of the practices of my life. It was also there that I was forced to examine closely my racial identity. During my first year there, I was dismissed by many of the students as an Oreo (black on the outside and white on the inside): most of my friends from home were not black, I did not listen primarily to "black" music, I talked "white," and I loved philosophy. I had failed the authenticity test. I considered leaving Spelman, but after many tearful conversations with my family and friends, I decided to stay and do what a Spelman English professor said that Spelmanites should do: claim our space. I threw myself into enacting the theory of the liberal arts education. My goal was to infuse my entire life with learning and to create a life that was geared toward pushing the limits of my strengths and weaknesses.

Though I had not read any Nietzsche yet, I was engaging in an active dismissal of outside expectations as to who I should be and what I should do, and a conscious exploration of who I was and what I wanted to do—I was building my own raft. I sought out other students who had similar interests and managed to create a support community. I reveled in having so many close women friends with whom I could talk about race issues as well as ideas from class. I had found a group of traveling companions in our journey to "claim our space" and to fill it with our newly discovered essences.

It was an intense time, and for the first time in my life, I really liked myself. I felt as though I had come close to becoming that independent woman of my younger fantasies. I felt full of myself; full of a person who I was coming to know and love deeply. I no longer felt inauthentic.

I had determined my own standards and was striving to live up to them. It was at Spelman that I established my first guidelines for my practice of the art of living: search for continual challenge (to avoid getting stuck in ruts); live a multifaceted life (academics, sports, nurturing friendships, novels, etc); avoid sacrificing my authentic self (meaning my conception of it) in the name of pleasing or placating someone else; surround myself (physically and emotionally) with people who nourished my soul, were serious, reminded me to laugh at myself and life, and were impatient with the standards of normality; remember that perfection is an illusory and not very interesting goal; heal oneself into wholeness by celebrating life and the good and beautiful in oneself.

My upbringing in a family shaped in part by feminist ideas, and my subsequent coming into adulthood in a historically black college for women that not only taught me theories of feminism, but also provided a nurturing environment in which to experiment with enacting them, have largely influenced my adoption and continuing practice of the art of living. In so many ways, I had little choice (due to the lack of ready role models) but to try to actively shape, and continually refine, my own identity. At the same time, I was not immune from the social forces that as a black woman pressured me to see myself and to enact that identity in prescribed ways. The art of living has helped me to negotiate this space between the rock of societal stereotypes and the hard place of few ready alternatives. I credit the theories and practice of feminisms (particularly feminisms of women of color) with introducing me to the *possibility* of taking charge of my identity formation.

PHILOSOPHY

There are few black women with doctorates in philosophy in the United States. In fact, as I write this at the beginning of 2000, I would estimate the number to be below thirty. I do not revel in being among such an elite group. My membership in this group does not indicate me as chosen, particularly gifted, or radical. I do not revel in being one of the "first"; I would have much preferred to be safely number 500. At philosophy meetings, I get puzzled, curious, and surprised stares; my students often have trouble fully comprehending that I am a professor with a doctorate,[9] and I am often invited to attend events, be on committees, and participate in conferences because I am a "twofer" and my mere presence can offer the patina of diversity in a field and academy dominated by white males.

I do not enjoy this "celebrity" status. There are some who seem to be born rebels, and who love to stand out, introduce paradigm shifts, cause conflict, and blaze new trails. I am in awe of these people. I am shy. I am a classic middle child whose first urge is to mediate conflict and make everyone feel comfortable. I prefer to work in groups and to do the less glamorous behind-the-scenes work (I dislike playing individual sports and prefer being a member of the stage crew as opposed to acting on stage). I am not a risk taker. I chose to be a philosophy professor *despite* the fact that I would be placed in the role of trailblazer. I expect this is the case for many others who have chosen lives that put them in such positions. Despite the common portrayal in made-for-TV movies, many of those people of color and/or women who have been "firsts, seconds, thirds" are not born rebels who thrive on conflict. I would guess that my case is the same as many of theirs: it is a role that we have accepted because it allows us to "become who we are." I accept the roles of representing both a race and a gender (and, recently, a religion), of acting as a role model for others who might follow my lead, and of explaining who and what I am for those who have never seen my kind before, because it allows me to do that which I love—teach and study philosophy. I accept those roles because I would not have gotten to practice my dream if others had not accepted those roles on my behalf.

If I could teach and study philosophy without the "celebrity" of being one of very few women of color, I would do it. Nevertheless, I am a woman of color, and I would not wish to be anyone else (at least not most of the time). It is who I am, so this is what I do. I do not want to opt out of the responsibility of representing a race and a gender, and yet I do not revel in it either. I long and work for the day when women of color will be among the many in philosophy and in the Academy. I am trying to work my way out of my job as spokesperson.

I suppose I could have chosen a field of study in which I could have enjoyed more of the anonymity I like, but that would have meant betraying a key tenet of my practice of the art of living: systematically following your passions. In other words, philosophy chose me, and because of my decision to follow my passions, I had no choice but to choose it. I took my first philosophy class during my first year at Spelman in a seminar required of members of the Honors Program. The entire semester was dedicated to reading Plato's *Republic,* and on the first day the professor requested we move our desks into a U-shape and then asked us to comment on the first assignment: Book I. The fifteen eager honors students were stunned into a silence that quickly became long and uncomfortable. Already this class was proving to be the collegiate challenge we craved but were unsure of how to negotiate: the class met two times per week for two hours (so different from high school classes), the professor was a white southern male who did not seem to like us, and the reading contained more questions than answers. I broke the silence by reading from my copious reading notes in which I had summarized the plot of Book I. The professor quickly interrupted me and asked me why particular questions had been asked, and what the answers meant.

I was both scared and elated by this class. Safe and ready answers culled from the text were not the end but the beginning. The professor did not fill in silences; instead he looked out of the window until someone offered a comment. I loved the idea that rote memorization was not prized (I have always had a lousy memory for facts), and that we were expected to *think*. It sounds like such a cliché now, but it truly revolutionized my whole view of college. It was the one class that semester that really challenged me because I could not do well primarily by reading more carefully or by memorizing more facts. Reading the assignment was only the beginning of class preparation. I also had to *think* about the ideas I had read and try to plumb their depths. By the third week, one of my classmates and I had further embodied the cliché of neophyte philosophy students by spending two hours in the cafeteria trying to define the Idea of Beauty, and then presenting it to the professor, thinking that we had been successful.

I was quickly smitten with the class (the use of the erotic term is not wholly metaphorical), while most of my classmates complained about it and the white southern male professor who was aloof and at times seemingly hostile. I think that I was not turned off by the class because it played to my intellectual strengths (making connections between abstract ideas as opposed to memorizing facts) and because I had loved the TV series *The Paper*

Chase. I recognized our professor as being like the crotchety law professor in the series who was the best and hardest professor. In the year-long class, I learned the basic skills and importance of analytical reading, and I fell in love with the exploration of abstract ideas about "living well."

At end of the first year, the philosophy professor requested that I come to his office. I was apprehensive about talking to him face to face, but I was shocked when he praised my work in the class, proceeded to talk about the difficulty of philosophy, and then suggested that I consider taking another philosophy course the next year. I was flattered, and that, combined with both the challenge he had leveled with his suggestion and my growing infatuation with the discipline, was the reason that I registered for another philosophy course in the fall of my second year. By the third week of that class, I had decided to major in philosophy, with the Honors Seminar professor (Dr. Westbrook) as my advisor. So here I was, a student at a historically black college for women who had chosen the unlikeliest of majors and who was being advised by the unlikeliest of mentors. Most of the other Spelman students thought I was crazy for choosing a major that had nothing to do with black people, and for having an aloof white man as an advisor.

I did not see it this way. Philosophy (by that point I had read a few Platonic dialogues, Rousseau, Descartes, Dewey, and Aristotle) was about figuring out what "living well" meant by moving outside of quick, easy categories to the abstract Idea of Living Well. This journey entailed questioning accepted beliefs in order to get at foundational truths. This seemed to me precisely what black people should be worried about, and especially black women at Spelman who were trying to move beyond the stereotypical categories of black womanhood that are usually based on myopic assumptions. While I was still scared by Dr. Westbrook, as I got to know him (there were only two philosophy professors at Spelman then, and only five students—including me—who regularly took upper-level philosophy classes), he proved to be the most ideal of mentors. He cared about me as a student, yet respected my individuality. He remains a model that I emulate in my roles as professor and mentor.

I spent my junior year in Strasbourg, France, on a study abroad program (I had chosen to double major in philosophy and French). Because the program did not offer philosophy courses, I directly enrolled at the Université de Strasbourg in two philosophy courses. For one of these courses, I was required to present an oral commentary on two pages of Hegel's *Aesthetics,* as well as write a paper on the book. In order to do both of these assignments, I had to cancel my vacation travel plans to Paris and northern Europe. I had never worked so hard on an academic assignment in my life, and I had never enjoyed it so much. It was then that I decided that I *had* to continue my study of philosophy after college, and I could think of no better way to live a full life than to expose others to the potential joys of studying philosophy. I had completely and unadulteratedly fallen in love. Philosophy had chosen me, and I had chosen it.

I spent my senior year applying to graduate school and writing a thesis for the Honors Program. I had trouble choosing a topic for my thesis, so Dr. Westbrook asked me to name the last philosophy book I had read that I really liked. I said it was Nietzsche's *Thus Spoke Zarathustra*. He asked me why, and my answer was the main idea behind my thesis. I was taken with Nietzsche's untraditional styles of writing and the question of their relationship to the content of his philosophy. I concluded (not very originally) that these styles were devices used both for communication of his ideas and as defenses against misinterpretation. In short, Nietzsche's writings were both a description and an example of how one might engage in the art of living in a culture in which one is discouraged from thinking critically and creatively and is expected to stay within prescribed limits—within nooks. As is the case with so many undergraduates, I read Nietzsche's writings very personally and modeled my own practice of "becoming what one is" on his prescriptions for his *Übermenschen*.

When I entered Stanford's doctoral program in philosophy, I had thought that I would specialize in ancient political philosophy, and yet when it came time to begin formulating my dissertation topic, I returned inexorably to Nietzsche. I was still compelled by Nietzsche not only because of my personal interest in his ideas, but also because of the potential revolution they presented for the discipline. After three years of coursework in the most popular aspects of contemporary analytic philosophy, I had come to the conclusion that the discipline had nooked itself. Most contemporary analytic philosophy had become so focused on a few areas that it seemed far removed from "the art of living." In general, anything that fell outside of those areas was not deemed "real philosophy." As a result, for my undergraduate students, philosophy was full of interesting mind and language games that had little to do with real life; with the practice of living. While I do not think that all philosophy must directly pertain to the art of living, the overemphasis on theoretical philosophy prompted the neglect of the philosophy of the art of living. It was precisely my interest in philosophical approaches to the art of living, and my desire to introduce it to undergraduates, that had drawn me into philosophy as a profession. Therefore, I decided to specialize in Nietzsche as a way of fulfilling this goal.

I would be disingenuous if I left my choice of specialty with this explanation. In graduate school I had found myself drawn to Nietzsche's prescriptions for how those on the margins of society could flourish on their own terms. During my first year, I was cowed by the intelligence and undergraduate philosophical training of my fellow graduate students. I was convinced that I was an intellectual fraud who had been accepted by mistake, and that they would soon realize their error. I worked hard to read for the first time many of the articles and books my colleagues were re-reading, and I tried to keep a low profile. The doubt spiders had returned with a vengeance. To fight them off, I worked on cobbling together a community of graduate students (many of them women and/or people of color) who could help me through the hard times because we could empathize with each other. I discovered professors both within and outside of the philosophy department whom I could trust and ask for help. I also discovered the writings of many feminists of color, and they were literally my saving grace—less because their work informed my own than because their ideas emboldened me personally.[10]

During those first years in graduate school, I often felt like a walking contradiction and felt that at almost any moment those contradictions would split apart and I would disassemble before my very eyes. I felt as though I had become a fusion of disparate traits which most did not see as naturally going together: black/woman/graduate student/philosopher/feminist/athlete. Others saw me with those slashes between the words—as deeply, indelibly inscribed slashes. On the other hand, I viewed those words as running together, a continuum of traits with no slashes separating them. The problem was that I had trouble maintaining that view. I would go to one group, and they could accept one or two of my traits, but they had to put a slash between those traits and the others. The philosophy graduate students understood my love of, and frustrations with, philosophy, but did not understand my experiences as a black woman, and so they inserted a slash. The predominantly male Black Graduate Students Association accepted me as a black woman, but inserted the slash between those two traits and philosophy and feminist. There did not seem to be one established group in which my view of myself was readily accepted, and I questioned the validity of this view.

It was my created communities that helped me to turn that questioning gaze away from my own reflection to those inserting the slashes; to those who were unable to see, feel, and learn beyond proffered categories; to those who accepted the surface at the expense of the soul. My communities kept me from becoming schizophrenic. I learned to avoid spending so much time explaining myself in order to help cure *their* myopia that I devoted all of *my* energy and time to translating myself, and left little time for doing that which I needed to do. In short, I learned to heal myself into wholeness, to inoculate myself against their disease.

By the time I graduated from Stanford, I had become more confident of the identity I had created for myself. I spent less time fighting my doubt spiders and their entangling webs and more time on creating a full life for myself. For instance, upon starting my first tenure-track position, I decided that I needed to balance my academic pursuits with other interests. I did not want to, and in fact did not think that I could, become one of those academics whose lives were almost entirely defined by teaching, research, and service to the Academy. I must admit that I was not sure quite how to achieve this balance. In graduate school, I had been so focused on mastering my chosen field that I was not sure how to "have a life." So I started small: I would avoid working at night, exercise regularly, read novels again, volunteer my time, learn to play the cello, meet academics from other departments as well as people outside of the university, and sustain a long-distance relationship with a man I had met in graduate school and who lived in California. Even these small steps have proved hard to follow. I do exercise regularly, do read novels, do not work at night, and the relationship is flourishing, but I have not taken any steps toward learning the cello, and I do not do any volunteer work.

Part of the problem was that these steps were too small. I had not articulated a larger picture of who I was as a well-rounded person, and so I found myself flailing about in despair as I wondered what I was doing with my life—because I did not know what my life meant. I felt lonely as I moved from school, from California, from my friends outside of the Academy, and from my family. I had rejected most of the academic role models I knew, had not found any models with which to replace them, and did not know how to create my own. In short, those coping mechanisms I had created in college and further refined in graduate school no longer seemed to work. Even finding fellow artists of living as I had done in graduate school did not work. I needed more.

JUDAISM

It was at this time that Judaism came into my life. I would love to say that I realized that religion would help provide the overarching guide that I needed to shape a vision of a fuller self, and that after long consideration I realized that Judaism would be that particular guide. I wish I could say that I had a spiritual conversion experience that provided me with a revelatory new vision of myself. It would be so much easier to explain both to myself and to others how it is that I became a Jew if I had followed that more "authentic" route to religious conversion. The primary impetus for my conversion was that my partner in California, David, and I decided that we wanted to get married and begin a life together. In order to do that, we decided that because of the added pressures of being an interracial couple and hopefully bringing biracial children into this world, we would have to contend with many issues. In particular, we would need to consider how to combine the various cultures from which we spring into a whole meaning-ful life.

For these reasons, we wanted to create a life and home together that re-flected these values. We could have worked at cobbling together a value sys-tem, and I felt that I had done this in my own life (though not always successfully), but we decided that it would be difficult to create, learn, em-body, and teach our children a suitable self-styled value system. Instead, we decided to join a value system in which we saw many of these values already formalized. We found this in Judaism—David's religion, and a religion that I have always respected.

Previously I had not chosen to be a part of an organized religion because I thought I had managed to cobble together a good ethical worldview that worked for me. As my life has become more complex, I see the failings of this approach. It was sometimes hard to remind myself of the most impor-tant things in life, and as a result, I found myself swimming in a sea of con-fusion. I began the conversion process primarily for the sake of our rela-tionship. I did not anticipate that it would have such a profound effect on me personally. I thought that living as a Jew might aid me in my practice of the art of living—that it would help fill out the life I was already living. I have to admit that I was skeptical about the ability of an organized religion to provide meaning in my life. Even though I was respectful of its ability to do so for other people, I had thought that my study of Nietzsche's criticisms of religion when combined with an academic's generally cynical views about religious practices would prevent me from becoming a true believer.

Instead I initially adopted a more scholarly approach to becoming a Jew. I thought of it as a system of values that had proved itself as an effective means for becoming a moral person. It would help me in providing a re-newed *theoretical* basis upon which I would carry on my practice of the art of living. After a year of intensive study and practice, I realized that while Judaism has provided a theoretical basis for my art of living, it has even more profoundly shaped my *practice* of the art of living. As a result, many of the values that I believe characterize the art of living well have begun to infuse my entire life—and not just my philosophical writings. I began this process primarily as preparation for my life with David, and, a year later, I did it primarily for me. I cannot imagine not living as a Jew. Through this process, I have been transformed, as has my relationship with David, my family, and the world around me. I feel more firmly implanted in a larger vi-sion of who I want to be as well as infinitely more sure of what I need to do to become that person. I find myself less often plagued by doubts as to how I am shaping my life, because Judaism has provided me with rituals that en-courage me to reflect on how one shapes one's life as well as concrete steps as how to make the vision concrete.

A Jew is supposed to put into practice the 613 *mitzvot* (command-ments) in one's daily life in order to carry out the task of *tikkun olam* (heal-ing/repairing the world). As I understand it, the reception of the Ten Com-mandments on Sinai bestows on the Jews the primary responsibility for the task of working with God to repair the world. This task is not left to Jews alone, as stated in Isaiah (42:6): "I the Lord have called thee in righteous-ness, and will hold thine hand, and will keep thee, and give thee for a covenant of the people, for a light of the nations." I read this quote less as a proclamation of the "chosenness" of Jews and more as an acceptance of the responsibility, while we are here on this earth, to make it a better place. Just as I understand the art of living as shaping oneself by shaping the world around one, I see a similar injunction in Judaism. There are many aspects of Judaism which I have always found compelling and that have helped me to see my conversion as being "natural": the emphasis on deeds over beliefs; the emphasis on study and learning; the idea that anyone can study Torah and Talmud and offer an interpretation (as evidenced by the Talmud—thousands of years of debates on interpretation); the emphasis on doing good deeds in this life; the importance of creating an ethical home and being part of an ethical community; the emphasis on family and communi-ty as equally important to (if not, more so than) what goes on in a house of worship; knowing that inhumanity and pain exist in this world, having the faith that one can emerge from a personal experience of them and find love and peace in one's heart, while also taking seriously the responsibility be-stowed on those who have survived them to prevent this inhumanity and pain from happening to others.

There were many other aspects of Judaism that seemed less "natural." How in the world could I pray to a God in whom I could not wholeheart-edly believe? How would I undertake the rituals prescribed by *halacha* (Jewish law)? What would I do about the limited role afforded women by traditional Judaism? I have not fully addressed these concerns, but I was sur-prised at the relative ease with which I have undertaken the practice of Jew-ish ritual. Leon Weiseltier wrote that "ritual is the conversion of essences into acts,"[11] and it is in my practice of Judaism that I have enacted, for the first time in my life, a reliable connection between my theory and practice of the art of living.

Judaism necessarily entails putting words into deeds. One's faith is mea-sured primarily by one's acts as opposed to beliefs. The understanding is that carrying out the ritual of certain actions will aid in developing the at-tendant beliefs. One works from the outside to the inside. Because I was not expected to "believe," it was not difficult for me to undertake the practice of certain rituals. I have found ritual to be immensely comforting. In my prac-tices of the art of living, I have continually created systems of ritual for various aspects of my life. As I demonstrated above, it has been an ever-present struggle to create and refine rituals that are effective and, at the same time, adhere to them. So I don't find the rituals of Judaism to be confining. In fact, I have welcomed many of them. They already exist as part of a formalized system, and I "only" have to follow them. I don't have to conceive them, create the theory supporting them, or monitor their effectiveness. Moreover, as Arnold Eisen has pointed out, I can get them right—such a relief for a philosopher.

> Ritual, we might say, touches life but is not life; it marks out bounds within which life can be lived well. It is a sort of art. We need that art because, no matter how complicated its details, it has one supreme advantage over life: *we can get it right.* I know that I will never live up to ethical ideals, even my own, in my relationships with other people. I will always "sin," which in Hebrew literally means missing the mark, falling short. I will not always be the spouse I should be to my wife, the father I want to be to my children. But I can get the Bach invention right, if I practice it long enough. I can leave Yom Kippur *Ne'ilah* service, after twenty-five hours of following the prescribed ritual, with the precious sense of having at least done that much right. The ritual gives us a sense of rightness that is meant to inspire us to try to attain it outside the bounds of art as well.[12]

It was through the enactment of ritual that I found my entrée into the more spiritual aspects of Judaism. It is through the following of various rituals (observing *shabbat,* attending services, praying before meals, observing the holidays, etc.) that I have learned to carve out a part of my life and sanctify it. In such a way, I place a higher value on it, and try to keep it from being sullied from the other parts. I try to sanctify not only places (my home, the synagogue), but also time (*shabbat*) and actions (eating). I try to look on these as being sacred, and thus as goods-in-themselves, and thus untouchable by my doubt spiders.

For instance, *shabbat* signals the separation of one day of the week from the rest, and the sanctification of it. It is a day away from the pressures of work, errands, chores, etc. For twenty-four hours, I have permission from a higher source to take time off from my everyday life. From the time we light candles on Friday evening until *havdalah* (sundown on Saturday), I try to turn my eyes to matters I have put aside during the busy week: relaxing, slowing down time, assessing the whole of my life, reveling in silence, community, and all that is good in the world. I look forward to *shabbat*—it is a big sigh and a comforting pat on the shoulder at the end of the week. Observing *shabbat* reminds me of that which is important in life: living nobly, that living is a miracle and living well the ultimate achievement, celebrating the good, and actively shaping my life as well as the world around me.

Ritual has also allowed me to confront the issue of God—a most Jewish undertaking. *Yisrael* ("Israel" in Hebrew) means "one who wrestles with God," and Jews (Israelites) wrestle with God as partners in the covenant. I feel as though I have already engaged in this activity in my study of philosophy. So much of Western philosophy has been engaged in attempts to understand and prove the existence of transcendent Truth and/or God. My personal view has been that many in the discipline have lost the forest for the trees—meaning that understanding and proving the existence of Truth and/or God has been divorced from the meaning of this search for our lives now. In short, many have attempted to live in the *a priori* realm and have forsaken their lives in the subjective realm and the practice of living well.

I cannot say definitively that there is a God, but I do believe that if God does exist, we as human beings do not have direct access to God. At best we can only feel God's pull on us. Since undertaking the practice of Judaism, I feel more assured about recognizing and appropriately responding to this pull. I have found myself searching for and reveling in the awe produced by acts of love, the power and beauty of nature, the selflessness of kindness, and the righteousness of justice. I have found this awe to be both empowering and humbling as it reminds me both of how far I have yet to go to attain the ideal, and how far I have come. I cannot say with any surety that I believe in God, but I can say that I am both humbled and emboldened by the idea of God. Moreover, it is the struggle with this enigmatic and often problematic notion that guides me in envisioning myself within a larger context. In this sense, I read the Torah as a teaching document. It teaches me, not how to be a perfect person, but rather, how to be imperfect and still be a good person. The Torah is the story of the first Jews coming to terms with their covenant with God and with God coming to terms with them. In it, the moral exemplars are not perfect. They make mistakes, do not follow the word of God perfectly, are angry at God—they wrestle with God. Yet it is their attempts at shaping themselves as Jews, as human beings, that make them stand out.

I have become a person of faith, and one of the chief benefits of this new identity is that it does not require me to be wholly rational. I do not try, and am not expected, to be able to *explain* rationally my beliefs and practices. While I entered into the process of conversion as a theoretical, academic exercise, I have emerged from it focusing on the practical and spiritual. Unlike with the philosophical and even feminist aspects of my art of living, I do not feel constrained to be able to understand fully varying points of view and to come to a conclusion as to which ones are best. I do not feel constrained to be rationally consistent in terms of the rituals I adopt or the way in which I practice them.

I think the reason I have so taken to Judaism is that, through its ritual, it helps me to address the existential crisis I faced after graduate school: I had grave doubts about the life I had created for myself, and because of these doubts I no longer trusted my ability to re-adjust either my identity or my methods for identity creation. In other words, I had come to question both my theory and practice of the art of living. My doubts left me frozen in in-action. Judaism has helped bolster my confidence in my theory of the art of living, and it has guided me in specific practices that have transformed the essence of the theory in acts.

I am a Jew, and yet I struggle with that designation—just as it struggles with me. I am only just beginning to try to fit into Jewish communities, and as with my experiences in the philosophical and feminist communities to which I also belong, the fit is not perfect. Many people, Jews and non-Jews alike, do not assume that I am Jewish, and even after learning of my official conversion, they are unwilling to accept me as a full-fledged Jew. Just as when I go to philosophy meetings, when I attend services at a synagogue, people stare at me, and I can see them trying to come to terms with the cognitive dissonance that my presence invokes in them. I do not like the generally secondary role afforded women by many synagogues, and as both David and I become more observant, it is harder to find the combination of a more traditional yet egalitarian approach to Jewish practice that we prefer. I also worry that my Jewishness will further distance me from my non-Jewish family and friends.

In short, there has been a symbiotic relationship between my practice of the art of living and my commitments to feminism, philosophy, and faith. On one side, I first conceived of, and developed, an art of living (in both theory and practice) because of my commitments to these three areas. My encounters with feminism provide me with reasons for engaging in identity creation. Philosophy, and especially Nietzsche's philosophy, has helped me to develop the theory behind the practice, and Judaism has guided me in the particular aspects of practicing forms of identity creation that work well for me. On the other side, my conceptions and ways of exercising the art of living have had an impact on the feminist, philosophical, and Jewish communities with which I have allied myself.

This symbiotic relationship has not been a stable one. Changes in my life have necessitated changes on both sides of the equation, and these changes have also introduced tensions. I have found myself struggling with the ideas, people, and activities to which I have made commitments, and this struggle has caused me to re-evaluate my identity as a feminist, philosopher, and Jew. In short, my skirmishes with these communities often mirror interior skirmishes with the concomitant disparate parts of my identities. Out of this struggle comes my practice of the art of living, and therefore it is a necessary part of my life. Yet this struggle also presents the danger of the disintegration of the ties that bind these parts of my identity. Just as fire melds the items in a crucible into a new substance, it also carries the potential danger of destroying them. The art of living then can be understood as playing with fire. Doing it well entails wielding a power over which one does not ultimately control. At the same time, for me, to decline to engage this power offers its own danger: if the struggle were to end, so would my practice of the art of living.

NOTES

1. Friedrich Nietzsche wrote of philosophers as being like tragic asses in the sense that they are "crushed by a burden one can neither bear nor throw off" (Nietzsche, "Maxims and Arrows," in *Twilight of the Idols*, trans. R. J. Hollingdale [London: Penguin Books, 1968], p. 11). I have argued elsewhere that this burden was the philosopher's task of creating rationales for existence that will always eventually become ineffectual. See my "Nietzsche and Decadence: The Revaluation of Morality," *Continental Philosophy Review* 31 (1998): 59–78.

2. Friedrich Nietzsche, *Beyond Good and Evil*, trans. Walter Kaufmann (New York: Vintage Books, 1955), p. 198.

3. Alexander Nehamas, *The Art of Living* (Berkeley: University of California Press, 1998).

4. *The Art of Living*, pp. 1–2.

5. Friedrich Nietzsche, *On the Genealogy of Morals*, trans. Walter Kaufmann (New York: Random House, 1967), III 28.

6. *On the Genealogy of Morals*, III 28. One way to understand this connection between nihilism and the despair for which suicide seems to be the only answer is to think of them in terms of clinical depression. Many people who are depressed experience despair over the lack of meaning in their lives. They cannot think of any reason to get out of bed in the morning and go about their daily lives. When taken to an extreme, they feel that their only recourse, in light of this lack of purpose in their lives, is suicide.

7. The subtitle of Nietzsche's book *Ecce Homo* is *How One Becomes What One Is*.

8. In particular, Nietzsche cited religious believers as paradigmatic passive types. See his criticisms of Christianity in *On the Genealogy of Morals* and *The Antichrist*.

9. Even though I refer to myself only as Professor or Doctor Scott in class, at least 60 percent of my students in a given semester call me Mrs. or Ms. Scott. I am often asked if I will ever get my doctorate. While these incidents might be attributed to my relative youth, I wonder how many of my white male colleagues of the same age experience the same treatment.

10. *Making Face, Making Soul*, ed. Gloria Anzaldúa (San Francisco: Aunt Lute Foundation, 1990); *This Bridge Called My Back*, ed. Cherríe Moraga and Gloria Anzaldúa (New York: Kitchen Table Press, 1983); *Homegirls*, ed. Barbara Smith (New York: Kitchen Table Press, 1983); *Black Women Writers at Work*, ed. Claudia Tate (New York: Continuum, 1988).

11. Leon Weiseltier, *Kaddish* (New York: Knopf, 1998), p. 46.

12. Arnold Eisen, *Taking Hold of Torah* (Bloomington: Indiana University Press, 1997), p. 74.

EIGHT

Learning to Question

PATRICIA ALTENBERND JOHNSON

> Questions always bring out the
> undetermined possibilities of a thing.
> —*Hans-Georg Gadamer,* Truth and Method

> Interrogation itself becomes an act of critical intervention,
> fostering a fundamental attitude of vigilance rather than denial.
> —*bell hooks,* Yearning

> The Queries enable Friends, individually and corporately,
> to examine themselves.
> —Book of Discipline, *Ohio Valley Yearly Meeting*

Beginning graduate school in philosophy was a deciding point in my life. I majored in philosophy as an undergraduate, went on to a masters degree in comparative religion, married, taught pre-school, and worked as a live-in house-parent for ten boys, most of whom were young teenagers. The first day of the graduate program at the University of Toronto was spent taking written examinations. The following day, students faced a short oral examination based on those written examinations. At the end of the oral examinations determinations were made as to what each student would be required to take. Connected with the oral examination was a more informal conversation with the examiners. My examiners asked me what I wanted to get from doing graduate work in philosophy. Many answers would have been appropriate and perhaps expected at the time, but the one that I found myself speaking was simply, "I want to learn how to question."

Since that day I have grown in my philosophical, feminist, and religious commitments. Representatives from each of these communities to which I belong suggest that a life cannot be lived with commitments in all three of these areas. Certainly I have experienced discomfort from time to time in being at home in all of these communities. Yet, when I reflect on these commitments as part of my life, I understand each of them as contributing to my learning to question. Moreover, I have learned that the process of questioning can place me in a position of holding these seeming contradictions in balance. In the following essay, I will explore how philosophy, feminism, and religious practice have all helped me learn how to question and how questioning has helped me understand the commitments I have made as complementary and interrelated.

LEARNING THE ART OF GENUINE QUESTIONING

Much of my doctoral training in philosophy did, of course, focus on questions and on asking and answering questions. Two seminars stand out in particular as providing me with the experience of the role of questions in gaining knowledge and understanding. Fr. Joseph Owens regularly taught a seminar on Aristotle's *Nichomachean Ethics*. The course met for two hours each week. During the first hour a student gave a presentation on a particular portion of the text. We were expected to have consulted all secondary sources on the text and to give a presentation that set out the major issues and discussions. We took a ten-minute break after the presentation and then returned to the seminar room for an open discussion on the text and the issues raised. Fr. Owens always had the option of asking the first question. If he asked a question, you knew that you had missed something that you should have found in preparing for the class. Similarly, Emil Fackenheim regularly taught a seminar on Hegel's *Phenomenology of Spirit*. He also required student presentations, and also always asked the first question. In his case, you knew that no matter how well you prepared, he would ask the "difficult" question. He always asked the question you could not answer, not because you were not well-prepared, but because he always seemed to know the question that would take you beyond your current understanding.

Later, as I read Hans-Georg Gadamer's *Truth and Method* in preparation for writing a dissertation, I understood more fully what I had learned from my teachers and came to a better understanding of what I still take to be the role of philosophy. Gadamer stresses that to learn to question is not to learn a methodology. Rather questioning requires "the knowledge of not knowing."[1] This is, of course, the lesson that Plato teaches us through the Socratic dialogues. Gadamer understands Socratic dialectic as setting up the "presuppositions of the question."[2] We must come to recognize that we do not know, we must admit our ignorance, before a genuine question can be asked.

As I reflect back on my experience, I think that both Professors Owens and Fackenheim were teaching their students how to admit to our own ignorance in order to open us to the possibility of genuine questions. To recognize that we do not know is to recognize the need to ask further.

Once we know that we do not know, we are in a position to learn the art of genuine questioning. Gadamer's reflections are helpful for both understanding and learning this art. He suggests that a genuine question "presses itself on us."[3] I take this to mean that a genuine question is one that is motivated by a sincere desire to know—it moves us out of ourselves. A genuine question sets us in a direction, on a search, into a conversation. A genuine question also is directed toward a decision, toward taking a position.

Gadamer further distinguishes genuine from false and distorted questions. A false question "pretends to an openness and susceptibility to decision that it does not have."[4] Philosophers, perhaps most particularly in our roles as teachers, often ask false questions. We ask questions that do not allow our own presuppositions to be questioned. Certainly, we have a knowledge that our students do not have, and some of our questions are asked out of our own knowledge in order to try to convey that knowledge. But we can also ask questions, some of them on examinations, that clearly require that our own unexamined prejudices be accepted. For example, a philosopher might accept Kant's critique of the ontological argument. On an examination such a professor might ask a student to explain and critique the ontological argument and only accept a Kantian critique. A student who has practiced or studied Buddhism and who offers a critique from this position might be judged as shallow or not philosophical in this critique. There is no genuine question here, for there is no openness on the professor's part. The question is not really intended to help a student decide on a commitment of action, nor is it intended to facilitate growth or authenticity. Learning the art of questioning means being self-vigilant so as to avoid such false questions. It also means recognizing that such questions usually serve to reinforce a dominant position or allow a dominant position to suppress genuine questions that might challenge that position.

Learning the art of questioning also means recognizing distorted questions. Gadamer says that there is a question behind a distorted question, but the question "leads us only apparently, and not really, through the open state of indeterminacy in which a decision is made."[5] Students often ask such questions. "Why would anyone want to call herself a feminist?" Part of the art of questioning is to find ways of strengthening or redirecting these questions. Providing students with the opportunity to learn about women who have been and are feminists and for seeing how the goals of these women are admirable and socially important is a way of strengthening such a question. As professional philosophers, we need to learn to consider the direction that is opened by our questions. This may well mean that we need to examine the focus of our research projects, of our professional meetings, and of our class syllabi. To learn the art of asking questions is constantly to reflect on how our questions might distort the discussion. For example, in contemporary philosophy of religion, which is heavily dominated by analytical philosophy, questions of theodicy are a regular part of the curriculum. Many of the readings that are used really ignore the existential realities of the question of evil for an individual's religious practice and address the question as a logical puzzle or game. This approach does more to distort the issue than to help us address evil.

The art of questioning also requires understanding the many sides of a question. If we are to avoid false and distorted questions, we must include what Gadamer terms both "negative and positive judgments." The medieval form of disputation is helpful for demonstrating and learning this aspect of asking genuine questions. This format requires that a philosopher clearly and concisely articulate the positions and arguments that support those positions for the range of directions that can be taken from a question. The philosopher must be able to articulate his or her own position clearly, and must be able to reply to all of the counter positions. While using this format does not totally exclude the possibility that false and distorted directions will be pursued, it does provide a disciplined structure for reviewing the basis for particular answers to questions. This is a particularly helpful format to use with students, since it shows them the importance of becoming informed when addressing a question. This approach can help us understand more clearly where to stand on an issue and what the appropriate next question may be.

Finally, the art of questioning must be developed and carried out in community. Questions are not problems that can be addressed abstractly and removed from their living situation. Nor can community here be treated in abstraction. To develop questioning in community means to engage in conversations in the communities in which we find ourselves or into which we move. It means learning to identify questions that address the community in its historical and temporal particularity. Such questions also ask that community, and the individual members of the community, to develop in certain directions. Asking questions in community encourages the community to develop in particular directions. While I am a Quaker woman philosopher, I teach at a Catholic university run by Marianist brothers. Some of the questions that emerge in the context of that working community are quite different than what I would ask in other settings. Yet those questions are important in that community setting, both for me and for other members of the community. For example, I was recently involved in a discussion where the suggestion was made that forms of liturgy develop habits which can provide the basis for changed moral behavior. The question was raised: What form of liturgy could be developed or practiced if we want to move in the direction of more egalitarian communities? This question helped me to see the Quaker practice of gathering in silence as a form of liturgy that can lead to the development of moral habits of listening and waiting.

Philosophy has provided me with a framework in which to pursue my initial desire to study philosophy in order to learn how to question. I have learned that the beginning of questioning is to recognize that I do not know. I have learned the importance of being vigilant in order to raise genuine, rather than false or distorted, questions. I have learned the importance of recognizing that every question arises in the context of complexity and community. My commitment to feminism has pressed questions upon me and has especially required me to find ways of developing and understanding how to question within the context of community.

LEARNING TO QUESTION PLAYFULLY

On January 15, 1968 (so my button says), I joined thousands of other women from across the United States in Washington, D.C., to march in the Jeannette Rankin Brigade. My motivation for participating in the march was primarily my opposition, religiously based, to the war in Vietnam. This march was unlike any that I had participated in before, for it was all women. In Toronto, several years later, I participated with a group of women in starting a rape crisis center. During the several years that I worked with the center, I researched the issue of rape; worked on the hotline; accompanied women to medical examinations, police interviews, and court appearances; did presentations for various community groups including police and hospital staff; and did public relations work. All of these contributed to a growing identity as a feminist. But it was not until I began teaching that I fully realized how essential it was for me to be a feminist. What I eventually came to realize was that to be a feminist in the Academy required one to learn how to raise questions that others preferred not to address and did not even see as questions. I have also learned that as a feminist, my simple presence is sometimes a question.

When I first began teaching, I had worked for feminist political goals, but I had not read or studied much feminist philosophy. It was simply not part of the curriculum. I joined a department that had one other woman. She taught a course on philosophy and women, and she suggested that I work with her to further develop the course and to teach it. That was really the beginning of my education. I also started working with the Women's Studies Program that had just recently been approved. I read more, and read in a wide range of disciplines. As I reflected on what I was learning, I began to understand it in the framework of hermeneutics. Again, I was drawn to the importance of questioning, this time in the context of a hermeneutics of suspicion, and then a hermeneutics of transformation.

My understanding of a hermeneutics of suspicion was informed by the work of authors such as Paul Ricoeur, Juan Segundo, and Elizabeth Schüssler Fiorenza. Fiorenza and Segundo, in particular, emphasize that traditional beliefs and understandings are formulated by those in power. Because they are both theologians, they explicate this hermeneutic in the context of Biblical interpretations and the resulting positions of the Roman Catholic Church. A hermeneutic of suspicion begins from the position of the oppressed, of those who are dominated. The experiences of these people often do not fit well with the prevailing interpretation and so they begin to raise questions about the adequacy of the interpretation. Out of those questions new interpretations develop that fit more appropriately with the experiences of the oppressed or dominated. This way of looking at questions provided me with a framework for my emerging relationship with philosophy as a discipline and with the Academy.

My scholarly work turned to more of these questions. In 1986, as Director of Women's Studies, I organized a series that brought eight women scholars to campus to give public presentations. The series extended over most of the academic year and was received with overwhelming enthusiasm by women in the local community, as well as by those on campus. The series featured scholarly women in ways that had not occurred on our campus, and in ways that helped members of the campus community raise many important questions. In the book that emerged from this series, *With Both Eyes Open: Seeing Beyond Gender*, I articulated the process of questioning the given tradition as a hermeneutics of transformation. I saw this hermeneutic as a four-staged process that was both theoretical and practical:

> (a) Women enter and become skilled in fields or areas from which they have previously been excluded; (b) women reflect on these areas or disciplines from their own experiences, raise questions, and begin to do work that is influenced by their own experiences; (c) this work leads women to ask for and begin to make specific changes within the traditional framework or approach of the area or discipline; and (d) women recognize the inadequacy of these changes and begin working for transformation not only of the discipline or area, but also of the Academy and of the possibilities it provides for people.[6]

Thirteen years after having set this out, I still find it a helpful touchstone. I also recognize that the reflection required for transformation is very complex. The diversity of women's experiences based on race, class, sexual orientation, age, ethnic background, and religious commitment means that identification of specific changes and agreement on the direction of transformation requires both theoretical and existential work. Moreover, the process of transformation in most areas of women's lives also requires continued functioning in a fairly untransformed reality.

In this context, how can I continue to learn how to raise genuine questions? I have found it helpful to think about questioning as a matter of playfulness. In developing an understanding of playful questioning, I draw on the work of both Hans-Georg Gadamer and Maria Lugones. Lugones herself rejects Gadamer's account of play in her 1987 *Hypatia* article "Playfulness, 'World'-Traveling, and Loving Perception." Her argument in that essay, however, does not develop a full argument against Gadamer's position, but equates his position with Huizinga's and suggests that both have an agonistic understanding of play that supports hostility and conquering. While this may be an appropriate evaluation of Huizinga, it does not apply to Gadamer. Indeed, Lugones's work on play fits well within Gadamer's analysis of the concept. Both are helpful for developing an understanding of playful questioning.

Gadamer's work on play in *Truth and Method* is focused on the mode of being of play. He notes that *spiel* originally meant "dance." With this as a starting point for his analysis, he describes play as a to-and-fro movement. He writes, "The movement which is play has no goal which brings it to an end; rather it renews itself in constant repetition."[7] When play is understood as fundamentally this movement, then play is understood to be more than the attitudes and activities of players. Indeed, play absorbs the human players and relieves us from the "strain of existence."[8] This understanding of play contributes to an understanding of playful questioning. If genuine questions are to be raised playfully, this will mean that the questioner must understand herself as part of a totality that surpasses her. This understanding of the greater totality helps to remove the tension of the situation, the strain of existence.

Yet play is not just to-and-fro motion; Gadamer emphasizes that when we play we take up a particular attitude.[9] Lugones's work focuses on this attitude and is especially helpful in thinking about how to ask genuine questions within a context that is playful. Lugones summarizes her analysis of a playful attitude:

> [T]he playful attitude involves openness to surprise, openness to being a fool, openness to self-construction or reconstruction and to construction or reconstruction of the "worlds" we inhabit playfully. . . . playfulness is characterized by uncertainty, lack of self-importance, absence of rules or a not taking rules as sacred, a not worrying about competence, and a lack of aban-

donment to a particular construction of oneself, others and one's relation to them.[10]

Lugones emphasizes the importance of openness to the reconstruction of one's self and one's world. To adopt such an attitude is to facilitate the playful asking of genuine questions. Asking questions from the context of such an attitude facilitates change and relieves tension.

This is important for feminist reflection and social and political action. Feminist reflection requires women from diverse experiences and ages to question each other playfully. We come from backgrounds that are diverse in so many ways, yet we share a common commitment to women. We need to question each other in order to find the finest and the fullest answers, yet we need to do this in an open way, in a way that reduces tension. To bring a playful attitude to feminist discussion is to facilitate the asking of genuine questions. Lugones's approach is helpful within the diverse feminist community. As I grow older, I am more aware of the need for this playfulness. Young women did not march in 1968; they could not. They often see the world differently than I do. But they are nonetheless as committed to women as I am.

Contemporary feminism is also engaged in conversations about race and class. For example, bell hooks calls for the "production of a discourse on race that interrogates whiteness."[11] She notes that the concepts of "Other" and "difference" have become acceptable. They have become integrated into academic discourse. On my campus the term "diversity" is a popular catchphrase. However, the integration of these words into academic discourse may serve to prevent us from asking the difficult questions we need to ask about race and class on our campuses. hooks writes, "Too often, it seems, the point is to promote the *appearance* of difference within intellectual discourse, a 'celebration' that fails to ask who is sponsoring the party and who is extending the invitations. For who is controlling this new discourse?"[12] The mutual openness of play is necessary to find and address such genuine questions. As Lugones suggests, we need to be open to uncertainness, to be willing to be foolish, and to be open to reconstructing our worlds. One sign of the presence of genuine playful questioning is the humor that helps us to live with our still unsettled issues and to overcome tension.

But genuine questioning that arises out of feminist commitment needs also to take place in the context of the larger community that is not feminist, is not transformed, and may not be interested in being transformed. What does it mean to question playfully in this community? Gadamer's work on play is again helpful. He notes that play is always representation. He writes, "Only because play is always representation is human play able to find the task of the game in representation itself."[13] He reminds us that play does not depend on achieving goals, but is a "spending of oneself on the task of the game" where one plays oneself out. For example, in a range of philosophical and religious communities to which I belong, I represent a question about how to speak about human beings and about God. Should we speak of human beings and people instead of men? Can we speak of God as she and as mother? I, and many other women, have represented feminism in these communities long enough that our very presence asks these questions. And the longevity of our presence is part of the play that perhaps allows the questions to be asked playfully, in a way that gets rid of tension. This is not to say that the contexts or worlds have been transformed. If they were, questions of this sort would not be needed. But what we have come to represent is a question.

This representation is a representing for someone and so is like a theatrical play. One takes on a role and becomes absorbed in it. But what one is doing is representing. Another way to understand this form of representation is to see that sometimes one is a question in a world in which one is a player. I believe that many feminists function as questions in their communities, including philosophical and religious communities. This form of life has its risks. Kurt Vonnegut's admonition in *Mother Night* is worth heeding: "We are what we pretend to be, so we must be careful about what we pretend to be."[14] The task for feminists is often to represent, to be a question. The challenge is to do this in such a way that the person I become is someone with whom I am comfortable. The challenge is to represent a question that does not support hostility, but rather one that asks for openness and an ability to not take the rules too seriously. It is not always easy to be a genuine non-hostile question, but I have learned the importance of such living questions as a feminist.

LEARNING FROM QUERIES

My religious identity, like my philosophical and feminist identities, has involved a journey. I was raised Presbyterian in a small Midwestern town. Part of what this meant is that I grew up in a religious community that valued education and allowed me to ask questions. When I left home for college, I went to a new and experimental Presbyterian college. Much of my life there involved discussion of questions, including many theological questions. My roommate was my partner in conversations. Over the years, after college, we re-established those conversations every year or so. One year we were amazed and pleased to discover that we had separately joined the Society of Friends. We had both become convinced Quakers. At an earlier time we had both become feminists in our parallel, but spatially distant, paths and so it seemed most appropriate that we would have taken yet another step together.

My friend died far too young. But I have a picture that her husband composed from several photographs that is a very powerful symbol for me. It is a picture of her as a child, holding a candle, standing on a path with light streaming in from over her head. It is a great reminder to me to always listen to the query: Have you tried to see the light within each person, to see each as a divine child?

Quaker religious practice makes use of queries. These are questions that are formulated by Yearly Meetings (a geographical organization) and are read on a regular basis by the Monthly Meetings, which are the smaller local meetings. These queries are intended to help Friends, both individually and corporately, examine themselves in relation to standards of conduct that we espouse as Friends. For example, Friends are committed to a peace testimony. The query in the *Book of Discipline of the Ohio Valley Yearly Meeting Religious Society of Friends* related to this testimony reads:

> Do you live in the life and power which takes away the occasion for all wars? Do you, on Christian principles, refuse to participate in or cooperate with all military effort? Do you work actively for peace and the removal of the causes of wars? Do you endeavor to cultivate good will, mutual understanding and equal opportunities for all races, creeds and nations? Have you examined your life style and possessions to make sure that the seeds of war are not found within them?[15]

The query is not intended to be answered as a catechism question. Rather, the query is to direct the Meeting, both as a group and as individuals, to reflect upon their own lives and actions and to make changes where this query seems to direct the need for changes. Sometimes, in particular social circumstances, the query will call for a written or public response. In time of national wars, the query may lead a Meeting or an individual to write an explanation of what it means to take away the occasions for war.

Queries have also helped me to learn something about asking questions. Philosophy first led me to question and to ask about the nature of questioning. Philosophy taught me to recognize that I must know when I do not know. I must distinguish genuine from false and distorted questions. I must recognize that addressing a question requires investigating the many sides of a question. I must ask questions in the context of community. Feminism showed me the complexity of communities and the importance of being a question. Quaker religious practice has helped me to recognize the importance of self-interrogation in the context of spiritual waiting.

This self-interrogation shows me that I change when I am asked questions in a spiritual context. When I was still in college, and many years before becoming a Quaker, I remember a fellow student coming to ask me to help organize a protest against the Vietnam War because she knew of my religious commitments. At that point in my life, I had no conviction that this war was wrong. But that request served, in a sense, as a query for me. It asked me to examine my actions in light of my religious commitments. Two years later, I was marching, and several years later, I became a Quaker. The question set a context for self-examination in a spiritual context. What led me to this change was a question pressed upon me, a question that moved me out of my self. Queries press upon us and ask us to examine ourselves in the light.

The Quaker practice of query also makes evident the importance of reflecting on the commitments that form the context of questions. Queries are designed to help individuals and groups reflect on how best to live out their commitments in the context of a particular lived situation. The response a query elicits in a time of war will be different than the response in other times. But when a war ends, the query is not answered or irrelevant. To examine one's life and ask how to live so as to take away the occasion for war requires a continual search for ways to live one's commitment.

I think that bell hooks asks for a query when in *Yearning* she asks for a discourse that interrogates whiteness. She is asking for genuine questions to be raised and addressed. Such a discourse would benefit from a query or two. The query begins with a commitment to human equality and dignity, and asks us how it is that we live that commitment. Do you live in the life and power that takes away the occasion for racial domination? Are you vigilant about your own standpoints and practices to ensure that they do not perpetuate racist practices?

As I have lived as a philosopher, a feminist, and a Friend, I do think that I have at least begun to learn something about how to question. It is a more complex process than I envisioned when I first recognized the need. It requires continual examination of commitments. It requires the admission of ignorance and vigilance against false and distorted questions. But the initial quest has led me to recognize the playful possibilities of questions and the ways in which one's life can represent important questions. Moreover, I have learned that formulating questions as religious queries can lead to carrying out commitments in a more open manner, and in a manner that holds each person in the light.

Life can be lived as a philosopher, a feminist, and a person of spiritual commitment simultaneously. Living such a life, however, requires learning to question properly. I continue to question. A paper I presented at the Society for Christian philosophers, "Feminist Christian Philosophy?" is an example of an attempt to raise a genuine question as a query for people who belong to a philosophical and religious community of which I am a part.[16] My hope is that as people like me raise such questions, we will be able to construct and reconstruct our communities in ways that will result in more opportunities for genuine and playful questions. Learning to question is not easy, and it requires perseverance. But it also opens one to the fullest possibilities of human existence.

NOTES

1. Hans-Georg Gadamer, *Truth and Method* (New York: Seabury Press, 1975), p. 325.

2. *Truth and Method,* p. 329.

3. *Truth and Method,* p. 330.

4. *Truth and Method,* p. 327.

5. *Truth and Method,* p. 327.

6. Patricia A. Johnson, "Possibilities and Promise for Seeing Beyond Gender," in *With Both Eyes Open,* ed. Patricia A. Johnson and Janet Kalven (New York: Pilgrim Press, 1988), p. 167.

7. *Truth and Method,* p. 93.

8. *Truth and Method,* p. 94.

9. *Truth and Method,* p. 96.

10. María Lugones, "Playfulness, 'World'-Traveling, and Loving Perception," *Hypatia* 2, no. 2 (1987): 17.

11. bell hooks, *Yearning* (Boston: South End Press, 1990), p. 54.

12. *Yearning,* p. 54.

13. *Truth and Method,* p. 97.

14. Kurt Vonnegut, *Mother Night* (New York: Delta Publishing Company, 1966), p. v.

15. *Book of Discipline of the Ohio Valley Yearly Meeting,* Religious Society of Friends (1978), p. 67.

16. Patricia A. Johnson, "Feminist Christian Philosophy?" *Faith and Philosophy* 9, no. 3 (1992): 320–34.

NINE

I Can't Say No:
Self-Sacrifice and an Ethics of Care

RUTH E. GROENHOUT

> Whoever seeks to gain his life will lose it,
> but whoever loses his life will preserve it.
> —*Luke 17:33*

> Apprehending the other's reality, feeling what he feels as nearly
> as possible, is the essential part of caring from the view of the
> one-caring. For if I take on the other's reality as possibility and
> begin to feel its reality, I feel, also, that I must act accordingly;
> that is, I am impelled to act as though in my own behalf,
> but in behalf of the other.
> —*Nel Noddings,* Caring, *p. 16*

> For women to affirm difference, when difference means domi-
> nance, as it does with gender, means to affirm the qualities and
> characteristics of powerlessness.... Women value care because
> men have valued us according to the care we give them....
> —*Catharine MacKinnon,* Feminism Unmodified, *p. 39*

Care ethics strikes a deep chord with me. It picks out aspects of ethics that have been overlooked or downplayed in most contemporary ethical theories, it arises out of a concern for building a theory from the perspective of women's experiences, and it mandates behavior that seems the behavior an ethical theory ought to require. More than this, it meshes fairly well with my faith; the call to Care and the call to love one's neighbor as oneself are very close, and Care's emphasis on meeting the needs of the other fits well with the portrait of Christ one finds in the Gospels. The two quotes above from Nel Noddings and the Gospel of Luke suggest the close relationship between an ethics of Care and Christian ethics.

Developed by theorists who were concerned to listen to a woman's voice in ethics, Care stresses the emotional connections and relationships out of which flow our ethical responsibilities. It identifies the central moral imperative as the obligation to care for the other in his or her particularity, and the maintenance of relationships as one primary expression of that care. The mothering relationship has provided the primary paradigm for a relationship in which Care is seen most clearly (although some theorists have advocated friendship as a healthier paradigm), and a mother's willingness to give up everything for the sake of her children is idealized as the pinnacle of caring behavior.

Care ethics also seems deeply problematic. The political, economic, and personal gains that women have made in this century have been made because women have refused to submit and be self-sacrificial and have instead decided that the time has come to fight for their rights. How can a feminist advocate an ethical theory that not only seems to reinstate women's sacrificial attitudes, but seems to pronounce that sacrifice morally obligatory? As expressed in the quote from Catherine MacKinnon which begins this essay, Care ethics seems to glorify the very caring, self-sacrificial traits that make women suitable subjects for cooperative, willing subordination. Not only can they be subordinated, they will participate in their subordination and call it virtue.

But the problem does not occur just at the social level. On a personal level, the tension between pursuing career goals and caring for others is fierce. At work I feel guilty for failing to care properly for my children. Even when this worry is squelched, time spent in the office with my door closed is time during which I feel guilty for excluding my students. The student whose mother is dying from cancer needs to talk just when the deadline for that important paper is looming. Caring for others is a moral imperative; but my own professional life requires me to refuse to care.

This conflict between the responsibility I feel to care and my need to develop professionally is not felt only by women, but it is felt with particular poignancy by women because of the cultural identification of women's virtues with self-sacrificial care. Our natural image of a good man easily accommodates professional success. The cultural images of good women that arise spontaneously involve self-effacement and sacrifice for others.[1] So the context within which Care theory is heard is one in which women, more than men, hear the call to care as a call to give up legitimate concerns for their own development and subordinate their own talents and abilities in the service of others.

In the context of this cultural symbolism it is easy for critics of Care to dismiss it as a standard, reactionary, cultural conception of femininity dressed up in feminist clothing. Although developed by feminist theorists interested in exploring women's moral reasoning, in practice it seems to obligate women to care, to devote themselves to the maintenance of the familial relationships in which they stand, to service others' emotional needs. The consequences seem to be that women who accept this feminist ethical theory are by that theory prevented from the work of self-development, the political activism, and aggressive confrontation needed for feminist activism. A moral theory developed by feminists, and purporting to offer one feminist perspective on ethics, seems to undermine feminist aims by its endorsement of caring, self-sacrificial activities.[2]

But this quick dismissal is unsatisfactory. Care theory does seem to capture important features of our moral experience in ways that other theories fail to do, and I am loath to reject it. An alternative to rejection is to attempt to address more directly the issue of self-sacrifice and gender. In order to do this, I would like to discuss the connections between Care theory and Agapic ethics. Agapic ethics is an ethics developed in the Christian tradition and centered on the love commands of the gospel; it is another paradigmatically self-sacrificial ethics, without the overtly gendered status of contemporary Care theory. Care theory can learn from Agapic theory and can resolve some of the problems surrounding self-sacrifice by developing analogous concepts to some of those found in Agapic theories.

I. SELF-SACRIFICE

What is it about self-sacrifice and Care ethics that makes charges such as MacKinnon's, quoted earlier, so problematic for the project of developing an ethics of Care? The problem is not simply that an ethics of Care requires self-sacrifice; any number of theories require that and are not picked out for criticism on that score by feminists. Care theory, however, is regularly and explicitly criticized for precisely this feature.[3]

All ethical theories require a denial of self-interest at some level, either short-term self-interest for the sake of long-term self-interest, or denial of the self for the sake of the greater good, or denial of the self for the sake of the law of reason. But there are two features of these theories which, taken together, make them less problematic (on this particular issue)[4] than Care theory. The first is that the conception of self-denial at issue in these theories is one that accommodates a broad range of behavior. On a Utilitarian view, for example, one can deny one's desires and throw oneself into one's work for the sake of the greater good. But given Care's use of the maternal image as the paradigm of Care, this is not the image of self-sacrifice it produces. The mother who denies her emotional attachment to her children for the sake of professional advancement, even if her profession is one that brings great benefit to the world, will hardly be held up as an exemplar of care. Our cultural images of motherhood preclude it. So the image of self-sacrifice generated by Care is an image of the denial of the development of one's own talents and future prospects for the sake of another.

Added to this construal of the very notion of self-sacrifice is the fact that Care is presented as a woman's voice in ethics. Women's morality, this suggests, which arises from women's nature, requires an ethics of caring for the other, of maintaining relationships, and of nurturing, even at fairly great expense to oneself. But who is it who hears the call to care? If care is a woman's ethic, then presumably it is by and for women. And from this conclusion it is but a short step to complementarity theories of human ethical responsibilities.

The call for self-sacrifice in Care theory comes from a theory developed by paying attention to women's experiences and moral reasoning. This seems to imply that women are naturally more self-sacrificial than men; when we listen to women's voices, rather than men's, we hear the call to self-sacrifice in the particular way our culture assumes mothers should self-sacrifice. Men are good at claiming their rights (hence justice-based theories), women are good at maintaining relationships and taking care of others (care-based theories), and the two sexes are thus suited to occupy complementary (but not equal) niches in human society. Because Care theory is often presented as a woman's voice in ethics, it can very easily lend itself to stereotypical assumptions about women's nature that entrench beliefs about complementary roles for men and women.

But feminist theorists reject normative complementarity almost universally.[5] It is rejected for two reasons. The first is that complementarity theories are asymmetrical, in practice if not in theory. That is, women are taken to complement men (and thus be suitable as servants for them) while men are not taken to be suitably placed at the service of women. The asymmetry of complementarity seems to be generalizable beyond the bounds of gender. Whenever two diverse social groups are defined in terms of general characteristics that are claimed to be complementary, there is a very good chance that one of the groups is being used by the other. Apartheid in South Africa operated partly on an assumption of complementarity, slavery in the American South was frequently justified on that basis, and the contemporary denial of women's basic rights in countries such as Afghanistan, Saudi Arabia, and the Sudan likewise relies on the complementary natures of men and women. Participants in such practices often claim that the complementary roles are different but equal, or that the subordinate role is really the better one. The best response to such claims comes from Simone de Beauvoir's wry discussion in *The Second Sex:*

> There are American sociologists who seriously teach today the theory of "low-class gain." In France, also, it has often been proclaimed—although in less scientific manner—that the workers are very fortunate in not being obliged to "keep up appearances" and still more so the bums who can dress in rags and sleep on the sidewalks, pleasures forbidden to the Count de Beaumont and the Wendels. Like the carefree wretches gaily scratching at their vermin, like the merry Negroes laughing under the lash and those joyous Tunisian Arabs burying their starved children with a smile, woman enjoys that incomparable privilege, irresponsibility. Free from troublesome burdens and cares, she obviously has "the better part." But it is disturbing that with an obstinate perversity—connected no doubt with original sin—down through the centuries and in all countries, the people who have the better part are always crying out to their benefactors: "It is too much! I will be satisfied with yours!" But the munificent capitalists, the generous colonists, the superb males, stick to their guns: "Keep the better part, hold on to it!"[6]

Separate but equal somehow always becomes separate and unequal in actual practice.

A second problem with complementarity theories is a general lack of an adequate statistical basis for the delegation of separate roles to men and women. It may be, for example, that there is a general, small, statistical tendency for women to be more proficient verbally than men, and men more proficient in mathematics than women. From that small statistical fact, however, nothing follows about individuals such as myself or my husband. For us to assume that I cannot balance the checkbook, and that he should be responsible for all financial decisions because of complementarity would be ludicrous; I might very well be far more proficient than he is at mathematical (and economic) decisions. From statistical differences one cannot simply infer individual differences. Further, and more importantly, from statistical differences, even large statistical differences, one cannot infer that enforcement of difference is morally acceptable. The social enforcement of complementary sex roles that is central to complementarity theory, however, relies on such inferences.[7]

In addition to its natural connection to complementarity theory, Care theory's call to care is also suspect, from a feminist perspective, because of the cultural context in which it occurs. Care theory occurs in the context of a society that encourages women to be far more submissive and self-denying than men. In that context, critics charge, women already have very little sense of self. The call to self-sacrificial care, in the specific context in which it occurs, exacerbates women's tendency to submissiveness, self-denial, and enabling masculine oppressiveness. Care theory's encouragement of self-sacrifice counters feminist aims of political justice and professional fulfillment for individual women.

There are cultural differences in the way men and women hear the call to self-sacrifice. Men rarely seem to think, first, that their sacrifice should be for the sake of women's intellectual or developmental benefit.[8] The masculine paradigm of self-sacrifice can involve giving up time, energy, even one's life for another man, as in the case of the Good Samaritan or the soldier in the foxhole leaping on a hand grenade to protect his fellow soldiers. It can also involve giving up money or energy for the sake of children; the prevalence of children's faces in pleas for charity indicate the centrality of this image in our culture. But giving up one's job so that one's wife can more freely pursue her own career has never, in my own experience, been offered as an emulable example of self-sacrifice.

Second, men's glorification of self-sacrifice rarely leads them to reject the service and sacrifice of women for their sake. One exception to this rule is Christ's gentle rebuke of Martha's service in the story of Mary and Martha found in Luke; but this story is rarely held up as a model for men's and women's relationships. In both of these respects, women experience the call to self-sacrifice radically differently than men do. Women do regularly assume that the call to self-sacrifice, in their case, does require that they sacrifice their own intellectual and career development for the sake of men or children. And their acceptance of the norm of self-sacrifice regularly leads them to reject others' service, or to make it impossible for others to serve them.

When these two features are juxtaposed, so that women who already lack a sense of duty to self are told that morality is a matter of self-sacrificial giving, and that message is overlaid with the implication that women are naturally suited to such caring behavior, or, worse, women are told that the essential nature of "woman" involves sacrifice of the self for another, Care ethics becomes a conceptual barrier to women's defense of their own rights and freedoms.

So the problem with Care theory and the endorsement of self-sacrifice, from a feminist point of view, is not that self-sacrifice can never be advocated. Nor is the problem that only women are directed to sacrifice themselves; that claim could hardly be substantiated by references to the writings of those who advocate care. The problem is the differential impact the directive to self-sacrifice has on women as compared to men. Critics of Care theory charge that men, directed to self-sacrifice, begin to occasionally care for others. Women (the charge continues), when directed to self-sacrifice, are likely to feel compelled to serve the needs of everyone and everything that crosses their path.

For clarification I should emphasize here that I am not claiming that women are more self-sacrificing than men. I do claim, however, that women and men who do self-sacrifice do so in different ways, and those differences are morally significant. I have known many men who sacrificed their lives by working far too many hours for too little pay in order to provide a chance at a happier life for their children. It is far rarer to find a man who sacrifices his career for a family. Acts of physical self-sacrifice by men for women (I think of this as the Titanic case) are fairly frequent, as is the portrayal of soldiers as sacrificing for their wives or mothers. So what does seem correct is that the ways in which men and women may be expected to sacrifice themselves differ in Western culture; whether or not the actual incidence of self-sacrifice is greater in one gender than another is unclear. But whatever the truth of the general claim about levels of self-sacrifice, there does seem to be some legitimacy to the charge that an ethics of Care can encourage unhealthy patterns of self-sacrifice in women's lives, where that self-sacrifice is the peculiarly gendered sacrifice of failing to stand up for or fully develop the self.

A third layer of connection between women and self-sacrifice is added to this scenario, according to Grace Clement, by the symbolic linking of social practices of caregiving with the feminine in our culture, and the further linking of those practices (again at a symbolic level, as well as a practical level) with a lack of autonomy. Clement argues that social practices of caregiving (nursing, teaching, child care, and the like) are first, symbolically linked with cultural conceptions of the feminine, and second, strongly defined in terms of a lack of autonomy. These linkages are not accidental; the social construction of femininity in Western culture involves a close connection of femininity with passivity and a lack of self-directedness.[9] At the level of the cultural imagination, then, the picture we hold unconsciously of what a good woman is is inextricably linked to notions of being under the direction of an authority, of obedience, and of lacking autonomy. Again, these traits connect with the concept of care in ways that diminish women's sense of entitlement, of a right to self-fulfillment, and of the appropriateness of women's autonomy.

At the symbolic level, furthermore, the self-sacrifice critique of care draws our attention to the ways in which a symbolic connection between self-sacrifice and women's nature can legitimate the assumption that women are naturally suited to self-sacrifice so that sacrificial actions are, first, expected of women and, second, attributed to their nature so that they are not given credit for those actions, in much the same way that the "natural athletic ability" of African American athletes is used to diminish the credit the athletes receive for their skills.

II. CARE THEORISTS' PROPOSED SOLUTIONS TO THE PROBLEM OF SELF-SACRIFICE

Critiques of Care theory that focus on self-sacrifice seem to raise a legitimate and serious problem for Care theorists. A natural way of resolving the problem of self-sacrifice is to set limits on the care that one is required to give, and several different accounts of those limits have been offered. Unfortunately none of the proposed limitations completely resolves the problem. They tend to fall into one of two camps: a limitation on the obligation to care based on the caregiver's own limitations and relationships, or a limitation on the obligation to care based on the need to develop social structures of care. While both of these limitations are important, neither of them is entirely satisfactory.

Both Rita Manning and Nel Noddings limit the call to care first by the natural limits faced by the caregiver herself in terms of time, energy, and resources, and second by making care dependent on the type of relationship that holds between caregiver and care receiver. Unceasing care is self-destructive of the caregiver; after a certain point giving too much destroys the capacity to give. When the demand for care becomes so oppressive that it destroys one's ability to care, one must turn away. So care is limited in the first instance by the physical and emotional limits of the caregiver. It may be too strong to conclude that one *should* stop caring when this point is reached (since Noddings considers stopping a failure of care, but one which needs to be accepted as part of the human condition),[10] but these practical limitations do represents one way of limiting the care one can give.

Secondly, Noddings and Manning both argue that the closeness of the relationships in which we stand to others places limits on our responsibility to care. Noddings phrases this in terms of circles of responsibility, a phrase which has been criticized by a number of theorists, but which captures the basic notion that we have differing levels of responsibility to others based, in part, on the closeness of our relationship to them.[11] Obviously the content of our responsibilities to others depends on the type of relationship; it seems reasonable that the degree of responsibility should change as well.

Both of these points are important, and worth making, but they fail to solve the problem of self-sacrifice. The first fails, in part, because it offers too little too late. If it is acceptable for me to limit care only when I have reached the absolute limits of my physical and emotional resources, then care really does demand more than an ethical theory can rightly demand. Nor does the addition of the second limitation solve the problem. It seems correct to say that my responsibilities to those closest to me are the greatest, but that hardly gives me grounds for refusing to sacrifice myself for the other, it merely ensures that the other for whom I sacrifice is close to me.

These limitations fail, most importantly, because neither of them requires the agent to accord herself independent value for her own sake. Both limit the requirements of care by an attempt to get more long-range care-value from the agent, so to speak, rather than limiting care by the inherent worth of the caring person herself. That is, both limitations assume that the only valid reason for limiting the call to care is for the purpose of generating more (future) care. But the call to care should sometimes be limited by the agent's legitimate interests in her own development, her concern for her own needs, and (though I realize the dangers in using this language) her rights.

A further problem is this. Because of the emphasis on the care given rather than the person of the caregiver, neither of these limitations encourages a careful critique of the relationships that limit care. Care is an appropriate response in the context of certain relationships. But relationships in which the caregiving is inappropriately one-sided[12] (or pathological in other ways—there are many ways in which relationships can go wrong) should not be supported by care. They should be ended. As Grace Clement points out in a discussion of this type of case, Care theory needs a way to separate caring from enabling.[13]

A third method, and again an important but inadequate way of limiting care, can be found in Joan Tronto's discussion of the political and social dimensions of care. Tronto argues that when care is conceptualized purely as private, emotionally motivated service, service that individual women are expected to offer voluntarily, care will be offered inadequately in society. That is, the way in which care work is conceptualized leads to it being offered at an inadequate level. This is because private resources are inadequate to the task of fulfilling all the care needs that exist in our society. The stress experienced by middle-aged couples trying to cope simultaneously with teenage children and aging parents indicates the extent to which the privatization of care in society leaves important needs unmet—individual caregivers lack the resources to offer the needed care at an adequate level. So Tronto concludes that society needs to think of care in terms of social structures of care—structures that don't exclude private care relationships, but which supplement and support those relationships while providing a fallback set of structures for those without caregivers.[14]

Tronto's point is vital for thinking about the ramifications of Care theory for social structures. Without the resources for generating broadly based social directives, Care theory is an inadequate account of the ethical life. But for our purposes in this paper, it is inadequate, since it fails to address the problem with which we began—how to deal with the issue of self-sacrifice in a satisfactory way from within Care theory. Care can have social implications—Tronto seems exactly correct in drawing this conclusion. But even after we have drawn those conclusions we are still left with the problem of how to put limits on the care that individuals are to offer to others. Social structures or no, the individual still has to decide when she will care and when she will not.

Further, none of the limitations discussed so far go any distance toward solving the peculiarly gendered nature of the self-sacrifice critique of care. The first two seem instead to entrench it, since if it is the case that women understand themselves and are understood by others to be naturally suited to sacrificial care, then the relationships women are in will be ones that require high levels of caring sacrifice, and the point at which burnout is seen as incipient will be fairly late. Tronto's move to a political solution, while it is an important modification of care theory, nonetheless occurs in the context of a society in which public care work as well as private care work is carried out predominantly by women. Public care work simply exploits women's willingness to undervalue themselves at a different level than private care work,[15] but it certainly doesn't resolve the gender problem.

As an alternative to setting limits on Care, Noddings also points out in a more recent article that Care is an ethical ideal for both men and women, and so should not pose a uniquely gendered call to self-sacrifice.[16] She makes the claim, but does not develop it extensively in that context. I think this response is heading in the right direction, and I will return to it at the end of this paper. At this point, however, and without further support, the attempt to include men in an ethic of Care does not resolve the issue of care and women's self-sacrifice because it does not offer any way to change the differential impact the command to care has on men and women in our society.

III. CARE AND AGAPE:
SIMILARITIES AND DIFFERENCES

It seems to me worthwhile to look at a moral theory that is quite similar to Care theory, but which does not suffer from the same gender-differentiated notion of self-sacrifice, to see what resources that theory might have for a better treatment of self-sacrifice. So I turn now to consider the similarities between Care and Agape, and the natural affinity the two theories have for each other. There are, of course, some important differences between the theories. But even with these differences, both accounts of ethics make many of the same assumptions, and the large areas of agreement suggest that there is a basic compatibility between them. Since Agapic ethics does not share the same sort of gender baggage as an ethics of Care, an examination of Agape may suggest some ways of avoiding the gendered self-sacrifice problem that Care faces.

But first, a quick discussion of points of similarity and dissimilarity. The most obvious area of overlap between a Care ethics and Agapic ethics is that both are relational ethics. Both make ethics a matter of relationships, both understand humans as beings who stand in relationship to others, both focus on the multiple ways in which right and wrong are determined by the relationships in which one stands, and both de-emphasize the issue of choice in regards to those relationships. This is not to say that freedom and choice do not play important roles in both theories, but to make the point that many of the obligations and responsibilities we have arise out of the relationships in which we stand, and we do not always choose either the relationship or the obligations. As a daughter, for example, I have any number of responsibilities to my mother that I did not choose, but which are nonetheless obligatory. In the case of Agapism, the doctrine of grace is the clearest example of the fact that choice, while important, is not determinative of moral responsibility.

Mothering has been a central paradigm in Care theory since its inception. In *Caring* Noddings uses the mother-child relationship as her central motif in developing the notion of care, though she moves to a broader variety of relationships in *Women and Evil*. Sara Ruddick develops her entire ethical theory from an examination of maternal thinking, and focusing on mothering has been central to much of Care thinking in general.

Agapic ethics is likewise based in a relationship, but the relationship taken as paradigm is either God's relationship with humans, particularly as exemplified in Christ's incarnation, bridging the gap between God and humans by becoming human himself, or (in some versions of Agapism) the Trinitarian relationship among the various persons of the one God.

So both theories emphasize the relational aspect of human lives. However, the nature of the relationships taken to be paradigmatic is clearly different. Care ethics begins from human relationships, while Agapic ethics begins with a discussion of the relationship between humans and God. The central importance of the "Father" motif in both the Old and New Testaments suggests, of course, that even here there may be areas of overlap.

A second similarity can be found in that both Care and Agapism emphasize particularity. In both cases, the love or the care for the other must be a love or care for the other in his or her particularity, not care or love generalized across all of humanity. In an interesting departure from his generally Augustinian account of human life, for example, Anders Nygren argues that love for the other cannot be understood as love for the image of God in the other—love must be directed at the other in her/his particularity.[17] In the case of some theorists (most notably Joseph Fletcher) this attention to particularity shades over into a full-fledged situationalism. In others, such as Paul Ramsey, the emphasis on particularity is used to bolster a respect for principles, since Ramsey argues that absolute principles protect and support respect for the particularity of individuals. (The Ramsey-Fletcher debate in the Agapic tradition has recently been echoed in Care theory by Noddings and Tronto, with Noddings firmly rejecting principles (at least in her earlier work) and Tronto arguing for social structures that bear a striking resemblance to Ramsey's defense of human rights.)

A third obvious area of comparison between an ethics of Care and an ethics of Agape is the centrality of the motif of love/compassion/care. Both theories place other-regarding love or care at the heart of what it is to be moral, rather than a concept such as rationality, or universality, or rights. Both theories, then, operate with a picture of human life that allows a central place for the emotions. Further, the affective aspects of human life are not denigrated, but are considered essential aspects of human flourishing.

Finally, both theories emphasize the extent to which morality requires one to live for the other, rather than emphasizing or starting with responsibilities to the self, as, for example, Kant's account of ethics does. Both theories begin with the assumption that the moral imperative is a command to care for or to serve the other, and both thus face the need to account for limitations on self-sacrifice from that starting point.

So, for example, Paul Ramsey begins by arguing that the Christian, faced with a life-threatening attack, cannot kill the other in order to preserve the self, since that would be to treat another in a way that fails to respect the sacredness of human life. In self-other relationships, he argues, the self can never take precedence over the other.[18] If he had stopped there in his ethical analysis, of course, he would have had to advocate pacifism, which he famously did not. When we move from individual relationships with a single other person to the more complex relationships between several people, or in the context of social structures, Ramsey argues, pacifism becomes unacceptable because it represents a failure to respect the sacredness of those others who may be unjustly hurt or killed. Christian charity calls me to lay down my life for another, but it never permits me to lay down someone else's life.[19]

The similarities between this account and Noddings's are striking. Noddings, likewise, believes that prior limitations cannot be placed on the care I owe to the one cared for. She speaks, in fact, of the fact that a stranger in need may generate in us a sense of dread at the prospect of an unbounded call to care.[20] (And her discussion here is phenomenologically perspicuous.) She also recognizes the existence of conflicts of care and the need to choose when two others call for my care.[21] While she rejects the principles approach that Ramsey embraces, her discussion, nonetheless, bears a striking resemblance to Agapic thinking.

Given these similarities, is it fair to charge, as Sarah Lucia Hoagland has,[22] that Care simply is an Agapism developed by feminist theorists? There are several reasons why I think this charge is mistaken. The most obvious is that Agapic ethics arises out of a specific religious tradition, and is not appropriate for translation into completely secular terms.[23] It has been developed from a specifically theological perspective. Care theory, on the other hand, is probably best described as humanistic; it depends, theoretically, on human relationships, and some fairly strong claims about human nature, and is explicitly free of any theistic grounding.

Secondly, Agapic ethics has been developed, by and large, by male theorists, writing in many cases (more so in the past, less so today) for male readers. Perhaps because of this, perhaps because of assumptions common at the time when some theorists were writing, many Agapic theorists understand persons as largely self-sufficient male individuals.[24] Anders Nygren offers the most extreme example of this individualistic focus. Human ethics, for Nygren, involves the individual, his relationship to his God, and his relationship to other (presumably adult male) individuals. Families appear nowhere in the book, mothers and children are never mentioned, and the fundamental ethical issue for Nygren is whether or not actions are undertaken out of pure love for the other or out of self-love. The two loves are completely opposed; either one acts from the one or from the other.

This is both bad psychology and bad theology. Humans, of course, can act simultaneously out of love for the self and for the other, and parental actions offer one of the clearest cases in point. If asked why I make my daughter do her homework, whether I do it out of self-love or other-love, the either/or simply cannot be accepted.

Nygren's account of Christian ethics was criticized at a very early point for its unconscious individualism, most notably in the 1960 article by Valerie Saiving entitled "The Human Situation: A Feminine View." Saiving, like many feminist theorists, associates Nygren's individualism and stark "I or the Other" rhetoric with masculinity; I think, on the contrary, that it needs to be criticized for what it is, a false dilemma and bad human psychology. Even men whose rhetoric matches Nygren's do not live lives that exemplify the isolated individual, driven in all his actions by pure self-interest except when, by God's grace, he manages to deny the self and live for the other. Their day-to-day lives belie the truth of their claims, as do Gospel stories of Christ (the paradigm of self-sacrifice) accepting meals and care from others. The question is not whether we will love ourselves, but how we should love ourselves.

IV. AGAPE AND SELF-SACRIFICE

There are clearly differences between Care and Agapism, but the basic similarity between them remains. Given that similarity, it seems worthwhile to ask how thinkers in the Agapic tradition deal with the issue of self-sacrifice. There are some who don't deal with it very well at all. Nygren, for example, simply advocates it, and asserts that any actions motivated by any sort of self-love are unacceptable from an Agapic standpoint. This is not a terribly helpful position to take.

Paul Ramsey's approach to the issue of self-sacrifice begins in much the same way as Noddings's, as was briefly mentioned above. For Ramsey, justice is indirectly derived from the duty to love the other as oneself. When one is confronted with a choice between self and other, love requires that the self be sacrificed for the sake of the other. The situation changes, however, when I am not threatened, but perceive another threatening a third party. When there are others involved, justice comes into play for Ramsey. It is proper to defend an innocent person against unjust aggression, for example, even though it may require that I sacrifice another (i.e., the aggressor), rather than myself. Further, if my survival is necessary to defend an innocent, Ramsey argues, I am morally obligated to refrain from self-sacrifice.[25]

This is very similar to Noddings's limitations on Care. My obligation to Care can itself set limits on how much I care, since too much self-sacrifice makes care impossible, thus harming the very one I care for. But Ramsey adds to this another factor, missing in Noddings. He points out that since I know that there is a natural tendency in humans to sin, my willingness to sacrifice for the other must be limited by an intention to limit the effects of sin in the world. Ramsey terms this a preferential ethic of protection,[26] and provides a grounding for it by reference to the destruction and suffering that people regularly choose to cause to others. If we do not take seriously the difference between the innocent victim and the aggressor, Ramsey points out, we fail to live out the law of love. The presence of evil in the world, of sinful proclivities in human nature, requires that we struggle ourselves to limit the effect of evil on others, and that we work to create and maintain social structures that protect the weak and the innocent.

Gene Outka goes further than Ramsey in discussing the limitations on self-sacrifice. He agrees with Ramsey that love for the other can require us to choose between others; love can require that we kill the unjust aggressor to protect the innocent victim. Sin produces one set of limitations on how we love others. But he goes further than Ramsey in arguing that consistency requires that if we love the other as much as our self, we must be prepared to value the self as we do the other. His account of Agapic ethics thus offers a context in which care for the self can be developed. Such care is developed under the rubric of impartiality; the command to love must at some level be applied impartially, and so it requires both other-love and self-love to similar degrees.[27] Outka considers various objections to this obligation to self-love from some who say it allows for too little love for the self (because we ought to care for the self more than for others), and from some who say that it allows for too much love for the self (because there is a natural tendency to love the self too much, so that such love should not be commanded). He concludes that it is nonetheless an essential part of Agapic love.

There are two conceptual structures that underlie Outka's account of self-love. One is the conceptual trope of creation. All humans are created by God to live in relationship to God, so all humans share in the sacredness of relation to God. Based on this basic sacredness, it is necessary to affirm that one's own self should be valued as highly (though not more highly) than other selves. Outka continues on to argue that this can provide the grounds for a certain level of self-preference based on the responsibility each of us has to God for our own lives.[28] In saying this, Outka moves from what I would call the creation grounds for self-love to the vocation ground of self-love.

My love for my neighbor and my love for myself, based on our equality as loved children of God, ought to be largely identical based on an equal capacity for relationship with God. So if we begin and end with a creation grounding, self-love and other-love must be largely equal. But the further conceptual motif of vocation adds a heavier degree of responsibility that I have to God for my own life. That is, I am responsible to God for how I live my life in ways that I cannot be responsible (to God) for my neighbor's life and the choices she makes. This notion of responsibility is part of what we get when we develop a notion of vocation, of the idea that each of us has a unique responsibility to become a particular person, participating in a unique way in the human community.[29]

Both of these motifs, of the worth of each individual based on their creation by a loving God, and of the individual vocation to which an individual is called, provide a needed balance with respect to issues of self-sacrifice. If a theory has strong grounds for asserting the equal value, or equal sanctity, of each individual, then it cannot call for unrestrained self-sacrifice. The self should be valued as are others, and this places limits on the place of self-sacrifice in the theory.

Further, if each individual has a unique vocation, or life's work to which she is called, her responsibility to give up the self is again placed within limiting brackets. The vocation itself may require a particular sacrifice of the self, but other self-sacrificial actions will be ruled out. If an agent squanders her time and abilities in service to others' minor whims, her ability to carry out her true calling will be destroyed. The motif of vocation in Christian thought allows for fairly stringent limitations on when and under what circumstances self-sacrifice is morally acceptable.

V. CARE AND LIMITS ON SELF-SACRIFICE

There are three motifs, then, that figure in Agapic responses to the problem of self-sacrifice. Care theory requires a similar trio of concepts in its understanding of human nature in order to resolve the self-sacrifice dilemma with which we began. That is, Care theory needs analogous concepts to the ideas of creation, sin, and vocation if it is to offer a theoretically adequate account of care without advocating unceasing self-sacrifice.

How might such an account go? Care theory cannot fall back on a creation theology and remain theologically neutral. Nor can it fall back on a Kantian account of the equality of all humans based on their capacity for rationality. What is needed is an account of human nature that locates human identity in responsiveness to the other, and in relationality. That is, to be human is to find oneself in relationship with others, or face to face with the other who obligates me simply by existing as a fellow member of the moral community. Such an account of human existence has been developed in the work of Emmanuel Levinas, as well as in the work of Annette Baier, and it provides the grounding for the claim that the one-caring (to use Noddings's terminology) needs to accord herself the same measure of respect as is offered to other members of the moral community.

Both Levinas and Baier emphasize the extent to which human existence is grounded in the natural expression of and acceptance of an ethical relationship to others. Levinas's account starts from a first-person phenomenology of human existence, and Baier offers a more detached third-person account of trust, but both point to the centrality of emotional/moral commitments to human existence. If this account of human nature is correct, humans are fundamentally communal selves; to be human is to be in relation. Human existence is existence in ethical community with others. Placed explicitly in this context, however, the call to care loses some of its self-sacrificial character.

I experience myself as a member of the human community and I experience the call to care. If I were to understand myself as an isolated individual, that unmitigated call would require a total abnegation of the self. But I shouldn't understand myself as an isolated individual—I am always already a member of a community. The care I offer another can, first, strengthen the community and so strengthen me. Providing care need not be understood solely in terms of economic transactions where anything given to the other is lost to me. Instead, care given recirculates back through the community so that we all benefit from the care we all give.

But, further, my location within the community precludes complete self-sacrifice except under very exceptional circumstances. My own destruction harms the community of which I am a part. My own care for the self is required because of my position within the moral community,[30] a community marked by mutuality of moral concern and recognition of mutual worth.

An ethics of Care runs the risk of devolving into a sacrificial ethic only so long as it is understood individualistically. When, however, it is placed, as it originated, in a communal context, then the imperative to care applies to all, and all properly share in the benefits of care.

Further, a person who chooses to self-sacrifice may find that she is impeding others' ability to develop their own capacity to care. Self-sacrifice can be destructive of others' ability to have a realistic conception of their own place in the universe. Children who believe that their mother's life should revolve around them ceaselessly are being trained to be selfish autocrats. This is not healthy. It is only when children are raised to reciprocate the care they receive that they can grow up into healthy adults, capable of fully ethical relationships with others.

The concept of membership in the moral community, a concept that is analogous in many ways to the notion of humans as part of a created community, provides a partial solution to the problem of self-sacrifice. It also goes some way toward defusing the gender problem, since membership in the moral community is a human trait, not a female trait. Women are not uniquely called to care, and women's acceptance of an unfair share of caring work is destructive of a healthy moral community. It enables others to fail to care, which harms them as members of the moral community. It also overburdens those who do care, which again is harmful for the community as a whole.

I think some account of women's nature that resembles this has actually been operative in most Care theory. Care theorists' interest in hearing women's voices indicates a fundamental recognition of women's worth. But the tendency to term Care a feminine theory makes it harder to argue that it is a theory that speaks of the whole of the ethical community, and makes it easy to slip into thinking that care is women's responsibility.

Second, Care theory needs some analogue to the notion of sin, some explanation of the horrible things human voluntarily choose to do to each other. If it is human nature to care, and to respond affectively to fellow humans, then why are brutality and enslavement standard human responses to other humans? Noddings discusses evil extensively in *Women and Evil*, and while her focus there is mostly on the steps that can be taken by individuals and societies to prevent, ameliorate, or ward off evil, she does suggest that a Jungian account of the shadow side of one's own psyche goes some way toward explaining evil.[31]

Jean Grimshaw has argued that feminist theory has a tendency to assume a simplistic, unified, rationalist picture of the self in its explicit theorizing about women's experiences and lives (a tendency, I should note, to which Noddings does not seem particularly susceptible). In contrast to this, she argues, feminists need a complex notion of subjectivity in which the self is understood to be "always a more or less precarious and conflictual construction out of, and compromise between, conflicting and not always conscious desires and experiences."[32] Such an account of subjectivity need not be Freudian, Jungian, or Lacanian, though it might have similarities, but it is, I think, a necessary part of any ethical account of both the moral ideals to which we are called and our impulses and choices that act against morality.

Humans, as Noddings has argued, do naturally care, and that natural care provides the context for ethical caring. But humans also naturally act in malicious ways; they are naturally destructive. These tendencies are almost as deeply rooted in human nature as the urge to reach out in love,[33] and an account of ethics that does not recognize them lacks the ability to explain an essential part of human nature.

When humans' natural proclivity to hurt others, to bear them malice, and to delight in tormenting others is paired with the natural tendency to care, and the complex whole of subjectivity that is formed by these contradictory tendencies is kept in mind as an ethics is developed, the call to care can be constructed in a way that is less prone to advocate self-sacrifice.

Other humans need, and legitimately expect, care from me. Other humans, however, are not always caring themselves. They may use my care for them as a resource on which to draw as they cause harm to others, or they may see a refusal to harm them as license to harm others with impunity. An active recognition of human tendencies to choose evil pushes Care theory to develop social structures that prevent the expression of such evil, but it also places important limitations on the individual's self-sacrifice. If my care for this person contributes to the destruction of other people, then I should not engage in that sort of care. I may, in fact, have a duty to preserve myself so that I can continue to fight against evil.

But there is a second corrective of care that arises from this more complex psychology. Care itself can be perverted, and can serve evil. An individual can, while intending the best for another, cause the other great harm. This is a difficult phenomenon to explain from a Care perspective. If care is the central ethical imperative, then it would seem that actions arising from the desire to help another should be good actions.

This paradox can be partly explained if human nature is not assumed to be morally neutral or morally good. If humans have the capacity for good, but also a tendency to do evil, the ways in which care can be misused, and can turn destructive, can be accounted for. The impulse to care is good in and of itself, but as expressed by humans who are tempted to choose evil it can be destructive and productive of horrible results. An account of human emotional drives that pairs the natural affective tendencies humans have with a death drive, or a desire for destruction, offers a necessary explanatory structure for an adequate account of care. And such a will to destruction provides more of the needed limits on self-sacrifice. It provides a needed corrective to the notion that any and all actions arising from natural caring are ethical. When natural caring serves evil it is evil itself. And natural caring can be true care only when it serves the needs of those who can be harmed rather than those who want to harm.

Both membership in the moral community and a natural tendency of humans to choose evil place needed limits on the obligation to care. Neither of them goes far enough, however. Both allow for the same degree of concern for the self as one has for others, but neither of them can justify a higher degree of responsibility for the self that could counter social expectations of women's self-sacrifice. Care theory needs something analogous to Agape's concept of vocation. It needs some theoretical support for the idea that each individual has the responsibility to develop her capacities and abilities into a complete and flourishing life. In the case of Agape, of course, this flourishing life involves a joyous relationship with the Creator, but such an account is not available to a non-theistically based theory.

Providing a concept that can do the theoretical work of vocation is difficult in the framework of Care theory, however. In the context of a world that is not inherently meaningful, it is difficult to provide a conceptual grounding for the idea that each person has a specific life to which she is called. Noddings's advocacy of humanism as a non-theistic religion seems to me the most promising response to this problem.[34] But there is a faintly tautological flavor to this response as well. It seems to require that we assert and respect the value of each individual because we are, ourselves, individuals.

A second problem with this response is that it provides no context for judgments about which lives are legitimate developments of ability and which are not; as Outka points out, the uniquely developed individuality of a Caligula or a Stalin does not deserve our moral approbation.[35] An account of the individual telos which can justify caring for the self in morally acceptable ways poses a problem for Care theory in its current form.

Agapic ethics is valuable in thinking through the nature of care since it offers an example of an ethics that does require self-sacrifice, but places that sacrifice in a context in which the individual is not solely responsible for meeting all the needs of every one needing care with whom she comes into contact. The notion that we are called to love the other within the context of a moral community puts limits on the obligation to care for the other. The natural desire humans have to cause harm and destruction requires further limitations on the obligation to care. Finally, Agapic ethics also has room for the notion of a vocation, of a calling or responsibility which may very well require self-sacrifice, but not just any self-sacrifice, and not for just any reason. It requires that one subordinate oneself to a higher purpose, rather than to accept any and all claims others make on one's time. This contextualizes self-sacrifice in a way that is needed in Care ethics, preventing the call to care from becoming oppressive and destructive of the self. It seems to me that the first two can be provided relatively straightforwardly by the Care theorist, but that the third presents a problem.

Does this resolve the problems with which I began? Does it put to rest my own concerns about how to balance my professional and personal life, or my duties to my students with my need to do research? Well, frankly, no. I am left to struggle with these problems, as is every person whose commitments pull her in conflicting directions. But it does help to contextualize these struggles. When I am faced with a needy student, I do have an obligation to listen, to provide a space in which she can mourn, and so on. But to imagine that I am the solution to her problem would be wrong as well. Caring requires, among other things, that I recognize her strength and ability to deal with the troubles life throws at her. Further, I have my own obligations that must be met, including the obligation to develop the gifts I have been given, and the continued involvement in student problems may actually be a running from my responsibility for that development.

A simplistic command to care, heard in our individualistic cultural context, accompanied by a gendered subtext, may encourage self-sacrifice. A Care theory developed more fully can have the opposite effect. It can energize women and men to change oppressive social structures that damage the moral community. It can strengthen them to resist evil in themselves and in others. And it can, perhaps, bring them to recognize the responsibility they have to themselves to become the people they were meant to become.

NOTES

This chapter was partly funded by a summer Calvin Research Fellowship. My thanks to Calvin College for supporting my research in this way. The essay has also benefited from comments on an earlier draft that passed through the Philosophy Departmental Colloquium; thanks to my colleagues for their careful reading and perceptive comments.

1. Just how deep this cultural imagery runs was brought home to me during a Mother's Day sermon I listened to a few years ago. The text for the sermon concerned Hannah, the mother of Samuel. Hannah had prayed for a child for years, her prayers are finally answered when Samuel is born, and in a grateful response she gives the child back to the service of God, sending him to live at the temple as a servant from about the age of four or five. The preacher somehow managed to construe Hannah's sending Samuel to live and serve at the temple as a paean to mothers who give up careers to stay home and care for their children. His complete obliviousness to the inappropriateness of the text to the message brought home to me the depth of our cultural association of good women (Hannah is a good woman, after all) with subordinating professional goals to service to the family (if she is a good woman, she must be an at-home mom.) I was the only member of the congregation who found the text and the sermon to be at odds.

2. Patricia Ward Scaltsas titles an essay discussing this issue "Do Feminist Ethics Counter Feminist Aims?" in *Explorations in Feminist Ethics: Theory and Practice,* ed. Eve Browning Cole and Susan Coultrap-McQuin (Bloomington and Indianapolis: Indiana University Press, 1992), pp. 15–26. Scaltsas discusses three themes: a rejection of abstract reasoning in favor of contextual reasoning, an emphasis on natural empathetic emotions, and a de-emphasis of choice in the sorts of theories I discuss in this paper. Her argument concludes that all of these themes could, in theory, be important ethical starting points, but in practice all of them serve to support sexist allocation of social roles. I am sympathetic to her concerns, as I hope is clear from the rest of this paper.

3. MacKinnon, of course, is not the only feminist critic who rejects an ethics of Care because of its connection with women's self-sacrifice. See also Sarah Lucia Hoagland's "Some Thoughts on 'Caring,'" in *Feminist Ethics,* ed. Claudia Card (Lawrence: University Press of Kansas, 1991), pp. 246–63; Jean Grimshaw's discussion of maternal thinking in *Philosophy and Feminist Thinking* (Minneapolis: University of Minnesota Press, 1986), pp. 227–53; Marcia Homiak's "Feminism and Aristotle's Rational Ideal," in *A Mind of One's Own,* ed. Louise Antony and Charlotte Witt (Boulder, Colo.: Westview Press, 1993), pp. 1–18; Jean Hampton, "Feminist Contractarianism," in *A Mind of One's Own,* pp. 227–255; and John Broughton's "Women's Rationality and Men's Virtue: A Critique of Gender Dualism in Gilligan's Theory of Moral Development," in *An Ethic of Care,* ed. Mary Jeanne Larrabee (New York: Routledge, 1993), pp. 112–39. This is by no means an exhaustive list.

4. Feminist theorists have criticized most traditional ethical theories on a number of points; I don't intend to imply that the standard theories are unproblematic, merely that they do not have the same problem faced by Care theory.

5. There are some exceptions to this rejection. Mary Stuart VanLeeuwen claims to defend a complementarity position in *Gender and Grace* (Downers Grove, Ill.: Intervarsity Press, 1990), 76, but her arguments in that book focus exclusively on providing equality of opportunity for men and women to parent, and to engage in professional development, and to develop their abilities to serve the Kingdom of God; it is unclear how this can be taken as an argument for complementarity

6. Simone de Beauvoir, *The Second Sex,* trans. H. M. Parshley (New York: Alfred A. Knopf, 1993 [1949]), pp. 211–12.

7. For more extended arguments concerning sex roles, see Joyce Trebilcott's "Sex Roles: The Argument from Nature," reprinted in *Philosophy of Woman,* ed. Mary Briody Mahowald (Indianapolis: Hackett, 1994), pp. 349–56, or Mary Midgley "On Not Being Afraid of Natural Sex Differences," in *Feminist Perspectives in Philosophy,* ed. Morwenna Griffiths and Margaret Whitford (Bloomington and Indianapolis: Indiana University Press, 1988), pp. 29–41; and Alison Jaggar "Sexual Difference and Sexual Equality," in *Theoretical Perspectives on Sexual Difference,* ed. Deborah Rhode (New Haven, Conn.: Yale University Press, 1990), pp. 239–54.

8. Examples of men's sacrifice for the physical benefit of women, on the other hand, are more widespread. (A modern example that springs to mind is that of the men who gave up lifeboat seats to women on the Titanic.)

9. Grace Clement, *Care, Autonomy, and Justice: Feminism and the Ethic of Care* (Boulder, Colo.: Westview Press, 1996), pp. 22–27.

10. Nel Noddings, *Caring: A Feminine Approach to Ethics and Moral Education* (Berkeley: University of California Press, 1984), pp. 100–101.

11. *Caring,* pp. 11–12.

12. Some relationships are appropriately one-sided to some degree, such as those between parent and infant, caregivers and the severely mentally handicapped, and so on. The one-sidedness becomes inappropriate when the participants in the relationship stand on a fairly equal footing.

13. *Care, Autonomy, and Justice,* p. 38.

14. Joan Tronto, *Moral Boundaries: A Political Argument for an Ethic of Care* (New York: Routledge, 1994), pp. 165–66.

15. Nurses, aides, child care workers, and similar public caregivers are predominantly female and are usually paid at close to the prevailing minimum wage. A newspaper article recently quoted a manager for an in-home nursing care provider as lamenting the fact that it was difficult to find workers. Women used to work because they felt for the patients, the manager explained, but now they were beginning to expect a living wage. Tronto, clearly, is aware of these issues (see, for example, pp. 116–17), and I do not mean to imply otherwise. Her analysis, however, is aimed at a different issue than the one I am concerned about here.

16. Nel Noddings, "Ethics from the Standpoint of Women," in *Theoretical Perspectives on Sexual Difference,* ed. Deborah L. Rhode (New Haven, Conn.: Yale University Press, 1990), p. 171.

17. Anders Nygran, *Agape and Eros,* trans. Philip S. Watson (New York: Harper & Row, 1969), pp. 98, 214–16.

18. Paul Ramsey, *Basic Christian Ethics* (Louisville: Westminster/John Knox Press, 1993), p. 167.

19. *Basic Christian Ethics,* p. 171.

20. *Caring,* p. 47.

21. *Caring,* pp. 54–55.

22. Sarah Lucia Hoagland, "Some Thoughts on 'Caring'," in *Feminist Ethics,* ed. Claudia Card (Lawrence: University Press of Kansas, 1991), p. 253.

23. See Stephen Post's discussion in *A Theory of Agape: On the Meaning of Christian Love* (Lewisburg, Pa.: Bucknell University Press, 1990), p. 80.

24. Barbara Hilkert Andolsen makes this charge in "Agape in Feminist Ethics," *The Journal of Religious Ethics* 9 (1981): 69–83.

25. *Basic Christian Ethics,* p. 177.

26. *Basic Christian Ethics,* p. 169.

27. Gene Outka, "Universal Love and Impartiality" in *The Love Commandments: Essays in Christian Ethics and Moral Philosophy,* ed. Edmund Santurri and William Werpehowski (Washington, D.C.: Georgetown University Press, 1992), p. 11.

28. "Universal Love and Impartiality," pp. 51–53.

29. For further discussion of the notion of vocation and its importance for an Agapic ethics, see Douglas Schuurman's "Protestant Vocation under Assault: Can It Be Saved?" in *The Annual of the Society of Christian Ethics* (Washington, D.C.: Georgetown University Press, 1994), pp. 23–52.

30. There are, of course, actual communities in which this mutuality is not present, and in which my own sacrifice will not be seen as detrimental to the community as a whole. So this is only true with regard to the moral community. Speaking of the moral commu-

nity in this way has its own dangers, perceptively discussed by Noddings in *Women and Evil* (Berkeley: University of California Press, 1989), p. 147. Community provides the grounds for both inclusion and exclusion, she comments, and I would concur. Nonetheless, a community which truly exemplifies mutuality is one within which self-sacrificial actions are no longer necessarily destructive.

31. *Women and Evil,* pp. 200–201.

32. Jean Grimshaw, "Autonomy and Identity in Feminist Thinking," in *Feminist Perspectives in Philosophy,* ed. Morwenna Griffiths and Margaret Whitford (Bloomington and Indianapolis: Indiana University Press, 1988), p. 103.

33. On both theological grounds and psychological grounds I believe a case can be made that love precedes maliciousness. Theologically I would argue that our creation by God makes love prior to malice. On psychological grounds I would argue that a baby's first impulses are ones of love and trust, though malice makes its appearance more quickly than one might hope. But a psychology that made distrust and self-protection the primary human motive would simply be false; Hobbesian babies would starve, as Annette Baier has noted.

34. See, for example, her discussion in this volume.

35. "Universal Love and Impartiality," p. 57.

TEN

Seduction: Does How You Get to "Yes" Still Matter?

CAROLINE J. SIMON

Do not arouse or awaken love until it so desires.
—*Song of Songs 8:4*

"Whatever we wear, wherever we go, 'yes' means yes and 'no' means no!" So goes the chant heard at many a "Take Back the Night" march. The slogan is meant as a corrective to centuries of enculturated misunderstanding between the sexes.[1] Male sexuality does not underwrite a "point of no return" in arousal; women should renounce coy negatives that are meant as implicit come-ons; everyone should be emphatically discouraged from taking refusal for assent.

Issues of assault and acquaintance rape are important. Explicating the sort of ethic of consent needed to adjudicate such issues is useful and necessary. For the last two decades, projects related to such explication have received considerable philosophical attention.[2] Yet an exclusive focus on such issues would lead to an impoverished view of sexuality. "Was there consent?" is a judicial question; even when broadened from settings involving courts and sexual harassment hearings to less formal interpersonal interaction, the question sets a minimalist and quasi-legal tone for sexual mores.

Such "thin" concepts as consent may be all that the public square in a pluralist society can allow in the framing of social policy. Yet we need not live the whole of our lives in the public square. Within the neighborhoods and courtyards of our varied traditions and subcultures we can look to thicker concepts that more adequately express the substance and texture of our sexual ideals and our embodied lives.

Seduction is certainly a thick concept; some would see it as altogether too weighed down by the accretions of its mottled history to be fit for anything but the conceptual archives. Quaint? Straight-laced? Sexist? Perhaps; but there may be salvageable elements of the concept of seduction that can be retained in a useful term of negative moral evaluation. Some philosophers have tried to explain what is problematic about seduction by appeal to the wrongness of deception or manipulation. This will be an adequate explanation of wrongness of seduction in some cases, but it leaves others untouched. The Christian tradition provides resources for explaining why getting to "yes" is still problematic in many cases even when it does not involve deception. While not all feminists will find the explanation presented here appealing, I have feminist, as well as Christian, reasons for finding it preferable to alternative accounts.

CHRISTIAN FEMINISM

Christianity is a complex tradition that has had severe public relations problems connected with its supposed stances toward sexuality. Certainly it is possible to amass a large collection of bizarre, benighted, unhealthy, and repugnant comments made by Christian thinkers about sexuality and most especially about women as seductresses or as easily seducible. While some would take this as ample evidence that Christianity should be rejected, especially by feminists, I take the sadly mixed history of Christianity as a confirmation of Christianity's own anthropology. The Christian tradition from its inception has predicted that the flawed humanity and finitude of Christian individuals and institutions would give rise to a flawed Christian tradition.[3] Among the tradition's flaws has been its (at times) rampant sexism. This is unsurprising, both theologically and socio-historically.

Feminism's history, on most tellings, is shorter than that of Christianity, but it is not necessarily less complex. Perhaps there is but one thing that all feminists agree upon: Things could be and should be better than they are for women. Beyond that, feminists disagree with one another about most of the vital issues related to feminism. At times there seems to be as much or more disagreement among those who call themselves feminists as there is between feminists and non-feminists. Liberal feminists berate radical feminists for wanting to impose their personal agendas on all women, regardless of what other women say they want.[4] More radical feminists doubt whether liberal feminists are feminists at all, implying at times that they may instead be dupes of patriarchy.[5] Younger feminists call older feminists "conservative" and accuse them of being retrograde.[6]

Given these flaws and fissures, it may be tempting to eschew both "Christian" and "feminist" as uninformative and unhelpful labels. What, after all, is one saying of oneself by calling oneself a Christian or a feminist? In my own case, I am stating the simple truth that Christianity and feminism have contributed to making me what I am. I do not call myself a Christian or a feminist because I agree with all that is maintained by others who also identify themselves as such. Rather, in both cases, I use these terms of myself because distancing myself from the Christian tradition or from the feminist movement would be rank ingratitude, like disavowing my family because I sometimes find some of my relatives irritating, distressing, silly, or embarrassing.[7]

Moreover, by my lights, Christianity and feminism are not incompatible. There are three great movements in the central narrative of the Christian tradition. The first involves the creation of the world and of humanity by God, who pronounces creation "very good." The second is the subsequent fall of humanity into alienation from God. This alienation results in human estrangement from one another and from the created order. The third is the gracious working of God to bring about the reconciliation between humanity and God in a new creation. Christianity proclaims how this reconciliation is brought about through the incarnation, crucifixion, and resurrection of Christ, and the ongoing activity of the Spirit of God in the world. Feminism fits within this narrative. Christian feminism takes gender inequalities to be an aspect of our alienation from God, and the healing of those inequalities to be part of God's redemptive purpose for humanity. As a Christian feminist I am interested in exploring how the concept of seduction can shed light on sexuality's role in a well-lived human life.

THE TRADITIONAL CONCEPTION OF SEDUCTION: FEMINIST MISGIVINGS

"Seduce" has its root in the Latin *seducere,* to lead away or separate. The *locus classicus* of seduction is the figure of Don Juan. The classical male seducer deliberately sets out to separate women from what was traditionally considered to be their chief virtue: chastity. Betty Becker-Theye observes,

> The myth of the seducer always touches upon the myth of the virgin. In order to seduce to "knowledge," the seducer must find a woman in a state of unknowing innocence who can be seduced. The mythic virgin is inaccessible to man; she is not always physically virgin . . . but she must also be untouched in some way so that the seducer can attempt to bring her to some new knowledge about her own sexuality. At the same time, she must offer resistance to his efforts since it is precisely her inaccessibility, her virginity, that challenges and interests him.[8]

Traditionally, the concept of seduction is intertwined with a sexual standard that assumes that women, in contrast to men, should value their chastity.[9] Seduction is a male achievement because conquest is hard-won and not something that just anyone could achieve. The highly successful seducer shows himself to be more attractive, more charming, and more clever than other men who have not been able to possess the particular women or the number of women whom he has been able to bed. Classically, male seducers set out with a deliberate program aimed at the goal of sexual intercourse.

Often running parallel to the picture of the male seducer is the assumption that women are inherently seductive. Don Juan sets out to bed women, cultivating and deploying tactics that are predictably effective. In contrast, Bathsheba goes about her own business and, when accidentally seen by King David, captivates him just by being who she is. The tradition teaches that a woman, in order truly to be chaste, must cultivate strategies to counter her inherent seductiveness. Not only must she not deliberately "lead men on," she must learn how to keep her distance and damper her powers, else she will be accused as a temptress who leads men astray.

From a feminist point of view, the problematic elements of the traditional concept of seduction abound. It seems closely tied to a sexual double standard: chastity as *the* paramount feminine virtue. It is also naturally linked with a vocabulary of sexuality as war, property acquisition, or competitive sport that many feminists find distasteful: sex as conquest, captivation, winning, having, possessing. Moreover, the conceptual system in which the traditional concept of seduction is embedded seems a morass that bodes nothing but ill for women. It casts women in a sexually passive role; it sets women over against men toward whom they must constantly be on guard; it damns women if they do and if they do not succumb. A woman who successfully resists seduction is virtuous but suspected of frigidity. A woman who is seduced is cast as complicitous victim. She was pursued, therefore, she was seductive; should a man captivated by her charms really be blamed for doing what comes naturally to him?[10] She was not, after all, raped. She ceased at some point to resist, therefore she was a willing participant. She wanted what she got when she got it.[11] Moreover, while the existence of female seducers is acknowledged, the tradition evaluates them by a very different standard than males. Don Juan may be a rake and a libertine, but a female Don Juan is a witch and a man-eater, not just weak, self-indulgent, or irresponsible, but beyond the pale.

Katie Roiphe's complaints about what she calls "rape-crisis feminism" indicate that she thinks that its proponents have views of sexuality which are far too indebted to those which nourish the traditional concept of seduction. She says,

The American College Health Association's pamphlet tells men: "Your desires may be beyond your control, but your actions are within your control." And it warns the female student to "communicate your limits clearly." According to this picture of sexual relations, her desires are never beyond her control. The assumption embedded in the movement against date rape is our grandmothers' assumption: men want sex, women don't. In emphasizing this struggle—he pushing, she resisting—the rape-crisis movement recycles and promotes an old model of sexuality. . . .

By protecting women against verbal coercion, these feminists are promoting the view of women as weak-willed, alabaster bodies, whose virtue must be protected from the cunning encroachments of the outside world. The idea that women can't withstand verbal or emotional pressure infantilizes them. The suggestion lurking beneath this definition of rape is that men are not just physically but intellectually and emotionally more powerful than women. Printing pamphlets about verbal coercion institutionalizes an unacceptable female position.[12]

Roiphe deplores the implications she attributes to rape-crisis feminism: Women are so fragile and naive that they need special seminars and special protections in order not to be persuaded into accepting "bargains" that are no bargain from their point of view.

I agree with Roiphe when she maintains that the term "rape" is unhelpfully distorted when those who wheedle others into regrettable sexual activity are called date rapists. But it would be equally unhelpful to conclude that rape is the only category of negative moral evaluation needed in thinking clearly about sexuality. In reflecting on the current broad definitions of "date rape," which include having sex when intoxicated or in situations in which one feels pressured, Roiphe frankly reports:

People have asked me if I have ever been date-raped. And thinking back on complicated nights, on too many glasses of wine, on strange and familiar beds, I would have to say yes. With such a sweeping definition of rape, I wonder how many people there are, male or female, who haven't been date-raped at one point or another. People pressure and manipulate and cajole each other into all sorts of things all the time.[13]

Should we conclude that because "all sorts of things" happen "all the time" our moral attitude toward them should be a shrug? The commonplace may still be highly problematic.

Roiphe, with other younger feminists like Sallie Tisdale,[14] seems to look forward to a day when women will be encouraged to be just as self-interested in their sexual aggressiveness and just as "tough" as men were permitted to be under the old double standard. Roiphe and Tisdale do not view sexuality as a Hobbesian state of nature; they acknowledge that such concepts as consent and rape avoidance should still have moral purchase.[15] However, they do appear to see sexuality as appropriately a libertarian zone in which consent to individually negotiated contracts is the only relevant consideration. However, a sexual environment in which "Let the 'consenter' beware!" forms the basic, and perhaps only, guiding principle is, on my view, far too likely to approximate a war of all against all. Whether the war will see more female than male casualties is a matter of sociological speculation; as a moral philosopher I am concerned about ameliorating its human toll.

GETTING DOWN TO CASES

From a feminist point of view, can seduction continue to function as a useful term of negative moral evaluation? Part of what will be crucial in answering this question is the extent to which seduction can be characterized without appeal to traditional gender roles and a sexual double standard. In exploring this issue, it will be helpful to examine cases that display various salient features of seduction.

Let us first turn to a literary example. The play *Les Liaisons Dangereuses* is adapted by Christopher Hampton from the eighteenth-century novel of the same name by Choderlos de LacLos.[16] Hampton's characters the Vicomte de Valmont and Marquise de Merteuil are old friends with a common hobby—seduction. For years they have compared notes on the conquests they have made. As the action of the play begins, they make a wager: Merteuil will go to bed with Valmont if he succeeds in seducing Madame de Tourvel, who is a woman famous for her "strict morals, religious fervor and the happiness of her marriage" (11).

Valmont relishes the challenge of seducing someone who appears unseducible. This will be the supreme demonstration of his irresistibility. Early in the play he tells Merteuil, "I have no intention of breaking down her prejudices. I want her to believe in God and virtue and the sanctity of marriage, and still not be able to stop herself. . . . I want the excitement of watching her betray everything that's most important to her" (13). Valmont relishes watching Madame de Tourvel being torn between her growing interest in him and her personal integrity.

Valmont sets out to systematically undermine Madame de Tourvel's defenses. He arranges to be a houseguest where Madame de Tourvel is staying and soon declares his love for her. When she asks him to leave her alone, he agrees to vacate the house, but begs her to accept his correspondence. When his letters become too passionate for her to find acceptable, Valmont connives to have her confessor insist that she allow Valmont an audience in order to beg her forgiveness for offending her. Again and again he uses her sympathy for his plight as an unrequited lover as an opening to pursue his goal. As he tells his friend the Marquise:

> It is true that she's resisted me for more than two months now; and that's very nearly a record. But I really don't want to hurry things. We go for a walk together almost every day: a little further every time down the path that has no turning. She's accepted my love; I've accepted her friendship; we're both aware how little there is to choose between them. Her eyes are closing. Every step she tries to take away from the inevitable conclusion brings her a little nearer to it. (73–74)

He finally convinces de Tourvel that if she does not sleep with him, he will commit suicide. This brings about her tearful acquiesce; she sacrifices her integrity for his life and happiness. The Marquise, who has by now become jealous of what she suspects is a real attachment of Valmont to Madame de Tourvel, refuses to "pay off" on their wager. Instead she indicates that Valmont must break off his connection with Madame de Tourvel or risk looking ridiculous—conquered rather than a conqueror. He coldly breaks with de Tourvel.

Hampton's dark play displays sexuality used in the service of raw power. For Vicomte de Valmont and Marquise de Merteuil, sex is a competitive sport where the point is to see how many others one can enthrall without becoming enthralled.[17] Valmont's cold-bloodedness, his relishing of the very features of the case that will render the situation most devastating for Madame de Tourvel, his calculated exploitation of her virtues to maneuver her to his goal, his holding her up to the scrutiny and ridicule of the Marquise, all make his behavior more odious than it would be otherwise.

Valmont's seduction of Madame de Tourvel involves the following features that are present in a broader spectrum of cases of seduction:

(1) There is mutual consent to all sexual activities at the time of participation.

(2) The pursuer seeks knowledge of the pursued in order to use that knowledge for purposes of obtaining consent to sexual activity.

(3) Deception is used as a means of obtaining consent to sexual activity.

(4) The pursuer is indifferent to the welfare of the pursued, or at least takes the pursued's welfare only as an easily overridden priority.

(5) The pursuer's motives in the pursuit are personal pleasure and/or self-aggrandizement.

(6) The pursued person consents to sexual activities which he or she was adverse (at least initially) to engaging in or which are at odds with his or her principles or priorities.

(7) The pursued person would not consent to all the activities engaged in unless he or she were deceived or manipulated.

Note that, as these features are characterized here, no assumptions are made about gender roles.[18]

What is the status of this list? Does it constitute necessary and sufficient conditions for seduction? How are each of the features relevant to the wrongness of seduction?

The presence of consent does appear to be essential to seduction, for consent is what distinguishes seduction from rape. Consent is also part of what normally makes the situation enjoyable for the seducer. Getting to "yes" is intrinsic to the game; being able to get a "yes" where others would meet continued resistance is what makes the seduction an ego-enhancing experience for the seducer.

It follows that (1) and (5) are connected, though not in a way that would make (5) also a necessary condition for seduction. One can imagine a dutiful and somewhat bored Mata Hari, who, while glad of her competence, pursues targets for the sake of her employers' goals rather than for pleasure. We can also imagine that she has nothing to prove to herself or anyone else about her powers, and thus does not seek self-aggrandizement. Her activities would still be seduction. I think, in fact, that with the exception of item (1), the rest of the features I have listed are best seen as comprising a family resemblance cluster rather than as a list of severally necessary and jointly sufficient conditions. In order for an encounter to be a seduction, it will need feature (1) and some indeterminate number of the others. That seduction is such a family resemblance term presents complications for explanation of its wrongness.

To see this, consider the following passage from Jane Tompkins's *A Life in School,* describing an episode that occurred when she was a first-year student at Bryn Mawr dating a senior English major:

> After a couple of dates he wanted me to go to bed with him, and I, flattered by his attentions but with no desire to comply, tried to keep him interested without giving in. One night we were in his room, sitting on his bed necking. As usual, it started to get too hot for me, so he proposed a bargain. He would turn the lights out and promise to be good if I would hold "it." Well, I agreed, reluctantly. So there we are in the dark, lying down now, my hand wrapped around this *thing.* . . . "What does it feel like?" he said. Oh, no, please, this is embarrassing enough already, I thought. . . . I don't remember what I said, but I'm sure it failed to meet his expectations.[19]

Tompkins's description of this incident is instructive in its commonplaceness: one person consents to sacrifice her dignity and her desires for those of another. One is reminded of Roiphe's observation discussed earlier that people "pressure and manipulate and cajole each other into all sorts of things all the time." As Tompkins describes the encounter it has much of the same phenomenological "feel" to it as one would attribute to Madame de Tourvel's situation in *Les Liaisons Dangereuses,* though in a milder form. Yet it is obvious that (3), the element of deception, is completely lacking in this case, nor are calculation, indifference, and manipulation (features 2, 4, and 7) obviously present.

This is significant because many philosophers have attempted to explain the wrongness of seduction by appeal to the deceptiveness or manipulativeness of the seducer. David Archard claims that:

> The practiced seducer falsely but successfully represents sex to his victim as demanded by the love they both feel for each other, or as a prospect of barely imaginable joy. Neither love nor transport of delight are forthcoming. The woman is induced to consent to that which she then experiences as considerably less and other than her seducer led her to believe it would be.[20]

Yet Tompkins does not seem to have been deceived in this situation; she strikes a bargain under no illusions of her part of it being required by love or its likelihood of yielding delight. Was she manipulated? Archard himself contrasts manipulation with persuasion. He maintains, "Manipulation seeks not to argue for its end, but to exacerbate any weaknesses of will, emotions, or psychological irregularity which would secure consent. It is this that makes it morally suspect."[21] Persuasion is rational, manipulation appeals to non-rational elements. Archard's diagnosis of what is morally objectionable in manipulation and seduction bears similarities to Anne C. Minas's account of coercion. She connects the psychological condition of the coerced with Aristotle's references to weakness of will as "the condition of men under the influence of the passions."[22]

Leaning heavily on the element of manipulation, and identifying manipulation with weakness and emotionalism, in order to explain what is morally problematic about seduction seems misguided for two reasons. First, characteristically, sexual encounters are imbued with passions, desires, and complex emotions. Normally this is just as true of morally unproblematic encounters as it is of seductions. In situations that are characteristically emotionally loaded, it will be difficult, if not impossible, to distinguish subversions of rationality from situations where rationality just seems beside the point. Second, the emphasis on the primacy of rationality in these standard characterizations of manipulation and coercion bifurcates human beings into minds and emotions. The view that human beings are made up of distinguishable faculties of reason and emotion, and that reason should always rule the emotions, is not only questionable philosophical psychology,[23] it has been subjected to considerable feminist suspicion, with good reason.[24] While I do not want to claim that these problems are intractable, they do warrant the exploration of alternatives. What follows is an adumbration of a Christian view of personhood which is more holistic and which provides a cogent explanation of the wrongness of seduction.

CHRISTIANITY AND SEDUCTION

Elsewhere I have explicated a concept of personal destiny rooted in the Christian tradition.[25] Along with other Christian thinkers such as Stanley Hauerwas and Glenn Tinder, I maintain that a full understanding of ourselves and others involves a grasp of ourselves as creatures whose story is comprehended within God's story.[26]

A narrative understanding of personhood acknowledges that people inhabit history, that who we are unfolds over time. Because of this, a person's life can be seen as a narrative account of how our potentials become actual. No person's story can include realizing all his or her potentials, because such a narrative would be impossible and incoherent. It is part of the human condition that not all of the potential properties we are born with can be brought to fruition in the life span of a single individual. A destiny is a range of possibilities that should be brought to fruition but which a person can choose not to cultivate. Destinies are inherently both goal-oriented and normative. To see people as having a destiny is to see them as having a responsibility for a task. The task is to become our true selves.

A Christian conception of selfhood sees a person's destiny as what God intends, but does not compel, her or him to be. A destiny is unlike a fate in that a destiny can be failed or refused. God grants people not only the freedom to reject their destiny, but the freedom to shape it. While there is a core of potentials that constitute God's intentions for each person, this core is compatible with his or her life's taking on any number of different shapes. God confers on humans the dignity of being creators of their own destinies within the limits set by God's intentions. Thus, one's destiny is a range of possible lives all of which would be different ways of becoming one's "true self."

Christianity also acknowledges human finitude. When we try to discern the "meaning of our life" we can at best arrive at an intuitively convincing account of the whole in light of its constituent parts. This will be only one among many possible "readings," none of which, from a human point of view, can be decisively determined to be privileged.

Our finitude and fallenness imply that not every tale we tell ourselves about our own or others' stories is true; often we are makers of fictions. We often desire more creative license in authoring our own and another others' stories than God's intentions allow. Fiction making is the construction and projection of a narrative for oneself or another which is unconnected with that person's destiny. No matter how generous fiction making may be, it is at best a pleasant entertainment. At worst, if acted on and lived out, it may seriously interfere with someone's attaining his or her destiny.

Against this background it is easy to see what is wrong with seduction. Seducers show a negligent or callous disregard for the central good of those whom they pursue. Our central good is the fulfillment, or at least the approximation, of God's intentions for us. The seducer sets out to procure consent to sexual activity without caring whether this will compromise elements that are integral to the other's true self.

The seducer lives as if he or she is ignorant of the truth that each of our lives is lived with and among others who have their own stories to live out and tell. The seducer's purposes and plans fail to take into account the fact that others also have purposes and plans. The seducer's version of how things are does not take into account that others have differing versions of their story.

The seducer who sets out to acquire knowledge of the pursued for the purposes of seduction often connives to abuse the power which intimate knowledge of another confers. Within the Christian story, loving knowledge involves and makes possible the work of attention necessary for insight into the loved one's destiny. The seducer uses his or her knowledge, not for the purpose of aiding the other in discerning and pursuing his or her destiny, but to win compliance with the seducer's own agenda, whether or not that agenda is likely to conflict with the other's destiny. Seduction breeds fiction making in a particularly invidious form.

This explanation of seduction's wrongness is a near neighbor to the Kantian account given by Onora O'Neill. She points out that detailed knowledge of another's character and desires, together with the intertwining of desires which is a natural part of intimacy, makes it all too easy to make someone of whom one is cultivating intimate knowledge of "an offer he or she cannot refuse" without deceiving, coercing, or manipulating.[27] Her diagnosis of the wrongness of seduction sees it as a failure of Kantian respect and benevolence. And so, of course, it is.

The Christian account given here does not displace a Kantian account, it deepens and extends it. People should be treated as ends and never as mere means *because* they have destinies to fulfill. To show Kantian respect and benevolence requires giving due attention to the plans and projects which people consciously pursue and acknowledge as their own. Christians will want to practice Kantian respect and benevolence as appropriate responses to the freedom and dignity which each person has to shape his or her own destiny. So, Christians will have reasons to avoid setting out to win consent without regard to its incompatibility with another's central plans or projects. But Christians will also have reasons to go beyond this. Christians know that we all "see through a glass darkly,"[28] and that it is all too easy to lose track of one's true self. Christians can see the seducer as more than a violator of the Categorical Imperative; the seducer is a person mired in fiction making, not just about others, but about himself or herself. On the Christian story, resistance to the seducer is not just standing up for oneself; resistance to being co-opted into someone else's fiction making is the most loving response one can make to someone who has lost his or her way.

Some may find my account of why seduction is wrong from a Christian point of view strange because it does not make explicit mention of the traditional Christian ideals of chastity in singleness and fidelity in marriage. Surely, someone might say, the reason seduction is wrong is that it involves extramarital sexual activity. Why complicate matters with all this business about destiny? I have two reasons: First, it is useful to leave conceptual room for the possibility of being seduced into marriage. The idea that the pursuer's "intentions are honorable" if the pursuer intends marriage is a holdover from the sexual double standard and goes hand-in-hand with the idea that a seducer can repair things by "making an honest woman of" the object of his seduction. It is healthier to see that courtship is as morally problematic as seduction if it is pursued with a flagrant disregard for whether marriage is compatible with the destinies of both parties. Second, the following observations by Jeffrey Weeks strike me as sociologically accurate:

> Simone de Beauvoir distinguished between long-term loving relationships, "essential love" (which she enjoyed, if that is the correct word, with Sartre), and what for her were more short-term passionate sexual involvements, what she called "contingent love." It is at least arguable, however, that in the Western world, contingent love is not very far removed from becoming the norm. The stress now, I have argued, is not so much on the qualities that make for a lifetime's sexual partnership but on the pleasures and satisfactions that can be obtained from the particular relationship—so long as it lasts. Meaning resides less in the "ties that bind" than in the passions that unite, until they fade; then we start all over again.[29]

In the twentieth century, this description is almost as true of American Christian subculture as it is of Western culture as a whole. If such a culture is going to become more self-critical of its "norms," it needs deep explanations of why one might want to or be obliged to refrain from acting on "passions that unite, until they fade." An account of human destiny, and of the role of our sexuality in living out our destinies, offers some hope of making sense of the biblical Song of Song's refrain "Do not arouse or awaken love until it so desires" (8:4). Such an account thus offers hope of explaining why ties that bind are not arbitrary or antiquated constraints. While I have only been able to hint at such an account here, I hope that what I have said may make those who are weary of the pluralistic public square think that the neighborhood of the Christian tradition is worth at least an afternoon walking tour.

NOTES

1. The views that the chant are meant to counter are at least as old as Ovid:

> A man who kisses a girl and goes no further deserves to forfeit even the plea-sure of kissing her. Obviously one wants to do a great deal more than that, and if one does not, one is not civilized, but silly.
>
> "Oh, but I should hate to use brute force," you say. Why, that is exactly what girls like: they prefer to enjoy themselves under duress. The victim of a sexual assault is generally delighted, for she takes your audacity as a compli-ment; whereas the girl who could have been raped but was not is bound to feel disappointed. . . . (*The Technique of Love,* trans. Paul Turner [London: Panther, 1968], p. 46)

These views are encouraged and reinforced by such important subsequent thinkers as Rousseau. (See Carole Pateman's discussion in "Women and Consent," in her book *The Disorder of Women: Democracy, Feminism, and Political Theory* (Stanford, Calif.: Stanford University Press, 1989), pp. 76ff.)

2. See, for example, David Archard, *Sexual Consent* (Boulder, Colo.: Westview Press, 1998); Susan Brownmiller, *Against Our Will: Men, Women, and Rape* (New York: Simon and Schuster, 1975); Catherine MacKinnon, *Toward a Feminist Theory of the State* (Cambridge, Mass.: Harvard University Press, 1989).

3. See, for example, Jesus' parables in Mt. 13:24–30 and Mt. 25:31ff, as well as por-traits of the flawed nature of the disciples in the gospels and the early church in Acts, the Epistles, and Revelation.

4. See Christina Hoff Sommers, *Who Stole Feminism? How Women Have Betrayed Women* (New York: Touchstone, 1995).

5. See Susan Faludi, *Backlash: The Undeclared War against American Women* (New York: Crown Publishing, 1991).

6. See Sally Tisdale, *Talk Dirty to Me* (New York: Doubleday, 1994), p. 147, and Katie Roiphe, *The Morning After: Sex, Fear, and Feminism on Campus* (Boston: Little, Brown and Company, 1993).

7. Here I resonate with remarks of Kathleen Norris: "In the suspicious atmosphere of the contemporary Christian church, it is good to know one's ground. When others label me and try to exclude me, as too conservative or too liberal, as too feminist or not feminist enough, as too intellectual or not intellectually rigorous, as too Catholic to be Presbyterian or too Presbyterian to be a Catholic, I refuse to be shaken from the fold. It's my God, too, my Bible, my church, my faith; it chose me." *Amazing Grace* (New York: Riverhead Books, 1998), p. 143.

8. Betty Becker-Theye, *The Seducer as Mythic Figure in Richardson, Laclos, and Kierke-gaard* (New York: Garland Publishing, 1988), pp. 6–7.

9. David Hume states the situation current in his time with great clarity:

> The greatest regard which can be acquired by [the female] sex is derived from their fidelity; and a woman who becomes cheap and vulgar, loses her rank, and is exposed to every insult, who is deficient in this particular. The smallest failure is here sufficient to blast her character. A female has so many opportu-

nities of secretly indulging these appetites that nothing can give us security but her absolute modesty and reserve; and where a breach is once made it can scarcely ever be fully repaired. If a man behave with cowardice on one occasion, a contrary conduct reinstates him in his character. But by what action can a woman whose behavior has once been dissolute be able to assure us that she has formed better resolutions and has self command enough to carry them into execution? (*An Inquiry Concerning the Principles of Morals,* ed. Charles W. Hendel [Indianapolis: Bobbs-Merrill, 1957 (1751)], p. 63)

10. See Patricia M. L. Illingworth's helpful discussion of contemporary spins on these traditional ideas in "Explaining without Blaming the Victim," *The Journal of Social Philosophy* 21, no. 2–3 (Fall 1990): 117–26.

11. "[I]f seduction is stealthy and stolen it is also, necessarily, seductive and delightful, so that women are required to concede above all that seduction is quite different from rape, that they have wanted it and that their complicity has, more often than not, had dire consequences for men." Jane Miller, "The Seductions of Women," in *Don Giovanni: Myths of Seduction and Betrayal,* ed. Jonathan Miller (Baltimore: Johns Hopkins University Press, 1990), p. 49.

12. Roiphe, *The Morning After,* pp. 65, 67–68.

13. Roiphe, *The Morning After,* p. 79.

14. See Tisdale, *Talk Dirty to Me,* pp. 33–37, 95–100, 117–121.

15. Thus, if they thought that Jeffrey Weeks were right that "Sex today exists in a moral vacuum" (*Sexuality and Its Discontents* [London: Routledge & Kegan Paul, 1985], p. 3), they would presumably be as concerned as he is to rectify the situation. While Tisdale's core values are self-determination and avoiding harm (*Talk Dirty to Me,* pp. 15–16), Weeks advocates the more humane values of care, mutuality, responsibility, and love. (See his *Invented Moralities: Sexual Values in an Uncertain Age* [New York: Columbia University Press, 1995].)

16. Christopher Hampton, *Les Liaisons Dangereuses* (Boston: Faber and Faber, 1987). Page numbers to subsequent references to this play are included in the text.

17. One is, of course, reminded of Sartre's famous analysis of this dynamic in *Being and Nothingness.*

18. I chose Hampton's play as a central narrative in part because the features its situation displays are more susceptible to analysis without regard to gender roles. There are, of course, many other interesting seduction narratives. For example, one of the subplots of George Eliot's *Adam Bede,* first published in 1859, concerns the romance between Arthur Donnithorne and Hetty Sorrel. Arthur is the son of a wealthy landowner, Hetty is the daughter of one of his father's tenants. Arthur finds himself attracted to Hetty and struggles unsuccessfully against this attraction. Eliot portrays Arthur and Hetty as equally infatuated and equally weak. Yet the prevailing narrative voice underlines Eliot's clear evaluation of Arthur as more responsible and more blameworthy for their liaison than Hetty. His greater responsibility arises partly from his greater age, but especially from his class standing and from his greater knowledge. Arthur is portrayed as a seducer because his greater ability to understand and avoid a situation likely to have disastrous consequences gives him a greater burden of responsibility to do so. Though it is more his class and education that make him wiser than Hetty, the situation in *Bede* could more easily be construed as portraying women as in unequal need of protection. The Marquise's role in Hampton's play makes the play less susceptible to Roiphe-type objections.

19. Jane Tompkins, *Life in School* (New York: Addison Wesley Publishing, 1996), p. 70. This fragment of Tompkins's description of dormitory and dating life is a very small part of her ruminations about the nature of education, which is framed in an autobiographical setting. Tompkins, a literary scholar, describes her own education from grade school on, as well as her own career as an academic and teacher. Her focus is on intellectual

autobiography, but her frank disclosures reflect the embeddedness of her intellectual life in her familial, cultural, occupational, affectional, and embodied existence.

20. Archard, *Sexual Consent,* p. 47. Archard alludes to deceptiveness again in connection with seduction on p. 75, where he claims that "the seducer cannot be honest and his intentions transparent to the other without defeating his purposes."

21. David Archard, "Exploited Consent," *The Journal of Social Philosophy* 25 (Winter 1994): 93.

22. Anne C. Minas, "Coercion and Consciousness," *Canadian Journal of Philosophy* 10, no. 2 (June 1980): 304–308.

23. See, for example, Ronald de Sousa, "The Rationality of Emotion," in *Explaining Emotions,* ed. Amelie Oksenberg Rorty (Berkeley: University of California Press, 1980), pp. 127–52, and Robert C. Solomon, *The Passions* (Notre Dame, Ind.: University of Notre Dame Press, 1983).

24. See Lorraine Code, *What Can She Know? Feminist Theory and the Construction of Knowledge* (Ithaca, N.Y.: Cornell University Press, 1991), for a good summary discussion of the literature on this subject.

25. See my "On Seeing What Does Not Yet Appear: Reflections on Love and Imagination," *Faith and Philosophy* 10 (1993): 311–29, and *The Disciplined Heart: Love, Destiny, and Imagination* (Grand Rapids, Mich.: Eerdmans, 1997).

26. See Stanley Hauerwas, *The Peaceable Kingdom* (Notre Dame, Ind.: University of Notre Dame Press, 1983), especially pp. 25–27; Glenn Tinder, *The Political Meaning of Christianity* (Baton Rouge: Louisiana State University Press, 1989), especially Chapter 1. Alasdair MacIntyre is committed to a narrative understanding of personhood, but the connections between Christianity and his philosophical anthropology are somewhat oblique; see *After Virtue* (Notre Dame, Ind.: University of Notre Dame Press, 1981), especially p. 204.

27. Onora O'Neill, "Between Consenting Adults," *Philosophy and Public Affairs* 14 (1985): 270.

28. I Corinthians 13:12.

29. Weeks, *Invented Moralities,* p. 174.

ELEVEN

Living within Tradition

LAURA DUHAN KAPLAN

A colleague invited me to write an essay about some of the difficulties I face in trying to reconcile my philosophy, my feminism, and my faith. After two botched attempts to outline such an essay, I came to realize that I had nothing to say on the topic because I have no difficulties reconciling philosophy, feminism, and faith. Instead, all three pursuits converge in my understanding of tradition. This understanding is not an intellectual achievement, but a way of life. It is difficult for me to rip this way of life far enough out of its context to articulate it in words. But perhaps I do not have to, as the words of other writers can serve me well here.

For example, Hans-Georg Gadamer has written that "understanding is not to be thought of so much as an action of one's subjectivity, but as the placing of oneself within a tradition, in which past and present are constantly fused."[1] In my philosophy, my faith, and my feminism, I practice understanding as Gadamer has described it. I place myself within a tradition, and then continuously fuse past and present as I negotiate a modern life within traditional horizons.

PHILOSOPHY

In his book *The Poetics of Space,* philosopher Gaston Bachelard tells readers that philosophers have expended a great deal of energy crafting a phenomenology of the mind, but very little energy crafting a phenomenology of the

A revised version of this essay appears under the title "Three Applications of Gadamer's Hermeneutics: Philosophy-Faith-Feminism," in *Feminist Interpretations of Hans-Georg Gadamer,* ed. Lorraine Code (University Park: Pennsylvania State University Press, 2002).

soul. Let me intertwine my words with Bachelard's as I try both to under-stand and explain what he means. In both the phenomenological and ana-lytic traditions, philosophers generating theories of knowledge and philosophies of mind have focused on the mind's active agency. Analytic philosophers have described the processes by which the mind molds the raw data of perception into a web of concepts. Phenomenologists have observed the ways the mind reaches out into the world to prejudice even our raw per-ceptions of it. But little attention has been paid to the moments in which the world itself seems to reach out and touch a human psyche. In these mo-ments, the world arrests and transfixes our attention; we say our senses have been "transported"; some artists and writers speak of "the aesthetic mo-ment." Bachelard calls such a moment a "poetic moment" and says the study of poetic moments is what he means by a "phenomenology of the soul." A poetic moment, says Bachelard, burns an image into a person's mind, and this image becomes a template for future images, understand-ings, and interpretations. But the poetic moment itself, the moment that seizes the soul, is not interpreted. Only later does the mind engage in inter-pretation, as a person attempts to reconstruct or analyze the moment through the filter of words and concepts.[2]

Philosophy, for me, begins in poetic moments, as Bachelard describes them. A poetic moment enwraps me in a new and surprising vision. Even after the intensity of the moment fades, I still find myself under its sway, as I come to see more aspects of life through the new lens. Self-conscious at-tempts to widen or refocus the lens, as well as attempts to articulate the vi-sion in public language are, for me, the main activities of philosophy. Spinning and sorting out the implications of such a new vision slide into the logical activity that many professional philosophers identify as "philos-ophizing," i.e., the testing of propositions about ethics, politics, or meta-physics through argument and counterargument.

But perhaps I have overestimated the importance of my own moments of original vision. Perhaps philosophy, for me, does not really begin in these poetic moments. Perhaps I begin, in a much more conventional way, with the discipline. Perhaps even the poetic moments that seize me are shaped by a discipline much larger than my own life encounters, a discipline powerful enough to have maintained an identity across twenty-five hundred years. Many of classical philosophy's great systematic treatises are attempts to ar-ticulate a vision of the world, as Stephen Pepper argues in *World Hypothe-ses*.[3] These visions, my experience as both a visionary and a reader of philos-ophy tells me, originate in a poetic moment. For example, Baruch Spinoza gives away the moment of insight that sparked his *Ethics* in that treatise's Appendix. (Of course, I read the *Ethics* from the end to the beginning, as I read all books.) How stupid, Spinoza notes, do people seem when they think the universe organizes itself around them when, in reality, the universe does not care. And from this insight Spinoza develops his own twist on the philosophical style of the day, writing pages of elegant ontological argument, describing a God who is seamlessly infinite, identical with the very laws of nature. This God, complete and self-sufficient in every way, does not have the capacity to respond to selfish human prayers.[4]

I believe I have learned much about the activity of looking for poetic moments from the philosophical tradition. I may have learned about this activity through a straightforward reading of the few philosophical texts, such as Spinoza's *Ethics,* that acknowledge it as part of the philosophical process. Or perhaps the activity of looking for poetic moments is itself part of my activity of reading. Most philosophical texts are doubly distant from me as a reader. They are written abstractly, and often about concerns unfamiliar to me. I myself must supply a living context if I am to "bridge the personal or historic distance between minds," as Gadamer defines hermeneutic (i.e., interpretive) activity. The poetic moment is that bridge, the spark that illuminates a reading, the moment in which I rearrange the familiar under the description the text offers. The poetic moments that seize me, or that I seize upon and take seriously, are often those that illuminate the very text I am reading. In this way, the philosophical tradition directs me to attend to specific poetic moments.

I find myself now in a hermeneutic circle. I am making an original interpretation of the philosophical tradition, yet the terms of my interpretation are drawn from tradition. As Gadamer puts it, "past and present are constantly fused," as I try to find a place for myself within the tradition. I find myself in the same hermeneutic circle when I think of my faith, and of my feminism.

FAITH

I am a Jew. I know no other life. "The soul of every living thing shall bless your name, Eternal One, our God, the spirit of all flesh shall glorify . . . you," says the Sabbath morning prayer, *Nishmat Kol Hay.*[5] One Sabbath morning, swayed by the magic of the poetry and my own sensation of the divine presence, I accidentally misread it. "Every living thing shall bless you in its soul, its spirit, and all its flesh," I sang. On that morning, every corner of my body, from my toes, to my fingertips, trembled with the divine presence. That sense of fusion with something much greater than myself is also my sensation of being Jewish. Oh, I can speak rationally about why the religion of Judaism appeals to me. Judaism emphasizes works over faith, prescribing a seemingly endless list of ethical rules designed to improve community life. It offers a rich tradition of song, story, and dance as modes of worship of a God who is too infinite to be pinned down in any single image. And it speaks of a long and complex history that indicates familiarity with challenges and changes to Orthodoxy. But it is not Judaism's rational advantages that move me. It is, instead, the sense of fusion.

Rabbi Mordecai Kaplan, founder of the Reconstructionist movement in Judaism, described Judaism as a civilization, with its own languages, literature, history, ethics, religion. I was raised within this civilization. I speak its languages, read its literature, know its history, practice its ethics, worship within its religion.[6] Yet it would be wrong for me to say that I live within the tradition. More accurately, the tradition lives within me. Sometimes I think I am driven by a blind imperative to preserve Jewish tradition at all costs. Perhaps this has become an imperative of self-preservation, as my present life is inseparable from the past that shapes it. In Gadamer's words, I have "placed myself within a tradition, in which past and present are constantly fused."

Feminist theologian Judith Plaskow has borrowed terms from phenomenologist Paul Ricoeur to articulate some of the dynamics of this fusion. My term "fusion" implies a seamless integration. But Plaskow sees fusion as an ongoing balancing act. Jews, particularly, says she, feminist Jews, must move between a "hermeneutic of remembrance" and a "hermeneutic of suspicion." The hermeneutic of remembrance honors the past, calling us to be moved by traditional interpretations of Jewish language, literature, history, ethics, and religion. The hermeneutic of suspicion calls us to question these traditional interpretations, measuring them against the imperatives of modern life. If the traditional interpretations are found to be irrelevant or even harmful within the contemporary context, they are to be at least temporarily revised or laid aside.[7]

For me, the balancing act Plaskow describes is certainly a feature of living within tradition. In fact, the balancing act is at the core of several contemporary Jewish movements. The Reconstructionist movement, for example, suggests that Judaism has always been syncretistic, that Judaism has continuously recast its basic theological and ethical understandings in terms accessible to Jews of the time. Rather than let this process be haphazard, members of the Reconstructionist movement try self-consciously to understand Judaism in terms of modern notions of spirituality, science, society, and personal identity. The movement calls upon Jews to reinterpret ideas, practices, and rituals in ways that honor contemporary liberal notions of social justice, including respect for individual autonomy and resistance against racism, sexism, and heterosexism.

The Jewish Renewal movement, sparked by Rabbi Zalman Schachter-Shalomi, offers a mystical counterpoint to the rationalism of Reconstructionism. Renewal shares the social and ethical values of Reconstructionism, as it seeks to anchor Judaism within the contemporary understanding of spiritual quest.[8] Both the Reconstructionist and Renewal movements recommend that reinterpretation take place in communities (*havurot*) small enough to invite participation and experimentation, but large enough for members to feel they are not alone. I am a member of one such community (*havurah*), and so I feel I am not alone in the task of fusing past and present within the Jewish tradition.

The balancing act that is at the core of Reconstructionism, Renewal, and feminist Judaism takes place within the context of its practitioners' pre-existing passion to find a way to honor tradition. In a sense, an existential fusion of past and present lays the foundation for self-conscious, public attempts to fuse past and present through reconstruction, renewal, or reinterpretation. Because members of these movements are shaped, in large part, by the very tradition they question, what practitioners perceive as new directions will be anchored in traditional meanings. Again I, along with many others, find myself twirling within a hermeneutic circle.

One of the complex twirlings within this circle involves the reinterpretation of language. As I (we) hold on to ancient metaphors, I (we) also give them new life, allowing our own spiritually potent poetic moments to renew them. A metaphor, according to Max Black's well-known philosophical analysis, consists of two terms, a focus and a frame. The focus is the term being described, and the frame is the descriptor that reflects upon the focus, showing it in a new light. The frame, says Black, carries with it a set of associated meanings, which, through the use of a metaphor, come to be predicated of the focus.[9] My favorite example of such a Jewish metaphor sits squarely within the Sabbath morning prayer service: "The Torah (the Five Books of Moses and all the customs and stories derived from it) is a Tree of Life to all who hold fast to her." No doubt the authors of the prayer saw the Tree as a life-giving organism, providing human beings as well as animals with air, food, and shelter, and the Torah as providing moral, social, theological, aesthetic, and intellectual sustenance. But the image of the tree comes alive in my own poetic moments, placing the focus "the Torah" within quite a different frame, a frame that, through its associations, highlights other dimensions of Jewish tradition.

Trees taught me to write evocative, sensual descriptions of the world around me. My earliest teenage journals include page after page of painstaking descriptions of trees in all their seasonal cycles, from the early spring weeks of their translucent young leaves to the winter months of their brittle gray branches framing bits of sky. Five years later, trees taught me another way to write the world, a way that lifts prosaic objects out of their mundane contexts and takes them soaring, pregnant with metaphorical possibilities. I liked to walk alone at night during those years. One late spring evening, a cedar tree caught my eye as it whirled in a wild dance under the thin night light. Fresh green needles tinged with blue edges overlapped to form the dancer's hoop skirt, twisting out from her tall straight torso. I understood, I thought, why some peoples worship the gods of nature: here was one dancing before me, infinite in its motion and completely self-sufficient in its beauty. All that summer, tree gods continued to reveal themselves to me. On a long mountain hike I saw birches streamside, their strong, sculpted legs splitting at the hips into branches reaching stalwart to the sky, virile guardians of the river. In my parents' yard I saw a tree with eyes, its knobs and knots all-seeing, all-knowing, judging the world with decades of quiet wisdom.

I draw my interpretation of the tree of life metaphor from my wildest visions of trees. The written Torah, the text of the Five Books of Moses, is the river guardian. His knobs and knots offer stability in a world of short-lived creatures and their social trends. But the oral Torah, all the actions, discussions, stories that Jews trace back to the Torah, is the dancing stream. She whirls and changes with the seasons, with the light, with the perspective of the observer. The written Torah is nourished by this flowing stream of life. He guards the stream, yet changes as it changes. He is virile, capable of growth, yet is young and immature, needing stimulation from the very lives he guards if he is to flourish. This symbiotic relationship again mirrors the hermeneutic circle: tradition lives only insofar as it is interpreted, yet those interpretations are made by people who surrender, at least in part, to the power of that tradition, fusing it with the other aspects of their lives.

FEMINISM

Definitions of feminism abound. Rosemarie Tong, in her book *Feminist Thought: A More Comprehensive Introduction,* offers no less than seven categories of feminism.[10] I would like to propose yet another definition: traditional feminism. Traditional feminism is a lived feminism, the continuous act of "placing oneself within a tradition where past and present are constantly fused." Traditional feminism is my daily practice of balancing a hermeneutic of remembrance with a hermeneutic of suspicion, as I try to find a morally and socially acceptable way to inhabit the category "woman."

The work is not so simple, of course, as fusing a progressive, feminist present with the legacy of an oppressive sexist past. The present is not simply progressive: many feminist authors have written about the deficiencies of gender and racial justice in the present. The past is not simply oppressive. In fact, the past is something of a mystery, as no adequate account of women's history is available. As feminist historians continue to sift through documents, artifacts, and stories, evidence of women's rich public contri-

butions piles ever higher. And alongside it piles evidence that women's contributions gradually disappear from the public record. As I try to understand the past, I am not sure who or what to trust. Should I trust the
somewhat fragmented tradition of brave women thinkers, activists, and
leaders, a tradition that is mythical in the sense that bits of written and oral
history are elaborated through imaginative fiction? Or should I trust the tradition in which women are chaste, homebound, and modest, a tradition
that is mythical in the sense that it misdescribes as many women as it accurately describes? Both of these traditions are complicated by overlapping
histories of race, class, gender, ethnicity, nationality—histories that are
themselves marked by vagaries and manipulations. For now, the only tradition of which I am certain is the tradition of struggle between these two
competing ideologies of what it means to live as a woman. In every era, the
two clash, and "the woman question" is raised anew. To live as a traditional
woman *is* to wander between these two, and perhaps many other, conflicting ideologies of women's nature. It is to fuse one's own ambiguous leaps of
fusion with a tradition of ambiguity for women.

Perhaps I can articulate some of the dynamics of these leaps of fusion
by referring back to my brief discussion of metaphor. In surveying the different ideologies of women's nature, I sometimes think of the word "woman" as the focus of an infinite number of metaphors. "A woman is strong,"
we say, and the associations of strength, physical and moral, become part of
the concept "woman." "A woman is modest," we say, and the associations of
modesty, from avoiding bragging to hiding one's talents, become part of the
concept "woman." Each new metaphor flashes into shape within a poetic
moment, a moment of strong passion that rearranges the familiar, coloring
the past into a new present. Sometimes these moments are tinged with joy;
sometimes they are tinged with anger. Sometimes they verify lived truths;
sometimes they reveal falsehoods. They can lead me to renew commitments, reconstruct them, and sometimes to reject them.

The starting point for saying something genuinely new is the web of existing meanings. So it is, I propose, with social behavior. Change begins
with the enactment of familiar routines. It begins to soar when a poetic moment reveals the deficiencies of the familiar, and takes concrete shape with
self-conscious deliberation about what ought to remain the same and what
ought to change. Change means that some familiar meanings should be enhanced at the expense of others. Feminist change works the same way: given
the ambiguities of women's history, it seems feminists are as much renewing
ancient meanings as they are rejecting contemporary ones. Even radical
change, it seems to me, can sometimes be understood as living within tradition. Once again, I find myself within the hermeneutic circle, as what is

conceptualized as resistance to tradition in one sense is recast as affirmation of tradition in another sense.

The hermeneutic circle is not a cause for paralysis. It is, rather, a way of life for social beings whose speech and behavior begin as enactments of routines we see in others. Initially we accept the accounts others offer of the meanings of these routines. Later we may come to question them. Moving with these meanings in order to move beyond them is the task of living within tradition. Ideally, past and present will be fused into a better future. This hope animates my philosophy, my faith, and my feminism, and animates this essay.

NOTES

1. Hans-Georg Gadamer, *Philosophical Hermeneutics,* trans. and ed. David E. Linge (Berkeley: University of California Press, 1976), p. xvi.

2. Gaston Bachelard, *The Poetics of Space,* trans. Maria Jolas (Boston: Beacon Press, 1994).

3. Stephen C. Pepper, *World Hypotheses: A Study in Evidence* (Berkeley: University of California Press, 1961).

4. Baruch Spinoza, *A Spinoza Reader,* ed. and trans. Edwin Curley (Princeton, N.J.: Princeton University Press, 1998).

5. *Kol Haneshama* (Wyncote, Pa.: The Reconstructionist Press, 1995).

6. Mordecai Kaplan, *Dynamic Judaism: The Essential Writings of Mordecai M. Kaplan,* ed. Mel Scult and Emanuel Goldsmith (New York: The Reconstructionist Press and Schocken Books, 1985). See also Rebecca T. Alpert and Jacob J. Staub, *Exploring Judaism: A Reconstructionist Approach* (Wyncote, Pa.: The Reconstructionist Press, 1988).

7. Judith Plaskow, *Standing Again at Sinai: Judaism from a Feminist Perspective* (San Francisco: Harper San Francisco, 1991).

8. Shohama Wiener, *The Fifty-eighth Century: A Jewish Renewal Sourcebook* (New York: Jason Aronson, 1996); Michael Lerner, *Jewish Renewal* (New York: Harper, 1994).

9. Max Black, *Models and Metaphors* (Ithaca, N.Y.: Cornell University Press, 1962).

10. Rosemarie Tong, *Feminist Thought: A More Comprehensive Introduction* (Boulder, Colo.: Westview Press, 1998).

TWELVE

Hagar on My Mind

AZIZAH Y. AL-HIBRI

A PERSONAL INTRODUCTION

I am an American Muslim immigrant. I come from an ancient corner of the world—the Middle East. My history goes back a few thousand years, for I am a descendent of Hagar, the mother of all Arabs. As years pass by in these United States, I find myself reading about Hagar, imagining her face, her hands, her life, her emotions. An Egyptian princess alone in the hot Arabian desert, twice an immigrant, with a crying infant and no food or water, not even breast milk to nurse. I close my eyes and feel the dry sand of the desert in my mouth. I hear Hagar running between two hills looking for water, food, people, anything. Seven times she runs back and forth. Her act is called *saʿi* in Arabic. It literally means to make an effort. You would think that one round of *saʿi* would have been more than enough to reach the inevitable conclusion—she was in trouble with no one in sight. But Hagar was an obstinate woman of faith who knew that in the end God would come through for her. He did, and thousands of years later I was born of her seed.

When I was in Lebanon, I lived a double life as a young woman. At home, I lived in highly religious surroundings, because I come from a house of learning and religious leadership. At the American University of Beirut (AUB), I stuffed my scarf in my briefcase and had American coffee with my classmates in the Uncle Sam restaurant. Two very different worlds that I tried very hard to keep apart, but in each I was privileged. At home, I was the descendant of major scholars and was seen as having inherited some of

This chapter was written before the events of September 11. Much has transpired since then, but it was too late to incorporate it into this essay.

their spiritual transparency. At the University, I had a rich modern uncle with a ridiculously expensive car and a chauffeur who often picked me up with my friends to spend the day at my uncle's chalet at the beach. My world was complex and contradictory, but whatever stress it placed on me, it never prepared me for the life of an immigrant.

I came to the United States to continue my higher education. As a result, my life suddenly changed. I faced serious challenges to my core values, to my dignity. I was emotionally shredded to pieces and thrown into the abyss. Till this day, I remember the departmental parties I attended when I began teaching in the seventies, and a certain colleague and senior administrator. He always reeked of alcohol in the afternoon. At parties, he held a drink in his hand and moved closer and closer to talk. Suddenly, the space would shrink and I would be backed slowly against the wall. "Be generous," he would whisper before I could wiggle out from my tight corner. One day, he stopped me to inquire: "I heard from the department secretary that you ordered an electric pencil sharpener for your office." "Yes," I answered, "the secretary told me it was not that expensive." He looked amused, then said with a grin: "Why don't you just order a manual one and hire an Arab to turn it? That would be much cheaper."

I turned to my feminist sisters. I remember around that time writing an article for a feminist socialist book. The latter half of the article was about the relationship of Marx and Lenin to the women in their lives. I had been introduced to Marxism only a few years earlier and was very proud of the research I had done. I had no agenda. I simply wanted to research and write about the topic. As it turned out, Marx in particular was a miserable male chauvinist. The article was accepted for publication, subject to the deletion and replacement of the part on Marx and Lenin. I was told to stick to writing about Arab women. Clearly, some Marxist feminist women did not want to destroy the image of their two patriarchal heroes, or take me out of the pigeonhole they assigned to me.

During that period, I remember lying in bed awake many nights. At times, tears ran down my cheeks like glittering sand particles from the beaches of Beirut. Then I would feel Hagar touching my shoulder, softly whispering: "You are an immigrant now, like me. You are all alone in this distant desert. Wipe up your tears. Get up and do your own *sa'i*. Run between these strange hills. In the end, God will be with you." Hagar was right, and this immigrant never gave up.

Luckily, I had the Society for Women in Philosophy (SWIP) to help me make an oasis in my desert. They were the finest group of women I ever had the privilege of working with in this country. A crazy bunch of women. We were crazy, because we would silence no one, and all ideas were placed on the table. There were no taboos, no restrictions on freedom of speech, no authority, but a great deal of honesty, love, and respect. When some of us violated these standards consciously or subconsciously, we stopped everything, discussed the problem and resolved it. Yes, some women viewed me as "exotic," but they loved me anyway. They listened to me. They embraced me with their thoughts and actions. I was no longer alone. These were the days SWIP asked me to become the founding editor of *Hypatia,* the first journal for feminist philosophy in the United States. I, the immigrant with the funny accent, was chosen by these brave women to give birth to our very special baby. I did and it lives till this day. Hagar, I am sure, is proud.

In the years that followed, I left teaching to go to law school and then to Wall Street before I returned to teaching. During that period, a lot had changed. I tried to get back into the feminist movement, but it was very different. There were now NGOs that went abroad and to the United Nations trying to mold the world in their own images. These were not the struggling anti-Establishment, anti-Patriarchy groups of the early seventies. These were "in" groups, heavily financed and backed by both the Establishment and Patriarchy. As I held the hands of Muslim women around the world and listened to their problems, I became more aware that the financing offered to some of them by American feminists was tied to a specific agenda. I realized then that I was looking at a new breed of American "feminists," women using feminism to achieve patriarchal goals.

My heart was, of course, broken. I thought of all the good times I had shared in the past with some of these women. I knew them personally. Decades earlier, we had held hands and sung feminist songs together, and we cried together. I wondered whether that old bond of sisterhood would not help them see what they were doing. I hoped that if they could see themselves through my Third-World-sensitive eyes, they would reform. So, one bright spring day in Washington, I stood at the podium of one such organization and spoke. The whole program was about Muslim women's rights. It was in preparation for the UN World Conference on Women held in Beijing. I was told that all the presentations would be published in a book to be distributed there. The major administrator of the organization was from my corner of the world, but every other leader of the organization was decidedly homegrown, as was the agenda. I looked at the audience. There were many women with head scarves, looking silenced and disempowered. I felt they needed my voice and I decided to speak for them. After all, wasn't the whole conference about their rights?

I turned to my old friends from the movement and reminded them of the basic principles of feminism: rejection of patriarchal and all other hegemonic hierarchical structures. I reminded them of our days of struggling together, of the good times and the bad times. I explained Islam to them from a feminist perspective, quoting the Qur'an. I reminded them of the pernicious effects of cultural imperialism and asked them to re-examine their current hegemonist behavior in the international arena. When I was done, my feminist friends sat eerily still, while the head-covered women rushed to the podium to thank me. My speech, they said, was the first in two days to address their concerns at the event. They had been rendered voiceless through a careful selection of speakers.

A few months later, I received a letter from the administrator of that organization informing me that the final version of my presentation was due in about a week. She also informed me that if I wanted the article to be published, I had to change the content. I responded by asking her about the concept of free speech. She invited me to exercise it in some other publication. This past year, I finally did just that when I published my response to Susan Okin, titled "Is Western Patriarchal Feminism Good for Third World/Minority Women?"

Hagar, I am still on track. I am continuing my *sa'i*. There will be water, there will be milk, and we, women of the trying desert, shall live and prosper for thousands of more years to come.

PHILOSOPHICAL AND RELIGIOUS REFLECTIONS

I am a logician. I love the certainty of a precise answer. I used to sit for hours solving problems for fun. Then I decided to apply logic to ethics. My system of deontic logic was "neat." It avoided all the pitfalls and paradoxes of earlier systems. But the only part of my system I ever used in real life was the foundational discussion on whether obligations conflict and what can we do about them. I have not been able to reduce a single ethical dilemma in my life to a set of premises with a precise conclusion. In a way, I look at my deontic logic as an exercise that keeps me in good ethical shape. It does not take me all the way to my answer, but certainly helps me avoid elementary mistakes.

I also dabbled in the philosophy of science and loved it. I loved all these theories about the world and the related measurements and paradoxes. This, I thought, was the real metaphysics. It told us about the real world. I was thus shaken when in the end, I discovered scientific as well as feminist critiques about the relativity and subjectivity of science. Science, it turns out, was about one more system of constructs masquerading as Reality itself. It works well for now, so we embrace it. It gives us power over nature, over others, so we idolize it. It has become the new religion in a world where hegemony is a primary value.

But then there were Marx and Hegel. My Marxist professor taught me about the "Early Marx," about Marxism with a humanist face. He denounced the repressive Soviet bureaucrats and their totalitarianism. I was spellbound, captivated. One wonders how much of the lessons he taught me informed his actions upon his return to his homeland, Serbia. There he became a major architect of the policy of ethnic cleansing. I look back at the old days at the University of Pennsylvania where he taught me. I look back at the many lunches, arguments, walks, even revolutionary music we shared. He was a partisan in Tito's army but had risen, so we were told, against totalitarian rule. He was my hero! My hero turned out to be a mass murderer of women and children. How can you ever go beyond that?

I learned from Hegel about the value of contradiction, and that patience with a text could lead to great rewards. These lessons were very helpful in my later life. Together with my feminist training, they taught me never to dismiss a text too soon, or an idea too quickly. I learned to look for hidden value and not be averse to alien thoughts. Despite appearances, humanity was indeed one, and the Other was I. Suddenly, I could hear the rhythmic chants of the sufis flowing back from the distant streets of Damascus: "Allah Hayy (God is alive), Reality is one."

I was told that God was the opium of the people. I was also told that all those who tried to prove God's existence failed. In fact, this logician went through a whole course of these proofs, dispensing of them one after the other. For my classmates, the failure showed the outrageousness of the belief in a God. For me, it showed the limitations of symbolic logic. Early on in life, I had experienced the world of spirituality and knew it was very hard to capture in a beaker or a formula. I had prayed to God and felt his love around me. I had related to others through that love, and I saw the world differently. We had peace. But as I became more philosophically educated, I was becoming conflicted, lonely, disillusioned, betrayed, unhappy. The theories I was applying in my own life, of unbridled materialism and secularism, were coming home to haunt me.

I remember a feminist discussion group where women spoke about the emptiness they had in their lives. Curiously, they reported that this emptiness was accompanied by the feeling of a hole in their bodies. It was right there in the middle of their chests, under their bosoms. It was painful, empty, and getting larger. Many of us agreed with that observation. I, too, had developed this hole, this painful sense of emptiness. It was a new feeling in many ways, and I hated it. All these theories had succeeded in doing was to rip me away from my intuitions and my heart. They impoverished the nature of my relationship to others and condemned me to a one-dimensional existence after which I would collapse into dust. The modern technological society had given me a mechanical heart, and it was tired of beating. I had no ancestors, no traditions. I did not have a history that extended thousands of years. Hagar was just one hapless woman. I, on the other hand, lived for the moment and was holding the whole world in my hand, with a gaping hole in my guts.

One night, I drove my Mercedes into the rain. There was a heavy Texas storm. I could not care less. The pain in my guts was too intense. I could not see the road. So what? I could crash and things would come to an end. I was young and attractive. I had a good job and lots of friends. But the hole kept getting bigger. The tears kept running down my face. The car kept moving faster on the highway. Then it occurred to me that I was given by God this valuable gift of life, this talent. I should not be an ingrate. I wiped my tears and went back home. A few days later, I woke up in the early morning and did a very primitive thing—I fell on my knees and prayed. Immediately, I felt the peace come back. I was whole again.

But how could I, a feminist, accept a patriarchal God who created me inferior to men? How could I submit to authority when I had fought it half my life? Had I truly lost my mind in exchange for spiritual peace? The answer is the rest of this story.

WEAVING THE STRANDS OF MY LIFE TOGETHER

It was hard to return to my faith if only because in my youth it was used to restrain me. I remember hearing repeatedly that the Qur'an states that men are superior to women. My choices, movement, actions, had all been restricted, and all in the name of religion. In the end, I had decided to leave it all and find my own way in life. Coming back to my faith was, therefore, a profound decision.

But you never cross the same river twice. The next time around, I was a mature and independent woman, a logician no less. I had seen the world and had lost my naïveté. I had seen good ideas poorly applied and insightful statements distorted. Through sheer obstinateness, I had retained my full knowledge of the classical Arabic language, the language of the Qur'an. Understanding that Islam has no ecclesiastical structure, I decided to read the Qur'an directly for myself. That would not have been the first time. As a child, I studied it with a sheikh for years. This time, however, it was different. I immersed myself in my project with a great deal of enthusiasm and hope. I did not have to work very hard before my efforts were thoroughly rewarded.

I remember a quiet summer afternoon on my family's estate in Maryland. The Grand Mufti of Lebanon, Sheikh Hassan Khalid, had come to the Washington area during the holy month of Ramadan to collect donations for the orphaned children of Lebanon. He was the guest of my family that afternoon. We strolled on the grounds talking about many issues, mostly religious ones. At one point, he turned to me and said, "Study the story of Iblis (Satan) in the Qur'an. It is most instructive. Iblis disobeyed God because Iblis believed that he was better than Adam. His arrogance caused his downfall. Examine that Iblisi logic in our modern context. For example, when a person thinks he is better than another because of money or race, isn't he engaging in Iblisi logic?" Soon thereafter, Sheikh Hassan Khalid was blown to pieces in Beirut by a car bomb.

The words of Sheikh Hassan Khalid echoed in my mind. I went back to the Qur'an. I read ancient commentaries, and I reached a very important conclusion. Islam has no ecclesiastical structure because it does not support any innate hierarchies, except that between Creator and created. The Qur'an is clear. All of us, males and females, nations and tribes, were created from the same *nafs* (soul, spirit). The claim that Eve was created from Adam's rib is not in the Qur'an, the primary source of Islam, at all. The Qur'an says repeatedly that women and men are created from the same *nafs*. I was dumbfounded! Doesn't the Qur'an say, however, that men are superior to women? Isn't that the refrain every Muslim woman hears daily?

I turned to the famous Qur'anic verse only to discover that the word "superior" is not even in it. Another word, *qawwamun,* is part of the verse, and most male jurists have *interpreted* it to mean superior. This is not the place to analyze that verse. I have done that elsewhere. But it turned out to be a verse that imposed *limits* upon men of ancient times who believed that they could interfere with every woman's business by virtue of their male gender alone. In fact, elsewhere, the Qur'an again clearly states that men and women believers are (equally) each other's *walis,* meaning guardians or caretakers. It is a basic rule of jurisprudential interpretation that Qur'anic verses must be interpreted in ways that render them internally consistent. Despite all these verses, men chose to interpret *qawwamun* to mean superior and from that derived significant legal privileges over women.

Worse yet, the male-oriented interpretation appeared to me to fall into Iblisi logic. So, let me recount briefly the story of Iblis. In that story, we are told that God created Adam and ordered Iblis (Satan) and the angels to bow to Adam. The angels bowed immediately, but Satan refused. His reason was simple: How could he bow to Adam if he was better than Adam? After all, Adam was created of clay, while Iblis was created of fire. And isn't it clear that fire is superior to clay? Satan tells God directly in the Qur'an: "I am better than he is." This Satanic logic, rooted in arrogance and a false hierarchy posited by Iblis, caused Satan to disobey God and incur his wrath. By disobeying God, Satan also posited his own will as equal or superior to the divine will. He thus violated the basic principle of Islam, namely the unicity of God, and the absolute superiority of God's will. Iblis thus fell into *shirk* (polytheism).

Based on this story, the medieval jurist al-Ghazali concludes that a rich person who thinks he is better than a poor one, or a white person who thinks he is better than a black or red person, is guilty of Satanic logic. By the same token, I add that a man who thinks he is better than a woman is guilty of Satanic logic. For after all, the Qurʾan is clear about the basis for the divine preference of one person over another. It is simply piety.

As I arrived at this conclusion, I started seeing my feminist thought revive and blossom. Having spent two decades rejecting patriarchal hierarchies, it was a relief to see my views affirmed by the Qurʾan. At that moment I realized that I had a calling. I was put on this earth both in Lebanon and the United States, in my religious family and in the feminist movement, given talent in the Arabic language, in logic and later in law, so that I could help Muslim women around the world who had become victims of an increasingly patriarchal society. They had been denied their rights in the name of religion, and I had the duty to unmask that monumental deception.

This deception was more monumental than appeared at first blush. Muslim men also had been victimized in the name of religion. Their democratic rights along with those of women had been stripped away, and they were taught that religion expected them to show obedience to the ruler, regardless of how corrupt that ruler may be. The Muslim's right to election and consultation was emptied of all meaning and limited to a favored few in some countries. Those jurists who dared to object, and it turns out there were many, ended up tortured or in jail. The history of Muslim societies turned out to be the history of how secular forces, barely disguised as religious ones, took over the power from the people and the religious scholars. Force was used blatantly in order to sow fear in the hearts of the citizens. So power-hungry were these forces that very early on they massacred members of the very House of the Prophet, killing all but one of his male descendants.

I did not know that. I did not know that Zainab, the granddaughter of the Prophet, shielded with her own body her remaining teenage nephew to save his life. I did not know that Zainab and all the women of the House of the Prophet were forced to march on foot from Karbalá in Iraq all the way to Damascus. I did not know that upon her arrival, Zainab's little sister was trembling in the palace of Yazid, the power-hungry usurper, for fear of being taken as prisoner of war. Zainab publicly comforted her, citing the Qurʾan to ensure her liberty. Then in the middle of all the tragic loss, the blood, the palpable fear, Zainab dared to speak out in a hall full of men who dared not speak. She stood up and branded Yazid as an oppressive ruler. She delivered a spontaneous, well-reasoned, and articulate speech, citing the Qurʾan repeatedly to denounce Yazid's rule. In the face of Zainab's courage, Yazid bowed his head in silence, perhaps in shame.

Zainab was not an exception. Before that, her mother Fatimah gave her own well-reasoned, defiant speech when her inheritance was denied to her after the death of her father, the Prophet Muhammad. Based on a reported statement of the Prophet, the leaders of the community had argued that children of prophets do not inherit. She refuted these claims with Qur'anic verse, but lost her case anyway in the face of a rampant patriarchy. Before her was her mother Khadija, who seems to belong to our century. Khadija was a wealthy and successful businesswoman. She hired the Prophet when he was still a young man to conduct some business for her. Khadija was so impressed by his honesty and manners that she proposed marriage to him. She was twenty years his senior, and they lived happily until her death.

Further research showed me many other basic facts. The Qur'an itself recognizes the right of the Muslim woman to participate in the political process, yet many Muslim countries continue to prohibit women from that participation. In one instance, the Prophet appointed a woman to lead prayers, yet men continue to question the Muslim woman's right to lead her community. The Qur'an repeatedly praises knowledge, and the Prophet declared the pursuit of education to be the duty of every Muslim, male and female. Yet the Taliban have severely restricted women's access to education. The Qur'an guarantees women a share of the inheritance, yet many women are left destitute when men refuse to give them their due share. I could continue multiplying examples. So, I packed my bags and went around the world to speak to my Muslim sisters.

I discovered both the achievements and misery of many Muslim women. We hear only of the latter in the United States. In the United Arab Emirates, for example, I was told by women that the number of female graduate students far surpassed that of men. Because of affluence in that part of the world, men gravitated to easier alternatives. The educational advantage has opened to the Emirati woman many doors in government, but at the same time, it may have created problems in her personal life. Despite the unfortunate debacle about her voting rights, the Kuwaiti woman has a great many rights and protections. For example, the Explanatory Memorandum to the Kuwaiti Personal Status Code (family law) quotes directly from the Qur'an when it defines the spousal relation as one of affection and mercy. It also follows the Qur'an by making verbal abuse a sufficient ground for divorce!

At the same time, there were deeply entrenched cultural views in various Muslim countries that had been unquestioningly accepted by both men and women as religious requirements. This unfortunate conclusion gave these views and the related laws a power of their own in Muslim societies, which, despite all their shortcomings, continue to value piety. To liberate women, it was thus important to strip the religious disguise from these views and force the community to re-evaluate the related customs in light of basic Qur'anic principles. How does a woman coming from the United States do that?

My task was complicated by the work already done by American NGOs in some Muslim countries. As I had stated in my suppressed speech in Washington, these NGOs had poisoned the well for Muslim feminists. They were amateurs who took their secular perspective abroad and thought they could change the world with it. Instead, they sowed a great deal of suspicion about the women's rights movement in societies that are deeply religious. Ultimately, some countries closed down NGOs altogether. Traveling again into these territories to defend Muslim women's rights was no small feat. I first had to undo prior damage before I could launch my own project. I understood that nothing could be achieved unless I tried to convince the women, the mullahs and sheikhs (religious scholars), and the legislators of the correctness of my Islamic position. I also decided to focus on one demand at a time. It appeared that the most urgent priority was that of ensuring the Muslim woman a fair marriage contract. The problem, in the United States and elsewhere, was that Muslim women were getting poor settlements upon divorce, often leaving them destitute. That was clearly contrary to Qur'anic teachings, and it had to change.

I leaf through a United States Information Agency (USIA then, now the Office of Public Diplomacy) report of a recent trip of mine it sponsored. It describes vividly one memorable scene at a meeting with assembly members of a Muslim province. I was explaining my views on the marriage contract and seeking support. A sheikh entered the meeting and sat demurely at one end. He was somewhat old with a white beard and probing eyes. He seemed powerless, kind, and soft-spoken. But I immediately understood that if I did not win him over, I would lose everyone. So I directed most of my remarks to him. According to the USIA report, "[a] most rewarding exchange occurred between Dr. al-Hibri and a sheikh, a religious leader, who was invited to join the discussion. He tested Dr. al-Hibri's understanding of the Qur'an during a dialogue in Arabic. Dr. al-Hibri fully won his confidence and the sheikh smiled and touched his heart."

As I was leaving the room, the assembly's secretary shook my hand and invited me to share my final proposals with him. "If your proposals are properly based on the Qur'an," he said, "we would consider revising our laws accordingly." Hagar, I am continuing my *sa'i*.

On another occasion, I met a mullah whose criticism and denunciation of feminists filled the morning papers. I was warned that he might not look me in the face, that he might not shake my hand, and that it would be futile to talk to him. I took my chances, however, and attended a dinner with him and a group of leaders. Initially, he was extremely formal, polite, and cold. Then the testing process started. It went so well that we turned to a discussion of my views on the marriage contract. The feminists had raised objections to certain consequences of the contract and were demanding change, but they had no knowledge of Islamic law, so they were making secular demands. That is why the mullah denounced them. When I met with some of these women, they explained to me that they were not secularists. They simply wanted change but did not have sufficient Islamic jurisprudential knowledge to know how to go about getting it. I told them that I thought I could help. That evening, I discussed with the mullah my views. I made the same demands, this time based on a thoughtful Islamic analysis. He listened, then he said, "If you can fully articulate a valid Islamic argument in support of this position, I am willing to consider it seriously." One of the supportive men sitting next to him asked, barely disguising his amazement: "Is that a 'yes'?" The mullah confirmed: "Yes."

The American press and feminists make sheikhs and mullahs look like irrational patriarchs. That may be true of many. The real ones, however, understand the story of Iblis very well. It is not their will that counts but God's. God's will is reflected in the Qur'an. If I can show that a certain practice is contrary to the Qur'an or even contrary to the spirit of the Qur'an, the religious person is bound to abandon it. In short, if you want to navigate your way around Kabul, you do not use the map of New York. Western feminists were doing exactly that. Luckily, I had the local map.

At the end of an exhausting summer, I passed by Beirut. I collected my thoughts and reflected on my whirlwind tour of nine Muslim countries. It was a tremendous success. How did that happen? Of course it was God's will. But God had prepared me for this. It dawned on me that finally my training in logic was paying handsomely. Often, the problems I posed to leaders at meetings were quickly disposed of by easy responses. I then tactfully exposed each response as inadequate. At that point, a more serious answer was proposed, only to be again disposed of. I had thought of all these answers long before I left the United States. None of them worked. My logical arguments, based on Qur'anic knowledge, soon won me the attention of those I was meeting. In the end, they either came up with valuable serious answers or gave up and asked me for my own. In each case, we achieved rapport, and they exhibited a great deal of respect and friendliness as I left the room. A very few evaded the challenge by promising to mail me the answer soon. I am still waiting for those.

So, after all these years, the lessons I learned and taught in class about argumentation, refutation by counter-example or otherwise, fallacies, and even *modus ponens* and *modus tollens* helped in my very concrete task of advancing the rights of women and promoting human rights. It is funny how the wheel of life turns. Who would have guessed?

Additionally, I could not have done all of this without my legal training. Logic helps me map my arguments properly. Law on the other hand makes me understand the complex subject matter I deal with. Islamic law is a combination of logic, law, and religion. It has evolved over fourteen hundred years, and many outstanding jurists have considered every single issue of their time. To introduce a feminist dimension to this tradition is to tread on very thin ice. How can I possibly measure up to those outstanding thinkers, such as al-Ghazali, Abu Hanifah, and Malik? My task, however, turned out to be less daunting than I originally suspected. These great thinkers themselves often supplied me with the arguments or views I needed. I said they were great thinkers, didn't I? All I needed to do was to revive some of their views, recast others, and deconstruct yet others. Law and logic, what a great combination!

The crux of this approach lies in the fact that Islam celebrates diversity. Based on this fact, Muslims jurists permitted the introduction of local customs into Islamic law, so long as these customs did not contradict it. As a result, Muslim cultures prospered. It is a basic tenet of Islamic jurisprudence that though Qur'anic principles remain absolute, laws change with changes in time and place. For this reason, when Imam al-Shafi'i immigrated from Iraq to Egypt, he revised his jurisprudence to make it more suitable to the culture and circumstances in Egypt. Clearly, then, all these major jurists would be appalled to discover that hundreds of years later, often thousand of miles away as well, we are still stuck on the jurisprudence they formulated for their own time and culture.

We have a duty to revisit this jurisprudence in light of the new historical era and new cultural circumstances in which we live. This is where deconstructing the old jurisprudence to separate its cultural components becomes necessary. Muslims are all bound by every word of the Qur'an, but they are not bound by cultural assumptions or biases. Engaging in Islamic jurisprudence is a whole other type of *sa'i* that Muslim women have to embrace in order to achieve their God-given rights. Very few can. For one, their education generally, and in religion especially, is limited in some countries. Luckily, al-Azhar al-Sharif of Cairo, the oldest Islamic University, has opened its gates to women. A deeper problem arises from the fact that the consequences of colonialism continue to unfold in Muslim countries. Given that many colonialist regimes prohibited the study of Arabic, the language of the Qur'an, and disadvantaged Islamic schools financially, a whole generation of Muslims has grown up without real knowledge of its heritage or religion. Angry with this deprivation, they continue to fight for their faith tooth and nail. Since they do not fully understand the flexibility of

Islam, their defense of Islam often becomes synonymous with the preservation of the status quo. This is why religious re-education is critical for the success of feminism in the Muslim world.

CONCLUDING REFLECTIONS

Today, all Muslims who go to Hajj (pilgrimage in Makkah) honor Hagar by repeating her *sa'i* between the same two hills for the full seven rounds. Men, women, and children remember her ordeal with this important symbolic ritual. Then they drink from the waters of Zamzam, the spring that miraculously gushed into existence, saving her and her baby Isma'il from thirst and certain death.

Yes, Hagar is my ancestral grandmother, and I am so proud of that. In a family whose family tree goes back over a thousand years, I know the name of every male ancestor I ever had and often something about his life story. I do not know the names of my female ancestors other than my immediate grandmothers Fihmiyah and Azizah (my maternal grandmother who gave me her name) and a handful of historically outstanding women, some of whom were mentioned in this story. For this reason, Hagar is very important to me. She is the mother of my whole family, the mother of my mostly unknown mothers. I do not know whose hair or eyes I inherited, but I do know that I have Hagar's determination for *sa'i*. It is this faithful *sa'i* that drove this immigrant female to study religion, logic, law, and feminist theory, to fight for other women around the world. Now, other women have joined my *sa'i*. Life is so beautiful!

NOTE

The author has chosen not to footnote this essay because of its intense personal nature. However, any information about Islam included herein is discussed more fully in the author's published articles and speeches. Many of these speeches can be found on the website of the organization the author founded, Karamah: Muslim Women Lawyers for Human Rights, www.karamah.org.

Part III

CHALLENGING TRADITIONS

THIRTEEN

A Skeptical Spirituality

NEL NODDINGS

When we try to answer the question whether philosophy, feminism, and faith can be reconciled, we see that many people have attempted the reconciliation, and quite a few have done so to their own satisfaction. Despite the multitude of personally satisfying accounts, no universally accepted reconciliation has ever been constructed. To argue for the compatibility of philosophy, feminism, and faith, then, is not a mathematical sort of task—one that can be completed to the satisfaction of some professionally constituted public. Part of the difficulty lies in the fact that neither philosophy nor feminism is a unitary body of thought. With which philosophies or feminisms is faith compatible? When one has identified a particular philosophical perspective or feminist orientation, one should at least be able to avoid gross logical errors. But, even so, philosophies and feminisms are less precise than mathematical frameworks, and people who share a basic philosophical framework may nevertheless disagree on what follows from it. Thus, it seems to me that the task of reconciliation is largely a personal one.

To grant that the task is personal is to recognize the subjectivity involved in it, but that is not to say that the job is irrational—a matter of unthinking preference. Taking the task seriously, one must work through the possibilities carefully, analyzing why one accepts or rejects various arguments. A credible account must demonstrate familiarity with the relevant arguments, but there will remain an element of the ineffable. What is it in *me*, in *my* life, that draws me toward or away from a particular argument? Thus, in addition to the sort of study that produces familiarity with existing arguments and a rationality that is ever watchful for logical errors, personal honesty is required. If we are confessed believers, do we still harbor doubts? If we are declared unbelievers, do we still embrace a form of spirituality? Locating myself in the second category, I need to say why I've abandoned formal belief, but I need also to explain why I retain a persistent and deepening spirituality.

WHY I AM NOT A BELIEVER

Both my husband and I were brought up in mainstream Protestant churches, but he had always looked at the church as a social organization, whereas I embraced it as primarily spiritual. In the early years of our marriage, when we had several small children, I began to feel uneasy with the Apostles' Creed, and I commented to my husband that I really didn't believe most of it. "Have you listened to what we say every week?" I asked him. His answer was, "You're not supposed to listen! It's just a ritual!" Well, of course, he did then begin to listen and agreed that he did not believe most of it either. Yet, the Creed begins, "I believe . . . "

Rejection of the Creed was followed by the realization that getting the kids ready for Sunday School every Sunday was ruining our family life. At that time, we had five children, the oldest of whom was nine. By the time I had the last of them dressed, the first two were already disheveled. More than once, as we were about to leave the house, we discovered that one small boy had on two different colored socks. Then, one day, the older two came home upset by the Sunday School lesson. They had been taught the story of the wheat and tares, complete with the cruel idea that human tares would be cast into Hell. That did it. After that, we spent Sunday mornings reading the comics and doing light chores.

As time passed, I became acquainted with writers whose views supported my doubts. I read Bertand Russell's *Why I Am Not a Christian* and agreed with much of it.[1] I came to admire his fearless response to the question whether he was never afraid of God's judgment for his denial. Here is what Russell said:

> Most certainly not. I also deny Zeus and Jupiter and Odin and Brahma, but this causes me no qualms. I observe that a very large portion of the human race does not believe in God and suffers no visible punishment in consequence. And if there were a God, I think it unlikely that he would have such an uneasy vanity as to be offended by those who doubt his existence.[2]

It was this last sentence that seemed to me particularly sound. As a parent, I knew I could not visit any lasting punishment on my children, and God is supposed to be better than human parents. The God described in our church could not be God. Thus, for me, the parting of the ways came mainly from ethical objections. Much later, I learned that many well-educated people in the late nineteenth and early twentieth century left the church for similar reasons. James Turner wrote:

Declarations of unbelief often sounded more like acts of moral will than intellectual judgments. [Robert] Ingersol said that "I cannot worship a being" whose "cruelty is shoreless." Darwin was so appalled by the harshness of natural selection that he could no longer bring himself to believe in God: better that this horror should have sprung from blind chance.[3]

For me, the obvious cruelty of nature is the main barrier to conventional belief, and I have never encountered a convincing argument for the goodness of God. Yet there is that inside me that keeps looking. If there is something of goodwill out there in the universe, I feel quite sure that it does not reside in one omnipotent and omniscient God. Thus, I am not persuaded by Wendy Farley's lovely argument for the compassion of God:

> Faith might be understood as an ever-deepening sense of the long sorrow of the world together with a vision and enactment of the compassion of God for creation . . . Theodicy cannot explain away evil or make evil into anything good. It can only hope to illuminate the radical love of God that is not overcome by evil, that is poured out inexhaustibly over all creation.[4]

I see no evidence of this compassion and, in contrast, I have seen much compassion in unbelievers who are stirred by the condition of their sister beings. However, Farley at least avoids the great errors and horrors of traditional theodicy. She does not attempt to reconcile evil and good by invoking harmony (as Leibniz did), or by denying evil (what seems to be evil really is not, and some day we will understand), or by glorifying suffering. The glorification of suffering or even the insistence that it is inflicted for the sake of soul making is repellent to me. Here, for example, is C. S. Lewis trying to explain his wife's agony and death:

> But is it credible that such extremities of torture should be necessary for us? Well, take your choice. The tortures occur. If they are unnecessary, then there is no God or a bad one. If there is a good God, then these tortures are necessary. For no even moderately good Being could possibly inflict or permit them if they weren't.[5]

Lewis's argument is far too simplistic, but it is widely accepted by believers. The notion that the suffering we undergo on earth will eventually be shown to be necessary for a great future good (the Iraenian view) has been developed in opposition to the Augustinian idea that traces evil to the Fall.[6] Less condemnatory than the Augustinian view, the Iraenian view is, nevertheless, as Russell says, "only a rationalization of sadism."[7]

Theologians have struggled with the problem of evil for ages and in far more sophisticated ways than Lewis.[8] Some yield on God's omniscience, suggesting that God exists within time and cannot foresee everything; others relax the insistence that God is omnipotent and recognize limits to his power. Augustine considered this latter possibility (in the form of Manichaeanism) but finally rejected it as a heresy. A few have even considered the idea that God may be struggling to manage his power and knowledge and, thus, still learning to be moral.[9] In this struggle, he was taught a lesson by Job, a mere mortal. Jack Miles writes:

> After Job, God knows his own ambiguity as he has never known it before. He now knows that, though he is not Bertrand Russell's fiend, he has a fiend-susceptible side and that mankind's conscience can be finer than his. With Job's assistance, his just, kind self has won out over his cruel, capricious self just as it did after the flood.[10]

A morally fallible God, one still learning to be good, is attractive in many ways. Acceptance of such a God rescues us from the need to explain evil in terms of eventual good. It sets a better model of divinity before us and counsels us to curb our own passion for power. Similarly, feminist attempts to recast God as a feminine deity have enormous appeal, and they have some historical backing as well. Merlin Stone writes:

> For people raised and programmed on the patriarchal religions of today, religions that affect us even in the most secular aspects of our society, perhaps there remains a lingering, almost innate memory of sacred shrines and temples tended by priestesses who served in the religion of the original supreme deity. In the beginning, people prayed to the Creatress of Life, the Mistress of Heaven. At the very dawn of religion, God was a woman. Do you remember?[11]

I love reading such accounts, and I agree with Christine Downing that women "need images and myths through which we can see who we are and what we might become."[12] But the problem that drove me away from mainstream Protestantism remains. I see no more evidence for the actual existence of a benevolent "Creatress" than I do for an all-good male god. True, we can see female creatures (and a few male ones, too) tenderly caring for their young, but the young may still be torn to shreds by predators, stricken with horrible illnesses, or visited with lifelong ill-fortune. Ernest Becker's remarks seem accurate:

> Existence, for all organismic life, is a constant struggle to feed—a struggle to incorporate whatever other organisms they can fit into their mouths and press down their gullets without choking. Seen in these stark terms, life on this planet is a gory spectacle, a science-fiction nightmare in which digestive tracts fitted with teeth at one end are tearing at whatever flesh they can

reach, and at the other end are piling up fuming waste excrement as they move along in search of more flesh.[13]

William James, too, acknowledges that the horrors of the melancholiac are real enough, although they lack balance:

> The normal process of life contains moments as bad as any of those which insane melancholy is filled with, moments in which radical evil gets its innings and takes its solid turn. The lunatic's visions of horror are all drawn from the material of daily fact. Our civilization is founded on the shambles, and every individual existence goes out in a lonely spasm of helpless agony. If you protest, my friend, wait till you arrive there yourself![14]

But, of course, there is more to life than horror, failure, fear, misery, and death. There is also joy, love, small successes, great natural beauty, awe, and deep satisfaction in work we love. If a change in the image of deity can move us toward a greater appreciation for creation and kindness over destruction and cruelty, it is a change to be encouraged. However, in developing a feminist theology, it seems reasonable to avoid the basic errors for which feminists have castigated male theologians. Sheila Greeve Davaney emphasizes the need to avoid ontological claims.[15] If the traditional male theologies are products of human construction, so are the newer (or older) female views. Our symbols do not necessarily point to realities existing beyond ourselves. The value of feminist theologies has to be located in their consequences for human life. Thus, I agree with Davaney that a feminist-pragmatist theology is the best bet for an intellectual reconciliation of feminism, pragmatism, and faith.[16]

In what way would such a view incorporate *faith*? Here we encounter yet another difficulty, in addition to the charges of relativism so often directed at pragmatism. The difficulty is that a symbol system with no ontological base is somehow spiritually unsatisfying. Jung said, rightly I think, "Agnosticism maintains that it does not possess any knowledge of God or of anything metaphysical, overlooking the fact that one never *possesses* a metaphysical belief but is *possessed by it*."[17] This explains our discontent with philosophical systems and symbols that retain the language of religion but relinquish its claim to sacred ontology.

John Dewey tried to assimilate the language of religion to secular purposes and succeeded in satisfying almost no one. For me, Dewey is the twentieth century's greatest educational thinker, and I draw on his work again and again. But his treatment of religion leaves me deeply dissatisfied. Abandoning all reference to the supernatural, Dewey wanted to retain the language of religion but deny its roots in a reality that cannot be reached through science. *Religion* had to go, but the religious was to be encouraged.

Even God was redefined. Noting that ideals exist in human affairs, Dewey wanted to detach them from any supernatural origin:

> They [ideals] are further unified by the action that gives them coherence and solidity. It is this *active* relation between ideal and actual to which I would give the name "God." I would not insist that the name *must* be given. There are those who hold that the associations of the term with the supernatural are so numerous and close that any use of the word "God" is sure to give rise to misconception and be taken as a concession to traditional ideas.[18]

My objection to such use is different from the one Dewey cites. If we want to talk about the "active relation between ideal and actual," then we should do so using exactly that language. "God" belongs to those who are possessed by a metaphysical belief. Martin Gardner complains that Dewey is "the outstanding example of an atheist for whom a sense of the numinous was minimal."[19] Russell, for all his avowed atheism, retained a sense of the numinous, and his rhetorical style accommodated the language of mystery. In a letter to Lowes Dickinson, he wrote:

> And often I feel that religion, like the sun, has extinguished the stars of less brilliancy but not less beauty, which shine upon us out of the darkness of a godless universe. The splendor of human life, I feel sure, is greater to those who are not dazzled by the divine radiance; and human comradeship seems to grow more intimate and more tender from the sense that we are all exiles on an inhospitable shore.[20]

Many other atheists have acknowledged the mysteries that seem not to have troubled Dewey. Jean-Paul Sartre, for example, felt that too many secular ethicists tried to abolish God "with the least possible expense." In opposition, he (with Heidegger) traced our forlornness to the realization that God does not exist:

> The existentialist thinks it very distressing that God does not exist, because all possibility of finding values in a heaven of ideas disappears along with Him; there can no longer be an *a priori* Good, since there is no infinite and perfect consciousness to think it . . . Indeed, everything is permissible if God does not exist, and as a result man is forlorn, because neither within him nor without does he find anything to cling to.[21]

I am not so concerned with the ethical problems raised by the loss of God, and I do not believe the loss entails that "everything is permissible." I believe Russell was right to suppose that the loss should bring human beings closer in a shared sense of our utter dependence on one another. But the forlornness that Sartre mentions is another matter. Metaphysical belief may possess us, as Jung says, but I suspect that it is a metaphysical longing, more than belief, that seizes us, and those of us who espouse no formal belief are, nevertheless, subject to it. This is where honesty becomes of paramount importance. What is it we long for, and can it be satisfied outside the domain to which "faith" usually belongs?

BEYOND BELIEF

A reflective intellect is often repelled by dogma. The requirement to believe a whole body of doctrine that flies in the face of both logic and empirical evidence is too much for many of us, but a lively intellect also remains challenged by the existence and grandeur of the universe. One cannot prove the existence of God from either the need for a first cause or a designer. Kant's arguments are decisive on this: indeed, some of his loveliest lines address the basic mystery:

> That unconditioned necessity, which we require as the last support for all things, is the true abyss of human reason. Eternity itself, however terrible and sublime it may have been depicted by Haller, is far from producing the same giddy impression, for it only *measures* the duration of things, but does not *support* them. We cannot put off the thought, nor can we support it, that a Being, which we represent to ourselves as the highest among all possible beings, should say to himself, I am from eternity to eternity, there is nothing beside me, except that which is something through my will,—*but whence am I?* Here all sinks away from under us, and the highest perfection, like the smallest, passes without support before the eyes of speculative reason.[22]

Still, wonder and awe persist. These may indeed come from something beyond—a god or a whole community of gods. But, admitting this possibility, what do we do with it? Deism in its eighteenth-century form does nothing to satisfy metaphysical longing. That longing requires some form of communion or connection. When I observe the sun rising out of the sea or listen to the breakers in the dead of the night, I want to say "thank you," but to whom or what does one say it? On this, I have found Martin Buber most helpful. He insists that we cannot know or describe God:

> The eternal You cannot become an It; because by its very nature it cannot be placed within measure and limit . . . ; because by its very nature it cannot be grasped as a sum of qualities . . . ; because it is not to be found outside the world; because it cannot be experienced; because it cannot be thought; because we transgress against it . . . if we say: "I believe that he is"—even "he" is still a metaphor, while "you" is not.[23]

Buber answers my question directly by quoting Nietzsche: "One accepts, one does not ask who gives."[24] It is personal honesty that leads me to this position, not something like Pascal's wager, for Pascal intends to cure unbelief, and I am not interested in doing this.[25] I only admit that I enter into communion. That I may be talking to myself is surely a possibility, but I did not create the sunrise or the sea. When the spirit soars, it is lifted by something outside itself, but this something need not be a describable god nor need it be a single thing. Many things may trigger this soaring of spirit.

We are sent back into the world. Here, again, Buber is helpful. In contrast to Kierkegaard, whom he criticizes, Buber says that one does not need to transcend the ethical world to reach God. "Of course," he writes, "whoever steps before the countenance has soared way beyond duty and obligation—but not because he has moved away from the world; rather because he has come truly close to it."[26] I do not know whether this soaring beyond duty and obligation is a result of stepping before "the countenance" or whether it is as natural as mother love. I affirm the experience, but I confess ignorance as to its cause. I suspect that causation may run in the opposite direction; that is, when we are deeply moved by some encounter, we feel transported toward something we feel as God. In seeking an explanation for it, we seek its source. It may be better simply to accept the gift.

Jung says that God is a "psychic reality."[27] The psyche is non-physical but real. Clearly, something is "there" inside us, and this capacity or indwelling spirit responds to a host of stimuli. As I write this, I am listening to a recording of Maria Callas singing operatic arias. Whence such a gift? And why am I so deeply affected? Momentarily distracted by "Casta Diva," I glance up and see a fishing boat heading north on a calm sea. I have already walked along the shore this morning and felt the usual combination of wonder and contentment. And rising a little after sunrise, I was awestruck by the colors on our bookshelves and library walls. At that time of the day, every part of the house colored by the northeast light is like a Monet painting in pinks and gold. But there is no need to analyze any of these experiences. The aesthetic yields spontaneously to the spiritual.

Perhaps the spiritual impulse—or the poetic?—is primary and takes different directions in different people. One would be hard-pressed to find a poet with a finer sense of the numinous than Thomas Hardy; yet Hardy was an unbeliever. A reader hears the spiritual longing and appreciation when Hardy writes of the May month flapping its "glad green leaves like wings" or the "full-starred heavens that winter sees."[28] And one wonders whether a God-feeling inspired Bach or whether the music within him (and echoing in lofty places) created and sustained the God-feeling. Does it matter?

Many think it does matter. If God guarantees immortality, but only conditionally, it surely matters. But what sort of God would play such a game with his creatures? Russell was surely right to say that, if he encountered the God whose existence he had denied in life, he would ask him why he had hidden himself so well from the intelligent minds that sought him. We could, of course, settle for the God of Spinoza—a creator who cares nothing for the individuals created, any more than we care for the individual ants in a great colony, each working according to rule and plan. But that acceptance (is it ever total?) leads to what Miguel Unamuno called "God-ache." Spinoza, Unamuno said, suffered from God-ache as other people "have a pain in the hand or foot, heart-ache or head-ache."[29] Whether he experienced an ache or a happiness satisfied by reason, Spinoza might have been right, but Unamuno might also be right—that reason cannot satisfy the metaphysical longing. Does one admit the longing or deny it? Unamuno was surely right when he said of immortality that both believers and unbelievers hear a voice that murmurs, "Who knows!"[30] Again, it takes a certain courage or humility—or at least authenticity—to admit that one hears this voice.

Accept the gift—the spirit that pours out of us into the everyday world and is somehow replenished by our encounters in it. There is no decision to be made, no transcendence required. The realization that no decision on the source of our wonder or on immortality (Is there? Is there not?) needs to be made does not suggest that there is nothing to be done. There is still the problem of ethical life to which I will return in a moment but, also, one's spirituality—if it is treasured—must be nurtured. To find out what nurtures it is one of life's great tasks, one terribly neglected in today's schools.

Music, art, poetry, and literature are all possible sources for the nurture of spirit. How odd it is, then, that these are the first studies to be cut when school districts have financial problems. Odder still is the pedagogical habit of ignoring the great existential questions in literature to concentrate on technicalities. Katherine Simon describes her own handling of *Macbeth* in her early years of teaching. After reading the wonderful lines that begin "Life's but a walking shadow,"[31] she did what she had been taught to do:

> I helped the students understand the definitions of the words "struts," "frets," and "signifying." I asked them to comment on the central metaphor, in which "life" is compared to an actor. We pounded out the rhythm of the lines on our desks, noting that the first, fourth, and fifth lines do not fall neatly into iambic pentameter, and discussing why Shakespeare might have departed from his norm for these lines. We had a passably interesting discussion about the matter and the words.[32]

Simon, a superb teacher, wonders why it did not occur to either her or her students to discuss the central existential question: Does life have meaning? Then, sadly, she comments, "I was neither equipped nor expected to explore questions about what it means to be human."[33] Today, amidst appalling violence and alienation, many educators and policymakers still insist on concentrating on the "basics" and, especially, on raising test scores in those subjects. My contention is that we can do both and that, indeed, the achievement test score problem is subsidiary to the larger problem of educating for fully human life. If we address the truly basic questions of life, all the rest goes more easily. It has point.

Through literature, music, and art, we can even discuss the directly religious. Here, without neglecting the existential themes, we might address poetic expression. Students might be asked, for example, to compare newer versions of a psalm to the King James Version. In some cases, the poetic superiority of the King James Version is obvious; in others, both versions are lovely, as in:

> As the hart panteth after the water brooks,
> So panteth my soul after thee, O God.

or

> As the deer pants for water,
> So I long for you, O God.[34]

In addition to a comparison and discussion of poetic preference, there is, of course, an incidental vocabulary lesson. Although it is not reasonable to depend on incidental learning for everything that must be learned, much of importance is learned better this way than by deliberate instruction. It is entirely feasible to talk about spiritual longing and the ways in which people have expressed it. Literary selections can be made from a variety of religions but, of course, no one religion can be taught as *the* way, although expressions of belief should not be forbidden. As the discussion develops, all sorts of things may be learned: appreciation for poetry, vocabulary, lots of history, some philosophy, a little theology, appreciation for other religious positions, and perhaps a growing sense that the existential questions are worth exploring.[35]

While I was considering metaphysical longing as an example of human yearning that seems to touch atheists and theists universally, I revisited a Hindu tale, *The Ashes of a God*.[36] What struck me (besides its mystery and beauty) returns us to the main theme. In Hinduism, as in every world religion, women are portrayed as an impediment to spirituality. Like the ancient Greek philosophers, Hindu sages seek freedom and wide-awakeness; their ultimate condition is described in striking contrast to those "who still remain blinded by illusion."[37] However, memory gets in the way of progress toward freedom and enlightenment. Memory contains love and regret: "And, what, then, is it, that is of all things most peculiarly the object of regret; that laughs at all efforts to reduce it to oblivion and non-entity; that refuses to be driven into the *oubliettes* of any soul? Needless to say, a woman."[38]

The author could have said "love" instead of "woman." But the clear message in all of the world's great religions is that it is men who engage in spiritual quests; women are the great distraction. For Adam, Odysseus, and St. Anthony, woman is portrayed as the devil's gateway.[39] Referring to I Enoch, where the story of the watchers and their descendants is told, Bernard Prusak comments, "As in Genesis and the *Odyssey,* evil, women, and knowledge are a package deal. War, jewelry, cosmetics, and sex are Azazel's [a fallen watcher] lessons."[40] The treatment of women in religion is another important theme for the school curriculum. But in connection with the main theme of this chapter—metaphysical longing—this horrific history reveals vividly why many women who experience that longing nevertheless reject traditional religions. Many more would reject their religious traditions if they were taught the truth about them.[41] Another major dishonesty in education!

There are two main ways in which women have tried to reconcile their feminism with a traditional faith. Some writers try to show that a religion has departed from its origins when it discriminates against women.[42] The basic argument here is that the existing great religions started out as emancipatory movements. A return to original commitments would, then, restore the equality of women. The second approach is to claim that the religion in question is dynamic—that, as a religion for all times, it must be open to thoughtful change. Although I have the greatest respect for the women and men who are working along these lines, I find neither approach powerful enough to accomplish the task. If religions tend to be emancipatory in their origins, it might be more practical to start a new religion than to return an old one to its roots. The discontents that give rise to emancipatory movements change, and new language is needed to discuss them. With respect to the second approach, the voiced claim that a religion is dynamic is itself evidence that the religion is trying hard to maintain the status quo.

"Woman must come of age by herself," wrote Anne Morrow Lindbergh.[43] By this, Lindbergh did not mean to reject relatedness and interdependence. Her entire book is devoted to personal growth within developing relationships. She meant, rather, that a woman must find her own way spiritually toward wholeness: "She must learn not to depend on another, nor to feel she must prove her strength by competing with another. . . . She must find her true center alone. She must become whole."[44]

Lindbergh goes on to suggest that man also needs to undertake the task of becoming whole, and now we can see that she means for each person to listen but not follow slavishly, to feel but not wallow in sentimentality, to have courage but not to use it in overcoming others, to develop the capacity to look inward and work toward becoming whole while remaining in relation. When she describes a "perfect" day, she describes intervals of physical chores, intellectual work, conversation, play on the beach, swimming, sipping sherry by the fireside, lying on the beach under bright stars, silent communion with her companion. That whole perfect day might be described as an exercise in spirituality.

Every person has to find her own way to spirituality. Kathleen Norris describes her periodic stays in a Benedictine monastery as restorative.[45] The ritual, liturgy, and meticulous structuring of time induce a sense of peace and wholeness in her. Although I enjoy sacred music, I would be put off by the other things that nourish Norris. With Lindbergh, I prefer to walk on the beach or play in the waves. In any formal religious setting, I cannot shake off the hypocrisy and political oppression so characteristic of organized religion. Where Norris is immersed in a supportive sanctity, I am ready to run off with Bertrand Russell.

Yet my everyday life is flooded with spirit. From the colors of sunrise to the soft purring of my cat as we both fall asleep at night, the day is filled with moments of contentment and, sometimes, even spiritual ecstasy. Both Lindbergh and Norris write of the need for solitude, and, although I do not believe that long periods of silence and isolation are necessary, I do believe that moments of solitude are essential. When I am deeply affected by a sunrise or its spectacular pre-glow, there is always a moment of reflection— time to simply "be with" the beauty. It may be that others require longer periods of solitude for the recovery of their souls. Each of us has to find a way that fits her own life and, of course, what fits in one period of life may not fit in another.

Thus I have come to a skeptical spirituality. I think that we have much to learn from personal accounts of spirituality and from music, poetry, nature, fiction, and loving interpersonal relations. But religious claims to knowledge are all suspect and, with Buber, I fear that they lead us away from connection and into the uneasy or even violent separation so characteristic of battles over dogma. Whether the persistent longing and deeply satisfying communion I have described are artifacts of unpurged superstition, evidence of the supernatural, or a spiritual achievement, I do not know. With Buber and Nietzsche, I simply accept the gift. If the source is some day disclosed, I may be as surprised as Dickens's "Pip" at its identity.

Although decisions in the form of Kierkegaard's continual reaffirmations need not be made, decisions in the ethical world must be made. None of our best impulses and moral sentiments need the assistance of religion. Indeed, although I think Russell exaggerated a bit, I believe he was right that, on balance, religion has done more harm than good for the world. Probably every source of morality identified by philosophers has functioned effectively in the lives of some individuals. Some of us are motivated to seek the good by obedience to religion, some by motherhood, some by enlightened self-interest, some by friendship, some by universal compassion, some by combinations of many sources. A skeptical spirituality lacks certainty; it even lacks assurance. But if it adds vitality to personal life, if it adds joy, then it may also bring with it a gentle and awed compassion that enhances ethical life. The gift accepted may be passed on in countless ways.

NOTES

1. Bertrand Russell, "Why I Am Not a Christian," in Russell, *Why I Am Not a Christian* (New York: Simon and Schuster, 1957), pp. 3–23.

2. Bertrand Russell, "What Is an Agnostic?" in *Religions in America,* ed. Leo Rosten (New York: Simon and Schuster, 1963), p. 200.

3. James Turner, *Without God, Without Creed* (Baltimore: Johns Hopkins University Press, 1985), 207.

4. Wendy Farley, *Tragic Vision and Divine Compassion: A Contemporary Theodicy* (Louisville: Westminster/John Knox Press, 1990), p. 133.

5. C. S. Lewis, *A Grief Observed* (Toronto: Bantam, 1976), p. 50.

6. For a well-developed modern version of the Iraenian position, see John Hick, *Evil and the God of Love* (New York: Macmillan, 1966).

7. Bertrand Russell, "Has Religion Made Useful Contributions to Civilization?" in *Why I Am Not a Christian,* p. 30.

8. For a comprehensive and fascinating review of theodicies, see David Lee Griffin, *Evil Revisited* (Albany: State University of New York Press, 1991).

9. See Carl G. Jung, *Answer to Job,* in *Collected Works,* vol. 2 (Princeton, N.J.: Princeton University Press, 1969), pp. 357–470.

10. Jack Miles, *God: A Biography* (New York: Alfred A. Knopf, 1995), p. 328.

11. Merlin Stone, *When God Was a Woman* (New York: Dial Press, 1976), p. 1.

12. Christine Downing, *The Goddess* (New York: Crossroad, 1984), p. 2.

13. Ernest Becker, *Escape from Evil* (New York: Free Press, 1975), p. 1.

14. William James, *The Varieties of Religious Experience* (New York: Mentor, 1958), 138. Original published in 1902.

15. See Sheila Greeve Davaney, "Problems with Feminist Theory: Historicity and the Search for Sure Foundations," in *Embodied Love: Sensuality and Relationships as Feminist Values,* ed. Paula M. Cooey, Sharon A. Farmer, and Mary Ellen Ross (San Francisco: Harper & Row, 1987), 79–95. Davaney criticizes the work of Rosemary Radford Reuther, Elizabeth Schüssler Fiorenza, and Mary Daly for this slip into ontology.

16. Note, however, that the problem of avoiding both objectivism and relativism has not been solved to universal satisfaction. See Richard J. Bernstein, *Beyond Objectivism and Relativism: Science, Hermeneutics, and Praxis* (Philadelphia: University of Pennsylvania Press, 1986).

17. *Answer to Job,* p. 452.

18. John Dewey, *A Common Faith* in *The Later Works, 1925–1953,* vol. 9: *1933–1934,* ed. Jo Ann Boydston (Carbondale and Edwardsville: Southern Illinois University Press, 1989), pp. 34–35.

19. Martin Gardner, *The Whys of a Philosophical Scrivener* (New York: Quill, 1983), p. 335.

20. *Autobiography (1872–1914)* (Boston: Atlantic-Little, Brown, 1967), p. 286.

21. Jean-Paul Sartre, "The Humanism of Existentialism," in Sartre, *Essays in Existentialism,* ed. Wade Baskin (Secaucus, N.J.: Citadel Press, 1977), pp. 40–41.

22. Immanuel Kant, *Critique of Pure Reason,* trans. F. Max Muller (New York: Doubleday Anchor books, 1966), p. 409.

23. Martin Buber, *I and Thou,* trans. Walter Kaufmann (New York: Charles Scribner's Sons, 1970), pp. 160–61.

24. *I and Thou,* p. 158. The quote is from Nietzsche, *Ecce Homo,* Section 3.

25. For "Pascal's Wager," see Blaise Pascal, *Pensées,* trans. A. J. Krailsheimer (Baltimore: Penguin Books, 1966), pp. 149–53. Original published in 1662.

26. *I and Thou,* pp. 156–57. The criticism of Kierkegaard immediately precedes this.

27. *Answer to Job,* pp. 463–64.

28. See Thomas Hardy, "Afterwards," in Hardy, *Selected Poetry* (Oxford: Oxford University Press, 1996), p. 135. Many others of his poems express what I am calling "metaphysical longing," forlornness, or regret. See, for example, "Hap," "The Impercipient," and "Nature's Questioning."

29. Miguel Unamuno, *Tragic Sense of Life,* trans. J. E. Crawford Flitch (New York: Dover, 1954), p. 7.

30. *Tragic Sense of Life,* p. 118.

31. The reference is to Shakespeare, *Macbeth,* Act V, scene V.

32. Katherine Simon, *Moral Questions in the Classroom* (New Haven, Conn.: Yale University Press, 2001), p. 1.

33. *Moral Questions in the Classroom,* p. 1.

34. Psalm 42:1. The first is from the King James Version. The second is from *Living Psalms and Proverbs* (Wheaton, Ill.: Tyndale House, 1967), p. 56.

35. See Nel Noddings, *Educating for Intelligent Belief or Unbelief* (New York: Teachers College Press, 1993).

36. F. W. Bain, trans., *The Ashes of a God* (New York: G. P. Putnam's Sons, 1911).

37. *The Ashes of a God,* p. x.

38. *The Ashes of a God,* p. x.

39. See John Anthony Phillips, *Eve: The History of an Idea* (San Francisco: Harper & Row, 1984); also Nel Noddings, *Women and Evil* (Berkeley: University of California Press, 1989); for both discussion and illustration of St. Anthony's temptations, see Bram Dijkstra, *Idols of Perversity: Fantasies of Feminine Evil in Fin-de-Siecle Culture* (New York: Oxford University Press, 1986), pp. 254–56.

40. Bernard Prusak, "Woman: Seductive Siren and Source of Sin? Pseudepigraphal Myth and Christian Origins," in *Religion and Sexism,* ed. Rosemary Radford Ruether (New York: Simon and Schuster, 1974), p. 91.

41. I was introduced to this material through Mary Daly, *Beyond God the Father* (Boston: Beacon Press, 1974).

42. See the essays in Jeanne Becher, ed., *Women, Religion, and Sexuality* (Philadelphia: Trinity Press International, 1990); also *Women of Spirit,* ed. Rosemary Radford Ruether and Eleanor McLaughlin (New York: Simon and Schuster, 1979).

43. Anne Morrow Lindbergh, *Gift from the Sea* (New York: Vintage Books, 1978), p. 96.

44. *Gift from the Sea,* p. 96.

45. See Kathleen Norris, *The Cloister Walk* (New York: Riverhead Books, 1997). A similar reaction may be induced by Dorothy L. Sayers, *The Whimsical Christian* (New York: Collier Books, 1978).

FOURTEEN

Faith, Philosophy, Passions, and Feminism: Dangerous Attractions

IRMGARD SCHERER

I. INTRODUCTION

To "profess" *philosophia,* the love of wisdom, as a teacher in the classroom and as a scholar in intellectual pursuits, faithful to one's life experiences and deeply held private beliefs, can be a high calling, a sacred mission, and a great need all in one. But most of all it is a delicate balancing act of competing demands in one's own soul. The attempt to "steer one's own rudder true," for example to live a life of religious faith in private, but divorce it from one's public *profession* which is based on different categories is, as the Existentialists have insisted, not only "bad faith" and inauthentic, but also life-denying and, over time, not even possible. Sooner or later such fissures between inner conviction and outer professing lead to alienation from oneself and others, to a schizoid existence, even shipwreck in one area or both.[1]

This essay is about authenticity struggles in one of *Sophia*'s daughters[2] who has, on existential detours, become an academic philosopher. Her evolution toward greater self-fulfillment, a balance between the inner and outer that includes a fundamental religious as well as a philosophical commitment, is necessarily revealed. (The nature of this essay cannot avoid transparency about personal experiences.) The question this anthology explores is: How can commitments to both faith in God and the life of the mind of disinterested reason, traditionally mortal foes in need of a Hegelian *Aufhebung,* be reconciled? Or, how can the changing demands of the professional and the personal-private, a commitment to philosophical-scientific knowledge on one hand and an equally earnest devotion to religious belief on the other, be brought together in one life, one character, without contradiction? In addition, how can such a life incorporate what is valuable about feminist insights?

Biographical narration will permeate the texture and tenor of this essay as it attempts to reveal how the above tensions play themselves out and press toward harmony in a particular way in a particular life. The story pays attention to the psychological and existential development of this life—youth's *Sturm und Drang* in idealist yearnings; the *volte face* of a life-changing religious experience tested in a "householding stage," an extended path of obedience to society's expectations; the stage of inwardness and contemplation that sought to grasp the paradoxes of existence; and finally achieving the life of academic philosophy. Through unsuppressed personal existential data an attempt is made to indicate that the vagaries, insecurities, and the "thrownness" of life are not weakening agents but the necessary ingredients by which life's projects must be confronted and through which the soul's passional-religious and rational-philosophical oppositions can find denouement. Such unconcealment attempts also to show that religious faith is a legitimate, timely, perhaps even essential, response to break down ordinary logic, much like Zen *koans,* overcoming the reason-passion fissure altogether, and to embrace such paradoxes as "intellectual love" and "passionate understanding" as redemptive forces. Faith becomes an ultimate overarching posture, emerging stronger over time, in which the reason-passion enmity falls away and a true *philia* of *Sophia* transcends epistemological, ontological, and ethical ways of knowing reality. The religious-passionate (often close to the abyss of the irrational and absurd) is a life force yet to be taken fully seriously in philosophy proper, just as seriously as enlightened reason. To invoke a metaphor, as the timeless genius of a Vermeer painting exhibits a unified mastery of reality in the interplay between light and darkness on the canvas, so an individual has the potential of mastering the interplay between passion and reason, darkness and light. The scales in Vermeer's "Woman Holding a Balance" can be taken as a symbol of judgment or discernment, a power in the human soul to reconcile these opposing forces. In the intriguing title of her book, Catherine Elgin calls for finding a place "between the absolute and the arbitrary."[3] And that's what one must do.

II. REASON, FAITH,
AND THE PASSIONS IN HISTORY

It is a commonplace that the "Golden Age of Greece" spawned the hegemony of Reason in Western thought, valuing the exclusivity of the rational-scientific outlook. This led, so it is believed, to the demise of mythopoeic thinking, blocking access to the divine and diminishing the energy of faith.

Viewed through a certain historical lens, such a view holds some legitimacy, but the sweeping generalizations on a tendency in the history of Western thought cannot altogether stand the test of personal experience of the private individual. In the realm of private life this universal thesis must be re-examined and perhaps abandoned.

Alarmist views about the excesses of philosophy or the "wisdom of the West" have sounded throughout the history of religious thought, but especially so with the rise of Christianity.[4] The clash between Greek Reason and Christian Faith or Revelation came to a head in the late Middle Ages,[5] but some of the severest pronouncements about the harmful effects of a Greek rational understanding of reality came from the early Church fathers. Tertullian and St. Augustine (third and fourth centuries c.e.) warned about Greek Reason as "the whore of Athens" who deceives the faithful. In the thirteenth century the Reason-Faith conflict led to the removal of what was considered a particularly virulent version of Greek Reason taught at the early European universities, "radical Aristotelianism." Its teaching was banned from the curriculum by Papal edict, the "Condemnation of 1277," in 219 propositions. For a time Tertullian's question, "what does Athens have to do with Jerusalem?" was answered in an unequivocal negative. Jerusalem, symbolizing Judeo-Christian teaching, must not mingle with Greek Reason. Thomas Aquinas was the man of the hour, offering his "double-aspect theory" to heal the rift between reason and revelation, which simply held that God had given human beings two powers of the mind, the faculty of reason with which we can do science and the faculty of faith by which to access the divine; both powers are his gifts and in both modes we serve God equally well. But the perception of the fundamental dichotomy between reason and faith remained a ubiquitous, if subterranean, theme in philosophical thinking. It reappeared with a vengeance in the mid eighteenth century following the earthquake of Lisbon in 1756. This disaster not only decimated a vibrant city, but it killed thousands of religious leaders from Europe who had gathered for a conference. After the earthquake the famous reason vs. passion debate ensued, focusing on the general question: Which of the two faculties was more primary in solving the riddles of existence, the passionate-feeling response of faith that argued for divine providence despite suffering and chaos, or the rational-cognitive response promoted by the Enlightenment ideal of reason which made scientific progress and rational understanding of the universe more central?[6] Which of these postures should be guiding the conduct of life? With Kant's critical philosophy and post-Kantian agendas on the ascendancy, the reason-passion debate lost its fervor and vehemence, receding into the abstract domains of academic philosophy. For the most part the passion-faith-reason issue became distant from philosophical discourse, the faith issue a non-issue. This has been changing recently, however, most notably through the work of Alvin Plantinga. He argues for the legitimacy of Christian faith in his recent published work, and for a more openly activist stance on the part of Christian philosophers in his "Advice to Christian Philosophers."[7] Although religious belief is seldom raised to a status of respect in philosophical debate, the issue of the conflict between science and religion continues to receive attention, *viz.* the "creationist vs. evolutionist" debate in school systems, but also consciousness-raising in the scholarly media.[8]

For the purposes of this paper the power of faith is circumscribed by the notion of *Sophia,* which becomes a religious metaphor. Despite its female allusion, Wisdom is not an exclusively female domain, as her sons as well have significant stories to tell. Even though *sophia* is Greek in origin, there is a parallel concept found in the "Wisdom Books" of the Old Testament where it is intimately linked to the divine—Wisdom is a Divinity, a Personality of great status, sometimes synonymous with God. *Sophia* takes the daughter (or the son) by the hand, leading her/him through life's events to teach its lessons. Wisdom is a personal guiding power from which individuals stray only at great personal risk and loss of spiritual, even physical, well-being. This Judaic idea contrasts with the Greek understanding of wisdom, the latter associated primarily with universal abstract reason which can only be achieved through a denial of the sense world, freed from (mere) opinion and belief (*pistis*). The Greek understanding of *sophia* in terms of the centrality of "pure thought" is downplayed in this narration. The personal experiences of the narrating daughter of *Sophia* are more nearly in agreement with an Augustinian insight that argues, "*unless* you believe thou shalt not understand" or, "[philosophical] understanding is the *reward* of faith." Belief is the prerequisite of cognitive understanding. When Plato defines knowledge as "true justified belief" but then relegates belief/opinion to an inferior status, he missed an important reality. True knowledge, scientific or otherwise, *originates* from the energy of belief (or faith if you will; in German *Glaube* is the one and only term for faith *and* belief).

However, there is a yet deeper level in this spiritual path. This daughter of *Sophia* learned her Mother's mysteries first through presentiments in her youth, followed by the surprise of faith. Faith, at first small and glimmering, became the basis of a deeper mystery that did not exclude a conceptual understanding of reality in the philosophical-scientific sense. Later as a Kantian she grasped that faith and cognitive understanding were not antipodes, or rather *as* antipodes were reconcilable. Modifying Kant's famous passage in the *Critique of Pure Reason,*[9] she coined a reformulation: "Faith without Understanding is blind, and Understanding without Faith is empty." Such strange juxtaposition finds an echo in William James, who came upon the religious vision late in his life and was preoccupied with the question of the "ethics of belief,"[10] i.e., what is the range of "permissible" faith? Blind faith as an ideal ("it is wrong not to believe come what may") is as undesirable as the ideal of caution and skepticism ("never accept anything on insufficient evidence.") James meets these extremes somewhere in the middle. This complex issue cannot be explored here, but if she takes (according to her Kantian proclivities) faith and cognitive understanding as two distinct domains, the question must be asked: how can they be reconciled existentially in human conduct? A *prima facie* answer might be this: Reason and faith, while independent powers legislating over disparate mental domains (reason over the sensible and faith over the supersensible), can engage in a game of "to and fro," a "play of faculties" in which both powers interact and yield to each other depending on which is called for: sometimes faith is the appropriate response, while at other times the rational must be "trusted." However the wisdom to *discern* which response to take requires the human power of judgment, the highest faculty of all.

III. THE STORY

Early in life *Sophia*'s daughter fell among "lovers of wisdom," not as a deliberate and self-aware initiate but merely *ahnend* and pre-reflective. Her divine Mother of the netherworld had ordained an early, particularly harsh Persephone-like existence during which she gathered ephemeral flowers in clouded meadows, scattered ideas of the good and beautiful. A Hades-like reality ravished her childhood, a world ruptured by two great misfortunes: The outer world of Germany at war, sleep-depriving raids, nocturnal bombings, and bunkered stays, as well as Nazism dwelling within the shadowy walls of her own home; secondly, the inner world of a shattered trust when her natural parents divorced. However, she was a dreamer dreaming of joys, far-off pleasures, and a better world in some enchanted land. She held these ideas in secret parts of her soul, hoping to exchange them some day for their counterparts in the real world. There were also memories of her biological mother fleeing Berlin with two small children from her Nazi father's sphere of influence and back to safety to grandmother's home in southern Germany. Then followed more uprooting: in order to escape the bombs she was evacuated to Heidegger country, the Black Forest with its fairy-tale woods and dark playgrounds. This experience also harbored memories of fear and rejection, albeit of a different kind, playing make-believe games with strange, non-accepting local children and a loneliness caused by the long absences of her natural mother, who followed the circuit court proceedings in various cities to fight for custody of her two children.

Was divine Mother *Sophia* the cause *and* illuminator of events, parceling out hardships proportionate to the daughter's ability to grasp their significance? Or was there a pervasive caprice as chaotic as a throw of dice that determined her existence? The latter seemed to be the case and her future was beyond her grasp, continued instability and forlorn despair a more reasonable prediction. Environmental and hereditary forces were stacked against the possibility of a productive existence. On one hand there was the influence of the harsh environment of war, dominated by an evil political system, and on the other a particularly "dark drop of the blood," the burden of Nazism in her family that seemed every bit as deterministic as environmental forces. Nevertheless, her inchoate understanding of this early existence somehow gravitated toward an innermost belief in a *Sophia* presence and guidance. Amid existential upheaval there remained a core of her dream world: ideas of beauty, the good; joyful dreaming promised excitement and pleasure somewhere. These dream-filled moments gave her a sense of peace and assurance. Subconsciously and inexpressible to herself, she clung to memories of transcendent flower gathering, not based on anything empirically real, but real in her mental world.

After the war her natural mother remarried a hard-working, reliable man who possessed a Kantian-like good will toward his adoptive children. She was grateful, but life continued hard, meager, provincial, few books in the home to encourage thoughtfulness, and only her mother's playing piano provided intermittent pleasure and release through this particularly therapeutic Dionysian muse. One memory is significant: A grandfather on her natural mother's side had left a large bookcase through which she spied, behind locked glass doors, a world of books beckoning with mysterious titles and authors: Zola, Nietzsche's *Also Sprach Zarathustra*, Schopenhauer, de Sade. Like forbidden fruits these volumes lured, but her natural mother warned of the dangers of such books. Her words sounded like God's command from on high: "The day thou shalt read thereof thou shalt surely die!" The bookcase remained locked and she never was allowed to read a single one despite her pleadings and requests. Why was she denied this early philosophical pleasure? Did *Sophia* not realize that her future would be certain to be enriched through an early study of philosophy, books so palpably near yet so far and inaccessible? Was *Sophia* in charge, protectress of her daughter's life? Did she guard the interests of her future?

As a teenager *Sophia*'s daughter had made an intellectual decision: She was going to be an atheist. The supplicant prayers of her natural grandmother for her soul and the vicar's abstruse sermons on Sunday morning had filled her with contempt and strengthened her resolve that the religious hypothesis lacked evidence, was unexciting, defended the interests of the "will to power of the weak" (as she later learned formally in a Nietzsche class); it represented a "will to resentment," especially convincing in the face of so much unhappiness and suffering. Against her protests she was confirmed into the Lutheran Church at age fourteen and assigned a Bible passage: "For I am not ashamed of the gospel of Christ for it is the power of God to salvation for everyone who believes it" (Romans 1:16). This verse remained etched in her memory although it was an embarrassment to have to recite it at the time.

Through a sponsoring relative she had the opportunity to leave Germany and to live in Canada; just for a year to learn English was the pretext. Germans believed that America was "the land of unlimited possibilities" and she had to hide her excitement from her parents and her grandmother, all saddened and urging her to change her mind and to *bleibe im Land und nähre dich redlich* ("stay in the land and make an honest living"). But the prospect of escaping her limited existence and coming to the land of unlimited possibilities—rights, freedom, and the pursuit of happiness—were overriding all other considerations. The wheels of destiny, or divine *Sophia's* providential care, were at work with irreversible precision. The idea of pursuing her dreams in a better, more beautiful, and equitable world had worked as inexorably in her soul as a bird's yearning to fly back home at the first sign of spring.

Viewed *sub specie aeternitatis,* it seemed that circumspect Mother *Sophia* had divinely prepared her daughter's way to Canada where shortly afterwards the most riveting, life-changing experience of her life was to take place: her conversion experience to Christianity, an entirely unsuspected event with far-reaching consequences, restructuring and redirecting her life, her thought-world, and especially her personality. The first visible traces of *Sophia's* behind-the-scenes direction was beginning to take empirical shape, slowly dawning on her daughter's new seeing eyes of faith, opening up untold realms of awareness. She began to embrace realities which only months before she had dismissed with vehemence and contempt. She accepted the most paradoxical of propositions, the notion of "God died on the Cross for me," an unintelligibility for the thinking mind. A Kierkegaardian event had occurred: She broke with the "first stage" of her life, the life of the detached aesthete, the posture of a disinterested spectator unwilling to risk personal involvement in the stakes of living. While up to now she was tossed in directions beyond her control, the subsequent "leap of faith" was one of deliberation, experiencing the "passion of the Infinite" with keen personal awareness. It was an awakening to spiritual powers which had been absent from most of her life, except as remembered possibilities in a child's dream world. (But might one argue that the strength of dreams, ideas, passions, dictates the direction of our lives?) Now the task became to live more fully and authentically, to become transparent, open, even vulnerable to life, people, events, and *Dasein* as a whole. It was as if Mother *Sophia* had taken her by the hand in a remolding process of her life and character. The daughter sensed dimly that a string of sufferings unlike any experienced before lay ahead, suited to her capacity for new possibilities to expand her personality. She sensed subconsciously that her Christian pilgrim's progress was a matter of no return; whatever life brought it would be under new guidelines, but all administered for her benefit by a positive and loving presence.

She met a powerful man, a mercurial personality, a "preacher's son," himself formed by similar if not worse war experiences. He and his family, his parents a short time before German missionaries in Brazil, had been installed in the Church she attended after her conversion. She fell in love and her own devotion to spiritual realities was now matched by someone with equal if not more intense religious convictions. His passion for changing an imperfect world seemed to her right and admirable at first. In the early stages, their life together seemed neatly laid out: he would study medicine in the U.S., become a missionary (like his father), they would have children born in some exotic foreign country and they too would be instructed in a life of faith and service. In old age they all would look back on a life of grandly executed tasks, like having "saved" many souls and thus fulfilled the mission-command of God. In retrospect, the lack of a sense of reality, scant realistic assessment on their backgrounds and constitutions, being absorbed with pushing ahead with their idealized visions of attaining a "safe haven" from the world's ills by committing themselves to the healing of those ills, was palpable. Arguably, the inherent weaknesses of their marriage and future plans were scripted by the pre-givenness of their similar psychological and environmental backgrounds. Yet, leaving naturalistic-psychological explanations of their union aside (all incisive decisions in life are uncertain in nature) *Sophia's* daughter felt guided by her transcendent Mother (this hasn't changed in retrospect), a positive reality that gave her joy and stamina and strengthened her conviction that her difficult existence was always a prologue to a more authentic richer life and the steeling of her personality. She never second-guessed the wisdom of these paths the details of which could not be foretold or rehearsed. Thus began a life in marriage that was to prepare her, in twenty-five years of sometimes grotesque existential highs and lows, to become the individual *Sophia* had envisioned all along through a strong bond of divine Love.

For a while things went according to plan. He went to college in the U.S., majoring in pre-med, graduating *summa cum laude*. She joined him in college, taking a few courses herself. After graduation he was accepted to medical school. However, as her spiritual commitments deepened, he became more recalcitrant toward their original goals and ever more anti-religious, rejecting altogether his overly strict religious upbringing. His conflicts with the medical school faculty culminated in his being given a somber choice, either to "shape up or ship out." He opted for the latter and decided he had seen enough of what he viewed as a deeply flawed motive, greed, dominating the whole medical profession, its practitioners as well as educators; sadly, its select students also viewed their medical education primarily as a source of a lucrative future. He decided to make a radical career change, to become a businessman, a "printer with a mission," namely to publicize the story of the ways in which the medical profession had sold out to market economy values rather than be faithful to the Hippocratic oath, which they treated as an antiquated relic adorning an occasional wall of a doctor's office. Initially she was proud of him, a man of bright courage (*heller Mut*) "to fight city hall," a David against the Goliath of entrepreneurial medicine. However, in his headlong rush to become rich to fight the system (which is ironic given his goals just alluded to), certain purchases of printing equipment involved him in writing bad checks that landed him in jail for the first time. Successful extradition proceedings of her jailed husband to another state (the venue of the purchase) left her existentially vulnerable, with two small children and a third on its way. There followed two decades of existential upheaval of incredible scope and intensity, soured business ventures and entanglements with the law. The ensuing roller-coaster ride of financial turmoil—excesses of alternating periods of "feast and famine," including clandestine involvement with the CIA, FBI, IRS, and intermittent threats of or actual jail terms—was a nightmarish life. For most people such a life would be intolerable even in small increments and spread over several lifetimes. However, her belief in *Sophia's* presence, an all-knowing, all-encompassing, unerring *telos* or benign guardian of her life and those close to her, remained firm. But her ideas about the nature of romantic and nuptial love underwent a fundamental transformation and reordering: married life, children, the role of partners, no longer made sense in traditional terms.

Sometimes she watched with detached amazement the curious phenomenon that was her life, acknowledging, as from a safe distance, *Sophia's* gentle encouragement and leadership in small details and turns of events. It seemed to her that *Sophia* was intent on making the strange and sad events of her daughter's life intelligible to her so she could learn from them and become wise. However, these periodic insights did not last or prevent the daughter from feeling the weight of unanswered questions. She groped for answers: how all this made religious sense, from the God point-of-view, according to her original vision of their life together. Many dark nights of the soul were spent in thinking, doubting, feeling the loneliness expressed in Goethe's immortal words, taking on personal meaning: *Wer nie sein Brot mit Tränen ass, wer nie die kummervollen Nächte auf seinem Bette weinend sass, der kennt sie nicht, die himmlischen Mächte* ("who never ate his bread with tears, who never wept at bedside through grieving nights, knows not the heavenly powers.") Similarly, in *Nur eine Rose als Stütze,* Hilde Domin described with poetic poignancy how one learns to "build one's nest in the wind and sky, and on the farthest branches of existence."[11]

Her liberation and path toward autonomy came in learning to relinquish desires of security and comfort and glean strength and pleasure from simple, scaled-down existence. She followed Fulton Oursler's advice of "day-tight compartment" living and executed her perceived tasks as faithfully as possible, one at a time, with all the energy of her heart and mind, as mother of four, homemaker, neighbor, friend, chauffeur to the children's social and sports activities, but, to a lesser degree, as lover and doting wife to her husband, whose affairs remained tangled and murky, to her a moral miasma. She moved within the shelter of an otherworldly presence encircling her, going before and beyond the frustrating encounters of external chaos, and especially beyond all her reasoned sense-making attempts.

IV. HER RATIONAL PHASE:
THE LIFE OF THE MIND

Twenty-five years of marriage were nearly completed and with it a growing sense that an era had come to an end. The children were almost on their own and the need for her own autonomy through formal education of her mind grew stronger every day. She had given much, received much, learned many of life's lessons and remained, miraculously, free from bitterness or regret. (Evaluating her experiences through philosophical hindsight, she would shout a *da capo,* to do it all over again.) However, a time of great conflict and inner turmoil over thoughts of leaving her marriage followed. The marriage was a debacle, the financial chaos unending, and thoughts of having to make it on her own intruded with ever-greater regularity and urgency. To seek her autonomy, indeed survival, through a formal education seemed a practical necessity, prompting contemplations of leaving. Such thoughts however were in great conflict with her vows solemnly spoken almost twenty-five years before, namely "to honor, to love and to cherish her partner, for better or worse, in sickness and in health, for richer or poorer, until death do you part." The struggle with the decision to abandon the marriage, to seek an education on her own, was fought in a desperate inner seeking of guidance, in prayer and appealing to the *Sophian* presence (such matters hardly decidable through human advice). There was a deeper reason for leaving, albeit more tortured because it seemed self-serving, and that was the conviction that part of her spiritual development and calling was to discipline her emotions and passions through intellectual training. From past experiences she had learned that sometimes reason's control of the emotions was a good way to get through hard times. But the question of a clear and unambiguous justification for the most difficult decision of her life, to leave her marriage and family, left a scar on her soul. Is it possible to be on a spiritual path when one is willing to break, not an earthly-ethical law, but a sacred promise before God and men? Or for that matter, would a Kantian condone the breaking of *such* a promise? In the end one can only flee into the arms of a Pascalian answer: *Le coeur a ses raisons que la raison ne connait pas,* or, modified with a Kierkegaardian twist, "faith has its reasons which ethical lawfulness does not know." And so the ultimate judgment of her decision must be in God's hands.

She returned to school, a middle-aged woman, vulnerable and raw from life in a particularly muddy trench, but with an indomitable faith in her goal of an education. A trip to the friendly bank (the only one friendly enough to trust in her personal integrity despite the family's bad credit rating), assured her a small personal loan which paid the rent of a room near campus for a few months, food, and car payments. The attraction to the life of the mind was immediate, a kind of second "Damascus Road" experience of a rational kind. New intellectual vistas opened up with every class, vistas she consumed with a hungry mind as well as the senses, as she spent vast amounts of time, often with little sleep or food, in studying, learning, absorbing, contemplating, reflecting, on knowledge, all for its own sake. She adhered to her long-practiced, self-imposed regime of staying close to the task at hand, which helped her overcome bouts of sorrow for the loss of her former life. *Sophia's* closeness was a solace as she lived through her anguish of having willed this separation from her family and neighbors.

Besides her majors in philosophy and history, courses in literature, American and European history, geography, art history, a course in classic literature and mythology, formed a rich tapestry in her curriculum. As an "older" woman, *Sophia's* daughter, matured over time, possessed a certain critical mass of life experience; in instants of recognition she perceived as universal truths what for younger students was but "gray theory." She drew parallels from the great classics and works of literature to her own life; Aschylean and Sophoclean tragedies made personal sense in their stark moral messages. With a new awareness, she grasped that from intellectual ordering of her thoughts could come an ordering of her unruly emotions. From Plato she learned that her emotions and her appetitive drives were not just the great detractors of life but were needed to provide the energy for the soul and power for living, provided that reason gave proper shape and direction. And thus, *Sophia* clarified and personalized her goal ever more concretely, that her education would provide not only a conceptual framework, a sense-making mechanism for her life, but also a means of self-support in the future. As her intellectual understanding increased, she felt her faith— expressed in the joy and the excitement of learning to grasp the mind of

God as it was reflected in human mental activity—increase and deepen as well. *Sophia* remained close as the daughter developed the other side of her nature, the power of philosophical thought. To learn to think and understand (as Anselm long ago had claimed to be the reward of faith) for her was a gift from God and served as partial fulfillment and as a complement to faith. Contrary to what Tertullian had pronounced, she concluded that reason and faith were not polar opposites but could be integrated, or that a reflexive relationship between them could be established. Thus, part of her development was to learn to integrate her passionate nature and her faith with reason. This integration, as it slowly dawned on her, required the power of discernment or judgment, a powerful synthesizing faculty in human consciousness and catalyst to right action.

Her discipline in scholarly matters brought her academic achievements, awards of grants and fellowships. She was accepted to graduate school in philosophy and was thus on her way to becoming a professional philosopher, although obstacles of finances, age, and geographical constraints towered like mountains in her path. However, the *Sophian* presence and a pervasive confidence in the reliability of destiny and the guidance of a gentle power besouled her to continue her education and to follow the regime of living in day-tight compartments, and yet to live fully and to be a spendthrift with her energies and talents.

Inchoately and slowly her philosophical specialty emerged, a first brush with Kant in an undergraduate course and an awareness that his ideas fit well her general tendencies and queries of how to reconcile the passions/faith with reason. Was such a move conceptually possible? In a senior undergraduate course she had come upon Kant's famous acknowledgment that his primary project was "to limit knowledge in order to make room for faith." She was intrigued by this direct reference to two ways of grasping reality, one through rational understanding and another through faith. Here were the medieval adversaries and the antipodal forces in her own life confronting each other anew, with the old question, which of them is more adequate in grasping reality? If the knowing mode required "limitation" then what was the requirement of the believing mode? What did it mean to make room for faith? And how were the two, if at all, linked? Based on another curious statement in the *Critique of Pure Reason,* it seemed the link between faith and reason could be established through the mechanism of a third faculty—judgment—the adjudicating power to weigh and discern between alternatives. Of judgment Kant had made some puzzling observations: that among the powers of consciousness, the power of judgment was of greatest significance, more important than knowledge and reason, and indeed "its lack no amount of schooling can make good."[12] Upon reflection her life had often been shackled with instances of the adverse effects of the lack of judgment, or bad judgment, or weak moral judgments, her own and those close to her. Bad judgment was a great detractor from a good life in many areas of human experience, often leading to devastating consequences in the moral, political, cultural, social, and environmental arenas of life. Kant's passage on judgment and the allure of finding an answer hit a nerve touching on her own questions: "What constitutes good judgment? How does one judge events, people, states of affairs? Or, when at a crossroad, is there a conceptual mechanism for good or correct judgment?" In the philosophical context, Kant's pronouncement was elusive, complex, and all the more puzzling because he proceeded to *demonstrate in the course of three Critiques* (which his earlier statement seemed to rule out) how three different types of judgment were possible: synthetic judgments *a priori* in science, moral judgments *a priori* in ethics, and aesthetic judgments *a priori* in art. All of which seemed to point to a way, a special route, by which judgment was possible, in which case this important skill could be taught and its lack *could* be made good by *some* school. To be educated in such a school could aid a seafaring soul to negotiate, among other things, the stormy conflicts between faith in the supersensible and the rational understanding of the sensible worlds.

V. FAITH, PASSIONS, AND REASON RECONCILED: JUDGMENT AND FEMINIST THINKING

As her Kant studies revealed, there was one factor like no other playing havoc with human thinking processes as well as throwing judgment into "crisis," and that was the "aesthetic factor." The passions, the irrational human feelings intruded, sometimes for better and sometimes for worse, when it came to human thinking and judging.

Aesthetics, understood in its most simple Greek etymological sense— *aisthesthai,* to feel, sense, perceive, imagine—is the root from which grows the posture of faith or the "passion for the Infinite." Aesthetic theory is an area of inquiry not easily integrated into the logic and system of philosophy; traditionally it is more closely allied to descriptive psychology. As Kant had demonstrated, the aesthetic factor (in the First Critique treated in the "Transcendental Aesthetic") describes our faculty of sensibility as it is governed by certain *a priori* forms of our intuition through which we have our first contact with the material world. The aesthetic factor, as my studies have revealed, is inseparable from human judgment, even scientific judgment. Since judgment occupies such a central role in human conduct and is so intimately linked to our feelings, it is incumbent to find a legitimate niche for the aesthetic factor in human consciousness, one not easily incorporated in the logic of philosophical discourse. For several years now *So-*

phia's daughter has focused on these ideas as her entire existence groped toward a denouement between private feelings (which must be trusted) and the demands of abstract reason (equally legitimate), often at cross ends with each other and requiring a reconciliation through an adjudicating process.

Feminist themes thus far have only been implicit in this essay, but "shimmerings" of them should not be lost on the reader. Her scholarly interests have not yet fully recognized certain obvious feminist concerns imbedded in her work. To be sure, Kant is an unlikely candidate to promote explicit feminist themes; however, as her extended intellectual companionship with Kant's writings over time has shown, some of his deepest insights are consistent with feminist concerns, especially when one includes Kant's Third Critique. There he comes closest to reconciling the passions with reason. Unfortunately, his characteristic abstruseness of style has led to many caricatures, as the *Alleszermalmer,* the "All-Destroyer," his prose making one's brain freeze in abstract ice, etc. But if one breaks the Kantian code one may come to the refreshing realization that, as Kant sees it, cognition or categorical understanding cannot advance a single step without a sensuous-passionate component by which we judge not only beauty and art, but also make judgments in science and ethics. And so it is an important theme to acknowledge that analyses of the aesthetic component in thinking, willing, and judging provide an important and useful counterpoint to what has been held, rightly or wrongly, to be the "male exclusivity of reason" in Western culture. Among *Sophia*'s more famous daughters we count Hannah Arendt, who was very much aware of this strand of Kant's thinking. Her primary work, *The Life of the Mind,* points in his direction as she, similar to Kant, arranges her work in three parts. Only *Thinking* and *Willing* were completed, while *Judging,* its crucial conclusion, was not written because of her untimely death. There is much that needs to be done concerning the issues she raised in her unfinished trilogy that finds an echo in the work of this daughter.

A theory of judgment as a symbol of balance, not only in thinking but also in living, has much to offer to incorporate the passionate-feeling factor (traditionally seen as the province of the female temperament) and the rational-analytical factor (a male domain) within human consciousness and the philosophical enterprise. Feminist concerns have long recognized that aesthetics, broadly conceived, must play a vital cognitive role in knowledge acquisition and must find an appropriate status in the epistemological-metaphysical and ethical discourses of philosophical debates. Many feminist writers (including men) have done significant work to promote this line of argument. For example, Carol Gilligan and Nel Noddings have stressed the aesthetic component in cognitive processes. Gilligan, in her rebuttal of the Kohlberg model of the stages of moral development, argues for the implicit integrative factor of aesthetic thinking, such thinking adding a greater complexity to the analysis of moral issues and judgments. She has convincingly shown, for example, that girls and boys are capable of complex moral reasoning, but girls often see more clearly the complicating factors in moral situations due to their ability of comprehending the "gray areas" and their capacity for "empathetic" judging (which in turn makes them also vulnerable to the charge of being "fuzzy moral reasoners" in the Kohlberg model).[13] Noddings, similarly, in her Ethics of Care offers a moral theory which originates in an aesthetic-feeling component in thinking, serving an important alternative, she thinks, to the "language of the father" and to the ethics of "necessary propositions and principles" of utilitarian and deontological models of morality.[14]

As her story has unfolded, the existential and professional components of the life of *Sophia's* daughter have intersected and the theory of judgment became the "living" symbol of this development in her scholarship. It provided the balance for reconciling the passions and her faith with reason. But the source of finding such reconciliation was from the beginning something one might call Grace entering her existence from a divine reality. Grace, perhaps a sister to *Sophia*, entered at a certain point to guide her through life's cliffs and mysterious passages, luring her, perhaps from an early age, into particular inquiries to arrive at this juncture. For this *Philosophin* the conception of judgment, especially as expressed in the antinomies between supersensible and sensible domains of reality and their resolution, finds a rich existential justification. Having lived through some of life's vagaries and paradoxes, she finds that "intellectual love" and "passionate understanding" have indeed, like *koans,* the power to redeem and renew.

NOTES

1. Heidegger's life has been cited as an example. There are those who argue that no matter what inauthenticities, infelicities, immoral acts of betrayal of friends and colleagues he might have committed, his abstract thought and work as a philosopher remains a worthy monument of human excellence; one can accept Heidegger's philosophical legacy, at least, without reservation. However true this might be, Heidegger's existence as an individual cannot be said to have measured up in the end. It was a life sadly and fatally flawed because it fell short of the most crucial test of all: the courage to bring his thinking capacities as a philosopher in harmony with the outward expressions of his lived life.

2. Editor's note: The title of this volume was originally intended to be *Among Sophia's Daughters: Reflections on Philosophy, Feminism, and Faith.*

3. Catherine Elgin, *Between the Absolute and the Arbitrary* (Ithaca, N.Y.: Cornell University Press, 1997). See also *Considered Judgment* (Princeton, N.J.: Princeton University Press, 1996).

4. For example, the New Testament states: "Beware lest any man cheat you by philosophy and vain deceit; according to the tradition of men and not according to Christ" (Colossians 2:8).

5. For a particularly vivid account of this clash, see Etienne Gilson's classic *Reason and Revelation in the Middle Ages* (New York: Charles Scribner's Sons, 1938).

6. Well-known literary figures and *philosophes,* such as Rousseau and Alexander Pope on the side of the passions, Voltaire, d'Alembert, and Diderot on the side of enlightened reason, engaged in a debate about *raison et sentiment* after the Lisbon earthquake.

7. Plantinga's *Warranted Christian Belief* (Oxford: Oxford University Press, 2000) is the culmination of a trilogy. *Warrant and Proper Function* (Oxford: Oxford University Press, 1992) and *Warrant: The Current Debate* (Oxford: Oxford University Press, 1993) are the earlier volumes. Plantinga's "Advice to Christian Philosophers" is issued in *Truth Journal* on the internet at http://www.leaderu.com/truth/1truth10.html. See also William Alston's *Perceiving God* (Ithaca, N.Y.: Cornell University Press, 1991).

8. The April–May 1998 issue of *Civilization* (The Magazine of the Library of Congress) devoted its entire issue to the topic of "On Faith, Fanaticism, and the Future." The lead article was Vaclav Havel's "Faith in the World," an urgent call to transcend politics and to relegitimize spiritual values such as faith (this from the president of the Czech Republic!).

9. Immanuel Kant, *Critique of Pure Reason,* trans. Norman Kemp Smith (New York: St. Martin's Press, 1965), B75/A51.

10. "The Will to Believe," an address to the Philosophical Clubs of Yale and Brown Universities. First published in the *New World,* 1896.

11. Hilde Domin, *Nur eine Rose als Stütze* (Frankfurt a. Main: S. Fischer Verlag, 1959), p. 55.

12. *Critique of Pure Reason,* A 134/B174.

13. Carol Gilligan, *In a Different Voice: A Psychological Theory of Women's Development* (Cambridge, Mass.: Harvard University Press, 1984).

14. Nel Noddings, *Caring: A Feminine Approach to Ethics and Moral Education* (Berkeley: University of California Press, 1984).

FIFTEEN

On Being a Christian Philosopher and Not a Feminist

M. ELAINE BOTHA

In a democratic state with many crisscrossing interests,
there cannot and should not be a specific feminine politics, and
therefore no specific feminine science and epistemology either.
—*Mary B. Hesse*[1]

I. A PERSONAL PROLOGUE

I recall vividly the utter astonishment of a fellow traveler on a flight from New York to San Francisco, when she discovered that I claimed to be a believer, a philosopher, and a teacher of Christian philosophy at a Christian university in South Africa. In her perception, the mix of womanhood, philosophy, and religion seemed incongruous, not to mention the even stranger notion of a woman claiming to teach Christian philosophy at a Christian university in a country with a political reputation which at the time certainly raised questions about the authenticity of Christianity. In her mind none of this seemed coherent. Something of a similar enigma seems to underlie the project of this book. The enigma is the question of how philosophy, feminism, and faith could actually be comfortable bedfellows. Yet, I seemed to have shared my bed with at least two of these purportedly odd bedfellows for just about a lifetime, without too much discomfort. I do not claim to share the puzzlement about the tenuous relationship between religion and philosophy, or faith and philosophy, yet I do experience some distinct discomfort with the possibility of being labeled a "feminist" of some or other stripe.

What is it in feminism that does not attract me? Why does it not speak to or enlighten the experiences that constitute my personal history? The assignment to work through these questions and the relationship between my faith and my philosophical commitment have revealed a number of paradoxes in my own position that require reflection. I believe these paradoxes are to some extent the legacy of the Reformed philosophical tradition that I share. Whether I will be able to resolve these paradoxes in the context of this paper is doubtful, but articulating them might contribute to their eventual clarification. Two of these paradoxes are substantive philosophical themes requiring further elaboration. The first I would like to call a *paradox of disillusionment*—a disillusionment with a philosophical tradition that contributed very little to the understanding of the role and significance of gender either in society or in scholarship. I shall merely state the paradox and leave to others the exploration of why this is the case. The second paradox intrigues me even more. It is the *paradox of cognitive (gender) neutrality.* This paradox names the tension between two claims I subscribe to. The first claim states that knowledge cannot be religiously neutral. The second claim states that both cognition and knowledge are, in some qualified sense, gender neutral.

Feminism in all its variations has raised consciousness about the multifaceted lack of recognition of women in the workplace and in society and the perceived disregard of women in the church. No doubt many of these efforts to raise consciousness have been the direct result of personal and existential experiences of women in a multitude of life situations similar to my own. And these experiences have contributed to the vast array of intellectual debates about these issues found in the literature. But these issues have been discussed widely. I doubt that one more particular account of the disparagement of women or one more intellectual analysis of purported exclusion or suppression of women could contribute to any understanding of this phenomenon, or that another account could in any way change the way women are viewed or treated.

Further, when women in so many situations have succeeded in breaking free from the stranglehold of difficult life situations, often without the help of any feminist movement, intellectual insights, or theoretical analysis, does this not prove that intellectual consciousness-raising by feminists and feminism is not prerequisite for the emancipation and liberation of women? Or perhaps it merely means that deep down in the individual and collective feminine psyche there are forces that rebel against subjugation and discrimination without too much intellectual prompting. On the other hand, exploring the many unique contributions of women to societal life and to knowledge, in particular, could contribute substantially to the emancipation of both women and men in society. So perhaps such explorations are still worthwhile.

These questions compelled me to attempt to give an account of the reasons why I claim not to be a feminist, yet fervently believe in the liberation of women. But they also confronted me with the need to explain how religion (faith) and philosophy as I see them address some of the issues central to the feminist cause. And the particular and troubling issue of the validity and justification of a feminist epistemology is central to my own interests.

I stumbled/fumbled my way into philosophy at the intersection of very concrete existential struggles with my calling as a Christian, my own cultural identity as an Afrikaner woman, and the reconciliation of my faith commitment with the political realities of a racially, ethnically, and culturally deeply divided South Africa. Gender consciousness played a negligent but perhaps subconscious role in this whole process. An attempt to develop some coherent understanding or account of my role as a woman, a Christian, and a philosopher in this complex interrelationship was something that developed much later as I gradually came to terms with becoming a professional woman and with the consequences of remaining single in a society where marriage is the rite of passage to personal and social identity in church and society. I was very conscious that the mere fact of being a woman in a predominantly patriarchal, paternalistic, and authoritarian society had its distinct drawbacks. These drawbacks were far too real in the South Africa of the sixties, seventies, and eighties not to be aware of them. But being a woman also had its advantages, advantages that I would like to subsume under the ironic title—*the (dis-) comfort of subjugation.*

The Comfort (and Discomforts) of Subjugation

For the longest time I implicitly assumed that conforming to the demands of such a society was imperative and that women had little choice in the matter. For a short time I justified the subjugation of all women in all societal spheres with a very literal understanding of the Scriptural injunctions pertaining to being a "helpmeet" for (all!) men, the headship of men (in all spheres) and the calling to subordination and subservience of women to men in the church. As I acquired more and more leadership roles in a variety of situations, I came to see that this position was untenable. I taught Sunday school, pre-seminary students and pastors, adult women, and men in a variety of situations; was called to give leadership as deacon and as elder in the church; was professor of philosophy while being required to pay (lip) service to the notion of male headship!

I was a (single) woman in a predominantly male society where feminine position was determined by marital status, and specifically by the position of one's husband. I initially experienced and interpreted my experience of not fitting in as a sort of personal deficiency. The anguish I suffered at times in this process was exacerbated by deep feelings of personal inadequacy which may or may not have been fueled by internalized and socialized social norms about gender. Whether this was actually the case is hard to judge. Personal experiences are often too complex to extricate all the various threads that constitute them.

The marginalized position of a White, single female in the South African Dutch Reformed church had ironic consequences in my personal life. The limited space for visibility of women in the church—a feature that influenced the position of most women in all spheres of the South African society—constantly confronted me with the challenge to attempt to assert some space for visibility in a variety of situations. I found that there were advantages to the absence of a husband in the background whose position and connections would have determined my own and whose position in society would be endangered by speaking out too boldly about political or ecclesiastical matters. There was very little to lose, socially, if one was already marginalized. Moreover, because one's presence as a woman was virtually invisible and one's voice practically inaudible, one could speak quite "loudly" without too dire consequences . . . or so I thought.[2] Looking back on the gradual dawning of my own deep sense of anger at the personal injustices I believed I suffered in the church, in the broader society, and especially in the workplace, I realize the anger was accompanied by a concomitant growing awareness of the pervasive political injustice in South African society. What I was experiencing as a White woman in a predominantly White male–dominated society was only a small bit of the suffering of Black people in general, and more specifically Black women.

In the church I was baffled by the fact that elders acquired decision-making authority on the basis of their gender, that they pronounced authoritatively on all kinds of societal, political, and ethical matters, yet very seldom felt called to back these views up with solid knowledge of Scripture through participation in Bible study groups of any kind. Church bulletins often announced only the upcoming women's Bible study groups, very seldom those of men or those mixed Bible study groups that men were actually involved in. I was utterly amazed at so many of my colleagues both in and outside of South Africa who were willing to write voluminously about and wax eloquent on the liberation of women from "a Biblical or Reformed perspective," whereas in personal, professional, and everyday relationships with women very little of these insights were actually put into practice.

In the workplace I marveled that masculinity warranted higher salaries and other perks even when women had far better qualifications and more experience. I was astounded by so many women (including myself) who accepted the notion that women required more proof of qualifications than men but had to work twice as hard for half of the social recognition men received in similar situations. I accepted that the majority of reports and memos I wrote and proposals I developed were always channeled to a male supervisor—with similar credentials to mine—who had very few qualms about accepting the accolades for the work I had done, but was seldom willing to accept responsibility for any mistakes made.

These personal experiences did not drive me into the arms of feminism. But they did make me acutely aware of the invisibility of women in general and more specifically the invisibility of women in the Reformed tradition. They also did gradually sensitize me to the fundamental flaws in the so-called "Christian" policy of apartheid. I realized that "learning to see" the injustice suffered by others (Black others) was instrumental in a process that contributed to coming to terms with my identity as a (discriminated against) woman and vice versa. An incident might illustrate the point I want to make. I distinctly recall my instinctive reaction to the first sporadic bursts of stone throwing by Black schoolchildren in the middle seventies. As a White I was horrified by what was happening. It was unthinkable that "they" would pick up stones and throw them at "us." "After all, we had given them so much," I argued, as did most other South Africans at the time. When my own car was a target for such a stone-throwing attack, I was furious. Didn't they realize I was a White woman who, as a Christian, had devoted my whole life to the service of others? Yet, I knew on an experiential level that these children were using the only communication medium (weapon) available to them. This was the only "language" they knew their oppressors could hear and understand. White South African men in positions of power do not listen to the language or the voice of protest from those subservient to them. They "know" what is good for their subordinates. To the powerful, the voices of the voiceless are inaudible, their presence invisible or transparent, and their needs assumed known. The language of violence, on the other hand, speaks for itself. Out of sheer necessity it forces one to notice, to listen, and to respond. I could not, did not, do not condone violence, but I came to understand the deep sense of frustration that gave rise to it. It was akin to the sense of futility and frustration I experienced when asking for change and understanding in a variety of situations. It reminded me of my hopeless sense of frustration with the incredulous response of total incomprehension to a simple request such as: "Could I perhaps be paid the same salary and have access to the same benefits as my male colleagues?" (Who had far less qualifications, I knew and thought at the time, though I did not have the courage to say it!) I too knew the helpless sense of anonymity that enveloped me when I was confronted with the blank stare that inevitably follows a raised (feminine) hand indicating the need to participate in a discussion in a meeting. Assertive male interruptions were assumed perfectly acceptable. Yet a raised feminine hand often remains unrecognized. It chafed that I was invisible, that in so many situations the mere fact that I was a woman disqualified me *a priori* . . . until it became fashionable to recognize gender and I became the "token woman" —a situation that I find even more demeaning than the disqualification on the basis of gender.

What hurts most in these experiences is that one lacks the yardstick of honest, critical, and open evaluation of one's abilities and contributions. Such experiences cause a loss on three fronts: the loss of recognition, the absence of honest, open feedback, and an inevitable loss of integrity in relationships. Many of these experiences were the common and everyday experience of Blacks, experiences that I too contributed to because I also very often did not really "see" them or take them seriously. I "knew" what was good for them. My own experiences and frustrations helped me understand the invisibility and voicelessness of women and Blacks that are normative in authoritarian and patriarchal societies (an experience that seems to have been thoroughly underlined in recent events in Afghanistan).

It took a long time to come to the realization that "asking" for understanding or change inevitably sets the stage for refusal by those in power. They assumed that they not only had the God-given right but also the calling to make decisions on behalf of others—the paternalistic South African notion of guardianship.[3] A similar notion was claimed by Afrikaners to be at the root of a more benevolent reading of the policy of racial apartheid. Between this notion and the justification of the leadership role of men in general on the basis of the Biblical notion of "headship," a very thin line exists. Attempts to address the issue of masculine authority, either in writing or in personal conversations, inevitably drew a response that attributed such "difficulties" or questioning to some personal psychological flaw somehow related to "men in positions of authority." This response has an uncanny resemblance to the Foucauldian line of argument in which knowledge and power are interrelated—and the powerful therefore have the right to determine who suffers from an aberration! If one was Black and succumbed to the temptation to question the authority of those in positions of power, it would call forth heavy-handed and forceful actions of repression. When one was White and a woman, the repression was more subtle, but there nonetheless.

For the longest time the only response to this state of affairs on my part was passive and mute acquiescence or seething emotional aggression. Learning to channel these feelings into constructive and assertive action and behavior became a lifelong process, perhaps still not adequately mastered. The parallel with the situation and predicament of Blacks is obvious. Learning to become assertive without resorting to passive or active aggression only becomes possible when one gains insight into one's self and the nature of relationships. Lack of assertion is often closely related to deep-seated feelings of personal inadequacy exacerbated by the culturally embedded discriminatory practices and relationships characteristic to native Afrikaners. Agonizingly slow liberation from these feelings resulted in a new-found self-confidence, which to my amazement somehow also called forth an equivalent liberation in the men with whom I was called to relate. I had discovered a very profound truth about human relationships: both my bondage and my liberation are intimately related to the bondage and liberation of others.

This was a simple empirical demonstration of a profound anthropological and Biblical truth: human beings are created as male and female, relationally interdependent and mutually responsible to actualize their cohumanity. This interdependence and reciprocity also holds for the relationships between diverse ethnic, racial, and cultural groups. The liberation of one group necessarily affects the liberation of another. This was a lesson White Afrikaners in positions of power also had to learn.

My life, then, was that of a Christian, single, White, Afrikaner, woman philosopher in a predominantly male dominated, patriarchal culture and philosophical tradition. I was very seldom aided by feminism or feminist intellectual ideals in my encounters with the impenetrable wall of masculine dominance and power. Perhaps this was due to a lack of serious interest on my part rather than any actual lack of availability of feminist intellectual analyses and resources.[4] This lack of interest in the marginalization of women, the discrimination and oppression of women, and feminist analyses of such discrimination was perhaps true of Afrikaner culture as a whole.[5] It is remarkable that the divisive issue of women in office, which led to a schism in North American Reformed churches, has had minimal impact in the churches of the Afrikaans Reformed tradition.

Race and its political implications, on the other hand, played a decisive role in the schisms that took place in the churches of the Reformed tradition in South Africa.[6] What puzzles me when I look back at the drastic political and other changes which took place in the contours of a racist society dominated by powerful White Afrikaner males is that in spite of major shifts in the political structure of South Africa, the monolithic structure of male dominance in White Afrikanerdom in the Reformed philosophical tradition remained virtually unchanged. This is even more surprising when contrasted with the fact that when the Black African National Congress came to power in 1994 in South Africa, there was apparently no lack of Black female leaders to appoint to a whole host of important political, cultural, societal, and educational positions. Not only were there adequate numbers of Black, Colored, and Asian women available for these positions at the time of political transition, but they were also included in the new Black leadership of the country from the very inception of Black rule in South Africa. Why was there such a vast difference between the White and Black communities when it came to accommodating women in positions of leadership? Why did White Afrikaner women acquiesce in situations of oppression, neglect, and exclusion from leadership roles in church, politics, and education while Black women obviously didn't? This question remains puzzling. More puzzling to me is that at no time did I feel called to avail myself of theoretical feminism to attempt to resolve any of these issues.

II. A PHILOSOPHICAL INTERLUDE

I believe it has now become abundantly clear that feminism as a theoretical or intellectual pursuit never really captured my imagination. I can think of a whole host of very good reasons why I would not like to be called a feminist of any stripe, even more why I have never had any real inclination to submerge myself in feminist literature. Yet many of the issues that have occupied feminists have also been my own personal and philosophical concerns. The anecdotes and personal stories related in the "Personal Prologue" attest to the fact.

Some might argue that this mere fact already qualifies me as some brand of feminist, but I do not agree. The struggle for the recognition and liberation of women and the acknowledgement of their unique identity and equality with men, I believe, does not necessarily have to qualify as a feminism of some sort. "Feminism" does not have a monopoly on the recognition of the identity of women or the acknowledgement of their unique personhood and the liberation from societal practices and proscriptions that endanger their authenticity. I do not believe that feminism adequately accommodates the nuances of the legitimate liberation of women (which inevitably has to be accompanied by the corollary liberation of men) that I would like to subscribe to. Moreover, using this epithet to qualify both radical feminist positions and the softer type of "feminism" I might be comfortable with makes it difficult to rule out the extreme absolutization of gender often found in the positions of radical feminists, which I do not believe to be compatible with Scripture.

Nor do I believe that the privileged leadership position of men so often uncritically accepted as the Biblical view in Christian circles is commensurate with the Christian message. One of the teachings of Scripture that captures best what I believe about sex and gender is the following:

> There is neither Jew nor Greek, there is neither slave nor free, there is neither male nor female; for you are all one in Jesus Christ. And if you are Christ's, then you are Abraham's offspring, heirs according to promise. (Gal. 3:28)

This passage clearly recognizes the reality of gender, ethnicity, and social position but relates it to Jesus Christ and the unity in Christ, which implies that these realities are not eradicated "in Christ," but are transcended by this unity and therefore lose their *decisive* significance in human life in the presence of this deeper religious relationship. Obviously this confessional conviction needs to be unpacked to address the philosophical challenges posed by feminism in general, and a feminist epistemology specifically. It also needs to be articulated in such a way that it sheds light on the very harsh realities of oppression and discrimination against women with its detrimental consequences for human relationships in general and relationships between women and men specifically.

I appropriated the tradition of Reformational philosophy with a profound sense of gratitude for the depth of insights it provided in my quest for a Biblical understanding of the integrality of faith and knowledge and for the guidelines it gave for understanding the complexity of the cultural and societal dynamics at work in the South Africa I love. And yet, when it came to the complexities of gender and the power relations in which they were embedded, I discovered to my disillusionment that this philosophy was apparently silent.[7]

The Paradox of Disillusionment

Reformational philosophy has been my scholarly "home" for most of my academic career. In this tradition the rapprochement between philosophy and Christian faith was both a challenge and imminent reality. Its core assumption is that philosophy and faith are inextricably and integrally related, and that faith informs and conditions all knowledge including philosophical knowledge. Furthermore it claims that the development of a Christian philosophy in discussion with other philosophical traditions should be seen as an imperative.[8] This school of thought believes that all philosophical systems, traditions, and theories are rooted in faith assumptions. Christian philosophy, with its own faith assumptions, would have as one of its primary tasks the transcendental critique of, and dialogue with, the underlying assumptions of such systems or theories. The starting point of this philosophy is the recognition that all of life *is religion* and that philosophy as a part of human endeavor is as much subject to the claims of the Lordship of Jesus Christ as any other area of life. It argues that reality, human life, and thinking cannot be and never is self-sufficient, because as creation it is dependent on its Creator.[9] The direction of this creation has been radically altered by sin but it is redeemed in and through Jesus Christ, the new root of fallen humankind in Whom all of reality finds its unity and coherence and redemption from sin. Because all things are from Him, through Him, and called to exist to His honor and glory, He alone can provide an Archimedean point for all human relationships and human thinking. The core anthropological assumption of this Christian philosophy recognizes the relationality of humankind: In the Archimedean point Jesus Christ, the deepest central religious relationship of the self to God, to reality, and all interpersonal relationships are concentrated. Remarkable in this formulation is the absence of any reference to gender or gender relationship.[10] This confession requires the philosopher to work out the implications of this core conviction for human life in general and in all the various dimensions of philosophy and the disciplines.

Working out the implications of this confession was the challenge of my own scholarly work in a career as teacher of philosophy and in all the other academic, cultural, and political work that I was involved in. It also provided the framework within which I attempted to deal with a variety of practical issues. And yet the project of the thorough exploration of the rule of Christ for all dimensions of life seemed to leave issues related to gender both philosophically and in practice practically undisturbed. Many factors contributed to this. As I have already mentioned, there was a lack of personal and theoretical interest on my part, in part due to the absence of a sense that dealing with gender issues was important in the context of the large-scale racial and political issues that dominated social life in South Africa and impinged upon every single dimension of one's personal life. But the lack of interest was also because the Reformational philosophical tradition did very little to raise consciousness about these issues.

I was an active participant in the "Koinonia declaration," issued in November 1977 at the height of the political injustices in South Africa. This was a confessional protest by a group of Reformed believers against the injustices entrenched in the political system of apartheid. I am amazed that it makes no mention of the discrimination against women and includes no call to either church or state to address matters of this kind.[11] What amazes me even more is that none of the small group of women who participated in this project raised the issue of discrimination against women, and specifically Black women, as an issue of equal significance to the others raised in the document.

Why is it that the Christian philosophy I was taught seldom confronted me with the need to pursue issues related to gender? Why is it that my religious tradition, culture, and faith commitment to Jesus Christ seldom raised the need to question the position of women either in church or in society? Perhaps most puzzling of all: Why did both my faith tradition and the philosophy developed on the basis of this tradition raise so few questions about social justice in general? To some extent, these questions are unfair. The philosophy of both Herman Dooyeweerd and H. G. Stoker, in which I was educated, had as a core tenet the encompassing notion of *law,* which is inextricably bound to questions of justice. Yet in the work of both these philosophers, the original thinkers who developed the system of Reformational philosophy, down-to-earth practical issues of racial and gender justice seemed to be buried within the ponderous realms of intellectual analyses. Those analyses seldom touch the realities of oppression and discrimination so prevalent in the experiences of women and Blacks in the predominantly patriarchal South African culture. Some would argue that this was the inevitable heritage of the Kuyperian tradition.[12] This is possible, even plausible. But it is the silence about these issues amongst the heirs of the Kuyperian legacy that speaks louder than anything else.

Reformational philosophy did provide some parameters for the discussion of questions raised by racial, national, ethnic, and cultural identity and for the analysis of colonial oppression and discrimination of Blacks by Whites. These elements in its social philosophy were issues that I very quickly appropriated and attempted to apply in my concrete cultural experiences in a multicultural society.[13] They seemed specifically applicable to the questions raised in attempting to define my personal cultural identity in a multicultural society and to reconcile my allegiance to Christ and my own people amidst a growing sense of discomfort and disillusionment with the political climate in South Africa. But they seemed to provide little analytic help in dealing with more general questions of gender and racial justice.

Not that I did not struggle with the issues of justice toward women and people of color—on the contrary. But these struggles were often born out of discomfort and chafing with the Afrikaner culture that I was part of, and even more discomfort with the circles of the predominantly White male practitioners of the Reformed philosophical tradition. It certainly was not because the tradition as such provided any intellectual stimuli or pointers in this struggle. In retrospect, however, it seems to me that the chafing I experienced was not only the result of personal idiosyncrasies and experiences. It also arose because both the Reformed religious tradition, and the Christian philosophy that developed out of this tradition, had more than adequate resources available to tackle the issues at hand, yet seemed impotent to address these issues. It is this impotence that puzzles me. What puzzles me more is my acquiescence with this state of affairs at the time. Would I have been served in any way had I turned to the resources of feminist philosophy or epistemology? I am not sure. This raises the second paradox, a paradox of a different kind.

A Christian, but Not a Feminist, Epistemology?

I am puzzled by the fact that I never wondered about or pursued the need for or justification of any specifically feminist methodology or epistemology. I devoted much of my academic career to the pursuit of an understanding of the relationship between faith and knowledge, religion and science, Christian philosophy and scholarship and more specifically methodological approaches that claimed to successfully develop integrality of faith and scholarship in the social sciences. Although I fervently believe that there is no such thing as the religious neutrality of cognition or theories[14] and am convinced that deep confessional commitments permeate all cognition, I am very hesitant to buy into the large-scale socializing and "genderizing" of cognition.

Like most post-empiricist and feminist philosophers of science, I share an opposition to the empiricist and objectivist tradition of rationality. These developments have paved the way for the recognition of the role of other than "rational" factors in the process of cognition and a recognition of the theory- and value-ladenness of all theoretical endeavors.[15] Feminists have zeroed in on these developments and have used similar arguments to make the case for a recognition of the pervasive role of gender in cognition. Their grounds for opposition to an Enlightenment view of knowledge are its purported ahistorical character, its claim to neutrality and universality, and the equation of such neutrality and universality with the "masculine" perspective.[16] The recognition of the historical, cultural, and social embeddedness, as well as the embodiment of knowers, they argue, provides support for the claim that universal rationality is implicitly masculine. Feminine embodiment would presumably lead to different knowledge, to a different "voice," in Carol Gilligan's memorable phrase.[17] But as Lorraine Code rightly points out, it is *knowledge claims* that are at stake in epistemology, and an " . . . introduction of an other (feminist) perspective or voice into the rhetorical spaces where epistemology is made" does not adequately address the need to critically evaluate knowledge claims themselves.[18] Knowledge evaluation requires devising methods for analyzing knowledge that is socially constructed by historically situated knowers, "and is constrained by a reality which is not wholly compliant with their wishes."[19] Code argues for the epistemic potential of well-constructed stories. She believes this narrative conception of knowledge is different from a simplistic perspectivalism because it requires situating the self reflexively and self-critically.[20] On Code's account of knowledge there cannot be a single dominant epistemological paradigm, and therefore, by extension, no single feminist voice. "Because experiences, knowing, and theories of knowledge are embedded in community and social structures," she writes, "and because epistemic activities are interconnected across and among communities . . . there is no single Archimedean point from which analysis can begin."[21] This position echoes that of many other philosophers who argue on the basis of developments in post-modern philosophy of science that a "Gods' eye view" is not to be found, and that therefore there can be no justification for a view that argues that the feminine perspective should replace the dominant masculine view.[22]

As mentioned above, I share this opposition to the modernist faith in a neutral, universal reason. My opposition to the modernist project is based on recognition of the constitutive role that faith commitments play in cognition and theorizing. Cognition and theorizing cannot be religiously neutral. Yet I hesitate to make a similar statement with respect to the presence, significance, and influence of gender in and on cognition. While I see a religiously neutral epistemology as a contradiction in terms, I agree with Mary Hesse that a feminist epistemology is a contradiction in terms.[23] That is, I reject religious neutrality, but am committed to gender neutrality. I do not believe the former claim requires too much elaboration. Clouser has succinctly formulated the essence of a (note: not "the"!) Reformed philosophical position in this respect: Knowledge of the world entails beliefs about the world that are the outcome of religiously determined presuppositions.[24] Religious and confessional convictions permeate theories via metaphysical assumptions.

The claim that a feminist epistemology is a contradiction in terms, however, obviously does call for further elaboration. My grounds for this claim differ from those of Code, who states that "as long as 'epistemology' bears the stamp of the post-positivist, empiricist project of determining necessary and sufficient conditions to defeat skepticism, there can be no feminist epistemology."[25] She argues for a reconstruction of the epistemological project. Until such a reconstruction occurs, the question of whether a feminist epistemology is possible or desirable must be left unanswered. I share her strong reservations concerning the post-positivist epistemological project and the need for its reconstruction, but on differing grounds. Epistemology needs to re-*cognize* the notion of cognitive agency to include the role of religious direction and determination in the process of knowledge formation. Thus I reject cognitive neutrality on religious grounds. Opposition to post-positivist claims of neutrality/objectivity/value freedom need to be based on their lack of recognition of the religious determination of knowledge and not on their purported conflation with so-called "masculine" traits or metaphors.

Could one argue that gender is as pervasive in cognition as is religious convictions? I do not believe this to be the case. The universality of religion is not of the same order as the pervasive particularity of gender. Moreover, knowledge of the world is the outcome not only of the condition and abilities of the knower but also of the structure of the world. Human cognitive abilities are universal in spite of the presence of (partially universal) gender factors. The structure of God's creation presents itself to all in very much the same way, whether they are male or female. Their ability to discern this order of reality is an ability shared by both sexes.

In South Africa, Afrikaans-speaking Christians developed a unique way to accommodate their "Christianity" to their national and cultural allegiances. A "two realms" view of life and the world was developed and dubbed "Christian Nationalism." The argument was then often heard: One is *first* a Christian and *then* a nationalist. In this way space was created for a separate, autonomous realm of national and cultural allegiance that often showed very little actual constitutive influence of Christianity. When required, the "realm" of Christianity was added to either supplement or complement the neutral realm of public life.[26] The flaws in such a "two-realms" position are all too obvious. One cannot first be a Christian and then a father, democrat, or scholar. One is a Christian father, a Christian democrat, or a Christian scholar. Christianity is not a second tier of human existence, but permeates all of human existence.

Does the same argument hold for the relationship of gender to various dimensions of human life? One can obviously speak of a *Christian* woman or *Christian* man, a *Buddhist* woman or an *Islamic* man. In this case, priority is attributed to the religious qualification of human existence. To argue that gender is epistemologically as fundamental or even as primordial a reality as religion is, one would need to show that gender, too, permeates every single dimension of human life to such an extent that faith, morals, culture, social life, and knowledge formation bear the constitutive and distinguishing traits of gender. Now, while it is true there is a certain universality to the particularity of gender, it is not of the same order as the universality of religion. My most fundamental assumption is that religion and religious convictions are ultimate and transcend gender. This does not mean that natural human differences do not impact on cognition, but I agree with Mary Hesse that these are not necessarily the most crucial factors in the context of cognition.[27]

One might be tempted to locate the particular difference that gender makes in a narrative conception of epistemology. The very cogent and persuasive argument that storytelling and narration, with its typical emphasis on particular, local, geographical-cultural-historical location, could be regarded as the feminine contribution to the epistemic project is deceptively attractive.[28] Its emphasis on the concrete situatedness of knowers with their particular and concrete experiences broadens the range of epistemic factors operative in and acknowledged in cognition. It also broadens the scope of the definition of what constitutes *knowledge.* As in the contribution of the Historical school in Philosophy of Science, it presents a different picture of the knower and the epistemic product. Its attraction may be deceptive, however. It does not adequately differentiate between concrete, pre-theoretical (naive) experience and the abstraction required by scientific theorizing. If taken as a description of the whole of knowledge, this position does injustice to the typical nature of *scientific storytelling*. Scientific theories tell stories that attempt to capture something of the structure of the world,[29] and as such are "a certain type of story." The nature of scientific storytelling requires abstraction from full, concrete experience and from the particular and the contingent, and also requires focusing on the universal structural conditions that condition the patterns and regularities that characterize reality and human experience. Anecdote, storytelling, and narrative do not necessarily provide alternatives for *scientific stories*. This is the case even when purportedly "feminine" or poetic/metaphorical language is utilized by scientists.

But feminists argue that a conflation of the metaphors of reason and masculinity is prejudicial toward women. Code, for example, argues that reason persists as an "ideal articulated through the symbols and metaphors that also articulate ideal maleness."[30] Two issues have to be distinguished here. The first is the thesis that the recognition, use, and introduction of metaphorical language in science is a feminine trait or contribution.[31] The second is the identification of rationality and objectivity with typically male metaphors and symbols.

Feminism runs the danger of responding to chauvinism and androcentricity by reinstating the same one-sided, albeit opposite, extremism exhibited by the position to which it is responding. Critical rejection of the already existing gender stereotypes in culture can result in retaining the stereotypes, but flipping the valuation. Replacement of the gender duality template with another one that merely chooses to emphasize the other pole does not resolve the constitutive and often dialectical tension in the original template. To the extent that feminism remains merely a reaction to androcentrism, they are birds of a feather. To the extent that feminism replaces the predominantly masculine viewpoint with a predominantly feminine viewpoint, feminisms' vantage point is as myopic as that of androcentrism. Feminists who claim to possess a typical feminine form of knowledge that either supplements, complements, or replaces masculine knowledge need to justify the epistemological gender duality template they assume.

Knowledge is always bound to historically situated and geographically located (embedded) knowers related to other knowers within the communal framework of an interpretive tradition, whether it is knowledge of concrete life experiences or highly theoretical issues, whether it be related via anecdote or story or by theoretical analysis. Such an interpretive tradition implicitly or explicitly assumes a vantage point. This clearly implies that although all possible approaches provide some understanding of the world, they cannot supply an absolute perspective. Human knowledge is always provisional, limited, and perspectival. Does relativism follow from this? I do not believe so. It is true that there is no single Archimedean point to be found *in* the diverse features of reality. They are all possible avenues of access to the multifaceted world we live in. But there is an Archimedean point that transcends this diversity, in which all diversity is unified: Jesus Christ (Colossians 1). There is also a providential and covenantal ordering of the world we live in which provides constancy and reliability for all human knowledge, whether it be developed by men or women or from whatever vantage point.

NOTES

1. Mary Hesse, "How to Be Postmodern without Being a Feminist," *The Monist* 77, no. 4 (1994): 459.

2. The minimal leadership role I did play brought with it its own notoriety and attention from the authorities. Cf. June Goodwin and Ben Schiff, *Heart of Whiteness* (New York: Scribner, 1995).

3. In Afrikaans: "voogdyskap."

4. See my own contribution to the anthology of the Institute for Reformational Studies, titled "Die stereotipe vrou," in *Venster op die Vrou* (Potchefstroom: IRS, 1987).

5. *Heart of Whiteness,* pp. 90–96. P. J. J. S. Potgieter is quoted as saying, "the issue of taking women seriously into the system is not very important. We are not so concerned about that as the Americans are."

6. The Nederduitse Gereformeerde kerk (NGK) or Dutch Reformed Church split as the result of deep differences of opinion about the place of the church in society and especially the acceptability of racially mixed congregations.

7. In North America a number of Reformational philosophers gradually did begin to deal with these issues. See, for example, Jim Olthius, "Be(com)ing: Human Kind as Gift and Call," *Philosophia Reformata* 58, no. 2 (1993): 153–72, and *Knowing Other-Wise: Philosophy at the Threshold of Spirituality,* ed. James Olthius (New York: Fordham University Press, 1997).

8. Herman Dooyeweerd, *A New Critique of Theoretical Thought,* vols. 1 through 3 (Amsterdam: H. J. Paris, 1953, 1955, 1969), and H. G. Stoker, *Beginsels en Metodes in die Wetenskap* (Potchefstroom: Pro Rege Press, 1961), *Oorsprong en Rigting I en II* (Kaapstad: Tafelberg Uitgewers, 1967, 1970).

9. *A New Critique,* vol. 1, p. 506.

10. In the later development of this philosophy a number of scholars do address these issues. See, for example, Olthius, "Be(com)ing: Human Kind as Gift and Call"; Elaine Storkey, *What's Right with Feminism?* (Grand Rapids, Mich.: Eerdmans, 1985), part 4; and Mary Stewart Van Leeuwen, *Gender and Grace* (Downers Grove, Ill.: InterVarsity Press, 1990), part 1.

11. It was only ten years later that the Institute for Reformational Studies of the Potchefstroom University for Christian Higher Education published the anthology *Venster op die Vrou.* (Potchefstroom: IRS, 1987). My own contribution to this book, "Die Stereotipe vrou," was far more a reflection on personal experience than any attempt at an intellectual account.

12. It is not necessary to document here the strong racist and sexist elements of the Reformational philosophical tradition of Abraham Kuyper. They have been exposed adequately by others. See, for example, Russel Botman, "Is Blood Thicker Than Justice?" in *Religion, Pluralism, and Public Life: Abraham Kuyper's Legacy for the Twenty-first Century* (Grand Rapids, Mich.: Eerdmans, 1998). These elements, though present, were seldom part of my intellectual resources, and they were not extensively discussed by the proponents of the tradition at the time.

13. I devoted two Ph.D. dissertations to aspects of these issues: "Partikuliere volksorg in die Afrikaanse volkskultuur met verwysing na die A.T.K.V. (S.A.S. en H.) 1930–1964" (Potchefstroom University for Christian Higher Education, 1971) and *Sosio-kulturele metavrae* (Amsterdam: Buijten en Schipperheijn, 1971).

14. R. Clouser, *The Myth of Religious Neutrality: An Essay on the Hidden Role of Religious Belief in Theories* (Notre Dame, Ind.: University of Notre Dame Press, 1991).

15. See, for example, Marthina E. Botha, "Philosophy at a Turning Point of the 'Turns'? The Endless Search for the Elusive Universal," in *Wysgerige Perspektiewe op die 20ste eeu,* ed. M. E. Botha et al. (Bloemfontein: Tekskor, 1994), and *Philosophies in a Feminist Voice: Critique and Reconstruction,* ed. Janet Kourany (Princeton, N.J.: Princeton University Press, 1998).

16. Lorraine Code, "Voice and Voicelessness," in *Philosophies in a Feminist Voice,* pp. 206, 217.

17. Carol Gilligan, *In a Different Voice: Psychological Theory and Women's Development* (Cambridge, Mass.: Harvard University Press, 1982). See also *Women's Ways of Knowing: The Development of Self, Voice, and Mind,* ed. Mary Belenky et al (New York: Basic Books, 1986).

18. "Voice and Voicelessness," p. 224.

19. "Voice and Voicelessness," p. 225.

20. "Voice and Voicelessness," p. 208.

21. "Voice and Voicelessness," p. 208.

22. See, for example, Jane Flax, "Postmodernism and Gender Relations in Feminist Theory," in *Feminism and Postmodernism,* ed. Linda J. Nicholson (New York: Routledge, 1990), p. 48.

23. "How to Be Postmodern," p. 445.

24. *The Myth of Religious Neutrality,* pp. 66, 104.

25. Lorraine Code, *What Can She Know?* (Ithaca, N.Y.: Cornell University Press, 1991), p. 314.

26. See M. Elaine Botha, "Christian-National: Authentic, Ideological, or Secularized Nationalism?" in *Our Reformational Tradition: A Rich Heritage and Lasting Vocation* (Potchefstroom: Potchefstroom University for Christian Higher Education, 1984), pp. 470–509, and Andre Du Toit, "Puritans in Africa? Afrikaner 'Calvinism' and Kuyperian Neo-Calvinism in Late Nineteenth-Century South Africa," *Comparative Studies in Society and History* 27, no. 2 (1985): 209–240.

27. "How to Be Postmodern," p. 459.

28. "Voice and Voicelessness," p. 208. Code does not argue for the claim that narrative epistemology is the feminine epistemology, though she does argue that feminists could make fruitful use of such an epistemology.

29. "How to Be Postmodern," p. 447.

30. "Voice and Voicelessness," p. 21.

31. Mary Hesse, for example ("How to be Postmodern," p. 449, footnote 9) expresses puzzlement that the recognition of the role of metaphor in cognition seems to be recognized in the writings of a disproportionate number of women.

SIXTEEN

Toward a Visionary Politics: Phenomenology, Psychoanalytic Feminism, and Transcendence

MARILYN NISSIM-SABAT

We need, and our society needs, to create a vision of our human future and to actualize that vision in practice. I believe that just such a vision can emerge from a synthesis of feminist, philosophical, and spiritual resources. While the project of constituting such a vision is implicit in the work of writers and activists in a variety of fields, I hope in this paper to make a contribution by making the project of synthesis explicit and discussing some of its theoretical and concrete ramifications. The following remarks explain how I came to embark on this project.

I am now in the last third of my career as a philosophy professor; I am also a psychotherapist trained in psychodynamic psychotherapy. Beginning in my teen years and continuing to the present, I have been a political activist, especially in the struggle for an end to anti-black racism. My theoretical orientation is to the Marxist tradition, but especially the tradition of Marxist-Humanism founded by Raya Dunayevskaya.[1] As both teacher and therapist, I have attempted to actualize the ethical stance that motivates my activism. I have found it both undesirable and impossible for me to live without active engagement in the struggle for a world without exploitation, racism, and alienation.

On the other hand, I did not become a feminist, that is, I did not discover or uncover my own searing pain, a pain emanating from inner acceptance of my socially constituted inferior status as a female, until I was in my early thirties. Nor did I discover the orientation to spirituality expressed in this paper until I discovered the philosophy of Edmund Husserl, also in my early thirties. Each of these vital dimensions of my life—political activism, feminism, philosophy, and spirituality—came to me in relative isolation from the other.

As I have developed in the decades since all of these dimensions have become central to my existence, I have at the same time felt more and more deeply disturbed by the continuance and intensification of anti-black and other racisms, including anti-semitism, backlash against women, gays, and immigrants in this country and elsewhere in the world, and by the growing dominance of global capital. In my struggle to comprehend these things, I have come to see that victim-blaming is one of the most significant, if not the most significant, mechanism perpetuating our failure to create a more just, humane environment for all people. (Victim-blaming includes blame by perpetrators, self-blame by victims, and blame by public opinion.) For as long as victim-blaming pervades our lives, for so long we will be deflected from focusing on understanding the origins of the unnecessary suffering we inflict on ourselves and others. But that is not all. In addition, we will be deflected from doing anything constructive even where the origins of suffering are identified. In my struggle to understand victim-blaming,[2] a phenomenon everywhere in evidence yet profoundly difficult to comprehend, I have found it necessary to try to develop a synthesis of feminist, philosophical, and spiritual resources. It is my present view that such a synthesis provides the only adequate context for understanding the phenomenon.

I. PRELIMINARY CONSIDERATIONS

A. Victim-Blaming

Motivation for this synthesis of the philosophical, feminist, and spiritual dimensions of my thinking and living can be understood in relation to my present focus on the problem of victim-blaming. What is victim-blaming? The term is generally used pejoratively to refer to an act of blaming a person or group of persons for unjust actions committed against those persons or that group. Those who blame victims judge the ones blamed to be immoral and to deserve condemnation and punishment. Victim-blaming thus carries with it connotations of moral condemnation of the character of the victim, or the one who suffers harm.

Victim-blaming as a response to both personal and societal problems is a pervasive attitude in the United States (and many other countries as well). The dominance of this attitude is reflected in the scope of deployment and degree of social acceptance it currently enjoys. Even a cursory look at the contemporary scene reveals the growing prevalence of the victim-blaming attitude: pervasive social Darwinism; escalating anti-black racism, including both increased discrimination and increased violence; backlash against improvements in the lives of, and opportunities for, women; hate crimes against black women and men, and all women, as well as gays and lesbians, Latinas and Latinos, immigrants, native Americans, etc; an already massive, yet still growing, income gap between rich and poor; the increasing influence of the radical right; weak labor unions and movements for social and economic justice; attacks on the goal of free, democratic education for all; the persistence of a reactionary foreign policy; the killing rage of our children; growing recourse to imprisonment, harsh sentences, and capital punishment as means of responding to crime. These social phenomena all testify to the perdurance and intensification of needs and desires to find scapegoats, i.e., those who are perceived as relatively weak and unable to retaliate: women, blacks, gays, children, immigrants, the old, the sick, the poor. It seems, then, that the moral and political climate of our society is veering ever more intensely toward victim-blaming or scapegoating. To fix the blame for an injury on the one who has been hurt by another adds insult to injury in a way that crushes the spirit and engenders despair.

What factors motivate victim-blaming? Those who blame victims begin with feelings of unhappiness and a sense of hopelessness, as well as feelings of shame and rage. These feelings are denied, rather than acknowledged. Victim-blaming serves as a means of defense against overwhelming feelings when no other means of defense are believed to be available. Further, victim-blaming manifests inability to take responsibility for one's own actions and their consequences. An additional factor is the widely acknowledged and deplored lack of community and intersubjective interrelatedness in our social environment. Due to these factors, individuals identify other individuals and groups, usually ones perceived to be weak and inferior, as objects on whom to expel their own anxiety and rage.[3] This perception of weakness and inferiority usually identifies those who appear to be unable to conform to the characteristics of a successful person inscribed in American culture, especially the specious "ideals" of total self-sufficiency and the ability to overcome any and all adversity.

Victim-blaming, like victimizing, is usually not recognized as such, that is, as an unjust attribution of blame, by those who enact it. This unawareness allows victim-blaming to function as a rationale for the continuation of victimizing behavior, that is, for deploying the scapegoat mechanism, as if to say, "neither we, nor our social and economic systems, are doing these terrible things to you. You are bringing them on yourselves. We would be just fine if not for you!"

Philosophically, victim-blaming can be rationalized by Aristotle's claim that some people are slaves by nature because they appear to accept the condition of servitude. Just as it appeared to Aristotle that there are "natural" slaves,[4] so too it appears to very many people in the United States at this time that those who, like battered women, are in violent relationships, or live in dire poverty, or fall into crippling mental illness, or are chronically unemployed, or are drug addicts or alcoholics, etc. are in these conditions because of some flaw in their "nature." Without such a flaw, how could they tolerate such lifestyles? And the proponent of such views assumes that they have other lifestyle options. This form of victim-blaming stigmatizes victims as inherently inferior.

Aristotle's notion of *akrasia* or weakness of will can play a similar role.[5] The diagnosis of "weakness of will," implicit in the view that some people knowingly act against what is in their own best interest, is also a form of victim-blaming because it too establishes a category of people who are alleged to behave in a way that a free, fully human person would not behave.[6] The allegation that victims knowingly act against their own best interests presupposes that the victims in question do know what is in their own best interest. Yet this judgment is usually made on the most superficial basis and without regard for the dynamic character of the psyche.

As mentioned earlier, victim-blaming is most likely to occur in situations in which the blamers assume that lifestyle options exist for the victim. Assuming that these options exist, and assuming that the victim was free, it makes sense to claim that she should have chosen to escape her victimization. Like Aristotle, people today who blame victims seem unable to grasp that a person, though free, can nevertheless be so oppressed by adversity that she accepts her servitude, her oppression. In other words, victim-blaming, while ostensibly affirming the freedom of victims to reject their condition, in fact denies freedom by attributing to victims an inherent flaw, namely Aristotle's weakness of will, or more contemporaneously, lack of will power. Thus, the allegation of *akrasia* enables the one who blames the victim to deny the terrible reality that only the free can be, and are, enslaved or otherwise victimized. If one has an inherent flaw, then to that extent one is not free.

Further, those who blame victims cannot see that responsibility, including moral responsibility, does not necessarily warrant blame, though it does warrant an investigation of the factors leading to victimization. The inference that victims are less than human denies the universality of responsibility, one's own, for example, in allowing the oppressive conditions that lead to victimization.

However, despite the overriding significance of the problem, there seem to be enormous obstacles in the way of even reducing, not to mention eliminating, victim-blaming. Although many have struggled to reduce victim-blaming and the concomitant victimization of others that is either the precipitating cause or the consequence of victim-blaming, they have faced difficult barriers. One of those barriers has been the resistance to awareness that victim-blaming occurs, for example, when, rather than attacking the causes of crime in poverty, alienation, ignorance, hyper-competitiveness, exploitation, etc., society resorts instead to increasing the severity of the penalty for a crime. For example, those who promulgated the notorious "three strikes" legislation did not believe that they were victimizing anyone; rather, they believed that they were attacking those who would victimize others—the criminals. They did not see criminals as victims, as persons who reacted freely to oppressive conditions and are responsible for their manner of reacting, but nevertheless ought not to be blamed. Yet, criminals most often are victims, for example, of severe abuse in childhood, and to treat them vengefully is to practice and perpetuate victim-blaming. It is also to act reactively, that is, out of despair. Those who are committed to eliminating the victim-blaming stance need to investigate means of promoting awareness of individuals' and society's propensity for victim-blaming and of means of combating resistance to this awareness in oneself and others.

Given the monumental destructiveness of victim-blaming on both societal and individual levels and for both blamer and object of blame, I can think of no greater moral obligation nor more important task for us today than its elimination. It is in this context that the confluence of philosophy, feminism, and spirituality gains its motivation and its momentum. Thus, the goal of bringing together or synthesizing, philosophical, feminist, and spiritual concerns and resources is motivated by awareness of a situation that can be characterized as a pressing need to comprehend and create the conditions for the possibility of full realization of our humanity through the elimination of dehumanizing factors in our lives, one of the most important and pervasive of which is victim-blaming.

B. The Relevance of Psychoanalysis

In the context of the concerns described above, one specific way of posing the question addressed in this paper is: in what way or ways can the human disciplines of philosophy, feminism, and spirituality contribute to the project of combating victim-blaming through generating awareness of its pervasive and malignant presence in our psychological and social life? One possibility I will explore is through an engagement with psychoanalysis. I want to argue that, as a therapy, psychoanalysis should offer a method of healing, not of blaming. Psychoanalysis should free individuals from the crippling effects of mental disturbances, and, along with this, from self-blame on one hand and victimization of others on the other.

However, this faith in psychoanalysis may seem misguided. At first, and even second glance, psychoanalysis would seem to be a markedly unpromising approach. After all, it has been a highly successful purveyor of anti-religious, misogynistic, and anti-philosophical ideas. In addition, psychoanalysis has been widely attacked as itself being a profoundly victim-blaming approach to individual and social problems.[7]

Classical psychoanalysis had grave shortcomings of both theory and practice. However, a contemporary modality of psychoanalysis has developed in the United States, partly as a result of historical developments flowing from treatment experience, and partly as a consequence of the immense challenge posed by the attacks against classical psychoanalysis. This modality is currently called the "relational model" or "relational psychoanalysis." This relational model is far better suited than the classical model for the project of synthesizing feminist, philosophical, and spiritual resources in an effort to bring about awareness of victim-blaming. Those working within the relational model have (1) responded to the charges of systemic hostility to religion[8] and women[9] made against classical psychoanalysis, and (2) have acknowledged that classical psychoanalytic theory and practice were not free from victim-blaming.[10] The attitude of relational psychoanalysis to the third resource, philosophy, is more complex. Relational analysts have drawn heavily on the work of philosophers in their writings. In particular, they have shown marked preference for the work of hermeneutic philosophers such as Heidegger, Gadamer, Rorty, Habermas, and postmodern theorists such as Foucault, Kristeva, and Butler. On the other hand, a long-standing debate in the psychoanalytic literature, as to whether psychoanalysis is a hermeneutic discipline or a science, has been duplicated within the relational perspective. Some reject a hermeneutic perspective on the grounds that it leads to relativism, a danger to be avoided at all costs. Others argue that non-hermeneutic perspectives tend to slide into positivism, another problem that must be avoided.

Relational psychoanalysis moves beyond the misogyny, scientistic reductiveness, and victimization of patients that are liabilities of classical Freudian theory and practice. The goal of these theorists is to reconstitute psychoanalytic theory so as to account more adequately and more realistically for human intersubjective interaction. This is accomplished by replacing the subject-object relation (Freudian intrasubjective model) with the subject-subject relation, or the relational matrix itself. More specifically, building upon and moving beyond the post-Freudian object relations (Klein, Kernberg) and self-psychology (Kohut, Stolorow) models, relational theorists maintain that difficulties in living that stem from emotional and psychosocial factors are most accurately conceptualized and treated as originating in and sustained by interactions (interactive theory of mind; two-person psychology), not as rooted in intrapsychic developmental fixations (Freudian, monadic theory of mind; one-person psychology). The origin of disturbances is now viewed as rooted in a failure of the early milieu to provide adequate intersubjective, empathic experiences for the developing child. In line with their notion of "two-person" psychoanalysis, relational analysts emphasize the therapeutic value both of the analyst's empathic attunement with the client and the analyst's acknowledgment, through self-disclosure, of the inevitability of countertransference distortion.[11]

Jessica Benjamin's work is important in this context. Benjamin was trained in philosophy and critical theory before she became a psychoanalyst. She has attempted to orient the relational perspective more consistently and systematically toward an inclusive feminist perspective, and has engaged philosophy deeply and sympathetically. Indeed, she has gone so far as to propose, in a recent paper, that critical theory be part of the curriculum of psychoanalytic training institutes.[12] Benjamin has made important advances in synthesizing feminist and philosophical insights into the psychoanalytic understanding of the psychosocial and psychosexual processes that lead to the development of our capacity for authentic intersubjective interrelations. One significant aspect of Benjamin's positive theoretical innovations that I will focus on is the emphasis she places on the role of a dialectic of the real and the ideal in human development.

Discussions of the role of the ideal in human psychic development are interspersed throughout Benjamin's second book, *Like Subjects, Love Objects.* In her most explicit evaluation of the role of the ideal, she says,

> While I often emphasize raising to the surface of our knowledge the less explicated side of intersubjectivity, I am equally concerned that idealization/identification be articulated and examined for its positive as well as its negative valence. The matter to which I return again and again, in different ways, is the tension between intersubjectivity and the dimension of the intrapsychic that I call the Ideal. . . . The very word Ideal has more than one valence, referring both to idealization and to ideals or goals.[13]

In Section III of this chapter I will present an analysis and critique of Benjamin's work. I will show that her formulations finally do not come to grips with the relevant issues in a way that would move us closer to a full synthesis and thus to a fuller understanding of the potential of a philosophically informed feminist psychoanalysis to help us move beyond victim-blaming. In order to provide a foundation for that critique, however, I will first articulate my own understanding of spirituality, philosophy, and feminism.

C. Spirituality

I use the notion of spirituality in the sense of a transcendence that leaves open the question of divine presence or the existence of a supreme being. This openness is not a mere rhetorical stance but has existential depth. Its depth is shown by three considerations:

a. *The problem of the ground of value:* human discourse and behavior are replete with conceptualizations of, and efforts to instantiate, values. We say, for example, that life is valuable or is a value and we attempt to live in accordance with this value. Why is it so? Any response to this question seems to end in an infinite regress or untenable relativism unless we are open to the possibility that values that are indeed of value, or manifest or instantiate value, are grounded in the being of value itself. It is difficult to comprehend how value can be of value unless it is grounded in transcendence, in a mode of being that is the source of value. For this reason, I do not think that we can consistently profess values at all without implicating ourselves in openness to transcendence.

b. *Social conscience:* We seem to be bound to consider the consequences of our actions over the long and short range in terms of their effects on ourselves and others, now and in the future. We grasp ourselves as part of a more inclusive whole, of the continuity of generations of humanity. I cannot maintain my psychic and actional integrity without examining the possible consequences of my actions on the lives not only of my children, but of my children's children, and their children, and all present and future children, and the adults they become. That people experience themselves as members of a human community that existed in the past and will continue indefinitely into the future does not seem to me to be explicable except on the supposition of a transcendent aspect of human existence that grounds our being as beings-in-becoming.

c. *Intersubjectivity:* My experience of other persons is such that, through empathic identification with them, I am able to concern myself with their perceptions, their feelings, their wishes and desires, hopes and dreams, their psychic lives. I come to know other persons through my experiences of and with them, and my ruminations on what their existence is like for them. I experience them as subjects, like myself, as independent centers of initiative and action. Yet, at the same time, when they experience joy, so do I; when they are in pain and suffering, so am I. What are the conditions for the possibility of this phenomenon of empathic attunement? Empathic attunement would seem impossible without a form of communication that transcends the boundary of self and other, a form of communication that encompasses self and other without violating, rather making possible a form of communication that makes possible the dialectic of self and other.

All three of these considerations raise difficult existential questions. No completely satisfactory answers to these questions exist; yet, in posing them, are we not centering ourselves in a certain attitude toward actual experience that precludes explaining away what is given?

D. Philosophy

I work within a Husserlian conception of philosophy. Husserlian phenomenology is a matter of uncovering the primordial subjective, and intersubjective,[14] experience of freedom that has been covered over by historical sedimentations. Husserl attributes these sedimentations to the positivist relegation of human subjectivity to irrelevance and meaninglessness. Phenomenology enables subjects by motivating a new attitude toward themselves, others, and the world. This new attitude comes into existence in and through the phenomenological *epoche,* the voluntary suspension of ontological commitments. It allows for acknowledgment of both human freedom and the ways in which experience, on both the subjective and intersubjective levels, can and does occlude our sense of our own freedom and the scope of our ability to change ourselves and our world. This acknowledgment, this awareness, is just what the victim-blaming stance denies.

Moreover, unlike existentialism in either its Heideggerian or Sartrean manifestations, Husserlian phenomenology recognizes a *telos* of being-in-becoming for human beings that is manifested in the striving for ideals. Such a teleological account relies on essences, and essences do play a central role in Husserlian phenomenology. Such essences, however, are not at all closed, nor are they otherworldly, Platonic forms. Rather, they are open essences inscribed in the historicality of human becoming. Thus, the perspective of Husserlian phenomenology is one which recognizes the domain of the transcendental as both an *a priori* directionality and as the condition for the possibility of human becoming.[15] Husserlian phenomenology, like both Marxist-Humanism and feminist philosophy of science, radically calls into question metaphysical materialism and the scientistic, positivist reduction of reality to ultimate material entities. Moreover, even though Husserl's writings, both published and unpublished, contain few explicit discussions of human relatedness to the possibility of divinity, his phenomenology does not at all preclude such a possibility, and was construed by Husserl as the only proper context for an authentic philosophical engagement with metaphysics and the question of divinity.[16]

Husserlian phenomenology began with the most thorough defense of the being of ideality in the entire history of philosophy since Plato.[17] Just as it is incorrect to absolutize Husserl's essences, the correlates of essential insight or *wesenschau,* so too it is incorrect to absolutize Husserl's ideals. Such absolutization leads to the conclusion that to posit the existence of transcendent ideals necessarily abrogates human freedom. For Husserl, in contrast, positing transcendent ideals constitutes the condition for the possibility of freedom.[18]

Husserl's focus on exploring subjectivity led him to write extensive phenomenological analyses of empathy and intersubjectivity in which these phenomena are neither presupposed nor explained away.[19] His goal was to constitute phenomenology as the philosophical foundation for the humanistic disciplines.[20] Further, he declared that psychology is the central humanistic discipline. He hoped to constitute a way into phenomenology through psychology that would be mediated by phenomenological psychology.[21]

E. Feminism

The most succinct way to explain what feminism means to me is by reference to a book: *Ain't I a Woman* by bell hooks.[22] hooks wrote this book when she was an undergraduate at the City College of New York. I consider *Ain't I a Woman* to be one of the great books of the twentieth century. No feminist work, no book at all, has generated in me a sense of woman as subject as has *Ain't I a Woman*. The book is about the impact of slavery and reconstruction on female slaves. hooks explores the extraordinary degree to which, and the means by which, both male and female slavers and male and female historians and sociologists, both pro- and anti-slavery and discrimination, have ignored, despised, and denigrated the subjectivity of black females. Owing to its lucid style, comprehensive scope, analytic power, and insight born of compassion, the book generated in me (and in some of my graduate philosophy students) a liberating identification with both hooks and the black females subjected to slavery and its aftermath. Concomitant with this was a sense of the being of female subjectivity so authentic that reading the book engendered in me and my students a lived experience of female subjectivity as both the particular experience of being female and as the universal experience of subjectivity in general. It is not surprising that such a book was written by a young woman, for it bears within it the timeless passion and hopefulness of youth.

Feminism is for me the project of revealing the being of women as subjects, and of revealing women's subjectivity as capable of standing for human subjectivity, just as men's has. Feminism in this sense is grounded in the belief that acknowledgment of women's subject status would bring into existence a new, more human, more fulfilling society. A dialectical analysis of this project would show (as has been maintained by many feminist theorists) that the historical assimilation of humanness to maleness has generated a conception of male subjectivity that is a deformed, socially constituted imago. This distorted conception prevents males from experiencing their subjectivity in any authentic sense. Through this project, feminism has begun to rehabilitate human capacities such as empathy, care, and connectedness. These capacities have been crippled, distorted, and rendered impotent because they are identified with beings viewed as non-persons, beings viewed as incapable of agency, ownership, or responsibility. This rehabilitation produces a deconstruction of the notion, endemic to Western and other cultures, that women are natural victims. Consigning of women to the status of natural victims has had an incalculably vast negative impact on human life. Deconstructing this social formation will provide a model for understanding and undoing the victim-blaming formations that heretofore have infected the core of human existence.

II. TOWARD A SYNTHESIS[23]

I would like to return, now, to the work of Jessica Benjamin, particularly her treatment of the dialectic of real and ideal, which, she maintains, plays a crucial role in the theory and practice of psychoanalysis. Though emphasis on the dialectic of real and ideal is present in all three of her books, the focus here will be on Benjamin's most recent book, *Shadow of the Other*.[24] This book is both a succinct restatement and reformulation of Benjamin's previous work and a new and more intense engagement with feminist philosophy, including the recent work of Benhabib, Butler, Cornel, and others. It is in the nexus of her engagement with feminist philosophy that Benjamin's most concrete conceptualization of the role of the ideal emerges.

I will present a constructive critique of Benjamin's work, specifically of some of her formulations in "Shadow of the Other Object," the last chapter of *Shadow of the Other*. My aim is to show that this work, the product of a passionate intelligence and prodigious linguistic and conceptual skills, nevertheless falls short of its goal of creating a genuinely feminist and philosophically informed relational psychoanalysis. My claim is that Benjamin's perspective on psychoanalysis, in my view the most promising one extant today, is itself compromised by its failure to engage, or resistance to engaging, the phenomenon of transcendence.

Benjamin's goal is to formulate an intersubjective theory of the self which "poses the question of how and whether the self can actually achieve a relationship to an outside other without, through identification, assimilating or being assimilated by it." Relations of assimilation are said by Benjamin to be "complementary" rather than intersubjective. Related to this, Benjamin further asks, "From what position is it possible to respect difference, or rather multiple differences?"[25] Reflecting the influence of Hegel's master-slave dialectic, Benjamin's term for a relationship in which difference is respected is "recognition," i.e., recognition of the other as an independent center of self without threatening or feeling threatened by that other. For Benjamin, this problematic is also directly applicable to nation-states.[26]

Benjamin shows how Freud's theory of the self fixed classical psycho-analysis in the intrapsychic domain, and, at the same time, provided a ratio-nale for Freud's misogyny. Freud viewed the self as a residue of internalized identifications. Thus, since his view of interpersonal relations was that of complementarity, Freud never theorized intersubjectivity. For Freud, males internalize their identification with their fathers and actively seek the fa-ther's place in the world. In one of her most powerful analyses of classical psychoanalysis, Benjamin shows that Freud was aware that female children go through a phase of identification with their fathers. In spite of this he re-fused to acknowledge that this was an identification with an active subject, for, his disclaimers notwithstanding, Freud was convinced that female sub-jectivity is inherently passive.[27]

In addition, Benjamin shows that theorists after Freud, who attempted to do more justice to intersubjectivity, also fell short. Ultimately, Benjamin argues, these theorists failed to understand intersubjectivity because they failed to overcome the Freudian heritage of a passive view of female per-sons. As a result, they failed to consider the mother as an independent cen-ter of self, an authentic other, another person. In particular they ignored the developmental significance of a patriarchal society, and the way in which it makes both male and female children unable to perceive the mother as an independent center of self.[28] Contemporary relational theorist Louis Aron suggests that, "On a more deeply unconscious level, it may be that psycho-analytic theorists were unable to conceptualize early development intersub-jectively because they were avoiding the recognition of the mother as a separate subject."[29]

Like other relational theorists, Benjamin has welcomed and appropriat-ed aspects of the work of postmodernist theorists and philosophers. These writers maintain that the notion of the unitary subject as heretofore con-strued in philosophy and culture generally (the Cartesian heritage) has been a major force in repressing the mother and all women. Traditional thought has constituted the subject as masculinist, that is, as unitary and au-tonomous, with a fixed identity and with instrumental rationality as its prime function. In contrast, traditional thought has viewed mothers, and by extension all women, as incapable of fixed identity, of rationality, and of agency, and has thus expelled and marginalized the mother and all women from the position of subject.

Benjamin concurs with postmodern feminist philosophy's deconstruc-tion of the masculinist version of subjectivity and with its effort to show that the subject is not unitary and that rationality in the masculinist sense is a false ideal. According to postmodern feminism, the subject is a construct of language or discourse. Consistently with the Foucauldian and Derridean inspiration of much postmodern feminist philosophy, these philosophers maintain that either there is no domain of ideality, or, if there is, it too is a product of discourse or of the discursive character of human experience. However, as noted above, Benjamin sees an important role for a dialectic of real and ideal where the ideal is not reduced to discursivity. Thus, despite significant areas of agreement, Benjamin elaborates her own views through a critique of postmodern feminist philosophy.

Benjamin speaks of the philosophical subject and the psychological self, and critiques feminist philosopher Judith Butler for eliding the difference between subject and self. Benjamin's critical point is that in focusing exclusively on deconstruction of identity and the subject, Butler elides the self in failing to take account of human psychic development.[30] This effectively eliminates psychoanalysis, especially the relational perspective, which views its domain as the theory of self-development and the practice of restoring the self's capacity to flourish. Benjamin states explicitly that neither subject nor self is unitary, as alleged in masculinist discourse, that both the self and subject dimensions are multiplicities, and that she wishes to retain both dimensions.[31] In Benjamin's terminology, "subject" corresponds to the intrapsychic dimension whereas "self" corresponds to the intersubjective, or social, dimension.[32]

For Benjamin, intersubjectivity is a developmental achievement. Self and other (self) are co-constitutive in and through both mutual negation and survival of that negation (or destruction). Unless the other survives destruction, the self will be unable to construe the externality of the other as an independent center of self and will be left with no other option than to reduce itself to its intrapsychic life alone. In this case the self will either assimilate or be assimilated by the other. In traditional roles, women, as mothers and wives, do not survive negation or destruction, they are "selfless." The developmental process of construction of a self can be derailed when significant others do not "survive destruction" as an other but, on the contrary, respond to both the assertiveness and the aggression of the self with compliance, retaliation, or withholding emotional sustenance.[33] For Benjamin, Butler's philosophical, non-unitary subject as subject of discourse cannot encompass an "identifier behind the identification," that is, it cannot constitute the self that survives destruction, the inclusive self.[34]

Benjamin's main critique of previous theories is that they were unable to conceptualize difference adequately, and were therefore unable to conceptualize intersubjectivity. To do so requires conceptualization of "the externality of the other," i.e., of the other self whose externality and unknowability is its difference.[35] In Butler's feminist philosophy the critique of identity and identification is the focus, and the "other," to one degree or another, remains, as in Freudian theory, an intrapsychic construct or, to use the terminology of classical analysis, an "object," a version of the same self which can be assimilated to or by the other, but cannot recognize nor be recognized by the other as an independent center of self. Thus, the otherness of the other, its externality and unknowability vis-à-vis the self, is not theorized. As Benjamin interprets her, Butler claims that subjects are formed through exclusionary operations. Butler advocates dispensing entirely with subjects and thus with the alleged exclusionary operations. Benjamin responds:

> Butler seems to posit an exclusion that has no opposing terms, no *inclusion*, no formation of the subject through recognition. But if this were so, how could the "contesting and rifting" she calls for occur, how could the demand of respect for difference be posed? On what basis other than an ideal of inclusion, of recognition of the other's right to participate in the polity, on what grounds—besides the sheer self-interest or power of the excluded—is exclusion to be opposed? Surely this critique of exclusion implicitly functions to make inclusion of preserved differences a normative, universal demand? And why not, as long as it remains open to interrogation? . . . Why not an ideal of an inclusive self that is the condition of multiplicity, difference and incomplete knowledge of the other? Why, when it comes to ideals, no locus of self or subjectivity, only discursivity?[36]

Benjamin suggests here, correctly, that discursivity functions as an unacknowledged and exclusionary ideal in Butler's formulations.

But how then does Benjamin construe the difference or otherness that is to be encompassed by the ideal of inclusivity that is "the condition of multiplicity"? She addresses this issue later in the chapter in terms of the philosophical controversy between Derrida and Levinas regarding alterity. "At issue here is whether the reduction of the other to the same is to be avoided by declaring the other to be absolutely other (Levinas), positing a radical alterity outside a knowledge which inherently strives to control it; or whether it is to be avoided by recognizing that the other must also be an alter ego, irreducible to my ego precisely because it is an ego." Benjamin sides with Derrida: "The condition for the other being recognized is that the other also be a subject, an ego, capable of negating [and recognizing]."[37]

What then constitutes difference, or, of what is difference constituted? In what sense are other egos, alter egos, not the same, different? What differs when there are two different subjects, two different egos? Benjamin places great stress on negation—it is the other who resists destruction, who survives, who manifests difference. But then, in what way is difference related to the ideal of inclusion, or, in what is difference included? Can difference meaningfully be conceptualized in purely formal terms as externality and unknowability? An other who has achieved self-recognition as an independent center of self can include difference without compromising her or his own status as an independent center of self. How? Benjamin posits that there is an ideal of inclusion that can encompass difference. However, though she speaks of "the necessary tension between the real and the ideal,"[38] a tension that must be acknowledged if ideals are acknowledged, she provides no philosophical or, for that matter, psychological grounding for how the ideal is given or constituted, except to say that it is an innate capacity. Thus, in her most intricate and compelling path of reasoning, and in defense of psychoanalysis as a theory of the development of the self and of a feminist perspective that would overcome masculinist domination, Benjamin finds an ideal of inclusivity of difference that functions within a necessary dialectic of real and ideal. She provides, however, no insight as to how this dialectic enables us to understand the relation between inclusivity and difference. It seems to me that this aspect of Benjamin's work is importantly relevant to the ways in which she believes her analysis of the nature of intersubjectivity pertains to the critique of capitalism and all other forms of domination.

Many of Benjamin's most prominent critics have ignored her extensive comments regarding the dialectic of real and ideal in her work. While much of the debate regarding her work has involved the issue of the constitution of ideal norms, for example in contrasting Benjamin's version of intersubjectivity with that of Habermas, this debate has not focused at all on the philosophical grounding of any reference to the ideal as such. That it has not is indicative of common assumptions on the part of the contending viewpoints. Rather than discussing the epistemic and ontological issues relevant to positing ideality at all, the debate has focused on whether or not a normative ideal of rationality associated with an ideal of autonomy necessarily reinstitutes domination, as Benjamin has affirmed and Habermas and his student Benhabib deny. It seems to me, however, that the reemergence of the dialectic of real and ideal in Benjamin's mature formulations of the nature of intersubjectivity suggests that crucial features of the relation between ideality and the feminist relational theory of psychoanalysis have yet to be theoretically played out. In my view, Benjamin's responses to her critics are less effective than they might have been because she has not realized the full implications of her emphasis on the role of the real and the ideal.[39]

I propose that Benjamin's profound notion of intersubjectivity and her recognition of the necessary dialectic of real and ideal can be fully realized if placed within the framework of Husserlian phenomenology. Husserls' phenomenological analysis of the constitution of the other in consciousness in the fifth of his misleadingly named *Cartesian Meditations* is well known. But Husserl also wrote extensively about the problematic of the multiplicity of selves, of subjects and intersubjectivity, and of the problem of sameness and difference.[40] His approach to the problem is directly relevant to Benjamin's formulation of the problem of difference. For Husserl, each ego differs precisely in its relation to the ideal; in other words, each subject, each ego, is a unique mode of relatedness to the ideal of inclusion or the inclusive ideal; that is, each subject is a unique exemplar or instantiation of that ideal.[41]

Most importantly, however, everything depends upon how real and ideal are construed. If the ideal is construed as just a mode of the real, for example, as a brain state where "real" is understood as reductive materiality, how has difference been construed—as the difference between one brain state and another with physical locations in different bodies? Certainly Benjamin, who incorporates Hegel's dialectic of recognition into psychoanalysis, cannot mean "difference" in this sense. If there is a dialectic of real and ideal, then the ideal must be construed, in a non-dualistic sense, to be transcendental vis-à-vis the real. Where it is so construed, to posit the ideal authentically is to adopt an attitude that suspends commitment to a materialist ontology. If ideality has no being other than materiality, how, then, can we conclude that the self is anything other than the subject of discourse, constituted by that discourse, where discourse itself is, in both form and content, a mode of materiality and thus relative to all contingencies of time and place? It seems to me that unless Benjamin acknowledges a transcendental status for ideals and ideality, unless she acknowledges transcendence, or the spiritual dimension of human existence, including the existential desiderata outlined above, she cannot avoid relativism, nor can she encompass difference within an inclusive self.

Benjamin does not declare herself on the ontological status of the real and the ideal; nevertheless, her effort to bring the resources of critical theory to bear on the psychoanalytic theory of intersubjectivity suggests that she considers herself a materialist. Since critical theory accepts Marx's rejection of metaphysical materialism and reductive empiricism, however, "materialism" does not have the same meaning when employed in the context of critical theory that it has in other contexts. The question remains, nonetheless, as to what the implications of a rejection of metaphysical materialism are. A second question also remains: how consistently do theories and theoretical work, including Benjamin's, remain free from the presupposition built into Western culture, the presupposition of metaphysical materialism, of what Husserl called the "naturalistic attitude"? Husserlian phenomenology begins with the suspension of all ontological commitments. In such a framework, the dialectic of real and ideal can be described just as it gives itself in actual experience, including the givenness of the transcendental character of the ideal and the mundane character of the real. Benjamin needs an account of this sort for her development of the dialectic of real and ideal.

To illustrate, in her second book, *Like Subjects, Love Objects,* in the same section referred to above, alluding to her emphasis on the mutuality of recognition, of each self recognizing the other as an independent center of self, Benjamin maintains that the development of the ability to experience mutual recognition or intersubjectivity is a "material possibility." This means that we are not born with this ability; rather we are born with "some innate capacities for such development," and "when we postulate a psychological need . . . for recognition, we mean that failure to satisfy the need will inevitably result in difficulties or even damage to the psyche."[42] However, Benjamin says nothing about the ontological status of that "material possibility" or of those "innate capacities." Are they "material" in the sense of metaphysical, reductive materialism, or in some other sense? In positing the material possibility, Benjamin does not deny that intersubjectivity is a normative ideal, though she avers that she does not conflate the two (i.e., material possibility and normative ideal). But this leaves open the ontological status of the ideal and its relation to the material possibility.

Thus, I maintain that while Benjamin is one of the first theorists to ask the most meaningful questions, her effort to constitute intersubjectivity is problematic. Because she avoids thematization of the nature of ideality, she cannot adequately ground difference and thus fails to differentiate her stance from those she critiques.

Another way to formulate my critique of Benjamin is to call into question the split she institutes between the "philosophical subject" and the "psychological self." Benjamin agrees with Benhabib's critique of Butler for ruling out rationality *in toto* for the subject. Moreover, Benjamin is correct to see that the subject, construed as subject of discourse, has no developmental history, for there is no self to undergo development. But there are other philosophical stances that repudiate the masculinist subject that are hospitable to the reality of human development. Husserlian phenomenology acknowledges both the subject as reflexive and free and the self that is "constituted in the unity of a history,"[43] an "identifier" behind the multiplicity of identifications. But for Husserl subject and self are not radically split but are rather the transcendental and mundane correlates of a given transcendental ego as it functions intersubjectively.

III. CONCLUSION

From the perspective of the ideas developed above, the solution to the problem of raising awareness of the scope and devastating consequences of victim-blaming lies in creating a concretely persuasive analysis of the meaning of being a victim that would obviate the tendency to blame the victim. Such an analysis would have to show both that victims are responsible agents and that they must not be blamed for their status as victims. It is, it seems to me, the absorption of responsibility into blameworthiness, the conflation of the

former with the latter, that deflects attention from identification and elimination of the conditions that lead to unnecessary harm. This tendency to
conflate responsibility with blame is especially intense under circumstances
when persons are free and therefore responsible for their beliefs and actions,
even under conditions of severe coercion.

Let us examine the case of a woman who remains in a severely abusive
relationship. Many people (possibly including the victim herself), consciously or unconsciously, would maintain that by remaining in such a relationship the woman reveals that she desires to be a victim, that being a
victim makes her "happy," or that either she does not suffer at all, or, if she
does, she "has only herself to blame." How might we defend the victim in
response? Shall we respond by saying that she has been brainwashed, that
she no longer has the capacity to realize what is happening to her? But then,
these people might ask, how did this happen to her in the first place, before
she lost that capacity?

Our next move in defense of the victim might be to lay out in intricate
detail the process by which brainwashing coerces assent. However, this
move could be, or could be interpreted as, an effort to claim that the victim
did not give her assent, for by definition assent is a free act. Thus, claiming
that assent was coerced seems perilously close to complicity with the dehumanizing effects of victimization. A person who cannot assent is no longer
a person. Furthermore, in the case at hand, given that the woman has options and could leave the relationship, denial of assent seems incongruous
with the facts. Affirming the woman's free assent, on the other hand, hardly
seems a defense of the victim. So, one might feel trapped between the Scyl-
la of resorting to determinism and thus taking the risk of complicity with
victimization, or the Charybdis of affirming freedom and responsibility and
taking the risk of condemning the victim we purport to be defending.

The approach I am suggesting here is that in responding to the many
who believe that victims are responsible for their condition, our response
should be to grant responsibility. That is, she chose to assent because, given
her evaluation of her situation, and her beliefs regarding whether or not she
had viable options, she believed that assent was in her own best interest. But
this is all the more reason to determine what factors affected this woman so
that she believed that accepting her abuse was her best or only option, when
in actuality she was mistaken. *Mutatis mutandis*, the same response should
be given to the racist and to all those who rather condemn than seek to
know the reasons why.

The victim cannot recover from her state without gaining awareness
that she assented to it, no matter what conditions of adversity led her to that
assent. She needs to become aware that her conscious and/or unconscious
assent helps to perpetuate her situation. Secondly, she must come to see that

her assent, however necessary in reality or in fantasy to secure her survival, was an act which secured her physical and psychological survival at the cost of loss of her experience of herself as a self, as an independent center of initiative, which was viewed as too dangerous to her psychic or physical survival.

This same dialectic is played out in relation to the charge that psychoanalysis (and all psychotherapy) is inherently victim-blaming. The charge has been based on one hand on the psychoanalytic claim that the client's disturbance is generated by her inner conviction that she deserves what she gets. On the other hand, the charge is that psychoanalysis as a body of theory and practice denies all other factors, especially social, political, and economic factors, in the etiology of psychic disturbance and in so doing discourages efforts at reform. As pointed out above, while contemporary analysts have acknowledged their profession's history of victim-blaming, they have not acknowledged, nor should they, that psychoanalysis is inherently victim-blaming. It is not accurate to claim that locating the origin of the client's disturbance in her assent to her victimization is victim-blaming. (Focus on victim assent would only be victim-blaming if assent were alleged to be a manifestation of *akrasia,* i.e., weakness of will.) On the contrary, psychoanalysis is based on the idea that the client must become acutely aware of her assent in order to be freed from it and its devastating consequences for her. However, it seems to me that the same critique can be made of this claim as was made in the critique of Jessica Benjamin's perspective made above. The notion of assent used here, just as in the case of Benjamin's use of inclusivity and difference, is marred by an unacknowledged metaphysics, an unacknowledged ontology, possibly of reductive materialism, unless it is referred to a telic directionality of the subject toward freedom, toward transcendence, toward *a priori* possibilities to be, toward an ideal of full realization of human possibilities to be and become. Where this latter view obtains, there is no contradiction between the notion of inner assent as a crucial factor in generating mental disorders and the commitment to revolutionary change in social, political, and economic conditions that occlude the scope of options for human beings. Conditions that occlude the scope of human options constitute oppression.[44] All oppression oppresses by restricting our ability to gain awareness of the actual scope of our possibilities to be and become human. We do, and should, act in accordance with our own best interest. (And, from the perspective of psychoanalytic feminism, our own best interest, as Benjamin rightly insists, lies in the mature capacity for mutual recognition, for intersubjective interrelatedness.) But we need to exist in an environment that does not occlude the actual scope of our options, of our possibilities to be and become.

We live in an environment that has, as one of its dominant characteristics, the denial of transcendence and the repudiation of the ideality, or transcendent status, of our ideals of human potential. We need a more humane environment, one in which resources would be directed toward eliminating unnecessary human suffering. Because discourse about and awareness of the potentiality of ideals to function creatively in our lives has been virtually eradicated, the field has been left open for dominance of specious ideals, of the impulse to oppress concealed within talk of "family values," of cynical, tyrannical relativism parading shamelessly as defense of ideals.

Phenomenology reveals the being of the domain of ideality as an infinite *a priori* of becoming, and the primordiality of human freedom, incarnate in the embodied subject, beyond all sedimented layers of denial. Transcendence, including the desiderata specified above, is then understood to be an experience that enables us not to foreclose the question of the divine. Feminist psychoanalysis moves us, for perhaps the first time in human history, toward the possibility of becoming whole persons. But neither apprehension of the being of ideality, nor openness to the divine, nor a vision of wholeness, each taken by itself, can stand by itself, except in deformed modes, nor can we sustain the vision of their fulfillment in synthesis unless we strive to create the conditions for the possibility of living that vision in every dimension of our existence.

Thus, feminism (including feminist psychoanalysis), philosophy (Husserlian phenomenology), and spirituality (openness to transcendence and the divine) converge in a vision of the subject, the human person, that is inclusive of all persons and founds our determination to vindicate in our life-world praxis our quest for a home in which we shall overcome all victimization once and for all time.

NOTES

1. Raya Dunayevskaya was, until her death in 1986, a major figure in the history of left anti-totalitarianism. She is the founder of Marxist-Humanism, which she developed in her numerous writings and four books published during her lifetime. An evaluation of her work can be found in Adrienne Rich's foreword to the republished version of Dunayevskaya's third book, *Rosa Luxemburg, Women's Liberation, and Marx's Theory of Revolution* (Carbondale: Southern Illinois University Press, 1991 [1981]).

2. An extensive socio-political analysis of victim-blaming, including a taxonomy of types of victim, can be found in Marilyn Nissim-Sabat, "Victims No More," *Radical Philosophy Review* 1, no. 1 (1998): 17–34.

3. The interpretation of the nature of victim-blaming presented in this paper is broadly congruent with that presented by Sharon Lamb in her excellent book *The Trouble*

with Blame (Cambridge, Mass.: Harvard University Press, 1996). However, her approach differs in some ways from my own. Lamb's primary theoretical context is psychology, not philosophy, she does not distinguish between responsibility and blame as sharply as I do, and (though her views regarding punishment are enlightened and humane) she views punishment as having redeeming social value, and I do not so view it.

4. Aristotle, *Politics,* ed. and trans. Ernest Barker (Oxford: Oxford University Press, 1969), p. 11.

5. The *locus classicus* of Aristotle's discussion of *akrasia* is book VII of the *Nichomachean Ethics.*

6. See Marilyn Nissim-Sabat, "Addictive Disorders, *Akrasia,* and Self-Psychology: A Socratic View," paper presented at the Association for the Advancement of Philosophy and Psychiatry, 1996.

7. See, for example, Jeffrey Masson, *The Assault on Truth: Freud's Suppression of the Seduction Theory* (Toronto: Farrar, Straus, and Giroux, 1984).

8. See, for example, Stephen Friedlander's "The Confluence of Psychoanalysis and Religion," in *Soul on the Couch: Spirituality, Religion, and Morality in Contemporary Psychoanalysis,* ed. C. Spezzano and G. Gargiulo (Hillsdale, N.J.: The Analytic Press, 1997), pp. 147–61.

9. See, for example, Lewis Aron's *A Meeting of Minds* (Hillsdale, N.J.: The Analytic Press, 1996), p. 258.

10. Stephen A. Mitchell, *Influence and Autonomy in Psychoanalysis* (Hillsdale, N.J.: The Analytic Press, 1997), pp. 11–12.

11. *A Meeting of Minds,* pp. 31–64.

12. Jessica Benjamin, "Psychoanalysis as a Vocation," *Psychoanalytic Dialogues* 7, no. 6 (1997): 781–802.

13. Jessica Benjamin, *Like Subjects, Love Objects* (New Haven, Conn.: Yale University Press, 1995), p. 20.

14. Owing to the influence of Heidegger and post-Heideggerian hermeneutic perspectives, psychoanalysts frequently hold, incorrectly, that Husserlian phenomenology cannot ground intersubjectivity. See, for example, the two books by Stolorow and Atwood, *Faces in a Cloud* (New York: Jason Aronson, 1979), pp. 36–39, and *Structures of Subjectivity* (Hillsdale, N.J.: The Analytic Press, 1984), pp. 8–12. A thorough study of Husserl's works demonstrates that this is a misreading. See, for example, his *Cartesian Meditations,* trans. Dorian Cairns (The Hague: Kluwer, 1960), and *The Crisis of European Sciences and Transcendental Phenomenology,* trans. David Carr (Evanston, Ill.: Northwestern University Press, 1970). I have criticized Stolorow and Atwood in "Psychoanalysis and Phenomenology: A New Synthesis," *The Psychoanalytic Review* 73, no. 3 (1986): 273–99, and in my review of their book *Contexts of Being* (Hillsdale, N.J.: The Analytic Press, 1992) in *Psychoanalytic Books* 6, no. 1 (1995): 29–38.

15. A discussion of the significance and explanatory power of a correct understanding of Husserl's notion of essences as open horizons of constitutive possibilities, and as the grounds of the possibility of a reconstitution of human life, can be found in the works of Lewis R. Gordon, Husserlian phenomenologist and critical race theorist. Gordon's works include *Bad Faith and Antiblack Racism* (Atlantic Highlands, N.J.: Humanities Press, 1995), *Fanon and the Crisis of European Man* (New York: Routledge, 1995), and *Her Majesty's Other Children* (New York: Rowman and Littlefield, 1997). See also my interpretive reviews: "An Appreciation and Interpretation of the Thought of Lewis Gordon," *The CLR James Journal* 5, no. 1 (1997), and "*Her Majesty's Other Children:* An Invitation to Existential Sociology," forthcoming in *The CLR James Journal* 6, no. 1 (1998): 97–108.

16. *The Crisis of European Sciences,* p. 9.

17. Edmund Husserl, "Prolegomena to Pure Logic," in *Logical Investigations,* vol. I, trans. J. N. Findlay (New York: Humanities Press, 1970), pp. 53–247.

18. Edmund Husserl, *Formal and Transcendental Logic,* trans. Dorian Cairns (The Hague: Nijhoff, 1969), p. 279.

19. Edmund Husserl, *Ideas Pertaining to a Pure Phenomenology and to a Phenomenological Philosophy,* trans. R. Rojcewicz and A. Schuwer (Dordrecht: Kluwer, 1989), pp. 179–80. Husserl discusses empathy and intersubjectivity throughout this book and in many of his other published works.

20. Husserl's task of establishing phenomenology as the philosophical foundation of the human sciences has been taken up most authentically and effectively, in my view, by Lewis R. Gordon in his *Fanon and the Crisis of European Man* and his *Existentia Africana: Understanding African Existential Thought* (New York: Routledge, 2000).

21. "The Way into Phenomenological Transcendental Philosophy from Psychology," in *The Crisis of European Sciences,* pp. 191–265.

22. bell hooks, *Ain't I a Woman* (Boston: South End Press, 1981).

23. I have also discussed a synthesis of psychoanalysis, phenomenology, and feminism in "The Crisis in Psychoanalysis: Resolution Through Husserlian Phenomenology and Feminism," *Human Studies* 14 (1991): 33–66.

24. Jessica Benjamin, *Shadow of the Other: Intersubjectivity and Gender in Psychoanalysis* (New York: Routledge, 1998).

25. *Shadow of the Other,* p. 80.

26. *Shadow of the Other,* pp. 98–99.

27. *Like Subjects, Love Objects,* pp. 115–41.

28. *Shadow of the Other,* pp. 1–78.

29. *A Meeting of Minds,* p. 75.

30. *Shadow of the Other,* p. 87.

31. *Shadow of the Other,* p. 90.

32. *Shadow of the Other,* p. 83.

33. *Shadow of the Other,* pp. 90–91.

34. *Shadow of the Other,* p. 87.

35. *Shadow of the Other,* pp. 96, 101.

36. *Shadow of the Other,* p. 104.

37. *Shadow of the Other,* p. 100.

38. *Shadow of the Other,* p. 104. Benjamin points out that Butler is inconsistent on just this point. Butler suggests that the notion of a dialectic of real and ideal should not be dispensed with, but also that ideals cannot be separated from slave morality.

39. *Like Subjects, Love Objects,* pp. 20–23; *Shadow of the Other,* p. xviii.

40. Edmund Husserl, *Ideas Pertaining to a Pure Phenomenology and to a Phenomenological Philosophy,* trans. R. Rojcewicz and A. Schuwer (Dordrecht: Kluwer, 1989).

41. *The Crisis of European Sciences,* p. 259.

42. *Like Subjects, Love Objects,* pp. 20–21.

43. *Cartesian Meditations,* p. 75.

44. Lewis R. Gordon, *Existentia Africana: Understanding Africana Existential Thought* (New York: Routledge, 2000), pp. 86–91.

SEVENTEEN

My Life Speaks

SARA EBENRECK

S hortly after finishing my doctoral dissertation in 1976, I bought a small table loom and took a summer course in weaving. Quickly I saw how strikingly diverse colors drawn into a fabric brought it alive for me. So it has been for contrasting elements of my life. I am a feminist, a philosopher, and a woman of faith. Each of these strands of my life are enmeshed with the other, not out of their own inner necessity, but because I want to draw these aspects of my being into a fabric marked by integrity, beauty, and vivacity. Unlike the process of working with docile threads in a loom, however, this life-weaving is marked by the reality of strands that each have an energy and direction of their own. Quite unexpectedly, one element can yank on the weaver's hands, pulling the whole pattern off an intended course. External circumstances shift, reshaping the space in which the weaving takes place. Rather than a finished fabric that can be analyzed, what exists is simply my life, that speaks—or whispers, or stands in silent hope—of this always-still-incomplete integration.

While there is no stopping my life's witness from hour to hour, writing of it has its hazards. The complexity of a life defies theoretical description, including any single sketch of how three aspects of it are interrelated. For one thing, these aspects are singled out, while others such as family and friendships fade into invisibility. In this essay, my journey as an environmental philosopher has little direct presence. Moreover, as biographers have observed of many autobiographical writings, the latter often tend to create a persona that the writer herself desires to become. The very act of making one's life public may easily lead to repression of unwelcome portions of it.[1] Still, a precious form of education occurs in the telling of our life stories to each other; in the conversations that ensue, a welcome solidarity may arise among those who engage in comparable work. Thus, despite awareness of their partiality, and in a spirit of hope for this educational project, I tell my stories. Each section of this essay opens with an experience or question related to one of my three commitments (to faith, philosophy, and feminism), then reflects on how each of the other two commitments interact with the first. In the conclusion, I reflect on the importance of the difficult work of integration evident in these three vignettes of interaction.

I AM . . . A WOMAN OF FAITH

It was late afternoon on the turnpike in central Pennsylvania, where I had been driving eastward for hours. Behind me, in northwest Michigan, my eighty-eight-year-old mother lay on a bed in a nursing home, slowly traveling toward that mysterious letting-go that we call death. Two days earlier, I had sat with her, watching her shallow breath just barely stir the small quilt over her ninety-pound body. She would open her eyes and look out the window near the bed, where dark pine stood green against a cloudy sky. Then, her eyes closed again, she would sink into whatever warm silence held her mind, free, it seemed, from the agitation that had marked the advance of Alzheimer's disease over the past five years. Here, in Pennsylvania, it was time to stop for coffee and a brief respite and let my partner pick up on the driving. As I turned off the key in the car, I was suddenly and unexpectedly shaken by an anxiety so deep that my physical balance seemed altered. "Walk the adrenaline down, get fresh air for oxygen to your brain, something to eat to buoy up body chemistry, and rest," my mind told me—all the practical steps learned to cope with the physical signs of stress. But I knew something far deeper was at stake here: in the sudden sense of becoming a motherless being, I experienced the universe itself as threatening.

Back in the car, my partner driving now, I tried to relax with closed eyes. Opening them what seemed like a moment later, I emerged into a world transformed by the westerly sun's slant rays over the landscape: first deep golden light spread over the dark tree branches and rock faces, followed by gold tinted with rose. For forty miles or more, in minutes that held a sense of dropping out of time, I felt myself held within this skyscape of golden, then rose light streaming over the mountains. I have been a sunset watcher since childhood, learning over long years something of the language of those colors, but never had I been held in such a light. Intuitively, I knew: I am cared for here, by some power that knows beauty is the language to speak to me. "God," I thought, as my awareness of a spiritual presence of some sort grew, along with a sense that, at the other end of this time zone, that presence would be in the sunset-light that streamed through the window of my mother's room. "It is enough," I remember saying to myself. "I will accept this experience." Like others before me, I felt I had sensed what the poet Shelley called "that Light whose smile kindles the Universe."[2]

My faith community, members of the Religious Society of Friends (Quakers), has no difficulty with affirming the reality intimated by such experiences. Its fundamental belief, that there is "that of God" within "everyone," is easily expanded to include all beings in the universe. The traditional Quaker language about the Light within, as language for God's inspiration, may have made simple my link between experience of light and experience of God's presence. Moreover, the deep trust placed in spiritual insight that arises intuitively from within each person, rather than a focus on texts or tradition as the central place of divine revelation, tends to affirm that experiences like mine have a revelatory quality. While I have experienced Christians whose theology might interpret my description as "confusing God with the earth," this is not an issue with my Quaker Meeting. I can easily imagine myself sharing this experience, finding it met with appreciation rather than criticism.

Quakers who inhabit the community with which I meditate are, however, so oriented to an experiential process that they are often reluctant to theorize about conceptual frameworks. Philosophers, of course, have no such compunction. Almost too quickly for comfort, my philosophical mind began to question this sunset experience and my intuitive interpretation of it. Although I halted that questioning until the next day, these queries insistently intruded. Isn't it strange that my partner, next to me as he drove through the same sunset, did not experience this revelatory time? Isn't my interpretation the height of subjective fantasy, driven, as Freud might argue, by the need to experience security in a world made precarious by my mother's failing life? How, indeed, as a respectable philosopher, could I leave my own interpretation unchallenged by rational doubt? Surely it is the empirical and objective methods of science rather than the subjective imaginations of fuzzy thinkers that ought to guide our sense of what the universe (including my Pennsylvania skyscape) really is. What epistemological support could I possibly provide for my interpretation?

As a feminist philosopher, I am aware of conceptual support for my intuitive interpretation of that Pennsylvania sunlight. I have studied medieval Western ideas about God, and know Hildegard of Bingen's twelfth-century affirmation that "I, the fiery life of divine wisdom, . . . I burn in the sun . . . ," and Julian of Norwich's fifteenth-century vision of God's mothering power, a power that assures us that "all will be well."[3] Twentieth-century feminist philosophers of religion such as Hilde Hein and Mary Daly have critiqued the matter/spiritual dualisms that separate God's presence from the material world and spoken of embodied spirituality.[4] Still, even if it is possible to think of God being present in the universe, how might I philosophically consider testing the accuracy of my interpretation of this particular experience?

Although they may never have intended such extension of their concepts, such feminist epistemological work as that of Alison Jaggar and Lorraine Code suggests the relevance to my experience of their questions about the dichotomy between "objective" and "subjective" knowledge created by the Western philosophical and scientific traditions. As Code puts it, instances of knowing fall "along a continuum, where some are more purely objective; others manifest a greater interplay of subjectivity and objectivity; other again are more purely subjective."[5] While the sciences operate at a different point of the continuum than does religious experience, that difference ought not to be taken as the distinction between more or less adequate or important knowledge. Instead, what may be required of truth-seeking religious experience is a discipline that guides the knowing process, something comparable in scope to the disciplines that check error in scientific inquiries. On this matter, attention might be given to the question, raised by Iris Murdoch, of whether the knowing arises in a context of egoistic fantasy or as part of a "patient and just discernment and exploration of what confronts one."[6]

This last qualification, the requirement of patient, non-egoistic, and focused attention on the other, gives pause to a too-easy philosophical affirmation of my sunlight experience. As I sat in the car, I experienced release from my anxiety and the calming experience of Light; I was not carefully observing the sunlight on the mountains. Might this mean, as some nature mystics express it, that I was literally seized by some power in the universe that was reaching out to me?[7] The verification process for my experience, then, would clearly involve a discussion of how truth arises in a dialogue. Here feminist philosopher Lorraine Code provides an important insight when she notes how modern Western epistemology has built itself on the model of human observation of "things." As she writes, if the relational knowledge of other persons, beings with a partially hidden interiority, were the paradigm instance of knowing, we would see that such knowledge "is possible only in a persistent interplay between opacity and transparency, between attitudes and postures that elude a knower's grasp, and traits that seem to be clear and relatively constant."[8]

From this perspective, I decide that it is no problem at all to consider that I experience something in dialogue with another reality that an also-present third person does not experience at all. Nor is the content of this communication verifiable in the same way as checking the reality of falling leaves by asking another if they too see the event. What I gain from my philosophical reflections, then, is not certitude about my interpretation of the experience, but rather an epistemological framework that helps me see how I might understand it in the conceptual language of my profession. At the conclusion of those reflections, I also understand the degree to which I alone live within my subjective experience, being responsible for the interpretation of that Pennsylvania sunlight. Here philosophy may meet poetry and art, being, finally, not simply a matter of examined logic and "objective" knowledge but also responsible choice of what one affirms as intuitively seen. As a woman of faith, I choose to affirm my experience of a spiritual presence in that sunset; as a feminist philosopher, I understand the limits of certitude about that affirmation. The awareness of choice gives me strength; the understanding of limits, appropriate caution.

I AM . . . A PHILOSOPHER

Entering college classrooms, semester after semester, I am challenged to define to the uninitiated what this process called "doing philosophy" actually is. In one dominant explanation, philosophy involves rational questioning of the principles that guide judgment in areas as diverse as ethics, aesthetics, and theories of reality. As I have described it, this process requires studying conceptual frameworks (including one's own frameworks) in a way that clarifies their assumptions, the arguments made for them, and their implications for a way of living—all with the hope that such examination will reveal elements of a preferred framework. One can undertake such inquiries in a multitude of ways, however. "Philosophy is a kind of intellectual game," said one of my graduate school professors, articulating his sense that conceptual dialogue is an intricate mental chess game. But while such descriptions name a disciplined process that can be followed, they barely touch upon the difficulty of what it means to actually allow the process of philosophizing to challenge one's own conceptual frameworks. As Simone de Beauvoir wrote, referring to her early experience of questioning her own beliefs, this process involves risk: "I *tore myself away* from the safe comfort of certainties through my love for truth" (my italics).[9]

So arises a question that permeates my philosophical life: How is this love for truth, especially the truth that challenges "safe certainties," nurtured? Isn't it, as well as the tearing oneself away from safe comfort, a matter of emotional attitudes as well as logical analysis? I recall the moment in my first year of teaching when a student challenged me to really consider a position antithetical to my spiritual perspective: the idea that humans have no freedom of choice. The image of the cold gray-cement walled hallway in which we were standing rises in my mind to accompany the inner memory of an anxiety that enveloped me when I considered the potential of a universe in which I was simply acting like a complex automaton. At the time, I could not emotionally consider this position, so rather than being able to meet this student with openness to hearing more, my rational response was simply a defense of free will combined with a counter-attack on the determinist position. I have no memory of the face of the student who posed this question, simply a sense of an antagonist to a philosophical position dear to me, an opposition against which I needed to mount a defense.

In academic life, philosophical discussion has too often been defined by the process to which I resorted in that conversation, a stance that feminist philosopher Janice Moulton aptly named the "Adversary Paradigm." In this approach to philosophical methodology, it is assumed that "the best way of evaluating work in philosophy is to subject it to the strongest or most extreme opposition," requiring that philosophers in conversation operate by adopting adversarial positions in order to test the view of their opponent.[10] Entire textbooks in the profession have been organized by this paradigm, presenting extreme cases of oppositional viewpoints next to each other, leaving the reader to judge which side "wins" by the stronger argument. The value of such methodologies is related to the chess-game image of philosophy: one finds the weakest point of an adversary's argument and targets it for attack. The result can be a helpful clarification of the validity of claims that are part of an argument, leading to the development of a theory that is more comprehensive in its consideration of evidence. But, in my experience, actually moving to this more comprehensive theory has required that the attitudinal relationship between the adversaries be more one of felt partnership in the pursuit of truth than of opponents presenting inherently exclusive positions.

How, then, does one develop the emotional capacity to welcome the questions that might help one onward in the search for truth, welcome such questions in a way that includes an openness to be altered by the positions of a philosophical partner? To begin, one must do some philosophical thinking about emotions; on this matter, being a feminist provides assistance. Alerted by the pattern in the hierarchical dualisms that led many Western thinkers to value traits traditionally associated with men (thinking, being active) over those associated with women (feeling, being receptive), feminist philosophers have worked at reassessing the role of emotion in the constitution of knowledge. As Alison Jaggar notes, "just as observation directs, shapes, and partially defines emotion, so too emotion directs, shapes, and even partially defines observation."[11] The most rational of philosophers are passionately rational; stingingly rational opposition may be inspired by fear. Further, by calling for the linking of life and thought, feminist philosophers have encouraged the turning within to watch emotional process, not as something separated from the philosophical enterprise, but as an intimate part of it.[12]

Bringing emotional process into awareness and linking it openly with related intellectual insights is itself a radical undertaking in a profession traditionally defined by its purely rational analysis, yet, I think, something still deeper is required if one is to actually practice "welcoming the questions." The capacity to hear and consider questions in more than superficial depth requires a conscious stilling of habitual responses, both intellectual and emotional, so that the newness of questions can actually be heard. Then one must make a further choice: to allow the question a harbor within one's consciousness, to let it rest there long enough for one to become acquainted with it and appreciate it before beginning to formulate a way of relating to it, of possibly incorporating some of its insight into one's own position. Actual receptivity must be practiced.

In the fast-paced conversations of classrooms and discussions at professional meetings, where philosophical acuity often seems to be measured by speed of response, such slowed-down, receptive process is difficult. There are exceptions, of course. At some meetings of the Society for the Study of Women Philosophers, I have discovered empathetic listeners, philosophers who respond to professional presentations with friendly questions, motivated by a desire to help clarify and take forward interesting points of an argument. Rather than inspiring defensive justifications, such questions may provoke a round of thinking that engages speakers and audience. In the community created within some of these gatherings, trust is fostered that the process of philosophical questioning will ultimately be life-giving to thought rather than simply devastating to one's fundamental premises. My own classrooms, I hope, create a home for such exploratory philosophical process. Yet these communities of inquiry, of their nature, are temporary; severe time constraints limit the degree of openness and exploration, and even here moments of silence for pondering, while still in the company of the philosophical community, are rare.

In fact, my deepest experience of this listening practice within a group has come from the process of my Quaker Meeting. The Quaker ritual of settling into a meditative silence, in which one opens oneself to the voice of God, permeates not only our formal meeting for worship but prefaces business, committee, and discussion meetings. Meetings of an hour, in which only two or three short messages are voiced, allows time for their depth to be savored. Multiple times in the course of a year, I have experienced messages that, in ways apparently quite unintended by the speaker, have provided insight on an issue with which I'd been struggling. The practice in business meetings of waiting until everyone who wishes to speak is heard before one speaks a second time draws one out of advocacy postures and into careful listening. In this group, as in any other, actual differences on matters ranging from financial expenditures to ideas about global population control are real and could divide the group; but the commitment to listen openly and search for the light of some truth in alternative perspectives has often led to breakthrough insights that allow the group to move forward, united. Experience of such transformative moments adds to the impact of such "mystical" experiences as the one described in the first part of this essay and reinforces the values of the "deep listening" process.

With such experience and reflections, I now enter my philosophical classroom in a radically different way than when I began teaching. As I prepare to present the work of a contemporary determinist philosopher, for example, I am very aware of my own still strong emotional resistance and, knowing that some students will echo my resistance while others will delight in the determinist stance, ask myself: How can I welcome this position, knowing that some insight within it could aid my thinking? From that perspective, I can see the ability of this philosopher to point accurately to the many genetic and environmental factors that play into decision making—a point that illumines the depth of our interrelatedness to each other as members of a community. Focus on this deep interrelatedness is appealing to me, and I suspect it may be an insight appealing to my students as well. Then, I also ask, how can I present the stance of one committed to a spiritual view of life, so that some of its insight might appeal to the determinists in the class? Perhaps focus on the creative moments of decision making, moments that are experienced as leaping beyond their antecedents, might be attractive for the determinist to explore. If the determinist and spiritual positions do not cohere, might that be because of their focus, each discerning some reality that the other tends to ignore?

Having processed my own emotional as well as intellectual responses to the conceptual position our class is studying, I am better able to discern the emotion residing in the multiple responses that arise in the course of the class discussions. By openly welcoming, in my preparation, the questions of a position that first appears antithetical to my own, I am prepared to facilitate a discussion in which unexpected questions and insights will arise. The two perspectives can be introduced in a way that leads to searching for insight in each rather than forcing a choice between them. I may call attention to the way that emotional commitments affect our ability to consider certain philosophical questions. Above all, I try to practice listening carefully in my classroom work, so that students will know that what they say, especially when its positional stance is different from my own, is heard as valuable.

Slowly, out of this teaching process, I have gained a sense that doing philosophy as a truth search might be characterized as taking part in a living conversation about conceptual frameworks within a community of wildly diverse partners that stretches over time and geography. To engage students in philosophy is to ask them into such a community, one in which they are

speaking participants as well as listeners. To be involved in professional societies and to write for publication is to engage this process, however halt-
ingly and imperfectly, among peers. The "clarification of conceptual frameworks" definition of philosophy, offered at the beginning of this section, is
a rationally serene name for what is, in practice, an intense and unpredic-
tably insightful way of living in company with other wisdom seekers, others
also willing to trust that the truth emerging in the certainty-challenging
process will prove to be life-giving.

So the process of my inquiry moves, from an attempt to define philosophy to feminist insight to religious process and back again into the philosophical. The threads link, cross, and shape new patterns.

I AM . . . A FEMINIST[13]

When I finished my graduate philosophy courses in 1970, I had read small
portions of only two women philosophers: Susanne Langer and Hannah
Arendt. Philosophical insight, and the searching process, were studied as
gender-neutral, a practice that both Langer and Arendt themselves affirmed. Offensive textual passages about the inferiority of women were
omitted from discussion, as if these were only historical matters not relevant
to the larger ideas being pursued. In my philosophical studies, clearly, gender issues were not yet out in the open.

Looking back, I also recall the atmosphere of my graduate studies as
somehow sterile, despite warm contacts among students and with faculty,
but I was then far from making a connection between this sense of sterility
and gender-based issues. If I could not easily identify with Socrates,
Aquinas, Kant, or Marx as archetypal philosophers, as so many of my male
colleagues seemed to do, I did not speak of it lest I be perceived as something less than a philosopher in good standing. Lack of such identification
did not mean lack of interest in their work, but simply an inability to see
myself as a philosopher behaving like Socrates or Kant, in class or out of it.
I took pride in the ideas I developed both in classes and in my papers, but I
didn't tackle the misogynist slurs of thinkers I studied. *I* was thinking, after
all, and apparently as well as my male peers, so what did it matter if, in centuries long ago, Aristotle, Thomas Aquinas, Rousseau, or Nietzsche had
doubts about women's ability to think as well as men?

Yet silence about gender left deep issues simmering just below the level
of conscious attention to them. The absence of work by women philosophers produced its inevitable effect: a tacit assumption on my part that no
women had yet accomplished philosophical work significant enough to
warrant inclusion in a curriculum that studied important Western theories.
How great a burden this silence placed upon my own philosophical work I

recognized only later, as I experienced the liberating movements of feminist and eco-feminist philosophy as well as the study of women philosophers.

After finishing my course work, while teaching part-time and mothering a son, chance browsing through publication catalogues led me to the early work of contemporary women philosophers who were analyzing gender bias in the canon of philosophy and developing alternate insights. I began rereading some classic philosophical texts, asking questions that had remained muffled during my graduate studies. As I considered Plato's and Aristotle's ideas on the virtue of courage, for example, I found myself comparing the classic instances of men at war with my grandmother's courage in creating a vegetable market business from a small and sandy family farm in northwest Michigan early in the century, and with my mother's courage in supporting a family of four children while my father was off in the South Pacific during World War II. In a paper co-authored with a woman colleague, we looked at courage as exemplified by women in transition to a radically new understanding of personal, social, and professional possibilities for themselves. Instead of continuing to assimilate to an abstract "philosopher's voice," with the stimulus of feminist philosophy I began to link my personal philosophical interests with my life as a woman in community with other women, to develop my voice as a woman philosopher.

In 1987, when an announcement of the first meeting of the Society for the Study of Women Philosophers came to me in the mail, I found a second important community: women deeply committed to the affirmation of the voices of women thinkers from the past as well as the present. Work to recover and link women's insights over long stretches of history seemed to me an absolute necessity. Although I would quickly discover that the myth of a "woman's voice" with which I could easily identify was exploded simply by the diversity of women's voices, nonetheless the Society provided stimulus and support for this discovery. In a way that still surprises me, even when I found myself in forcible disagreement with the insights of a particular woman philosopher, I could sense myself in a conversation that began and continued with an empathy created by a feeling of sisterhood.

I am not only a feminist but also an eco-feminist. It is clear to me that a parallel exists between the patterns of thinking that produce sexism and thinking that fails to consider the life needs of non-human beings in our economic, social, and spiritual decision making. In both cases it is assumed that a dominant member of the community can speak for and assume control over a member who is denied specific "voice." Since childhood I have experienced myself as part of the larger community of Earth, Water, Sun, Moon, and Stars; as an adult, I am endlessly startled (and discouraged) by the way that human views treat these realities as "beautiful landscape" or "resources," rather than as the essential web of life forms with their own non-verbal "languages," a web within which we are a small part. Searching for wisdom is for me a search for wholeness of vision that includes both women's voices and the "voices" of the universe. How could anyone expect to understand humanity without understanding women? How could anyone expect to understand humanity without puzzling over our role on this bright blue Earth and in the universe as a whole, without examining our relationships and responsibilities to the Planet as well as to fellow humans?

These questions have irrevocably changed both my approach to the history of philosophy and my present conversation within this discipline. A stark truth has become visible: I have learned about many of the ways in which important but culturally non-dominant voices can be muted, rejected, or forgotten in a philosophical conversation, and about how much is lost when those voices go unheard. This tells me that learning to listen carefully to voices not considered "important" by a dominant professional culture is absolutely important in the practice of philosophizing. New questions then open up. In addition to the study of the classic philosophical texts and the work of analyzing the logic of arguments within positions, might philosophy become a discipline also marked by the work of listening for truth in voices and places that are all too easily ignored? Philosophizing this way, in a class or in a conversation, becomes more an art than a logical exercise, an art of helping the culturally (or academically) invisible become visible in our discussions. If we practiced philosophy in this manner, would the discipline be embraced more readily by those who perceive themselves on the margins of the worldview created by the dominant thinkers of the West? Would philosophy courses then be sought out more often by students hungry to discover if indeed they too could develop a voice in responding to the deep value conflicts that rend our culture?

It was as a feminist philosopher who was also hungry for spiritual community that I approached my first Meeting of the Society of Friends (Quakers) in the late 1970s. In a story too long to be told here, my feminism and my philosophical tendencies had accelerated my departure from a previous religious affiliation. Friends, I knew, affirmed the ministries of women equally with those of men; indeed, the clerk (formal officer for business) of the Meeting I first attended was a woman (a position in which, after some years of experience, I have also served). In its spiritual practices, the Society of Friends, like feminism, offers non-hierarchical process and excels in developing the "feminine" quality of receptive listening. My Meeting contains many others who join me in identifying strongly with a "universalist" stance—one that de-emphasizes Christianity and is open to spiritual insight from any source, religious or secular. Because I define "spirituality" as the capacity for developing relationships of loving understanding and response to the whole of what-is, my relationship to the Earth and the Cosmos are naturally part of my spirituality. I have found community with many Friends who recognize the spiritual teachings that arise when one is attentive to the movement of seasons and the presence of other life forms beyond the human.

Indeed, it seems easier for liberal Friends to be Earth-conscious than to be strongly feminist, especially if that feminism includes an openly critical stance toward male-oriented worldviews. I have been advised that my feminism may keep me from appreciating the more biblically based aspects of Quakerism. I agree; it does do that. In a community that has affirmed equality of ministry for women, there is often a post-feminist stance: the idea that, with clearly equal opportunities in place, a strong advocacy form of feminist critique is no longer essential within the group. But I cannot help noting, for example, that while nearly all Friends are familiar with and regularly quote the writing of early Quaker leaders George Fox and John Woolman, a recently published anthology of Quaker women's writings from the same time period is appropriately named *Hidden in Plain Sight*.[14] My universalism includes a feminist critique of exclusive spiritual focus on any male role model, whether that be Christ or Buddha, or even discussion of the spiritual-life implications of contemporary such as Carl Jung or Joseph Campbell. I have learned as a philosopher how male writers all too easily make pronouncements about truth for the entire human condition, based on extrapolation from the male condition. For example, I think that endless affirmations by male spiritual teachers of the importance of loving compassion and listening may fail to address women's need to be challenged to develop a strong personal spiritual voice and to "speak truth to power."

Becoming a conscious feminist liberated my life from many assumptions made within a patriarchal culture and has led me to positively redefine what it means to be a philosopher. Using my feminist insights to interrogate spiritual ideas has opened new questions about the importance of moving spiritually beyond what are often called the "great world religions," all of which center on a male voice. I live in a time of transformation; I hope for a future in which women's wisdom informs our lives as deeply as have the traditions originated by men.

INTEGRATION

The life stories I have shared here only begin to open the creative tensions that I experience between my feminist, philosophical, and religious life. It is, for example, my philosophical studies that have led me to question religious ideas about life after death. My feminist consciousness is always at work, actively scrutinizing philosophical and religious positions to see whose social power is reinforced, and whose situation remains unanalyzed by the theory in question. My eco-feminist consciousness always presses questions about how planetary life is seen and affected by decisions and theories. In turn, my religious commitments to a caring community lead me to question both the adversarial confrontations still present in some feminist discourse as well as the value of philosophy's insistently rational analysis, when this does not connect itself to life and action. Rather than leading to a serenely coherent intellectual life, the tensions between these aspects of my life constantly pressure me toward questioning and the intellectual, emotional, and personal shifts that follow that questioning.

As I work, I have become more aware of existing in a broad human community many of whose members are also struggling, more or less consciously, toward integration. In a society open to global communication, even small children are already beginning their journey into the awareness of the conflicts that arise from the clash of the diverse perspectives present in images and ideas from school, television, church, and their friends. At its worst, in this ever-faster-paced and future-oriented Western culture, human consciousness becomes fragmented, and the skill developed is that of moving from framework to framework in an adaptation to each that avoids the difficult questions of how central perspectives in one relate to the other. At its best, in a fast-evolving global culture, becoming conscious of our own work at integration may be a priceless skill, not only for helping ourselves stay sane, but for helping human consciousness grow ever deeper and more whole. As we move together into the next millennium, our lives will speak, simply and clearly, of what we have each discerned about how to be wholly human. Our integrations, what our lives speak, is the gift we bring moment by moment into the evolving universe.

NOTES

1. Compare the analysis of Elisabeth Young-Bruehl in "The Education of Women as Philosophers," *Signs* 12, no. 2 (Winter 1987).

2. The quote from Shelley is noted in F. C. Happold's *Mysticism* (London: Penguin, 1963), p. 43.

3. Gabriele Uhlein, *Meditations with Hildegard of Bingen* (Santa Fe, N.M.: Bear & Co., 1983), p. 30. Julian of Norwich, *Revelations of Divine Love,* trans. Clifton Wolters (New York: Penguin Books, 1966), Chs. 13, 27, 62.

4. Hilde Hein, "Liberating Philosophy: An End to the Dichotomy of Spirit and Matter," in *Women, Knowledge, and Reality,* ed. Ann Garry and Marilyn Pearsall (New York: Routledge, 1992), pp. 437–53. Mary Daly, *Beyond God the Father* (Boston: Beacon Press, 1973).

5. Lorraine Code, *What Can She Know? Feminist Theory and the Construction of Knowledge* (Ithaca, N.Y.: Cornell University Press, 1991), p. 30.

6. Iris Murdoch, *The Sovereignty of Good* (London: Routledge & Kegan Paul, 1970), p. 38. See also Murdoch's *Metaphysics as a Guide to Morals* (London: Penguin Press, 1992), Ch. 11. I develop this idea in more depth in "Opening Pandora's Box: Imagination's Role in Environmental Ethics," *Environmental Ethics* 18 (Spring 1996): 3–18.

7. See, for example, the descriptions of writer Annie Dillard on her experiences of some spiritual presence in the natural world in *Pilgrim at Tinker Creek* (New York: Harper and Row, 1974), pp. 13, 33. I examine this idea in more depth in a paper in progress titled "Unlicensed Metaphysics: Annie Dillard's Search for Meaning in Nature."

8. *What Can She Know?* pp. 32–39.

9. Simone de Beauvoir, *All Said and Done,* trans. Patrick O'Brian (New York: G. P. Putnam's Sons, 1974), p. 16.

10. Janice Moulton, "A Paradigm of Philosophy: The Adversary Method," in *Women, Knowledge, and Reality,* p. 14.

11. Alison Jaggar, "Love and Knowledge: Emotion in Feminist Epistemology," in *Women, Knowledge, and Reality,* p. 174.

12. See, for example, the work of Maria Lugones in tracing her relationship to her mother in "Playfulness, 'World'-Travelling, and Loving Perception," *Hypatia* 2, no. 2 (Summer 1987): 3–19.

13. An earlier version of the first part of this section was published as "Finding New Roots as a Woman Philosopher," in *Presenting Women Philosophers,* ed. Cecile T. Tougas and Sara Ebenreck (Philadelphia: Temple University Press, 2002), pp. 105–109. It is used here by permission of the author.

14. *Hidden in Plain Sight: Quaker Women's Writings 1650–1700,* ed. Mary Garman, Judith Applegate, Margaret Benefiel, and Dortha Meredith (Wallingford, Pa.: Pendle Hill Publications, 1996).

CONTRIBUTORS

Azizah Y. al-Hibri is Professor of Law at the T. C. Williams School of Law at the University of Richmond.

M. Elaine Botha is Professor of Philosophy at Redeemer University College, Ancaster, Ontario, Canada, and Professor Emerita of Philosophy at Potchefstroom University for Christian Higher Education, Potchefstroom, South Africa.

Marya Bower is Associate Professor of Philosophy at Earlham College.

Sara Ebenreck is Associate Professor of Philosophy at St. Mary's College of Maryland.

Jean Bethke Elshtain is the Laura Spelman Rockefeller Professor of Social and Political Ethics, the University of Chicago.

Ruth E. Groenhout is Associate Professor of Philosophy at Calvin College.

Patricia Altenbernd Johnson is Professor of Philosophy and Associate Dean for Connected Learning in the College of Arts and Sciences at the University of Dayton.

Laura Duhan Kaplan is Associate Professor of Philosophy at the University of North Carolina at Charlotte.

Winifred Wing Han Lamb is a visiting fellow in philosophy at the Australian National University and is completing her Ph.D. in philosophical theology in the School of Theology, St Mark's National Theological Centre, Charles Sturt University, Canberra, Australia.

Mary B. Mahowald is Professor Emerita, Department of Obstetrics and Gynecology and MacLean Center for Clinical Medical Ethics at the University of Chicago.

Sister Mary Christine Morkovsky is a General Councilor of the Congregation of Divine Providence of San Antonio, Texas, and Adjunct Professor at Oblate School of Theology in San Antonio.

Marilyn Nissim-Sabat is Professor of Philosophy at Lewis University and a clinical social worker.

Nel Noddings is the Lee L. Jacks Professor of Child Education, Emerita, in the School of Education at Stanford University.

Martha C. Nussbaum is the Ernst Freund Distinguished Service Professor of Law and Ethics, Department of Philosophy, Law School and Divinity School, the University of Chicago.

Marianne Sawicki is Associate Professor of Philosophy in the Department of Philosophy and Religious Studies at Morgan State University.

Irmgard Scherer is Associate Professor of Philosophy in the Department of Philosophy at Loyola College, Baltimore.

Jacqueline Scott is Assistant Professor of Philosophy at Loyola University of Chicago.

Caroline J. Simon is Professor of Philosophy at Hope College.

INDEX

Abraham, 16, 37n13
"Adversary Paradigm," 287
aesthetics, 239–241
agape, 161–167
agnosticism, 89, 217
Archard, David, 183
Arendt, Hannah, 240, 290
Aristotle, 262–263
atheism, 232
Augustine, Saint, 48, 97–100
authenticity, 227–228
autonomy, 43, 158, 236. *See also* freedom

Bachelard, Gaston, 190–191
Baier, Annette, 167
Becker-Theye, Betty, 177
Benjamin, Jessica, 266, 270–276, 278
Bible: as literature, 222; authority of,
    18–20, 26, 31
body, 111
Buber, Martin, 219–220, 224

Camus, Albert, 90
capitalism, 44–46, 48
care ethics: and agapism, 154, 161–165;
    limits on care, 159–161; and self-
    sacrifice, 154–161, 167–171; and
    "woman's voice," 152–154
Christianity, 40, 47–49; Catholicism,
    53–54, 76–84, 106–107, 114; and
    communalism, 47–49; conversion in,
    233–234 (*see also* conversion);
    Episcopalian, 10–13; and feminism, 43,
    176–177; and individualism, 47–49;
    and justice, 12–13; and philosophy,
    229–230, 251–253; Protestant, 48, 78,
    214, 216; Quaker, 148–151, 284, 288,
    292–293; rejection of, 214–219; and
    resurrection, 111; and sexism, 53–54;
    and sexual morality, 184–187; in South
    Africa, 243, 245–249, 256; and
    suffering, 65–66

Clement, Grace, 158
Code, Lorraine, 254–255, 257, 285
communalism, 40, 42–43, 47–49
community, 4, 47, 55, 98, 167–168, 262,
    267, 284; in the classroom, 288–290;
    and identity, 124, 132; and Judaism,
    135; and questions, 143–144; among
    women, 291–293
complementarity, 155–156
·conscience, 20
consent, ethic of, 175–176, 181–182
contemplation, 67
conversion, 10, 13–16, 133–134, 148,
    233, 292–293
Cooper, David, 60
cosmopolitanism, 10, 23–36, 39
creation, 166, 177

Davaney, Sheila Greeve, 217
democracy, and Islam, 205–209
Dewey, John, 217–218
difference, 50, 270–276; of the sexes,
    155–156
disputation, 143
diversity, and Islam, 209
Dooyeweerd, Hermann, 68, 252
Downing, Christine, 216
Dussel, Enrique, 83

eco-feminism, 291–292
Einhorn, David, 17, 21–22, 27, 30
emotion: and knowledge, 287–288; and
    reason, 183
Engels, Friedrich, 45–46
Enlightenment, 9–10, 89, 229; Jewish,
    17–29, 31–35
epistemology, 285; feminist, 253–258;
    narrative conception of, 256–257;
    standpoint of, 50–52
equality, 16, 43–45, 47, 49, 50, 155–156,
    166, 167; and Qurʿan, 203–205,
    207–208; of the sexes, 29–31

Erikson, Erik, 88–92, 95–96
ethics: of care, *see* care ethics; and logic, 201; and the personal, 51; and women, 152–159
evil, 143, 168–170, 215–216
existentialism, 90

faith: Christian, 67–68; and conduct, 14, 18–20; and experience, 283–285; and feminism, 76, 85–86, 191, 214, 293–294; of Hagar, 198; and identity, 105; and passion, 239–240; and philosophy, 85–86, 214, 227–228, 237–239, 243, 293–294; and pragmatism, 217–219; and reason, 81–82, 89, 137, 228–231
faithfulness, 63, 64–68
Farley, Wendy, 215
feminism, 1–5, 40–43, 50–55, 118, 125–128, 199–201; and academics, 114; and Christianity, 176–177; and faith, 76, 85–86, 191, 243, 284–286, 293; and identity, 105, 144–146; and Judaism, 9–10; and Kant, 240; and oppression, 83; and philosophy, 243, 290–294; as practice, 107–109; and questions, 144–148; and race, 147, 269; and spirituality, 260–261; and subjectivity, 269–270; traditional feminism, 195–197; and traditional religion, 222–224; and women's liberation, 244–245, 247, 250
feminist theology, 216–217
feminist theory, 153–154
freedom, 94, 263, 268, 278; and existence of God, 48–49, 218. *See also* autonomy
Freud, Sigmund, 271

Gadamer, Hans-Georg, 141–143, 146–148, 190, 192
Geiger, Abraham, 17, 19, 20, 21, 26, 27
Geller, Laura, 30–31
gender, 110, 255–256; and equality, 15–16, 25, 26, 29–31; and Western philosophy, 41, 290–291
Gilligan, Carol, 240–241, 254
God, 63, 67, 68, 72, 73, 77, 80–82, 84–85, 87, 106–107, 115–116, 118, 193, 202–203; belief in, 31–34; and destiny, 184–185; and evil, 214–216; existence of, 137; and faith, 217–219; and freedom, 48–49, 218; and Iblis, 204; Jesus Christ, 113, 251–252;

presence of, 283–285; as psychic reality, 220–221; quilts, 117; relation with humans, 162, 164, 166; and the "Selfsame," 98; Spinoza's, 192; and spiritual experience, 220–222; will of, 208
grace, 49, 241

Habermas, Jürgen, 2
Hagar, 198–199, 210
Haraway, Donna, 51–52
Haskalah. *See* Enlightenment, Jewish
hermeneutics, 110; of suspicion, 145, 193; and understanding, 192, 194, 196–197
hierarchy, and Islam, 204–206
Hirsch, Samson Raphael, 21, 24, 26, 27, 30, 32
Holdheim, Samuel, 17, 19, 20, 26
hooks, bell, 147, 150, 269
hope, 97, 100, 117–118
humility, 54–55, 64
Husserl, Edmund, 112, 268–269, 274–275

ideal, and real, 270, 271–272, 274–276, 279
identity, 1, 3–4, 90–94, 97–100, 105, 107; of category "woman," 195–196; and community, 132; and conflict, 120; creation of, 122–125; and feminism, 199; and narrative, 177, 184–186, 282–283; and race, 126–128; and self-sacrifice, 156–158, 160
identity politics, 95–97
immigrant experience, 91
individualism, 40, 167–168; and Christianity, 47–49; and feminism, 42–43; and socialism, 47–49
integrity, 92
interdependence, 98–99, 249
Islam, 200, 203–210; and democracy, 205–209; and diversity, 209

James, William, 217, 230–231
Judaism, 133–138, 192–195; and belief in God, 137; Conservative, 15–16; and conversion, 13–16, 133–134; and patriarchy, 29–31; Reconstructionism and Renewal, 193–194; Reform, 9–10, 13–35; and ritual, 15, 27–29, 34, 134–137; and values, 134
justice, 12–13, 21–23, 253; and feminism, 52–53

Kant, Immanuel, 18, 20, 33, 219, 229, 230, 238–239, 240
Kierkegaard, Søren, 63, 70–71, 72, 220, 224
King, Martin Luther, Jr., 81, 91–92
knowledge: and finitude, 99–100; and lived experience, 285; models of, 67; and power, 248; and questioning, 141–142; theories of, 191. *See also* epistemology
Kohler, Kaufmann, 17, 19, 20, 27, 30, 32

language: and oppression, 247; and reinterpretation, 194
Lenin, Vladimir I., 46–47
Les Liaisons Dangereuses, 180–182
Levinas, Emmanuel, 167, 273
Lewis, C. S., 215
liberation, 249
Lindbergh, Anne Morrow, 223–224
logic, and ethics, 201
love, 49, 57–58n46, 67–68, 100, 152–153, 223
Lugones, Maria, 146–147
Luther, Martin, 88–90

Maitland, Sara, 72
manipulation, 183
Manning, Rita, 159
marginalization, 85–86, 121
Marx, Karl, 43–45, 199, 201
maternal experience, 96
Mendelssohn, Moses, 9–10, 14, 19, 20, 24, 26
metaphor, 194, 196
Miles, Jack, 216
Montefiore, Claude, 19–20
morality, 21–23; and ritual, 19; and transcendence, 33–35; as universal, 23–26. *See also* ethics; justice
Moulton, Janice, 287
music, 11, 28–29, 34, 36n12

Nagel, Thomas, 50–51
Nehamas, Alexander, 120, 121–122
Nietzsche, Friedrich, 120, 122–123, 131, 220, 224
nihilism, 122
Noddings, Nel, 152–153, 159, 161, 162, 163–164, 168–170, 240–241
Norris, Kathleen, 224
Nygren, Anders, 162, 164

objectivity, 51–52

O'Neil, Onora, 185
oppression, 83
original sin, 49
Outka, Gene, 165–166

Paley, Grace, 13
passion, and faith, 239–240
patriarchy, and Judaism, 29–31
phenomenology, 111–112, 190–191, 268–269, 274–275, 279
philosophy, 1–5; and the everyday, 60–61, and faith, 76, 80, 85–86, 191, 214, 227–228, 237–239, 243, 284, 293–294; and feminism, 41–42, 76, 191, 214, 243, 290–294; nature of, 140; poetics of, 191; practice of, 62, 64–66, 105, 112, 120, 121–125, 131, 142, 286–290; as profession, 70–71; and Quaker queries, 149–150; and race, 128–129
Plaskow, Judith, 193
play, 145–148
poetry: and philosophy, 191; and transcendence, 220–222
power, 71; and knowledge, 248, and sexuality, 181
pragmatism, 54; and faith, 217–219
privilege, 52, 54–55
psychoanalysis, 264–266, 278

questions, 101, 106, 109, 141–144; and philosophy, 288–289; and Quaker practice, 148–150
Qur'an, 200, 203–210

race: and feminism, 269; and identity, 95–96, 126–128; and philosophy, 128–129; relations in South Africa, 246–250
Ramsey, Paul, 163–164, 165
reason, 2, 9–10; and emotions, 183; and faith, 81–82, 89, 137, 228–231; and gender, 257; and Judaism, 14–15, 18–20; and particularity, 65; perspectival, 254–255
Reformed philosophical tradition, 244, 251–253
relativism, 51
religion, 1–5; and faith, 217–218; and women, 222–223
religious neutrality, 255
responsibility, 263–264, 276–277
revelation, 20

ritual: and Judaism, 15, 19, 27–29, 34, 134–137; liturgy and practice, 143–144; Quaker, 288–289
Roiphe, Katie, 178–180, 182
Royce, Josiah, 47
Ruddick, Sara, 162
Russell, Bertrand, 214, 218, 224

Saiving, Valerie, 164
Schlesinger, George, 64
seduction, 175–176; and Christianity, 184–187; and moral evaluation, 177–184
self: intersubjective, 270–276; nature of, 1–4. *See also* identity; subject
self-interest, 154–155, 160
sexes, differences of, 155–156
sexual double standard, 178–179, 186
sexuality: and consent, 175–176, 181–182; and power, 181
Simon, Katherine, 221–222
socialism, 13, 43–47
Society for Women in Philosophy (SWIP), 40–41, 199–200, 288
Society of Friends. *See* Christianity, Quaker
Spinoza, Baruch, 191–192, 221
spirituality, 266–267, 283–286, 292–293; experience of, 219–222; and feminism, 260–261; skeptical, 224–225. *See also* transcendence
Stein, Edith, 111–113
Steiner, George, 65
Stone, Merlin, 216

subject: and feminism, 269–270; masculine, 271

testimony, 117
Tisdale, Sallie, 179–180
Tompkins, Jane, 182–183
totalism, and totality, 92–93
tradition, 190, 193–194
transcendence, 68, 266–267, 275, 279; and ideals, 268–269; and poetry, 220–222. *See also* God; spirituality
Tronto, Joan, 160–161, 163
trust, 94, 96, 97, 100, 196
truth, 3, 9; and authenticity, 70; and humility, 64; love of, 268–288, 289, 292; and objectivity, 72; and philosophy, 62–63; and responsibility, 116; and subjective values, 123

Unamuno, Miguel, 221
universalism, 18, 20, 23–27, 31

victim-blaming, 261–264, 276–279
violence, 92
vocation, 166–167, 170

wisdom, 230
Wolf, Arnold, 22–23, 31
women: as a category, 195–196; and courage, 291; and ethics, 152–159; and historical studies, 113–114; as impediment to spirituality, 222–223; as subjects, 269–270